TRAINING & REFERENCE

murach's
JavaScript
and jQuery

Zak Ruvalcaba

Mike Murach

MIKE MURACH & ASSOCIATES, INC.

4340 N. Knoll Ave. • Fresno, CA 93722
www.murach.com • murachbooks@murach.com

Editorial team

Authors:	Zak Ruvalcaba
	Mike Murach
Editors:	Anne Boehm
	Ben Murach
Cover design:	Zylka Design
Production:	Maria Pedroza David-Spera

Books for web developers

Murach's HTML5 and CSS3

Murach's JavaScript and jQuery

Murach's JavaScript and DOM Scripting

Murach's PHP and MySQL

Murach's Java Servlets and JSP (Second Edition)

Murach's ASP.NET 4.5 Web Programming with C# 2012

Murach's ASP.NET 4.5 Web Programming with VB 2012

Books on Java, C#, and Visual Basic

Murach's Java Programming

Murach's Android Programming

Murach's C# 2012

Murach's Visual Basic 2012

Books for database programmers

Murach's MySQL

Murach's Oracle SQL and PL/SQL

Murach's SQL Server 2012 for Developers

For more on Murach books, please visit us at www.murach.com

Contents

Introduction   iii

Section 1   JavaScript essentials

Chapter 1	Introduction to web development	3
Chapter 2	Getting started with JavaScript	49
Chapter 3	How to work with objects, functions, and events	91
Chapter 4	How to test and debug a JavaScript application	119
Chapter 5	How to work with arrays	141
Chapter 6	How to script the DOM with JavaScript	157

Section 2   jQuery essentials

Chapter 7	Getting off to a fast start with jQuery	195
Chapter 8	How to use effects and animations	231
Chapter 9	How to use the DOM manipulation and traversal methods	259
Chapter 10	How to work with forms and data validation	287
Chapter 11	How to create and use plugins	313

Section 3   jQuery UI essentials

Chapter 12	Get off to a fast start with jQuery UI themes and widgets	343
Chapter 13	How to use jQuery UI interactions and effects	379

Section 4   Ajax, JSON, and API essentials

Chapter 14	How to use Ajax, JSON, and Blogger	405
Chapter 15	How to use the APIs for YouTube, Twitter, and Flickr	439
Chapter 16	How to use the API for Google Maps	469

Section 5   jQuery Mobile essentials

Chapter 17	Get off to a fast start with jQuery Mobile	497
Chapter 18	How to enhance a jQuery Mobile web site	535

Reference Aids

Appendix A	How to set up your computer for this book	571
Appendix B	A summary of the applications in this book	581
Appendix C	How to resolve $ conflicts	585
Index		588

Expanded contents

Section 1 JavaScript essentials

Chapter 1   Indroduction to web development

How a web application works **4**
The components of a web application 4
How static web pages are processed 6
How dynamic web pages are processed 8
How JavaScript and jQuery are used for client-side processing 10

The components of a JavaScript application **12**
How the Email List application works 12
The HTML 12
The CSS 14
The JavaScript 16

The HTML and CSS skills that you need for this book **18**
How to use the HTML5 semantic elements 18
How to use the div and span elements 20
How to use the basic HTML attributes 22
How to provide CSS styles for an HTML page 24
How to code the basic CSS selectors 26
How to code CSS rule sets 28

How to test a JavaScript application **30**
How to run a JavaScript application 30
How to ensure cross-browser compatibility 32

How to use Aptana to develop JavaScript applications **34**
How to create or import a project 34
How to open or close an HTML, CSS, or JavaScript file 36
How to change the colors that highlight the syntax 38
How to edit a file 40
How to run a JavaScript application 42

Chapter 2   Getting started with JavaScript

How to include JavaScript in an HTML document **50**
Two ways to include JavaScript in the head of an HTML document 50
How to include JavaScript in the body of an HTML document 52

The JavaScript syntax **54**
How to code JavaScript statements 54
How to create identifiers 56
How to use comments 58
How to use objects, methods, and properties 60

How to work with JavaScript data **62**
The primitive data types 62
How to code numeric expressions 64
How to work with numeric variables 66
How to work with string and Boolean variables 68
How to use the parseInt and parseFloat methods 70

How to code control statements **72**
How to code conditional expressions 72

How to code if statements..74
How to code while and do-while loops 76
How to code for loops 78

Two illustrative applications **80**
The Miles Per Gallon application...80
The Test Scores application 82

How to find errors in your code...**84**
How to get error messages with Firefox 84
Common JavaScript errors..84

Chapter 3   How to work with objects, functions, and events

How to use objects to work with data..**92**
How to use the window and document objects...92
How to use Textbox and Number objects 94
How to use Date and String objects...96
How to use DOM objects to change the text for an element 98

How to use functions..**100**
How to create and call an anonymous function 100
How to create and call a named function 102
When and how to use local and global variables 104

How to handle events **106**
How to attach an event handler to an event 106
How to use an onload event handler to attach the other event handlers....108

Two illustrative applications **110**
The Miles Per Gallon application..110
The Email List application 112

Chapter 4   How to test and debug a JavaScript application

An introduction to testing and debugging.....................................**120**
Typical test phases for a JavaScript application 120
The three types of errors that can occur...120
Common JavaScript errors..122
How top-down coding and testing can simplify debugging........................124

How to debug with Firebug..**126**
How to enable Firebug and find errors 126
How to use breakpoints and step through code..128

Other debugging methods..**130**
When and how to get error messages with other browsers 130
A simple way to trace the execution of your JavaScript code 132
When and how to view the source code 134
When and how to validate the HTML...136

Chapter 5   How to work with arrays

How to create and use an array...**142**
How to create an array and refer to its elements 142
How to add and delete array elements 144
How to use for loops to work with arrays...146
How to use for-in loops to work with arrays..148
How to use the methods of an Array object 150

An enhanced Email List application **152**
The user interface and HTML...152
The JavaScript..154

Chapter 6   How to script the DOM with JavaScript

DOM scripting properties and methods.....................................**158**
DOM scripting concepts 158
The Node interface 160
The Document and Element interfaces... 162

The FAQs application **164**
The user interface, HTML, and CSS.. 164
The JavaScript... 166
Another way the FAQs application could be coded 168

Two critical issues for JavaScript applications **170**
Usability.. 170
Accessibility.. 170
The FAQs application with improved accessibility...................... 172

DOM scripting skills for links and images **174**
How to cancel the default action of an event 174
How to preload images... 176

The Image Swap application..**178**
The HTML and CSS 178
The JavaScript... 180

How to use timers **182**
How to use a one-time timer.. 182
How to use an interval timer.. 184

The Slide Show application **186**
The HTML and CSS 186
The JavaScript... 188

Section 2 jQuery essentials

Chapter 7   Get off to a fast start with jQuery

Introduction to jQuery...**196**
What jQuery is... 196
How to include jQuery in your web pages.................................... 196
How jQuery can simplify JavaScript development 198
How jQuery can affect testing and debugging 198
How jQuery UI and plugins can simplify JavaScript development 200

The basics of jQuery programming **202**
How to code jQuery selectors.. 202
How to call jQuery methods 204
How to use jQuery event methods 206

The Email List application in jQuery..**208**
The user interface and HTML.. 208
The jQuery 210

A working subset of selectors, methods, and event methods ..**212**
The most useful selectors... 212
The most useful methods 214
The most useful event methods 216
Other event methods that you should be aware of........................ 218

Three illustrative applications **220**
The FAQs application in jQuery 220

The Image Swap application in jQuery 222
The Image Rollover application in jQuery 226

Chapter 8 **How to use effects and animations**

How to use effects **232**
The jQuery methods for effects 232
The FAQs application with jQuery effects 234

A Slide Show application with effects **236**
The user interface, HTML, and CSS 236
Two ways to code the jQuery 238
How to stop and start a slide show..240

How to use animation..**242**
How to use the basic syntax of the animate method 242
How to chain animate methods 244
How to use the delay and stop methods...246
How to use easings with effects and animations.................................248
How to use the advanced animate syntax
and the methods for working with queues..250

A Carousel application with animation **252**
The user interface, HTML, and CSS 252
The jQuery 254

Chapter 9 **How to use the DOM manipulation
and traversal methods**

The DOM manipulation methods..**260**
The methods for working with attributes 260
The methods for DOM replacement 262
The methods for DOM insertion and cloning.......................................264
The methods for DOM wrapping and removal 266

The TOC application **268**
The user interface and HTML...268
The jQuery 270

The methods for working with styles and positioning **272**
The methods for working with styles 272
The methods for positioning elements...274
The enhanced TOC application 276

The DOM traversal methods **278**
The tree traversal methods...278
The filtering methods..280
A Slide Show application that uses DOM traversal methods................282

Chapter 10 **How to work with forms and data validation**

Introduction to forms and controls...**288**
How forms work..288
The HTML5 and CSS3 features for working with forms 290

How to use jQuery to work with forms **292**
The jQuery selectors and methods for forms 292
The jQuery event methods for forms...294

A Validation application that uses JavaScript...........................**296**
The user interface and HTML...296
Some of the JavaScript for the application 298

How to use a plugin for data validation **300**
How to use the validation plugin 300
The options and default error messages for the validation plugin 302

A Validation application that uses the validation plugin **304**
The user interface 304
The HTML.. 306
The CSS 308

Chapter 11   How to create and use plugins

Introduction to plugins...**314**
How to find jQuery plugins.. 314
Some of the most useful plugins.. 316
How to use any plugin... 318

How to use four of the most useful plugins............................**320**
How to use the Lightbox plugin for images................................... 320
How to use the bxSlider plugin for carousels 322
How to use the Cycle plugin for slide shows 324
How to use the jLayout plugin for two-column layouts 326

How to create your own plugins..**328**
The structure of a plugin.. 328
How to code a plugin that highlights menu items 330
How to add options to a plugin 332

A web page that uses two plugins..**334**
The user interface 334
The script elements 334
The HTML for the elements used by the plugins........................... 336
The jQuery for using the plugins.. 336

Section 3   jQuery UI essentials

**Chapter 12   Get off to a fast start
with jQuery UI themes and widgets**

Introduction to jQuery UI **344**
What jQuery UI is and where to get it.. 344
The jQuery UI components 346

How to build and use a jQuery UI download..............................**348**
How to build a download 348
How to use ThemeRoller to build a custom theme......................... 350
How to use the downloaded folders and files 352

How to use jQuery UI widgets **354**
How to use any widget.. 354
How to use the Accordion widget.. 356
How to use the Tabs widget 358
How to use the Button and Dialog widgets 360
How to use the Autocomplete widget 362
How to use the Datepicker widget 364
How to use the Slider widget 366
How to use the Progressbar widget.. 368

A web page that uses jQuery UI...**370**
The user interface 370
The link and script elements.. 370

The HTML for the widgets 372
The jQuery for the widgets 374

Chapter 13   How to use jQuery UI interactions and effects

How to use interactions **380**
Introduction to interactions...380
How to use the draggable and droppable interactions.....................382
How to use the resizable interaction 384
How to use the selectable interaction 386
How to use the sortable interaction 388

How to use effects **390**
Introduction to effects...390
How to use individual effects 392
How to use color transitions..394
How to use class transitions 396
How to use visibility transitions 398

Section 4   Ajax, JSON, and API essentials

Chapter 14   How to use Ajax, JSON, and Blogger

Introduction to Ajax...**406**
How Ajax works..406
Common data formats for Ajax 408
The members of the XMLHttpRequest object 410
How to use the XMLHttpRequest object 412

How to use the jQuery shorthand methods for Ajax **414**
The jQuery shorthand methods for working with Ajax 414
How to use the load method to load HTML data 416
How to use the $.get or $.post method to load XML data 418
How to use the $.getJSON method to load JSON data.......................420
How to send data with an Ajax request 422

How to use the $.ajax method for working with Ajax **424**
The syntax of the $.ajax method 424
How to use the $.ajax method to load data.......................................426

How to use Ajax with the API for Google's Blogger...................**428**
Introduction to Google's Blogger..428
How to use the API for Blogger 430
How to use an online JSON editor to review the feed from a web site....................432
How to use Ajax and JSON to display Blogger posts.........................434

Chapter 15   How to use the APIs for Youtube, Twitter, and Flickr

How to use Ajax with YouTube **440**
How to use the API for YouTube 440
The query parameters and data items that you'll use the most 442
How to list videos by channel..444
How to list videos by search term..446
How to play videos in a video player on your site 448

How to use Ajax with Twitter **450**
How to use the API for Twitter..450
How to display the tweets for a user 452
How to convert the URLs within tweets to links 454
How to display a timestamp for each tweet.......................................456

How to use Ajax with Flickr **458**
How to use the API for Flickr..458
The query parameters and data items that you'll use the most 460
How to display titles and descriptions for a Flickr photo feed..................462
How to display a gallery of Flickr photos 464

Chapter 16   How to use the API for Google Maps

Introduction to Google Maps...**470**
Introduction to the Google Maps API 470
The classes for adding a Google map to a web page 472
The script element for the Google Maps API..474
How to add a Google map to a web page..474

How to display markers on a map..**476**
The classes and methods for geocoding and markers 476
How to create an address list that displays markers..................................478

How to display messages on a map **480**
The classes and methods for messages and markers 480
How to add messages to markers...482
How to add custom messages to markers 484
How to add Flickr images to messages..486

How to display driving directions **488**
The classes and methods for directions and listeners................................488
How to display driving directions on your own site..................................490

Section 5   jQuery Mobile essentials

Chapter 17   Get off to a fast start with jQuery Mobile

How to work with mobile devices..**498**
How to provide pages for mobile devices...498
How to use a JavaScript plugin to redirect mobile browsers to a mobile web site.....500
How to set the viewport properties..502
Guidelines for designing mobile web pages 504
Guidelines for testing mobile web pages 504

How to get started with jQuery Mobile **506**
What jQuery Mobile is and where to get it..506
How to include jQuery Mobile in your web pages 508
How to create one web page with jQuery Mobile 510
How to code multiple web pages in a single HTML file 512
How to use dialogs and transitions 514
How to create buttons 516
How to create a navigation bar 518

How to style web pages with jQuery Mobile..............................**520**
How to work with the default styles 520
How to apply theme swatches to HTML elements.....................................522
How to use ThemeRoller to roll your own theme.......................................524

A mobile web site for Vecta Corp...**526**
The layout of the web site 526
The HTML for the mobile web site 528
The style sheet for the mobile web site..528

Chapter 18   How to enhance a jQuery Mobile web site

How to use the jQuery Mobile documentation **536**
The components of jQuery Mobile...536
The data attributes of jQuery Mobile 536
The events and methods of jQuery Mobile....................................536

How to use jQuery Mobile for content formatting.......................**538**
How to lay out content in grids..538
How to use collapsible content blocks 540
How to use collapsible sets 542

How to use jQuery Mobile for list views **544**
How to use basic lists..544
How to use split button lists and inset lists...................................546
How to use list dividers and count bubbles 548
How to use search filter bars...550

How to use jQuery Mobile for forms **552**
How to use text fields and text areas 552
How to use sliders and switches 554
How to use radio buttons and check boxes 556
How to use select menus 558
How to submit a form 560

An enhanced mobile web site for Vecta Corp...........................**562**
The layout of the web site 562
The HTML..564
The style sheet..564

Introduction

jQuery is a free, open-source, JavaScript library that provides dozens of methods that make JavaScript programming easier. Beyond that, the jQuery methods are coded and tested for cross-browser compatibility, so they will work in all browsers. Those are just two of the reasons why jQuery is used by more than half of the 10,000 most-visited web sites today.

In fact, you can think of jQuery as one of the four technologies that every web developer should master: HTML, CSS, JavaScript, and jQuery. But don't forget that jQuery is actually JavaScript, and to use jQuery you need to know some JavaScript. That's one of the reasons why jQuery has been so hard to learn.

That's also why this book starts by teaching you the least you need to know about JavaScript for effective use of jQuery. This is essential for programming novices, but it's also useful for readers with some JavaScript experience. Then, this book uses a highly-structured approach to present all of the jQuery, jQuery UI (User Interface), and jQuery Mobile skills that you will need on the job, and it always presents these skills in the context of useful, real-world applications.

What this book does

- To make sure you have all of the JavaScript skills that you need for using jQuery, the six chapters in section 1 of this book present a crash course in those skills. If you already know JavaScript, you can skim this section, but you'll probably pick up a few new skills as you do that. If you're a programming novice, this section is especially designed to get you off to a good start.

- Once you have the JavaScript skills that you need, the five chapters of section 2 present the core jQuery skills that every web developer should have. Chapter 7 gets you off to a fast start with those skills, and the next four chapters focus on effects and animations, DOM scripting, working with forms and data validation, using the many plugins that are available for jQuery, and creating your own plugins.

- Besides the core jQuery library, jQuery provides the jQuery UI (User Interface) library. This library helps you build advanced features with just a few lines of code, and the two chapters in section 3 show you how to make the best use of jQuery UI. That includes the use of widgets like tabs, accordions, and datepickers...interactions like draggable, droppable, and sortable...and effects like color and class transitions.

- The three chapters in section 4 show you how to use Ajax and JSON to get data from a server and add it to a web page without reloading the entire web page. They also show you how to use the APIs for web sites like Blogger, YouTube, Twitter, Flickr, and Google Maps because that's a common use of Ajax and JSON.

- Last, the two chapters of section 5 show you how to use jQuery Mobile to develop web applications for mobile devices like iPhones and Android phones. As we see it, this is the best way to develop mobile web sites right now, so this too is something every web developer should know.

Why you'll learn faster and better with this book

Like all our books, this one has features that you won't find in competing books. That's why we believe you'll learn faster and better with our book than with any other. Here are a few of those features.

- Because section 1 presents a complete subset of the JavaScript that you need for using jQuery, you will be able to understand all of the JavaScript that's used in the jQuery applications in this book. In contrast, most jQuery books don't teach JavaScript, so you often need to refer to other sources when you don't understand the JavaScript that they use in their examples.

- If you page through this book, you'll see that all of the information is presented in "paired pages," with the essential syntax, guidelines, and examples on the right page and the perspective and extra explanation on the left page. This helps you learn faster by reading less...and this is the ideal reference format when you need to refresh your memory about how to do something.

- To show you how jQuery works, this book presents dozens of complete jQuery applications that range from the simple to the complex. To see how that works, take a quick look at the four applications that are presented in the first jQuery chapter: figures 7-7 and 7-8, figure 7-12, figures 7-13 and 7-14, and figure 7-15. This also shows how our paired pages make it easy to study the relationships between the HTML, CSS, and JavaScript code. Then, look at the summary of all of the book applications in appendix B.

- Of course, this book also presents dozens of short examples, so it's easy to find an example that shows you how to do what you want to do. Even better, our paired pages make it much easier to find the example that you're looking for than it is with traditional books in which the examples are embedded in the text. Incidentally, all of the examples in this book use HTML5 and

CSS3 so they illustrate the best web development practices of today.

- As you proceed through this book, you will learn how to use almost all of the selectors, methods, and event methods that jQuery provides. That means that you can use this book as a reference that will help you parse the code in any jQuery application. So, although no one book can present every type of jQuery application, this book prepares you to understand any application that you encounter on the job, on web sites, or in other books.

What software you need

To develop JavaScript and jQuery applications, you can use any text editor. However, a text editor that includes syntax coloring and auto-completion will help you develop applications more quickly and with fewer errors. That's why we recommend Aptana Studio 3 for both Windows and Mac OS users. Although Aptana is free, it provides many powerful features.

Then, to test a web page, Windows users can use Internet Explorer and Mac users can use Safari, because those are their default browsers. But we also recommend that you test your pages in a second browser like Mozilla Firefox, which is also free. In practice, you should also test your pages in Opera and Chrome, but that isn't necessary as you learn.

If you decide to use Aptana, chapter 1 presents a short tutorial that will get you started right. And to help you install Aptana and Firefox, appendix A provides the web site addresses and procedures that you'll need.

How our downloadable files can help you learn

If you go to our web site at www.murach.com, you can download all the files that you need for getting the most from this book. These files include:

- the files for all of the applications in this book
- the files that you will use as the starting points for the exercises
- the files that provide the solutions to the exercises

These files let you test, review, and copy the code. In addition, if you have any problems with the exercises, the solutions are there to help you over the learning blocks, which is an essential part of the learning process. And sometimes, the solutions will show you a more elegant way to handle a problem, even when you've come up with a solution that works. Here again, appendix A shows you how to download and install these files.

Support materials for trainers and instructors

If you're a corporate trainer or a college instructor who would like to use this book for a course, we offer an Instructor's CD that includes: (1) a complete set of PowerPoint slides that you can use to review and reinforce the content of the book; (2) instructional objectives that describe the skills a student should have upon completion of each chapter; (3) test banks that measure mastery of those skills; (4) extra exercises and projects that prove mastery; and (5) solutions to the extra exercises and projects.

To learn more about this Instructor's CD and to find out how to get it, please go to our web site at www.murach.com and click on the Trainers link or the Instructors link. Or, if you prefer, you can call Kelly at 1-800-221-5528 or send an email to kelly@murach.com.

Companion books

Since jQuery, HTML, and CSS are so tightly linked, we highly recommend that you know HTML5 and CSS3 as well as you know jQuery. To gain that expertise, you'll find that *Murach's HTML5 and CSS3* is the perfect companion to this jQuery book. With these two books at your side, you'll be able to develop web pages that use HTML5, CSS3, and jQuery the way the best professionals do.

If you want to learn more about JavaScript so you can do the type of client-side programming that jQuery doesn't provide for, we recommend *Murach's JavaScript and DOM Scripting*. It presents all of the JavaScript skills that aren't presented in this jQuery book, including how to use regular expressions, how to create and use your own objects, and much more. It is also a great reference.

If you want to learn server-side web programming when you finish this book, we offer several books that will help you. Our ASP.NET books will show you how to develop web applications with C# or Visual Basic. Our Servlets and JSP book will show you how to develop web applications with Java. And our PHP and MySQL book will show you how to develop web applications with PHP as the scripting language and MySQL as the database.

To find out more about our new books and latest editions, please go to our web site at www.murach.com. There, you'll find the details for all of our books, including complete tables of contents.

Please let us know how this book works for you

From the start of this project, we had three goals. First, we wanted to take a new approach to jQuery that lets you learn faster and better than ever. Second, we wanted this book to work for programming novices as well as it works for experienced JavaScript programmers. Third, we wanted to raise the skills of our readers to a professional level.

Now, we hope we've succeeded. We thank you for buying this book. We wish you all the best with your jQuery development. And if you have any comments, we would appreciate hearing from you.

Zak Ruvalcaba, Author
zak@modulemedia.com

Anne Boehm, Editor
anne@murach.com

Section 1

JavaScript essentials

In the six chapters in this section, you will learn all of the JavaScript essentials that you need for working with jQuery. To start, chapter 1 presents the concepts and terms that you need for developing JavaScript applications. It also shows you how to use the Aptana IDE that we recommend for developing JavaScript applications.

Next, chapter 2 presents a starting subset of the JavaScript language, chapter 3 completes that subset, and chapter 4 shows you how to test and debug a JavaScript application. At that point, you'll be able to start developing applications of your own.

Then, chapter 5 shows you how to use arrays, which are commonly used in JavaScript applications. Last, chapter 6 shows you how to use all of the JavaScript skills that you've learned thus far to do some DOM scripting with links and images.

When you complete these chapters, you'll be able to develop useful JavaScript applications. Beyond that, though, you'll have all of the JavaScript skills that you need for using jQuery. Then, you can master jQuery by reading the last four sections of this book.

1

Introduction
to web development

This chapter presents the background concepts, terms, and skills that you need for developing JavaScript applications. That includes a quick review of the HTML and CSS skills that you need. That also includes a quick tutorial on how to use Aptana Studio 3, which is the IDE that we recommend for developing JavaScript applications.

If you have some web development experience, you should be able to go through this chapter quickly by skimming the topics that you already know. But if you're new to web development, you should take the time to master the concepts and terms of this chapter.

How a web application works...4
The components of a web application 4
How static web pages are processed...6
How dynamic web pages are processed..8
How JavaScript and jQuery are used for client-side processing 10

The components of a JavaScript application..................12
How the Email List application works 12
The HTML..12
The CSS 14
The JavaScript..16

The HTML and CSS skills that you need for this book.....18
How to use the HTML5 semantic elements 18
How to use the div and span elements...20
How to use the basic HTML attributes 22
How to provide CSS styles for an HTML page..24
How to code the basic CSS selectors...26
How to code CSS rule sets...28

How to test a JavaScript application................................30
How to run a JavaScript application 30
How to ensure cross-browser compatibility 32

How to use Aptana to develop JavaScript applications...34
How to create or import a project...34
How to open or close an HTML, CSS, or JavaScript file...........................36
How to change the colors that highlight the syntax 38
How to edit a file..40
How to run a JavaScript application...42

Perspective 44

How a web application works

A web application consists of many components that work together as they bring the application to your computer or mobile device. Before you can start developing JavaScript or jQuery applications, you should have a basic understanding of how these components work together.

The components of a web application

The diagram in figure 1-1 shows that web applications consist of *clients* and a *web server*. The clients are the computers, tablets, and mobile devices that use the web applications. They access the web pages through programs known as *web browsers*. The web server holds the files that make up a web application.

A *network* is a system that allows clients and servers to communicate. The *Internet* is a large network that consists of many smaller networks. In a diagram like the one in this figure, the "cloud" represents the network or Internet that connects the clients and servers.

In general, you don't need to know how the cloud works. But you should have a general idea of what's going on.

To start, networks can be categorized by size. A *local area network* (*LAN*) is a small network of computers that are near each other and can communicate with each other over short distances. Computers in a LAN are typically in the same building or adjacent buildings. This type of network is often called an *intranet*, and it can be used to run web applications for use by employees only.

In contrast, a *wide area network* (*WAN*) consists of multiple LANs that have been connected. To pass information from one client to another, a router determines which network is closest to the destination and sends the information over that network. A WAN can be owned privately by one company or it can be shared by multiple companies.

An *Internet service provider* (*ISP*) is a company that owns a WAN that is connected to the Internet. An ISP leases access to its network to companies that need to be connected to the Internet.

The components of a web application

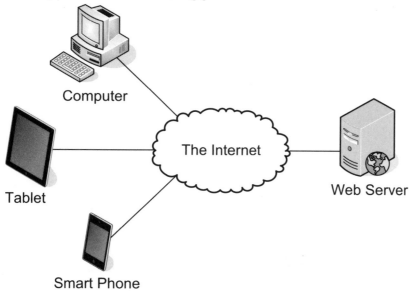

Computer

Tablet

The Internet

Web Server

Smart Phone

Description

- A web application consists of clients, a web server, and a network.

- The *clients* use programs known as *web browsers* to request web pages from the web server. Today, the clients can be computers, smart phones like the iPhone, or tablets like the iPad.

- The *web server* returns the pages that are requested to the browser.

- A *network* connects the clients to the web server.

- An *intranet* is a *local area network* (or *LAN*) that connects computers that are near each other, usually within the same building.

- The *Internet* is a network that consists of many *wide area networks* (*WANs*), and each of those consists of two or more LANs. Today, the Internet is often referred to as "the Cloud", which implies that you really don't have to understand how it works.

- An *Internet service provider* (*ISP*) owns a WAN that is connected to the Internet.

Figure 1-1   The components of a web application

How static web pages are processed

A *static web page* like the one in figure 1-2 is a web page that doesn't change each time it is requested. This type of web page is sent directly from the web server to the web browser when the browser requests it. You can spot static pages in a web browser by looking at the extension in the address bar. If the extension is .htm or .html, the page is a static web page.

The diagram in this figure shows how a web server processes a request for a static web page. This process begins when a client requests a web page in a web browser. To do that, the user can either type the address of the page into the browser's address bar or click a link in the current page that specifies the next page to load.

In either case, the web browser builds a request for the web page and sends it to the web server. This request, known as an *HTTP request*, is formatted using the *HyperText Transfer Protocol* (HTTP), which lets the web server know which file is being requested.

When the web server receives the HTTP request, it retrieves the requested file from the disk drive. This file contains the *HTML (HyperText Markup Language)* for the requested page. Then, the web server sends the file back to the browser as part of an *HTTP response*.

When the browser receives the HTTP response, it *renders* (translates) the HTML into a web page that is displayed in the browser. Then, the user can view the content. If the user requests another page, either by clicking a link or typing another web address into the browser's address bar, the process begins again.

A static web page at http://www.modulemedia.com/ourwork/index.html

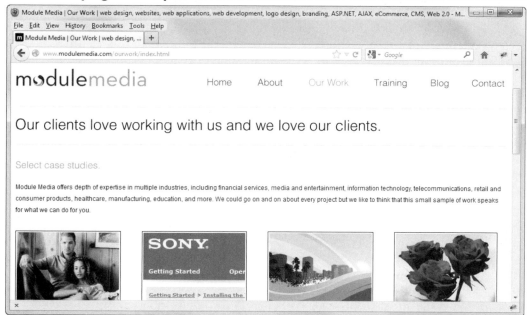

How a web server processes a static web page

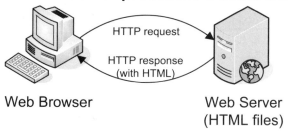

Web Browser

Web Server
(HTML files)

Description

- *Hypertext Markup Language* (*HTML*) is the language used to design the web pages of an application.

- A *static web page* is an HTML document that's stored on the web server and doesn't change. The filenames for static web pages have .htm or .html extensions.

- When the user requests a static web page, the browser sends an *HTTP request* to the web server that includes the name of the file that's being requested.

- When the web server receives the request, it retrieves the HTML for the web page and sends it back to the browser as part of an *HTTP response*.

- When the browser receives the HTTP response, it *renders* the HTML into a web page that is displayed in the browser.

Figure 1-2   How static web pages are processed

How dynamic web pages are processed

A *dynamic web page* like the one in figure 1-3 is a page that's created by a program or script on the web server each time it is requested. This program or script is executed by an *application server* based on the data that's sent along with the HTTP request. In this example, the HTTP request identified the book that's shown. Then, the program or script retrieved the image and data for that book from a *database server.*

The diagram in this figure shows how a web server processes a dynamic web page. The process begins when the user requests a page in a web browser. To do that, the user can either type the URL of the page into the browser's address bar, click a link that specifies the dynamic page to load, or click a button that submits a form that contains the data that the dynamic page should process.

In each case, the web browser builds an HTTP request and sends it to the web server. This request includes whatever data the application needs for processing the request. If, for example, the user has entered data into a form, that data will be included in the HTTP request.

When the web server receives the HTTP request, the server examines the file extension of the requested web page to identify the application server that should process the request. The web server then forwards the request to the application server that processes that type of web page.

Next, the application server retrieves the appropriate program or script from the hard drive. It also loads any form data that the user submitted. Then, it executes the script. As the script executes, it generates the HTML for the web page. If necessary, the script will request data from a database server and use that data as part of the web page it is generating. The processing that's done on the application server can be referred to as *server-side processing.*

When the script is finished, the application server sends the dynamically generated HTML back to the web server. Then, the web server sends the HTML back to the browser in an HTTP response.

When the web browser receives the HTTP response, it renders the HTML and displays the web page. Note, however, that the web browser has no way to tell whether the HTML in the HTTP response was for a static page or a dynamic page. It just renders the HTML.

When the page is displayed, the user can view the content. Then, when the user requests another page, the process begins again. The process that begins with the user requesting a web page and ends with the server sending a response back to the client is called a *round trip.*

A dynamic web page at amazon.com

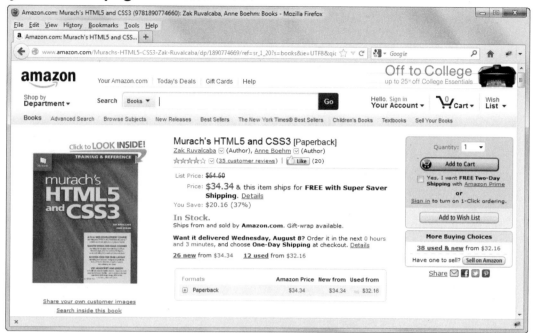

How a web server processes a dynamic web page

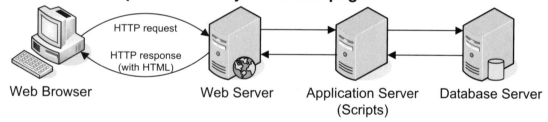

Web Browser   Web Server   Application Server   Database Server
                                                 (Scripts)

Description

- A *dynamic web page* is a web page that's generated by a program or script that is running on a server.

- When a web server receives a request for a dynamic web page, it looks up the extension of the requested file to find out which *application server* should process the request.

- When the application server receives a request, it runs the specified script. Often, this script uses the data that it gets from the web browser to get the appropriate data from a *database server*. This script can also store the data that it receives in the database.

- When the application server finishes processing the data, it generates the HTML for a web page and returns it to the web server. Then, the web server returns the HTML to the web browser as part of an HTTP response.

Figure 1-3   How dynamic web pages are processed

How JavaScript and jQuery are used
for client-side processing

In contrast to the server-side processing that's done for dynamic web pages, *JavaScript* is a *scripting language* that provides for *client-side processing*. In the web page in figure 1-4, for example, JavaScript is used to change the images that are shown without using server-side processing.

To make this work, all of the required images are loaded into the browser when the page is requested. Then, if the user clicks on one of the color swatches below a shirt, the shirt image is changed to the one with the right color. This is called an *image swap*. Similarly, if the user moves the mouse over a shirt, the image is replaced by a close-up image of the shirt. This is called an *image rollover*.

The diagram in this figure shows how JavaScript processing works. When a browser requests a web page, both the HTML and the related JavaScript are returned to the browser by the web server. Then, the JavaScript code is executed in the web browser by the browser's *JavaScript engine*. This takes some of the processing burden off the server and makes the application run faster. Often, JavaScript is used in conjunction with dynamic web pages, but it is also commonly used with static web pages.

Besides image swaps and rollovers, there are many other uses for JavaScript. For instance, another common use is to validate the data that the user enters into an HTML form before it is sent to the server for processing. This saves unnecessary trips to the server. Other common uses of JavaScript are to run slide shows and carousels and to provide data in tabs or accordions.

Where does jQuery fit into this picture? jQuery is actually a JavaScript library, which means that it is JavaScript. Today, because jQuery makes it easier to develop many common JavaScript applications, jQuery is the most popular JavaScript library. That's why the last four sections in this book are devoted to teaching you how to get the most from jQuery.

A web page with image swaps and rollovers

How JavaScript fits into this architecture

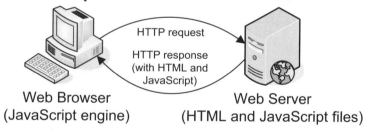

Web Browser
(JavaScript engine)

Web Server
(HTML and JavaScript files)

Three of the many uses of JavaScript and jQuery

- Data validation
- Image swaps and rollovers
- Slide shows

Description

- *JavaScript* is a *scripting language* that is run by the *JavaScript engine* of a web browser and controls the operation of the browser.
- *jQuery* is a JavaScript library that makes it easier to do many of the functions that JavaScript can be used for.
- When the browser requests an HTML page that contains JavaScript or a link to a JavaScript file, both the HTML and the JavaScript are loaded into the browser.
- Because JavaScript runs on the client, not the server, its functions don't require a trip back to the server. This helps an application run more efficiently.

Figure 1-4   How JavaScript and jQuery are used for client-side processing

The components of a JavaScript application

When you develop a JavaScript application, you use HTML to define the content and structure of the page. You use CSS to format that content. And you use JavaScript to do the client-side processing. This is illustrated by the Email List application that is presented next.

How the Email List application works

Figure 1-5 presents the user interface for an Email List application. It asks the user to make three entries and then click on the Join our List button. The asterisks to the right of the text boxes for the entries indicate that these entries are required.

When the user clicks on the button, JavaScript checks the entries to make sure they're valid. If they are, the entries are sent to the web server for server-side processing. If they aren't, messages are displayed so the user can correct the entries. This is a common JavaScript application called *data validation* that saves a trip to the server when the entries are invalid.

The HTML

HyperText Markup Language (*HTML*) is used to define the content and structure of a web page. In figure 1-5, you can see the HTML for the Email List application. In general, this book assumes that you are already familiar with HTML, but here are a few highlights.

First, note that this document starts with a DOCTYPE declaration. This declaration is the one you'll use with HTML5, and you must code it exactly as it's shown here. If you aren't already using HTML5, you can see that this declaration is much simpler than the declaration for earlier versions of HTML. In this book, all of the applications use HTML5.

Second, in the head section of the HTML document, you can see a meta element that specifies that UTF-8 is the character encoding that's used for the page. You can also see a link element that specifies the CSS file that should be used to format this HTML. And you can see a script element that specifies the JavaScript file that should be used to process the user's entries.

Third, in the body section, you can see the use of a section element. That is one of the HTML5 elements that we'll be using throughout this book. Within this section, you can see the use of h1, form, label, input, and span elements.

In this book, as you've just seen, we refer to *HTML elements* like the <link>, <script>, <section>, and <h1> elements as the link, script, section, and h1 elements. However, to prevent confusion when referring to one-letter elements like p and a elements, we enclose the letters in brackets, as in the <p> element or the <a> element.

The HTML file in a browser after CSS has been applied to it

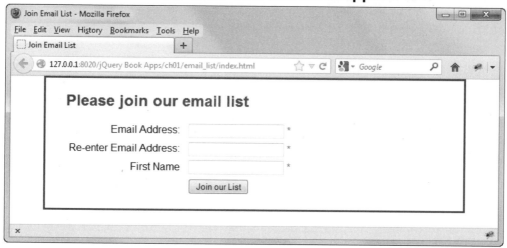

The code for the HTML file named index.html

```html
<!DOCTYPE html>
<html>
<head>
    <meta charset="UTF-8">
    <title>Join Email List</title>
    <link rel="stylesheet" href="email_list.css">
    <script src="email_list.js"></script>
</head>
<body>
    <section>
        <h1>Please join our email list</h1>
        <form id="email_form" name="email_form"
                action="join.html" method="get">
            <label for="email_address1">Email Address:</label>
            <input type="text" id="email_address1" name="email_address1">
            <span id="email_address1_error">*</span><br>

            <label for="email_address2">Re-enter Email Address:</label>
            <input type="text" id="email_address2" name="email_address2">
            <span id="email_address2_error">*</span><br>

            <label for="first_name">First Name</label>
            <input type="text" id="first_name" name="first_name">
            <span id="first_name_error">*</span><br>

            <label> </label>
            <input type="button" id="join_list" value="Join our List">
        </form>
    </section>
</body>
</html>
```

Description

- *HTML* (*HyperText Markup Language*) is used to define the structure and content of a web page.

Figure 1-5   The HTML for a web page

In practice, you'll often hear *elements* called *tags* so you can think of them as synonyms. In this book, we occasionally use the term *tag*, especially when referring to an opening tag like <h1> or a closing tag like </h1>.

The CSS

Not long ago, HTML documents were coded so the HTML not only defined the content and structure of the web page but also the formatting of that content. However, this mix of structural and formatting elements made it hard to edit, maintain, and reformat the web pages.

Today, *Cascading Style Sheets* (*CSS*) let you separate the formatting from the content and structure of a web page. As a result, the formatting that was once done with HTML should now be done with CSS.

In figure 1-6, then, you can see the CSS that's used to format the HTML in figure 1-5. Here again, this book assumes that you are already familiar with CSS, but here is a quick description of what this CSS is doing.

In the rule set for the body element, the font-family property sets the font for the entire document, the margin property centers the body in the browser window, the width property sets the width of the body to 650 pixels, and the border property puts a blue border around the body. This is typical CSS for the applications in the book, just to make them look better.

Similarly, the rule sets for the h1, section, label, and input elements are intended to make these elements look better. Here, the rule set for the h1 element sets the font color to blue. And the rule set for the section puts some space (padding) between the section contents and the right, bottom, and left border.

Next, the rule set for the labels floats them left so the text boxes will be to their right. This rule set also sets the width of the labels to 11em, and aligns the text for the labels on the right. Then, the rule set for the input elements sets the left margin so there's space between the labels and the text boxes, and it sets the bottom margin so there's space after each label and text box.

Last, the rule set for the span elements sets the text color to red. When the HTML page is first loaded, these span elements only contain asterisks (*). But the JavaScript changes that if one or more of the entries are invalid.

The web page in a browser after CSS has been applied to it

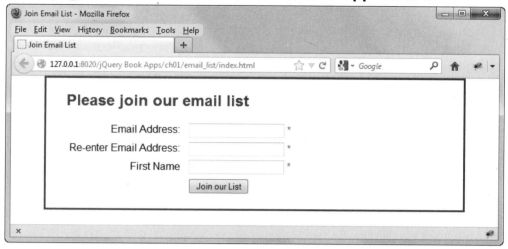

The link element in the HTML file that applies the CSS file

```
<link rel="stylesheet" href="email_list.css">
```

The code for the CSS file named email_list.css

```css
body {
    font-family: Arial, Helvetica, sans-serif;
    background-color: white;
    margin: 0 auto;
    width: 650px;
    border: 3px solid blue;
}
h1 {
    color: blue;
}
section {
    padding: 0 2em 1em;
}
label {
    float: left;
    width: 11em;
    text-align: right;
}
input {
    margin-left: 1em;
    margin-bottom: .5em;
}
span {
    color: red;
}
```

Description

- *Cascading Style Sheets* (*CSS*) are used to control how web pages are displayed by specifying the fonts, colors, borders, spacing, and layout of the pages.

Figure 1-6   The CSS for the web page

The JavaScript

Figure 1-7 shows how this application looks in a browser if the JavaScript finds any invalid data after the user clicks the Join our List button. Here, you can see that error messages are displayed to the right of the user entries for the second and third text boxes. In other words, the JavaScript has actually changed the contents of the span elements.

When JavaScript changes the HTML for a page, it is called *DOM scripting*. That's because the JavaScript is actually changing the *Document Object Model* (or *DOM*) that's generated by the browser when the page is loaded. This DOM represents all of the elements and attributes that are coded in the HTML. Then, when JavaScript changes any aspect of the DOM, the change is immediately made to the browser display too.

After the browser display, this figure shows the JavaScript for this application. Since you are going to learn how all of this code works in the next two chapters, you may want to skip over this code right now. But if you have any programming experience, it may be worth taking a quick look at it. In that case, here are a few highlights.

To start, this code consists of three functions: a $ function, a joinList function that is executed when the user clicks on the button, and a function that is run after the DOM has been loaded into the browser. Then, in the joinList function, you can see four if-else statements that provide most of the logic for this application.

Here, you can see that the if-else structures are similar to those in any modern programming language like Java, C#, or PHP. You can also see that declaring a variable (var) and assigning a variable is done in a way that's similar to the way that's done in other programming languages.

What's different about JavaScript is that it provides methods and properties that let you modify the DOM. For instance, the $ function uses the getElement-ById method to get the object with the id that's passed to the function. The first statement in the joinList function, for example, uses the $ function to get the object that represents the first text box in the HTML. Then, this statement uses the value property to get the value that the user entered into that text box.

Later, in the first if statement, if that value is an empty string (""), which means the user didn't make an entry, the JavaScript replaces the * in the span element for that text box with an error message. To do that, it uses this code:

```
$("email_address1_error").firstChild.nodeValue =
    "This field is required.";
```

Although this code may look daunting right now, you'll see that it's all quite manageable. You'll also come to realize that DOM scripting is where JavaScript (and jQuery) get their power.

The web page in a browser with JavaScript used for data validation

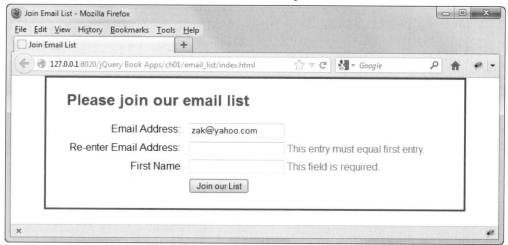

The script element in the HTML file that includes the JavaScript file

```
<script src="email_list.js"></script>
```

The code for the JavaScript file named email_list.js

```
var $ = function (id) {
    return document.getElementById(id);
}
var joinList = function () {
    var emailAddress1 = $("email_address1").value;
    var emailAddress2 = $("email_address2").value;
    var isValid = true;

    if (emailAddress1 == "") {
        $("email_address1_error").firstChild.nodeValue =
            "This field is required.";
        isValid = false;
    } else { $("email_address1_error").firstChild.nodeValue = ""; }

    if (emailAddress1 !== emailAddress2) {
        $("email_address2_error").firstChild.nodeValue =
            "This entry must equal first entry.";
        isValid = false;
    } else { $("email_address2_error").firstChild.nodeValue = ""; }

    if ($("first_name").value == "") {
        $("first_name_error").firstChild.nodeValue =
            "This field is required.";
        isValid = false;
    } else { $("first_name_error").firstChild.nodeValue = ""; }

    if (isValid) {
        // submit the form if all entries are valid
        $("email_form").submit(); }
}
window.onload = function () {
    $("join_list").onclick = joinList;
    $("email_address").focus();
}
```

Figure 1-7   The JavaScript for the web page

The HTML and CSS skills
that you need for this book

Although this book assumes that you are already familiar with HTML and CSS, the next six topics present a quick review of the HTML and CSS skills that you're going to need for this book. If you don't already have these skills and you can't pick them up from the topics that follow, we recommend that you use *Murach's HTML5 and CSS3* as a reference while you're learning JavaScript and jQuery.

How to use the HTML5 semantic elements

All of the applications in this book use the *HTML5 semantic elements* whenever they're appropriate. If you aren't already using them or at least familiar with them, figure 1-8 summarizes what you need to know.

In particular, the applications in this book use the section, aside, and nav elements. That makes it easier to apply CSS to these elements because you don't have to code id attributes that are used by the CSS. Instead, you can apply the CSS to the elements themselves.

Be aware, however, that older browsers won't recognize the HTML5 semantic elements, which means that you won't be able to use CSS to apply formatting to them. So, if you want your CSS to work in older browsers, you need to code a script element in the head section of the HTML document that provides a *JavaScript shiv* (also known as a *shim*). This shiv uses JavaScript to put the HTML5 elements in the DOM, which makes the browser aware of them.

The script element in this figure is one that you can use in all of your HTML pages. It gets the shiv from a Google web site and loads it into the browser. To save space and repetition, we don't always show this script element in the applications in this book, but it is used in all of the downloadable applications.

The primary HTML5 semantic elements

Element	Contents
header	The header for a page.
section	A generic section of a document that doesn't indicate the type of content.
article	A composition like an article in the paper.
nav	A section of a page that contains links to other pages or placeholders.
aside	A section of a page like a sidebar that is related to the content that's near it.
figure	An image, table, or other component that's treated as a figure.
footer	The footer for a page.

The JavaScript shiv that tells older browsers about the HTML5 elements

```
<script src="http://html5shiv.googlecode.com/svn/trunk/html5.js"></script>
```

A page that's structured with header, section, and footer elements

```
<body>
    <header>
        <h1>San Joaquin Valley Town Hall</h1>
    </header>
    <section>
        <p>Welcome to San Joaquin Valley Town Hall. We have some
            fascinating speakers for you this season!</p>
    </section>
    <footer>
        <p>&copy; San Joaquin Valley Town Hall.</p>
    </footer>
</body>
```

The page displayed in a web browser

San Joaquin Valley Town Hall

Welcome to San Joaquin Valley Town Hall. We have some fascinating speakers for you this season!

© San Joaquin Valley Town Hall.

Description

- HTML5 provides new *semantic elements* that you should use to structure the contents of a web page. Using these elements can be referred to as *HTML5 semantics*.

- All of the HTML5 elements in this figure are supported by the modern browsers. They will also work on older browsers if you include the *JavaScript shiv* shown above in the head section of the HTML5 document.

- Besides the HTML5 semantic elements, this book uses standard HTML elements like headings (h1 and h2 elements), images (img elements), links (<a> elements), and paragraphs (<p> elements).

Figure 1-8   How to use the HTML5 semantic elements

How to use the div and span elements

If you've been using HTML for a while, you are certainly familiar with the div element. It has traditionally been used to divide an HTML document into divisions that are identified by id attributes. Then, CSS can use the ids to apply formatting to the divisions.

But now that HTML5 is available, div elements shouldn't be used to structure a document. Instead, they should only be used when the HTML5 semantic elements aren't appropriate.

Note, however, that div elements are often used in JavaScript applications. If, for example, a section element contains three h2 elements with each followed by a div element, JavaScript can be used to display or hide a div element whenever the heading that precedes it is clicked. This structure is illustrated by the first example in figure 1-9, and you'll see how this works in chapter 6.

Similarly, span elements have historically been used to identify portions of text that can be formatted by CSS. By today's standards, though, it's better to use elements that indicate the contents of the elements, like the cite, code, and <q> elements.

But here again, span elements are often used in JavaScript applications, as shown by the second example in this figure. In fact, you've just seen this in the Email List application. In that application, JavaScript puts the error messages in the appropriate span elements.

The div and span elements

Element	Description
div	A block element that provides a container for other elements.
span	An inline element that lets you identify text that can be formatted with CSS.

Div elements in the HTML for a JavaScript application

```
<section id="faqs">
    <h1>jQuery FAQs</h1>
    <h2>What is jQuery?</h2>
    <div>
        // contents
    </div>
    <h2>Why is jQuery becoming so popular?</h2>
    <div>
        // contents
    </div>
    <h2>Which is harder to learn: jQuery or JavaScript?</h2>
    <div>
        // contents
    </div>
</section>
```

Span elements in the HTML for a JavaScript application

```
<label for="email_address1">Email Address:</label>
<input type="text" id="email_address1" name="email_address1">
<span id="email_address1_error">*</span><br>

<label for="email_address2">Re-enter Email Address:</label>
<input type="text" id="email_address2" name="email_address2">
<span id="email_address2_error">*</span><br>

<label for="first_name">First Name</label>
<input type="text" id="first_name" name="first_name">
<span id="first_name_error">*</span>
```

Description

- Before HTML5, div elements were used to define the structure within the body of a document. The ids for these div elements were then used by the CSS to apply formatting to the elements.

- Now, the HTML5 semantic elements are replacing div elements. That makes the structure of a page more apparent. However, you will still use div elements to define blocks of code that are used in some JavaScript applications.

- Before HTML5, span elements were used to identify portions of text that you could apply formatting to. Today, a better practice is to use specific elements to identify content. However, you will still use span elements for some JavaScript applications like the application in figures 1-5 through 1-7.

Figure 1-9   How to use the div and span elements

How to use the basic HTML attributes

Figure 1-10 presents the HTML *attributes* that are commonly used in JavaScript applications. You should already be familiar with the id attribute that identifies one HTML element and with class attributes that can be applied to more than one HTML element. You should also be familiar with the title attribute that can be used to provide a tooltip for an element and with the for attribute that relates a label to an input element.

When you use JavaScript, you will commonly use the id attribute to get or set the data in an input element. You will commonly use the name attribute so the server-side code can access the data that is submitted to it. You will sometimes add or remove class attributes to change the formatting of elements. And you will sometimes use title attributes to provide text that's related to elements.

In practice, you usually use the same value for the id and name attributes of an element. For instance, the example in this figure uses "email" as the value of both the id and name attributes. That makes it easier to remember the attribute values.

The basic HTML attributes

Attribute	Description
`id`	Specifies a unique identifier for an element that can be referred to by CSS.
`class`	Specifies one or more class names that can be referred to by CSS, and the same name can be used for more than one element. To code more than one class name, separate the class names with spaces.
`title`	Specifies additional information about an element. For some elements, the title appears in a tooltip when the user hovers the mouse over the element.
`for`	In a label element, this attribute specifies the id of the control that it applies to.
`name`	Specifies a unique name for an element that is commonly used by the server-side code and can also be used by the JavaScript code.

HTML that uses these attributes

```
<body>
    <h1>San Joaquin Valley Town Hall</h1>
    <h2 class="first_h2">Welcome to San Joaquin Valley Town Hall.</h2>
    <p>Please enter your e-mail address to subscribe to our
        newsletter.</p>
    <form id="email_form" name="email_form"
            action="join.html" method="get">
        <label for="email">E-Mail: </label>
        <input type="text" id="email" name="email"
                title="Enter e-mail address here.">
        <input type="button" value="Subscribe">
    </form>
</body>
```

The HTML in a web browser with a tooltip displayed for the text box

Description

- An *attribute* consists of an attribute name, an equals sign, and the value of the attribute enclosed in either single or double quotation marks.
- The id and class attributes are commonly used to apply CSS formatting,
- The name attribute is commonly used by the server-side code to access the data that is sent to it, but this attribute can also be used by the JavaScript code for a page.
- The for attribute in a label element is used to identify the control that it applies to.

Figure 1-10   How to use the basic HTML attributes

How to provide CSS styles for an HTML page

Figure 1-11 shows the two ways that styles are included for an HTML page in the applications in this book. First, you can code a link element in the head section of an HTML document that specifies a file that contains the CSS for the page. This is referred to as an *external style sheet*, and this is the method that's used for most of the applications in this book.

Second, you can code a style element in the head section that contains the CSS for the page. This can be referred to as *embedded styles*. The benefit of using embedded styles is that you don't have to switch back and forth between HTML and CSS files as you develop a page. Overall, though, it's better to use external style sheets because that makes it easier to use them for more than one page.

In some cases, you may want to use two or more external style sheets for a single page. You may even want to use both external style sheets and embedded styles for a page. In these cases, the styles are applied from the first external style sheet to the last one and then the embedded styles are applied.

If you want to provide an external style sheet for printing a page, you can code the media attribute in the link element. Then, when the user prints the page, the styles in that style sheet override the screen styles. This lets you provide the right formatting for printed pages.

Two ways to provide styles

Use an external style sheet by coding a link element in the head section

```
<link rel="stylesheet" href="styles/main.css">
```

Embed the styles in the head section

```
<style>
    body {
        font-family: Arial, Helvetica, sans-serif;
        font-size: 87.5%; }
    h1 { font-size: 250%; }
</style>
```

The sequence in which styles are applied

Styles from an external style sheet

Embedded styles

A head element that includes two external style sheets

```
<head>
    <title>San Joaquin Valley Town Hall</title>
    <link rel="stylesheet" href="../styles/main.css">
    <link rel="stylesheet" href="../styles/speaker.css">
</head>
```

The sequence in which styles are applied

From the first external style sheet to the last

How to specify the medium that an external style is for

```
<link rel="stylesheet" href="../styles/print.css" media="print">
```

Description

- When you use *external style sheets*, you separate content (HTML) from formatting (CSS). That makes it easy to use the same styles for two or more pages.

- If you use *embedded styles*, you have to copy the styles to other documents before you can use them a second time.

- If more than one rule for the same property is applied to the same element, the last rule overrides the earlier rules.

- When you specify a relative URL for an external CSS file, the URL is relative to the current file.

- You can use the media attribute of a link element to specify the medium that the style sheet is for. This lets you use different style sheets for different media.

- Since the default for the media attribute is screen, you don't have to use this attribute for a normal page. However, this attribute is commonly used to identify a style sheet that's used to format a page for printing.

Figure 1-11   Two ways to provide CSS styles for an HTML page

How to code the basic CSS selectors

Figure 1-12 shows how to code the basic CSS *selectors* for applying styles to HTML elements. If you don't already understand how these selectors work, you need to learn how because these selectors are commonly used by jQuery too.

To start, this figure shows the body of an HTML document that contains a section and a footer element. Here, the h1 element is assigned an id of "first_heading", and the two <p> elements in this section have class attributes with the value "blue". Also, the <p> element in the footer has a class attribute with two values: "blue" and "right". This means that this element is assigned to two classes.

The three rule sets in the first group of examples are *type selectors*. To code a type selector, you just code the name of the element. As a result, the first rule set in this group selects the body element. The second rule set selects the section element. And the third rule set selects all <p> elements.

In these examples, the first rule set changes the font for the body, and all of the elements within the body inherit this change. This rule set also sets the width of the body and centers it in the browser. Then, the second rule set puts a border around the section and puts some padding inside the section. Last, the rule set for the paragraphs sets the margin for the top, bottom, and left side of the paragraphs. That's why the paragraphs in the section are indented.

The rule set in the second group of examples uses an *id selector* to select an element by its id. To do that, the selector is a pound sign (#) followed by the id value that uniquely identifies an element. As a result, this rule set selects the h1 element that has an id of "first_heading". Then, its rule set sets the margins for the heading.

The two rule sets in the last group of examples use *class selectors* to select HTML elements by class. To do that, the selector is a period (.) followed by the class name. As a result, the first rule set selects all elements that have been assigned to the "blue" class, which are all three <p> elements. The second rule set selects any elements that have been assigned to the "right" class. That is the paragraph in the footer division. Then, the first rule set sets the color of the font to blue and the second rule set aligns the paragraph on the right.

One of the key points here is that a class attribute can have the same value for more than one element on a page. Then, if you code a selector for that class, it will be used to format all the elements in that class. In contrast, since the id for an element must be unique, an id selector can only be used to format a single element.

As you probably know, there are several other selectors that you can use with CSS (and also with jQuery). But the ones in this figure will get you started. Then, whenever an application in this book requires other selectors, the selectors will be explained in detail.

HTML that can be selected by element type, id, or class

```
<body>
    <section>
        <h1 id="first_heading">The Speaker Lineup</h1>
        <p class="blue">October 19: Jeffrey Toobin</p>
        <p class="blue">November 16: Andrew Ross Sorkin</p>
    </section>
    <footer>
        <p class="blue right">Copyright SJV Town Hall</p>
    </footer>
</body>
```

CSS rule sets that select by element type, id, and class

Three elements by type

```
body {
    font-family: Arial, Helvetica, sans-serif;
    width: 400px;
    margin: 1em auto; }
section {
    border: 2px solid black;
    padding: 1em; }
p { margin: .25em 0 .25em 3em; }
```

One element by ID

```
#first_heading { margin: 0 1em .25em; }
```

Elements by class

```
.blue { color: blue; }
.right { text-align: right; }
```

The elements displayed in a browser

Description

- You code a selector for all elements of a specific type by naming the element. This is referred to as a *type selector*.

- You code an id selector for an element with an id attribute by coding a pound sign (#) followed by the id value. This is known as an *id selector*.

- You code a selector for an element with a class attribute by coding a period followed by the class name. Then, the rule set applies to all elements with that class name. This is known as a *class selector*.

Figure 1-12   How to code the basic CSS selectors

How to code CSS rule sets

Figure 1-13 presents the CSS for the Email List application that was presented earlier in this chapter. This is typical of the CSS for the applications in this book. Since the focus of this book is on JavaScript and jQuery, not CSS, the CSS is usually limited. For instance, the CSS in this example doesn't require id or class selectors.

Just to make sure we're using the same terminology, this CSS contains seven *rule sets*. Each rule set consists of a selector, a set of braces { }, and one or more *rules* within the braces. Also, each rule consists of a *property name*, a colon, the value or values for the rule, and an ending semicolon.

The first rule set in this example applies to the seven HTML5 semantic elements. It is required for compatibility with older browsers. It tells those browsers that the semantic elements should be treated as block elements. Without this rule set, older browsers will treat these elements as inline elements, which is not what you want.

Although this rule set won't be shown in the CSS for the applications for this book, it is included with the downloadable applications. As a result, those applications should run on older browsers.

Beyond that, this book will explain any of the CSS that is relevant to the JavaScript for an application. So for now, if you know how to code rule sets, you're ready to continue.

The CSS file for a typical application in this book

```css
/* The CSS workaround so the HTML5 semantic elements can be formatted */
article, aside, figure, footer, header, nav, section {
    display: block;
}
body {
    font-family: Arial, Helvetica, sans-serif;
    background-color: white;
    margin: 0 auto;
    width: 650px;
    border: 3px solid blue;
}
h1 {
    color: blue;
}
section {
    padding: 0 2em 1em;
}
label {
    float: left;
    width: 11em;
    text-align: right;
}
input {
    margin-left: 1em;
    margin-bottom: .5em;
}
span {
    color: red;
}
```

Description

- Because the focus of this book is JavaScript and jQuery, not CSS, the CSS that's used in this book is usually simple. We just apply enough CSS to make each application look okay and work correctly.

- In fact, for most of the applications in this book, you won't have to understand the CSS so it won't even be shown. Whenever the CSS is critical to the understanding of the JavaScript application, though, it will be explained in detail.

- At the least, you should know that the CSS for an HTML document consists of one or more *rule sets*. Each of these rule sets starts with the selector for the rule set followed by a set of braces { }. Within the braces are one or more rules.

- You should also know that each CSS *rule* consists of a *property name*, a colon, the value or values for the property, and a semicolon.

Figure 1-13   How to code CSS rule sets

How to test a JavaScript application

Next, you'll learn how to test a JavaScript application. To do that, you run the HTML for the web page that uses the JavaScript.

How to run a JavaScript application

When you develop a JavaScript application, you're usually working on your own computer or your company's server. Then, to run the application, you use one of the four methods shown in figure 1-14. Of the four, it's easiest to run the HTML page from the IDE that you're using to develop the HTML, CSS, and JavaScript files. You'll learn more about that in a moment.

In the first of the four methods in this first list, File→Open File means to drop down the File menu from the menu bar and select the Open File command. Similarly, File→New→Web Project means to drop down the File menu, select the New command, and then select the Web Project command. This notation is used throughout this book.

After an application has been uploaded to an Internet server, you can use the second set of methods in this figure to run the application. The first way is to enter a *Uniform Resource Locator* (*URL*) into the address bar of your browser. The second way is to click on a link on a web page that requests another page. You can also use this method if an application is running on your own computer or server.

As the diagram in this figure shows, the URL for an Internet page consists of four components. In most cases, the *protocol* is HTTP. If you omit the protocol, the browser uses HTTP as the default.

The second component is the *domain name* that identifies the web server that the HTTP request will be sent to. The web browser uses this name to look up the address of the web server for the domain. Although you can't omit the domain name, you can often omit the "www." from the domain name.

The third component is the *path* where the file resides on the server. The path lists the folders that contain the file. Forward slashes are used to separate the names in the path and to represent the server's top-level folder at the start of the path. In this example, the path is "/ourwork/".

The last component is the name of the file. In this example, the file is named index.html. If you omit the filename, the web server will search for a default document in the path. Depending on the web server, this file will be named index.html, default.htm, or some variation of the two.

The web page at c:/jquery/book_apps/ch01/email_list.html

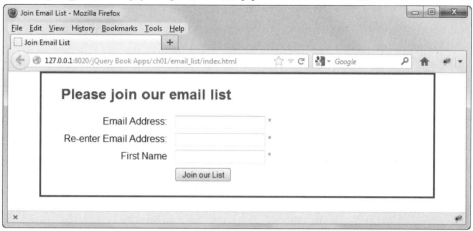

Four ways to run an HTML page that's on your own server or computer

- Use the File→Open command with Internet Explorer or the File→Open File command with Firefox.
- If you're using Windows, find the file in the Windows Explorer and double-click on it.
- Use the features of your text editor or IDE.
- Click on a link in the current web page to load the next web page.

Two ways to run an HTML page that's on the Internet

- Enter the URL of a web page into the browser's address bar.
- Click on a link in the current web page to load the next web page.

The components of an HTTP URL on the Internet

What happens if you omit parts of a URL

- If you omit the protocol, the default of http:// will be used.
- If you omit the filename, the default document name for the web server will be used. This is typically index.html, default.htm, or some variation.

Description

- When you are developing JavaScript applications, you usually store them on your own computer instead of the Internet. So when you test the applications, you run them from your own computer.
- Later, after the applications are deployed to your Internet web server, you can run the applications from the Internet.

Figure 1-14   How to run a JavaScript application

How to ensure cross-browser compatibility

If you want your web site to be used by as many visitors as possible, you need to make sure that your web pages are compatible with as many browsers as possible. That's known as *cross-browser compatibility*. That means you should test your applications on as many browsers as possible, including the five browsers summarized in figure 1-15, as well as the older versions of those browsers.

The table in this figure shows the current release numbers of these browsers and their rating for HTML5 support. To get an updated version of this information, though, you can go to the web site at www.html5test.com. This web site will also rate the browser that you're using when you access it.

In general, Internet Explorer (IE) gives web developers the most problems because it's the least standard. In contrast, the other four browsers generally support the same features so if a web page runs on one of them, it will also run on the others. The other four browsers also provide for automatic updates, but IE typically hasn't done that. As a result, the other four browsers are most likely to support the latest features of HTML5 and CSS3.

Incidentally, IE not only has some HTML and CSS incompatibilities, but also some JavaScript incompatibilities. In fact, one of the benefits of using jQuery is that its functions have already been tested for cross-browser compatibility. As a result, they will work on all browsers.

To provide for browsers that don't support the HTML5 and CSS3 features that are presented in this book, you need to use the workarounds shown in this figure. However, it is difficult to test your web pages in older browsers because (1) you can't get them anymore and (2) you can't put all versions of the old browsers on one system even if you could get them.

If you're a student, you probably won't need to test your web pages on old browsers. But for production applications, that type of testing is essential. To help you do it, you can search the Internet for web sites or software products that provide ways to test your pages on old browsers.

To do the exercises in this book, you can get by with just the current versions of IE and Firefox. But if you're using a Mac OS system, you won't be able to install IE so you can skip any steps that require it or substitute Safari for IE references. For a production system, of course, you need to install all five browsers and make sure your web pages work on all of them.

The current browsers and their HTML5 ratings (perfect score is 500)

Browser	Release	HTML5 Test Rating
Google Chrome	22	437
Opera	12	385
Mozilla Firefox	15	346
Apple Safari	6	376
Internet Explorer	9	138

The web site for these ratings

`http://www.html5test.com`

Guidelines for cross-browser compatibility

- Test your web pages on all of the major browsers, including all of the older versions of these browsers that are still commonly used.

- Use the HTML5 and CSS3 features that are supported by all of the modern browsers, which are the features that are presented in this book. But use the workarounds so these applications will run on the older browsers too.

The two workarounds for using the HTML5 semantic elements

The JavaScript shiv that lets older browsers know about the elements

```
<script src="http://html5shiv.googlecode.com/svn/trunk/html5.js"></script>
```

The CSS rule set that sets the semantic elements to block elements

```
article, aside, figure, figcaption, footer, header, nav, section {
    display: block; }
```

How to test your web pages in older browsers

- One of the problems in cross-browser testing is that you can't install all of the old browsers on one system. In particular, Windows doesn't let you install more than one version of IE at the same time.

- The solution is to use programs or web sites that offer this type of testing. To find out what's available, try searching for "browser testing software" or "cross browser testing".

Description

- Today, there are still differences in the way that different browsers handle HTML, CSS, and JavaScript. As a developer, though, you want your web pages to work on as many different web browsers as possible. This is referred to as *cross-browser compatibility*.

- One of the benefits of using jQuery is that it provides cross-browser compatibility for the JavaScript that it provides. However, the HTML, CSS, and other JavaScript can still cause compatibility problems.

- In general, Internet Explorer gives web developers the most problems because it is the least standard and hasn't provided for automatic updates.

- Eventually, all browsers will support HTML5 and CSS3 so the workarounds won't be necessary.

Figure 1-15   How to ensure cross-browser compatibility

How to use Aptana to develop JavaScript applications

Because HTML, CSS, and JavaScript are just text, you can use any text editor to create the files for a JavaScript application. However, a better editor or an *Integrated Development Environment* (*IDE*) can speed development time and reduce coding errors. That's why we recommend Aptana Studio 3. It is a free IDE that runs on Windows, Mac OS, and Linux, and it can greatly improve your productivity.

In the appendix for this book, you can learn how to install Aptana. You can also learn how to use Aptana for the common development functions in the topics that follow. If you prefer to use another editor, of course, you can skip these topics. But even then, you may want to browse these topics because they will give you a good idea of what an IDE should be able to do. They may also encourage you to give Aptana a try.

How to create or import a project

In Aptana, a project consists of the folders and files for a complete web application. Once you create a project, it's easier to work with its folders and files, to create new files for the project, and so forth.

To create a project, you use the first procedure in figure 1-16. The result of this procedure is that you end up with a named project that starts with the top-level folder for the application. Then, you can easily access the folders and files for the application by using the App Explorer window that's shown in the next figure.

To make it easier to work with the applications for this book, we recommend that you import them into one Aptana project that includes all of the book applications. To do that, you can use either the second or third procedure in this figure, depending on which Aptana release you're using. The dialog boxes in this figure import the downloaded book applications at this location

```
c:/murach/jquery/book_apps
```

into a project named jQuery Book Apps. Once that's done, you can easily access the applications by using the App Explorer window.

The dialog boxes for importing a project in Aptana 3.4

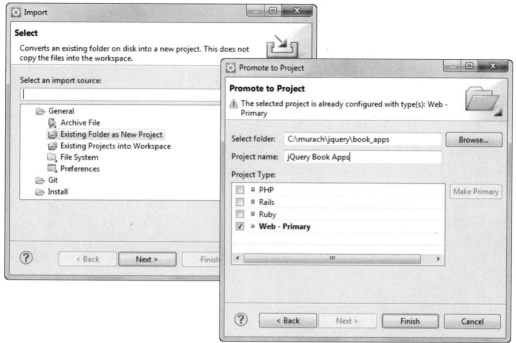

How to create a new project

- Use the File→New→Web Project command.

How to import a project with Aptana 3.4 or later

- Use the File→Import command to display the Import dialog box shown above, click on Existing Folder as New Project, and click Next. Then, in the Promote to Project dialog box shown above, browse to the top-level folder for the application, enter a project name, and click the Finish button.

How to import a project with Aptana 3.3 or earlier

- Use the File→New→Web Project command to display the New Web Project dialog box. Next, enter a name for the project, uncheck the Use Default Location box, and browse to the top-level folder for the project. Then, read the warning message that appears, and click the Finish button.

Description

- Aptana works the best when you set up projects for the web applications that you're developing and maintaining.
- In general, each Aptana project should contain the folders and files for one web application. For this book, however, you can set up one project for all of the book applications, one project for all exercises, and one project for all exercise solutions.

Figure 1-16   How to create or import a project in Aptana

How to open or close an HTML, CSS, or JavaScript file

Figure 1-17 shows how to open or close an HTML, CSS, or JavaScript file after you've created a project. Here, the jQuery Book Apps project is shown in the App Explorer window on the left side of Aptana. If you have created more than one project, you can switch from one to another by using the drop-down project list that's at the top of the App Explorer window.

Once you have the correct project open, you can drill down to the file that you want to open by clicking on the plus signs for the folders. In this example, the ch01 and email_list folders have been expanded so you can see the four files for the Email List application. Then, to open a file, you just double-click on it.

When you open a file in Aptana, it is opened in a new tab. This means that you can have several files open at the same time and move from one to another by clicking on a tab. This makes it easy to switch back and forth between the HTML, CSS, and JavaScript files for a web page. This also makes it easy to copy code from one file to another.

If you want to open a file that isn't part of a project, you can do that by using one of the methods shown in this figure. First, you can use the Project Explorer window to locate the file on your computer and then double-click on it. Second, you can use the File→Open File command to open a file.

To close one or more files, you can use one of the three methods shown in this figure. This makes it easy to close all of the files except the ones that you're currently working with. And that helps you avoid the mistake of making a change to the wrong file.

As you work with Aptana, you'll see that it has the same type of interface that you've used with other programs. So if you want to do something that isn't presented in this chapter, try right-clicking on an item to see what menu options are available. Check out the other buttons in the toolbar. See what's available from the drop-down menus. With a little experimentation, you'll find that this program is not only powerful, but also easy to use.

Aptana with the App Explorer shown and a JavaScript file in the second tab

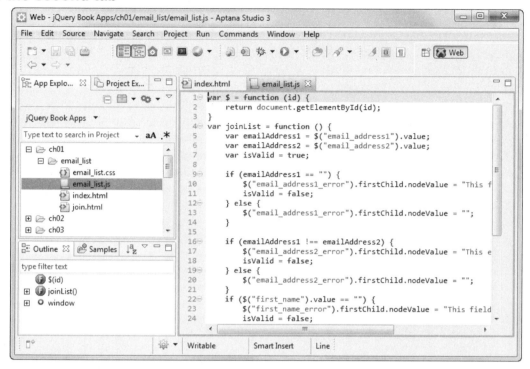

How to open a file within a project
- Use the drop-down list in Aptana's App Explorer to select the project.
- Then, locate the file in the App Explorer and double-click on it.

Two ways to open an HTML file that isn't in a project
- Use the Project Explorer to locate the file, and double-click on it.
- Use the File→Open File command.

How to close one or more files
- To close one file, click on the X in the tab for the file.
- To close all of the files except one, right click on the tab you don't want to close and select Close Others.
- To close all of the files, right click on any tab and select Close All.

Description
- When you open a file, the file is displayed in a new tab.

Figure 1-17   How to open or close an HTML, CSS, or JavaScript file in Aptana

How to change the colors that highlight the syntax

When you open a file in Aptana, one of the first things you might want to do is change the colors that are used to highlight the syntax of HTML, CSS, and JavaScript code. That's because the default settings are light colors on a dark background that can be hard to read.

To change the colors, you can use the procedure in figure 1-18. In this book, we use the Dreamweaver theme, but you can experiment with other themes until you find one that you like. If you click the Apply button after you select a theme, you can see the colors that are used in the window behind the dialog box. Then, if you like the colors, you can click the OK button to close the dialog box.

Aptana's Themes dialog box

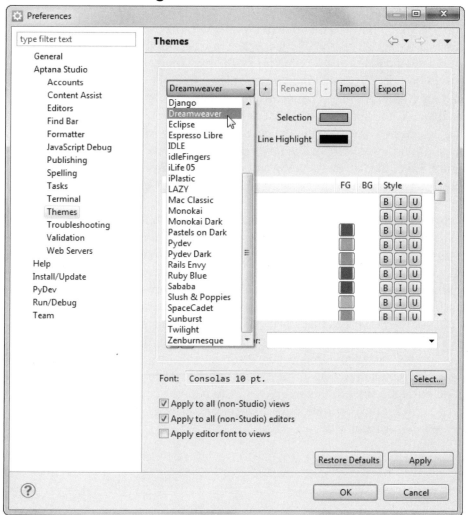

Procedure

- Use the Window→Preferences command to open the Preferences dialog box.
- Click on Aptana Studio, and then click on Themes to display the Themes dialog box.
- Choose a theme from the drop-down list.

Description

- Aptana displays different parts of the JavaScript statement in different colors so the statements are easier to interpret.
- If you don't like the colors that are used, you can change the colors by using the procedure above.

Figure 1-18   How to change the colors that highlight the syntax in Aptana

How to edit a file

Figure 1-19 shows how to edit a JavaScript file with Aptana, but editing works the same for HTML and CSS files. When you open a file with an html, css, or js extension, Aptana knows what type of file you're working with so it can use color to highlight the syntax components. The good news is that color coding is also used for CSS that's in a style element of an HTML document or JavaScript that's in a script element of an HTML document.

As you enter a new line of code, the auto-completion feature presents lists of words that start with the letters that you've entered. This type of list is illustrated by this figure. Here, the list shows the JavaScript choices after the letter *t* has been entered. Then, you can select a word and press the Tab key to insert it into your code.

This also works with HTML and CSS entries. If, for example, you type <s in an HTML document, Aptana presents a list of the elements that start with s. Then, if you select one of the elements, Aptana finishes the opening tag and adds the ending tag. This feature also works when you start an attribute.

Similarly, if you enter # to start a CSS rule set, Aptana presents a list of the ids that can be used in an id selector. If you enter *b* to start a rule, Aptana presents a list of the properties that start with b. And if you start an entry for a property value, Aptana will present a list of values. In short, this is a powerful feature that can help you avoid many entry errors.

Beyond that, Aptana provides error markers and warning markers that help you find and correct errors. In this figure, for example, you can see two error markers. Then, to get the description for an error or warning marker, you can hover the mouse over the marker.

Aptana with an auto-completion list for a JavaScript entry

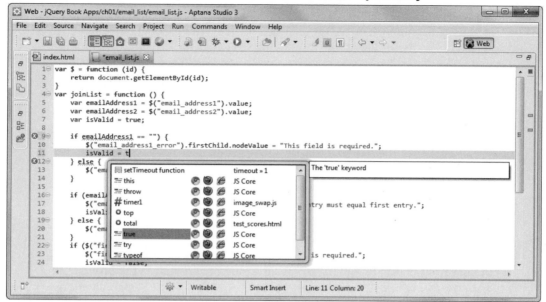

Description

- To expand the contents of a tab and hide the Project and App Explorers as shown above, double-click on the tab. To restore the Project and App Explorers, click the Restore icon at the top of the vertical bar that's to the left of the editing window.

- The auto-completion feature displays a list of elements that start with what you've typed. To insert one of those terms, double-click on it or use the arrow keys to highlight it and press the Tab key.

- An error marker is a red circle that contains a white X at the start of a line. A warning marker is a yellow triangle that contains an exclamation mark. These markers are displayed as you enter and edit code.

- To get the description for an error or warning marker, hover the mouse over the marker.

Figure 1-19   How to edit a file in Aptana

How to run a JavaScript application

Figure 1-20 shows how to run a JavaScript application from Aptana. To run the HTML file for the application in the default browser, you first select the tab of the open file. Then, you click on the Run button. This opens the default browser and runs the file in that browser. Or, to run an HTML file in another browser, you use the drop-down list to the right of the Run button.

Incidentally, if you click on the Run button when an HTML file isn't selected, nothing happens. Also, you need to save any changes to an HTML file and its related CSS file before you can run it. To do that, you can click on the Save or Save All button in the toolbar.

When you run a JavaScript application this way, a new browser or browser tab is opened each time you click the Run button. So, if you click on the Run button 10 times for an application, 10 browsers or tabs will be opened.

Another way to do this, though, is to run an application the first time by clicking on the Run button. Then, after you find and fix the errors, you can click on the Save All button in Aptana to save the changes, switch to the browser, and click on the Reload or Refresh button in the browser to reload the application with the changes.

Aptana's Run button

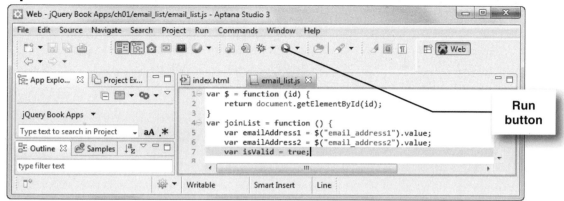

The web page in Firefox

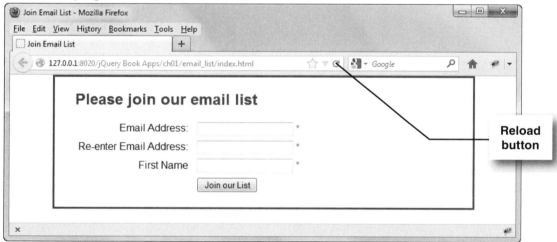

Procedure

- To run a JavaScript application in the default browser, open the HTML file for the application, select its tab, and click on the Run button.

- To run a JavaScript application in another browser, select the tab for its HTML file, click the down-arrow to the right of the Run button, and select the browser.

Description

- Before you run a file, you should save any changes that you've made to it or any of its related files. To do that, you can click on the Save or Save All button in the toolbar.

- When you test an application, you run its HTML page, note the errors, fix the errors in Aptana, save the changes, and run the page again.

- To run the page again, you can click on the Run button, which will open up another browser or browser tab. Or, you can switch to the browser and click its Reload or Refresh button. That way, another browser or tab isn't opened.

Figure 1-20   How to run a JavaScript application from Aptana

Perspective

This chapter has presented the background concepts and terms that you need for developing JavaScript applications. Now, if you're comfortable with everything that you've learned, you're ready for chapter 2.

But what if you aren't comfortable with your HTML and CSS skills? First, we recommend that you keep going in this book because you don't have to be an HTML or CSS expert to develop JavaScript and jQuery applications. Second, we recommend that you get a copy of *Murach's HTML5 and CSS3*, because every web developer should eventually master HTML5 and CSS3.

Terms you should know

client
web browser
web server
network
intranet
local area network (LAN)
Internet
wide area network (WAN)
Internet service provider (ISP)
HTML (HyperText Markup Language)
static web page
HTTP request
HTTP (HyperText Transfer Protocol)
HTTP response
render a web page
dynamic web page
application server
database server
server-side processing
round trip
JavaScript
JavaScript engine
scripting language
client-side processing
jQuery
image swap
image rollover

data validation
HTML element
tag
CSS (Cascading Style Sheets)
DOM scripting
Document Object Model (DOM)
HTML5 semantic elements
HTML5 semantics
JavaScript shiv or shim
attribute
external style sheet
embedded styles
selector
type selector
id selector
class selector
rule set
rule
property name
URL (Uniform Resource Locator)
protocol
domain name
path
cross-browser compatibility
IDE (Integrated Development
    Environment)
Aptana project

Summary

- A web application consists of clients, a web server, and a network. *Clients* use *web browsers* to request web pages from the web server. The *web server* returns the requested pages.

- A *local area network* (*LAN*) connects computers that are near to each other. This is often called an *intranet*. In contrast, the Internet consists of many *wide area networks* (*WANs*).

- To request a web page, the web browser sends an *HTTP request* to the web server. Then, the web server gets the HTML for the requested page and sends it back to the browser in an *HTTP response*. Last, the browser *renders* the HTML into a web page.

- A *static web page* is a page that is the same each time it's retrieved. In contrast, the HTML for a *dynamic web page* is generated by a server-side program or script, so its HTML can change from one request to another.

- *JavaScript* is a *scripting language* that is run by the *JavaScript engine* of a web browser. It provides for *client-side processing*. *jQuery* is a JavaScript library that makes it easier to develop JavaScript applications.

- Both JavaScript and jQuery are commonly used to modify the *Document Object Model* (*DOM*) that's built for each web page when it is loaded. This is referred to as *DOM scripting*. When the DOM is changed, the browser immediately changes the display so it reflects those changes.

- *HTML* (*HyperText Markup Language*) is the language that defines the structure and contents of a web page. *CSS* (*Cascading Style Sheets*) are used to control how the web pages are formatted.

- You can view a web page that's on your own computer or server or on an Internet server. To view a web page on an Internet server, you can enter the *URL* (*Uniform Resource Locator*) that consists of the *protocol*, *domain name*, *path*, and filename into a browser's address bar.

- When you develop a JavaScript application, you need to provide for *cross-browser compatibility*. That means you have to test your applications on all modern browsers as well as older versions of those browsers.

- One of the benefits of using jQuery is that its JavaScript functions have already been tested for cross-browser compatibility.

- To develop JavaScript applications, you can use a text editor or an *Integrated Development Environment* (*IDE*). For this book, we recommend Aptana Studio 3 because it's powerful, free, and runs on Windows, Mac, and Unix systems.

Before you do the exercises for this book...

Before you do the exercises for this book, you should download and install the Firefox browser as well as the applications for this book. If you're going to use Aptana, you should also download and install that product. The procedures for installing the software and applications for this book are in appendix A.

Exercise 1-1   Run the Email List application

In this exercise, you'll run the Email List application that's presented in figures 1-5, 1-6, and 1-7.

Open the application in Firefox

1. Start Firefox if it isn't already open. Then, use the File→Open File command to open this HTML file:

   `c:\murach\jquery\book_apps\ch01\email_list\index.html`

2. To test what happens when you don't enter any data, just click the Join our List button without entering any data. Then, you can see the error messages that are displayed.

3. Enter an email address in the first text box and invalid data in the second text box and click the Join our List button to see what error messages are displayed.

4. Enter valid data for all three text boxes and click on the button. Then, the data is submitted for processing and a new web page is displayed.

Exercise 1-2   Run other section 1 applications

This exercise has you run the applications presented in chapter 6. These applications will give you some idea of what you'll able to do when you complete this section.

5. Open this file in the Firefox browser:

   `c:\murach\jquery\book_apps\ch06\faqs_links\index.html`

   Then, click on one of the headings to display the text for it, and click the heading again to hide the text.

6. Open this file in the Firefox browser:

   `c:\murach\jquery\book_apps\ch06\image_swap\index.html`

   Then, click on the small images to see the large image get swapped.

7. Open this file in the Firefox browser:

   `c:\murach\jquery\book_apps\ch06\slide_show\index.html`

   Watch the slide show.

Exercise 1-3   Get started with Aptana

This exercise is for readers who are going to use Aptana with this book. It guides you through the process of creating projects that provide easy access to the book applications and exercises that you've downloaded.

Create the projects

1. Start Aptana, and use the procedure in figure 1-16 to create a project for the book applications that are stored in this folder:

   `c:\murach\jquery\book_apps`

   This project should be named jQuery Book Apps, and the entries for the last dialog box should be just like those in this figure.

2. Use the same procedure to create a project named jQuery Exercises for the exercises that are stored in this folder:

   `c:\jquery\exercises`

   as well as a project named jQuery Solutions for the exercise solutions that are stored in this folder:

   `c:\murach\jquery\solutions`

Test the Email List application

3. Use the drop-down list in the App Explorer to select the jQuery Exercises project. This provides access to all of the exercises that are in this book.

4. Click on the plus sign before ch01 to display the email_list folder, and click on the plus sign for the email_list folder to display the files for the Email List application.

5. Double-click on the file named index.html to open that file. Then, click the Run button in the toolbar to run the application in the default browser. That will automatically switch you to that browser.

6. Switch back to Aptana, and click on the down arrow to the right of the Run button. If the drop-down list offers Internet Explorer, click on it to run the application in that browser. Then, return to Aptana.

Edit the JavaScript code

7. In the App Explorer, double click on the file named email_list.js to open that file, and note the colors that are used for syntax highlighting.

8. If you don't like the colors that are used, use the procedure in figure 1-18 to change them.

9. In the JavaScript file, delete the right parenthesis in the first line of code. This should display two error markers. Then, hover the mouse over the markers to display the error descriptions. This illustrates Aptana's error-checking feature. Now, undo the change that you made. (To undo a change with the keyboard, press Ctrl+Z.)

10. In the JavaScript file, after the third statement that starts with var, start a statement on a new line with these characters:

    `if (e`

    This should display a list of the possible entries that start with the letter *e*. Here, you can see that emailAddress1 and emailAddress2 are included in the list. These are the variables that are created by the first two var statements, and this illustrates Aptana's code-completion feature. Now, undo this change.

11. Enter this statement on a new line that comes right before the last line of the JavaScript code, which consists of just a right brace (}):

    `alert("The DOM has now been built");`

    In other words, this statement will become the second last line in the file.

12. To test the statement that you've added, click on the Save All button in the toolbar to save your changes. Then, switch to your browser and click on the Reload or Refresh button to run the application with this change. This should display a dialog box that you can close by clicking on its OK button. After that, the application should work the same as it did before.

13. If you're curious, do more experimenting on your own. Then, close the files and exit from Aptana.

2

Getting started with JavaScript

The goal of this chapter is to get you off to a good start with JavaScript, especially if you're new to programming. If you have programming experience with another language, you should be able to move rapidly through this chapter. Otherwise, take it easy and do the exercises at the end of this chapter.

How to include JavaScript in an HTML document............**50**
Two ways to include JavaScript in the head of an HTML document...........50
How to include JavaScript in the body of an HTML document 52

The JavaScript syntax..**54**
How to code JavaScript statements 54
How to create identifiers...56
How to use comments..58
How to use objects, methods, and properties 60

How to work with JavaScript data **62**
The primitive data types..62
How to code numeric expressions 64
How to work with numeric variables..66
How to work with string and Boolean variables 68
How to use the parseInt and parseFloat methods.......................................70

How to code control statements.....................................**72**
How to code conditional expressions 72
How to code if statements..74
How to code while and do-while loops 76
How to code for loops..78

Two illustrative applications...**80**
The Miles Per Gallon application...80
The Test Scores application 82

How to find errors in your code **84**
How to get error messages with Firefox...84
Common JavaScript errors 84

Perspective **86**

How to include JavaScript in an HTML document

In chapter 1, you saw how the JavaScript for an application can be coded in a separate file. But there are actually three different ways to include JavaScript in an HTML document. You'll learn all three now.

Two ways to include JavaScript in the head of an HTML document

Figure 2-1 presents two of the three ways to include JavaScript in an HTML document. As you saw in the last chapter, one way is to code the JavaScript in a separate *external file*. Then, you code a script element in the head section of the HTML document to include that file.

In the script element, the src attribute is used to refer to the external file. For this element, you can also code a type attribute with the value "text/javascript" to tell the browser what kind of content the file contains. But with HTML5, that attribute is no longer needed because the assumption is that all files that are referred to in script elements contain JavaScript.

In the example in this figure, the src attribute refers to a file named calculate_mpg.js. The assumption here is that this file is in the same folder as the HTML file. Otherwise, you need to code a relative URL that provides the right path for the file. If, for example, the JavaScript file is in a folder named javascript and that folder is in the same folder as the HTML file, the src attribute would be coded this way:

```
<script src="javascript/calculate_mpg.js"></script>
```

This works the same as it does for any other file reference in an HTML document.

The second way to include JavaScript in an HTML document is to code the JavaScript within the script element in the head section. This can be referred to as *embedded JavaScript*. Note, however, that the application will work the same whether the JavaScript is embedded in the head section or loaded into the head section from an external file.

The benefit of using an external file is that it separates the JavaScript from the HTML. The benefit of using embedded JavaScript is that you don't have to switch between the HTML and JavaScript files as you develop the application. In the examples in this book, you'll see both uses of JavaScript.

Two attributes of the script element

Attribute	Description
src	Specifies the location and name of an external JavaScript file.
type	With HTML5, this attribute can be omitted. If you code it, use "text/javascript" for JavaScript code.

A script element in the head section that loads an external JavaScript file

```
<script src="calculate_mpg.js"></script>
```

A script element that embeds JavaScript in the head section

```
<head>
    ...
    <script>
        alert("The Calculate MPG application");
        var miles = prompt("Enter miles driven");
        miles = parseFloat(miles);
        var gallons = prompt("Enter gallons of gas used");
        gallons = parseFloat(gallons);
        var mpg = miles/gallons;
        mpg = parseInt(mpg);
        alert("Miles per gallon = " + mpg);
    </script>
</head>
```

Description

- A script element in the head section of an HTML document is commonly used to identify an *external JavaScript file* that should be included with the page.

- A script element in the head section can also contain the JavaScript statements that are included with the page. This can be referred to as *embedded JavaScript*.

- If you code more than one script element in the head section, the JavaScript is included in the sequence in which the script statements appear.

- When a script element in the head section includes an external JavaScript file, the JavaScript in the file runs as if it were coded in the script element.

Figure 2-1   Two ways to include JavaScript in the head of an HTML document

How to include JavaScript in the body of an HTML document

Figure 2-2 shows a third way to include JavaScript in an HTML document. This time, the two script elements in the first example are coded in the body of the HTML document. When a script element is coded in the body, the element is replaced by the output of the JavaScript code when the application is loaded.

If you want to provide for browsers that don't have JavaScript enabled, you can code a noscript element after a script element as shown in the second example. Then, if JavaScript is disabled, the content of the noscript element will be displayed. But if JavaScript is enabled, the script element is replaced by the output of the JavaScript code and the noscript element is ignored. This way, some output will be displayed whether or not JavaScript is enabled.

In the second example, the noscript element is coded right after a script element, so 2012 will replace the output of the script element if JavaScript isn't enabled in the browser. This means that the result will be the same in the year 2012 whether or not JavaScript is enabled. But in the year 2013, the year will be updated by the JavaScript if it is enabled.

You can also code a noscript element that doesn't follow a script element. For instance, you can code a noscript element at the top of a page that warns the user that the page won't work right if JavaScript is disabled. This is illustrated by the third example. In this case, nothing is displayed if JavaScript is enabled and the message is displayed if JavaScript is disabled.

In all of the applications in this book, the JavaScript is either embedded in the head section of the HTML or in an external file that's identified in the head section of the HTML. However, you shouldn't have any trouble including the JavaScript in the body of an HTML document whenever you want to do that.

JavaScript in the body of an HTML document

```
<p>
    <script>
        var today = new Date();
        document.write("Current date: ");
        document.write(today.toDateString());
    </script>
</p>
<p>&copy; 
    <script>
        var today = new Date();
        document.write( today.getFullYear() );
    </script>
, San Joaquin Valley Town Hall
</p>
```

The result of the JavaScript in a web browser

Current date: Mon Mar 12 2012

© 2012 , San Joaquin Valley Town Hall"

A noscript element in the body of an HTML document

```
<p>&copy; 
    <script>
        var today = new Date();
        document.write( today.getFullYear() );
    </script>
    <noscript>2012</noscript>
, San Joaquin Valley Town Hall
</p>
```

A noscript element at the start of an HTML document

```
<h2><noscript>To get the most from this web site,
    please enable JavaScript.</noscript></h2>
```

Description

- If a script element is coded in the body of a document, it is replaced by the output of the JavaScript code.

- The noscript element can be used to display content when JavaScript is disabled in a user's browser.

Figure 2-2   How to include JavaScript in the body of an HTML document

The JavaScript syntax

The *syntax* of JavaScript refers to the rules that you must follow as you code statements. If you don't adhere to these rules, your web browser won't be able to interpret and execute your statements.

How to code JavaScript statements

Figure 2-3 summarizes the rules for coding JavaScript *statements*. The first rule is that JavaScript is case-sensitive. This means that uppercase and lowercase letters are treated as different letters. For example, the names *salestax* and *salesTax* are treated as different words.

The second rule is that JavaScript statements must end with a semicolon. If you don't end each statement with a semicolon, JavaScript won't be able to tell where one statement ends and the next one begins.

The third rule is that JavaScript ignores extra whitespace in statements. Since *whitespace* includes spaces, tabs, and new line characters, this lets you break long statements into multiple lines so they're easier to read.

Be careful, though, to follow the guidelines in this figure about where to split a statement. If you don't split a statement at a good spot, JavaScript will sometimes try to help you out by adding a semicolon for you, and that can lead to errors.

A block of JavaScript code

```
var joinList = function () {
    var emailAddress1 = $("email_address1").value;
    var emailAddress2 = $("email_address2").value;

    if (emailAddress1 == "") {
        alert("Email Address is required.");
    } else if (emailAddress2 == "") {
        alert("Second Email Address is required.");
    } else if (emailAddress1 !== emailAddress2) {
        alert("Second Email entry must equal first entry.");
    } else if ($("first_name").value == "") {
        alert("First Name is required.");
    } else {
        $("email_form").submit();
    }
}
```

The basic syntax rules

- JavaScript is case-sensitive.
- JavaScript ignores extra whitespace within statements.
- Each JavaScript statement ends with a semicolon.

How to split a statement over two or more lines

- Split a statement after:
  - an arithmetic or relational operator such as +, -, *, /, =, ==, >, or <
  - an opening brace ({), bracket ([ ), or parenthesis
  - a closing brace (})
- Do not split a statement after:
  - an identifier, a value, or the *return* keyword
  - a closing bracket ( ]) or parenthesis

Description

- A JavaScript *statement* has a syntax that's similar to the syntax of Java.
- *Whitespace* refers to the spaces, tab characters, and return characters in the code, and it is ignored by the compiler. As a result, you can use spaces, tab characters, and return characters to format your code so it's easier to read.
- In some cases, JavaScript will try to correct what it thinks is a missing semicolon by adding a semicolon at the end of a split line. To prevent this, follow the guidelines above for splitting a statement.

Figure 2-3   How to code JavaScript statements

How to create identifiers

Variables, functions, objects, properties, methods, and events must all have names so you can refer to them in your JavaScript code. An *identifier* is the name given to one of these components.

Figure 2-4 shows the rules for creating identifiers in JavaScript. Besides the first four rules, you can't use any of the JavaScript *reserved words* (also known as *keywords*) as an identifier. These are words that are reserved for use within the JavaScript language. You should also avoid using any of the JavaScript global properties or methods as identifiers, which you'll learn more about as you progress through this book.

Besides the rules, you should give your identifiers meaningful names. That means that it should be easy to tell what an identifier refers to and easy to remember how to spell the name. To create names like that, you should avoid abbreviations. If, for example, you abbreviate the name for monthly investment as mon_inv, it will be hard to tell what it refers to and hard to remember how you spelled it. But if you spell it out as monthly_investment, both problems are solved.

Similarly, you should avoid abbreviations that are specific to one industry or field of study unless you are sure the abbreviation will be widely understood. For example, mpg is a common abbreviation for miles per gallon, but cpm could stand for a number of different things and should be spelled out.

To create an identifier that has more than one word in it, many JavaScript programmers use a convention called *camel casing*. With this convention, the first letter of each word is uppercase except for the first word. For example, monthlyInvestment and taxRate are identifiers that use camel casing.

The alternative is to use underscore characters to separate the words in an identifier. For example, monthly_investment and tax_rate use this convention. If the standards in your shop specify one of these conventions, by all means use it. Otherwise, you can use whichever convention you prefer...but be consistent.

In this book, we use underscore notation for the ids and class names in the HTML and camel casing for all JavaScript identifiers. That way, it will be easier for you to tell where the names originated.

Rules for creating identifiers
- Identifiers can only contain letters, numbers, the underscore, and the dollar sign.
- Identifiers can't start with a number.
- Identifiers are case-sensitive.
- Identifiers can be any length.
- Identifiers can't be the same as *reserved words*.
- Avoid using global properties and methods as identifiers. If you use one of them, you won't be able to use the global property or method with the same name.

Valid identifiers in JavaScript

```
subtotal          index_1              $
taxRate           calculate_click      $log
```

Camel casing versus underscore notation

```
taxRate           tax_rate
calculateClick    calculate_click
emailAddress      email_address
firstName         first_name
futureValue       future_value
```

Naming recommendations
- Use meaningful names for identifiers. That way, your identifiers aren't likely to be reserved words or global properties.
- Be consistent: Either use camel casing (taxRate) or underscores (tax_rate) to identify the words within the variables in your scripts.
- If you're using underscore notation, use lowercase for all letters.

Reserved words in JavaScript

abstract	else	instanceof	switch
boolean	enum	int	synchronized
break	export	interface	this
byte	extends	long	throw
case	false	native	throws
catch	final	new	transient
char	finally	null	true
class	float	package	try
const	for	private	typeof
continue	function	protected	var
debugger	goto	public	void
default	if	return	volatile
delete	implements	short	while
do	import	static	with
double	in	super	

Description
- *Identifiers* are the names given to variables, functions, objects, properties, and methods.
- In *camel casing*, all of the words within an identifier except the first word start with capital letters.

Figure 2-4   How to create identifiers

How to use comments

Comments let you add descriptive notes to your code that are ignored by the JavaScript engine. Later on, these comments can help you or someone else understand the code whenever it needs to be modified.

The example in figure 2-5 shows how comments can be used to describe or explain portions of code. At the start, a block comment describes what the function that follows does. This kind of comment starts with /* and ends with */. Everything that's coded between the start and the end is ignored by the JavaScript engine when the application is run.

The other kind of comment is a single-line comment that starts with //. In the example, the first single-line comment describes what the JavaScript that comes before it on the same line does. In contrast, the second single-line comment takes up a line by itself. It describes what the two statements that come after it do.

In addition to describing JavaScript code, comments can be useful when testing an application. If, for example, you want to disable a portion of the JavaScript code, you can enclose it in a block comment. Then, it will be ignored when the application is run. This can be referred to as *commenting out* a portion of code. Later, after you test the rest of the code, you can enable the commented out code by removing the markers for the start and end of the block comment.

When should you use comments to describe or explain code? Certainly, when the code is so complicated that you may not remember how it works if you have to maintain it later on. This kind of comment is especially useful if someone else is going to have to maintain the code.

On the other hand, you shouldn't use comments to explain code that any professional programmer should understand. Which means that you have to strike some sort of balance between too much and too little. One of the worst problems with comments is changing the way the code works without changing the related comments. Then, the comments mislead the person who is trying to maintain the code, which makes the job even more difficult.

A portion of JavaScript code that includes comments

```
/* this onload function sets up the events that display and hide
   the text that follows a series of h2 headings
*/
window.onload = function () {
    var fiveReasons = $("five_reasons");         // gets a div element

    // gets the h2 and div elements within the div element
    var h2Headings = fiveReasons.getElementsByTagName("h2");
    var divTags = fiveReasons.getElementsByTagName("div");

    var i, headingNode, divNode;
    for (i = 0; i < h2Headings.length; i++ ) {   // one loop for each h2
        headingNode = h2Headings[i];
        divNode = divTags[i];

        // Attaches an event handler for each h2
        headingNode.onclick = function () {
            var h2 = this;
            if (h2.nextElementSibling.getAttribute("class") == "closed") {
                h2.nextElementSibling.setAttribute("class", "open");
            }
            else {
                h2.nextElementSibling.setAttribute("class", "closed");
            }
        }
    }
}
```

The basic syntax rules for JavaScript comments

- Block comments begin with /* and end with */.
- Single-line comments begin with two forward slashes and continue to the end of the line.

Guidelines for using comments

- Use comments to describe portions of code that are hard to understand.
- Use comments to disable portions of code that you don't want to test.
- Don't use comments unnecessarily.

Description

- JavaScript provides two forms of *comments*, block comments and single-line comments.
- Comments are ignored when the JavaScript is executed.
- During testing, comments can be used to *comment out* (disable) portions of code that you don't want tested. Then, you can remove the comments when you're ready to test those portions.

Figure 2-5   How to use comments

How to use objects, methods, and properties

In simple terms, an *object* is a collection of methods and properties. A *method* performs a function or does an action. A *property* is a data item that relates to the object. When you develop JavaScript applications, you will often work with objects, methods, and properties.

To get you started with that, figure 2-6 shows how to use the methods and properties of the window object, which is a common JavaScript object. To *call* (execute) a method of an object, you use the syntax in the summary after the tables. That is, you code the object name, a *dot operator* (period), the method name, and any *parameters* that the method requires within parentheses.

In this book, the italicized words in a syntax summary are the ones that you need to supply. The words that aren't italicized stay the same. In this case, all of the words are italicized, so you need to supply all of them. In contrast, the syntax for the alert method in the first table shows that you code the word *alert* just as it is in the summary, but you must supply a string parameter.

In the first example after the syntax summary, you can see how the alert method of the window object is called:

```
window.alert("This is a test of the alert method");
```

In this case, the one parameter that's passed to it is "This is a test of the alert method". So that message is displayed when the alert dialog box is displayed.

In the second example, you can see how the prompt method of the window object is called. This time, though, the object name is omitted. For the window object (but only the window object), that's okay because the window object is the *global object* for JavaScript applications.

As you can see, the prompt method accepts two parameters. The first one is a message, and the second one is an optional default value for a user entry. When the prompt method is executed, it displays a dialog box like the one in this figure. Here, you can see the message and the default value that were passed to the method as parameters. At this point, the user can change the default value or leave it as is, and then click on the OK button to store the entry in the variable named userEntry. Or, the user can click on the Cancel button to cancel the entry.

The third method in the table doesn't require any parameters. It is the print method. When it is executed, it issues a print request to the browser. Then, the browser starts its print function, usually by displaying a dialog box that lets the user continue or cancel the print function.

To access a property of an object, you use a similar syntax. However, you code the property name after the dot operator as illustrated by the second syntax summary. Unlike methods, properties don't require parameters in parentheses. This is illustrated by the statement that follows the syntax. This statement uses the alert method of the window object to display the location property of the window object.

As you progress through this book, you'll learn how to use the methods and properties of many objects. No matter what kind of object you're working with, though, the syntax for using the methods and properties is always the same: object name, dot, and then the property or method name.

Common methods of the window object

Method	Description
alert(*string*)	Displays a dialog box that contains the string that's passed to it by the parameter along with an OK button.
prompt(*string,default*)	Displays a dialog box that contains the string in the first parameter, the default value in the second parameter, an OK button, and a Cancel button. When the user enters a value and clicks OK, that value is returned as a string. Or if the user clicks Cancel, null is returned.
print()	Issues a print request to the browser.

One property of the window object

Property	Description
location	The URL of the current web page.

The syntax for calling a method of an object

objectName.methodName(parameters)

A statement that calls the alert method of the window object
```
window.alert("This is a test of the alert method");
```

A statement that calls the prompt method with the object name omitted
```
var userEntry = prompt("This is a test of the prompt method", 100);
```

The prompt dialog box that's displayed

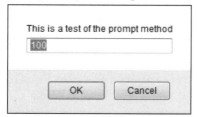

The syntax for accessing a property of an object

objectName.propertyName

A statement that displays the location property of the window object
```
alert(window.location);        // Displays the URL of the current page
```

Description

- An *object* has *methods* that perform functions that are related to the object as well as *properties* that represent the data or attributes that are associated with the object.

- When you *call* a method, you may need to pass one or more *parameters* to it by coding them within the parentheses after the method name, separated by commas.

- The *window object* is the *global object* for JavaScript, and JavaScript lets you omit the object name and *dot operator* (period) when referring to the window object.

Figure 2-6　How to use objects, methods, and properties

How to work with JavaScript data

When you develop JavaScript applications, you frequently work with data, especially the data that users enter into the controls of a form. In the topics that follow, you'll learn how to work with the three types of JavaScript data.

The primitive data types

JavaScript provides for three *primitive data types*. The *number data type* is used to represent numerical data. The *string data type* is used to store character data. And the *Boolean data type* is used to store true and false values. This is summarized in figure 2-7.

The number data type can be used to represent either integers or decimal values. *Integers* are whole numbers, and *decimal values* are numbers that can have one or more decimal digits. The value of either data type can be coded with a preceding plus or minus sign. If the sign is omitted, the value is treated as a positive value. A decimal value can also include a decimal point and one or more digits to the right of the decimal point.

As the last example of the number types shows, you can also include an exponent when you code a decimal value. If you aren't familiar with this notation, you probably won't need to use it because you won't be working with very large or very small numbers. On the other hand, if you're familiar with scientific notation, you already know that this exponent indicates how many zeros should be included to the right or left of the decimal. Numbers that use this notation are called *floating-point numbers*.

To represent string data, you code the *string* within single or double quotation marks (quotes). Note, however, that you must close the string with the same type of quotation mark that you used to start it. If you code two quotation marks in a row without even a space between them, the result is called an *empty string*, which can be used to represent a string with no data in it.

To represent Boolean data, you code either the word *true* or *false* with no quotation marks. As you will see, this data type can be used to represent data that is in one of two states: true or false.

Examples of number values

```
15                    // an integer
-21                   // a negative integer
21.5                  // a decimal value
-124.82               // a negative decimal value
-3.7e-9               // floating-point notation for -0.0000000037
```

Examples of string values

```
"JavaScript"          // a string with double quotes
'String Data'         // a string with single quotes
""                    // an empty string
```

The two Boolean values

```
true                  // equivalent to true, yes, or on
false                 // equivalent to false, no, or off
```

The number data type

- The *number data type* is used to represent an integer or a decimal value that can start with a positive or negative sign.

- An *integer* is a whole number. A *decimal value* can have one or more decimal positions to the right of the decimal point.

- If a result is stored in a number data type that is larger or smaller than the data type can store, it will be stored as the value Infinity or –Infinity.

What you need to know about floating-point numbers

- In JavaScript, decimal values are stored as *floating-point numbers*. In that format, a number consists of a positive or negative sign, one or more significant digits, an optional decimal point, optional decimal digits, and an optional exponent.

- Unless you're developing an application that requires the use of very large or very small numbers, you won't have to use floating-point notation to express numbers. If you need to use this notation, however, it is illustrated by the last example of number values above.

The string data type

- The *string data type* represents character (*string*) data. A string is surrounded by double quotes or single quotes. The string must start and end with the same type of quotation mark.

- An *empty string* is a string that contains no characters. It is entered by typing two quotation marks with nothing between them.

The Boolean data type

- The *Boolean data type* is used to represent a *Boolean value*. A Boolean value can be used to represent data that has two possible states: true or false.

Figure 2-7   The primitive data types

How to code numeric expressions

A *numeric expression* can be as simple as a single value or it can be a series of operations that result in a single value. In figure 2-8, you can see the operators for coding numeric expressions. If you've programmed in another language, these are probably similar to what you've been using. In particular, the first four *arithmetic operators* are common to most programming languages.

Most modern languages also have a *modulus operator* that calculates the remainder when the left value is divided by the right value. In the example for this operator, 13 % 4 means the remainder of 13 / 4. Then, since 13 / 4 is 3 with a remainder of 1, 1 is the result of the expression.

In contrast to the first five operators in this figure, the increment and decrement operators add or subtract one from a variable. To complicate matters, though, these operators can be coded before or after a variable name, and that can affect the result. To avoid confusion, then, we recommend that you only code these operators after the variable names and only in simple expressions like the one that you'll see in the next figure.

When an expression includes two or more operators, the *order of precedence* determines which operators are applied first. This order is summarized in the table in this figure. For instance, all multiplication and division operations are done from left to right before any addition and subtraction operations are done.

To override this order, though, you can use parentheses. Then, the expressions in the innermost sets of parentheses are done first, followed by the expressions in the next sets of parentheses, and so on. This is typical of all programming languages, as well as basic algebra, and the examples in this figure show how this works.

Common arithmetic operators

Operator	Description	Example	Result
+	Addition	5 + 7	12
-	Subtraction	5 - 12	-7
*	Multiplication	6 * 7	42
/	Division	13 / 4	3.25
%	Modulus	13 % 4	1
++	Increment	counter++	adds 1 to counter
--	Decrement	counter--	subtracts 1 from counter

The order of precedence for arithmetic expressions

Order	Operators	Direction	Description
1	++	Left to right	Increment operator
2	--	Left to right	Decrement operator
3	* / %	Left to right	Multiplication, division, modulus
4	+ -	Left to right	Addition, subtraction

Examples of precedence and the use of parentheses

```
3 + 4 * 5            // Result is 23 since the multiplication is done first
(3 + 4) * 5          // Result is 35 since the addition is done first

13 % 4 + 9           // Result is 10 since the modulus is done first
13 % (4 + 9)         // Result is 0  since the addition is done first

1000 + 1000 * .05    // Result is 1050 since the multiplication is done first
1000 + (1000 * .05)  // Result is still 1050
```

Description

- To code a *numeric expression*, you can use the *arithmetic operators* to operate on two or more values.

- The *modulus operator* returns the remainder of a division operation.

- An arithmetic expression is evaluated based on the *order of precedence* of the operators.

- To override the order of precedence, you can use parentheses.

- Because the use of increment and decrement operators can be confusing, we recommend that you only use these operators in expressions that consist of just a variable name followed by the operator, as shown in the next figure.

Figure 2-8   How to code numeric expressions

How to work with numeric variables

A *variable* stores a value that can change as the program executes. When you code a JavaScript application, you frequently declare variables and assign values to them. Figure 2-9 shows how to do both of these tasks with numeric variables.

To *declare* a numeric variable in JavaScript, code the *var* (for variable) keyword followed by the identifier (or name) that you want to use for the variable. To declare more than one variable in a single statement, code *var* followed by the variable names separated by commas. This is illustrated by the first group of examples in this figure.

To assign a value to a variable, you code an *assignment statement*. This type of statement consists of a variable name, an *assignment operator* like =, and an expression. Here, the expression can be a *numeric literal* like 74.95, a variable name like subtotal, or an arithmetic expression. When the equals sign is the operator, the value of the expression on the right of the equals sign is stored in the variable on the left. The use of this operator is illustrated by the second group of examples.

The second operator in the table in this figure is the += operator, which is a *compound assignment operator*. It modifies the variable on the left of the operator by adding the value of the expression on the right to the value of the variable on the left. When you use this operator, the variable must already exist and have a value assigned to it. The use of this operator is illustrated by the third group of examples.

The fourth group of examples shows three different ways to increment a variable by adding one to it. As you will see throughout this book, this is a common JavaScript requirement. In this group, the first statement assigns a value of 1 to a variable named counter.

Then, the second statement in this group uses an arithmetic expression to add 1 to the value of the counter, which shows that a variable name can be used on both sides of the equals sign. The third statement adds one to a counter by using the += operator.

The last statement in this group uses the increment operator shown in the previous figure to add one to the variable. This illustrates our recommendation for the use of increment and decrement operators. Here, the numeric expression consists only of a variable name followed by the increment operator, and it doesn't include an assignment operator

The last group of examples illustrates a potential problem that you should be aware of. Because decimal values are stored internally as floating-point numbers, the results of arithmetic operations aren't always precise. In this example, the salesTax result, which should be 7.495, is 7.495000000000001. Although this result is extremely close to 7.495, it isn't equal to 7.495, which could lead to a programming problem if you expect a comparison of the two values to be equal. The solution is to round the result, which you'll learn how to do in the next chapter.

The most useful assignment operators

Operator	Description
=	Assigns the result of the expression to the variable.
+=	Adds the result of the expression to the variable.

How to declare numeric variables without assigning values to them

```
var subtotal;                            // declares one variable
var investment, interestRate, years;     // declares three variables
```

How to declare variables and assign values to them

```
var subtotal = 74.00;                    // subtotal = 74.00
var salesTax = subtotal * .1;            // salesTax = 7.4
```

How to code compound assignment statements

```
var subtotal = 74.95;                    // subtotal = 74.95
subtotal += 20.00;                       // subtotal = 94.95
```

Three ways to increment a variable named counter by 1

```
var counter = 1;                         // counter = 1
counter = counter + 1;                   // counter now = 2
counter += 1;                            // counter now = 3
counter++;                               // counter now = 4
```

A floating-point result that isn't precise

```
var subtotal = 74.95;                    // subtotal = 74.95
var salesTax = subtotal * .1;            // salesTax = 7.495000000000001
```

Description

- A *variable* stores a value that can change as the program executes.

- To *declare* a variable, code the keyword *var* and a variable name. To declare more than one variable in a single statement, code *var* and the variable names separated by commas.

- To assign a value to a variable, you use an *assignment statement* that consists of the variable name, an *assignment operator*, and an expression. When appropriate, you can declare a variable and assign a value to it in a single statement.

- Within an expression, a *numeric literal* is a valid integer or decimal number that isn't enclosed in quotation marks.

- If you use a plus sign in an expression and both values are numbers, JavaScript adds them. If both values are strings, JavaScript concatenates them as shown in the next figure. And if one value is a number and one is a string, JavaScript converts the number to a string and concatenates.

- When you do some types of arithmetic operations with decimal values, the results aren't always precise, although they are extremely close. That's because decimal values are stored internally as floating-point numbers. The only problem with this is that an equal comparison may not return true.

Figure 2-9   How to work with numeric variables

How to work with string and Boolean variables

To declare a string or Boolean variable, you use techniques that are similar to those you use for declaring a numeric variable. The main difference is that a *string literal* is a value enclosed in quotation marks, while a numeric literal isn't. Besides that, the + sign is treated as a *concatenation operator* when working with strings. This means that one string is added to the end of another string.

This is illustrated by the first two groups of examples in figure 2-10. In the second group, the first statement assigns string literals to the variables named firstName and lastName. Then, the next statement concatenates lastName, a string literal that consists of a comma and a space, and firstName. The result of this concatenation is

`Harris, Ray`

which is stored in a new variable named fullName.

In the third group of examples, you can see how the += operator can be used to get the same results. When the expressions that you're working with are strings, this operator does a simple concatenation.

In the fourth group of examples, though, you can see what happens if the += operator is used with a string and a numeric value. In that case, the number is converted to a string and then the strings are concatenated.

The fifth group of examples shows how you can use *escape sequences* in a string. Three of the many escape sequences that you can use are summarized in the second table in this figure. These sequences let you put characters in a string that you can't put in just by pressing the appropriate key on the keyboard. For instance, the \n escape sequence is equivalent to pressing the Enter key in the middle of a string. And the \' sequence is equivalent to pressing the key for a single quotation mark.

The last example in this figure shows how to create and assign values to Boolean variables. Here, a variable named isValid is created and a value of false is assigned to it.

The concatenation operator for strings

Operator	Example	Result
+	`"Ray " + "Harris"`	`"Ray Harris"`
	`"Months: " + 120`	`"Months: 120"`

Escape sequences that can be used in strings

Operator	Description
`\n`	Starts a new line in a string.
`\"`	Puts a double quotation mark in a string.
`\'`	Puts a single quotation mark in a string.

How to declare string variables without assigning values to them

```
var zipCode;                          // declares one variable
var lastName, state, zipCode;         // declares three variables
```

How to declare string variables and assign values to them

```
var firstName = "Ray", lastName = "Harris";   // assigns two string values
var fullName = lastName + ", " + firstName;    // fullName is "Harris, Ray"
```

How to code compound assignment statements with string data

```
var firstName = "Ray", lastName = "Harris";
var fullName = lastName;               // fullName is "Harris"
fullName += ", ";                      // fullName is "Harris, "
fullName += firstName;                 // fullName is "Harris, Ray"
```

How to code compound assignment statements with mixed data

```
var months = 120;
message = "Months: ";
message += months;                     // message is "Months: 120"
```

How escape sequences can be used in a string

```
var message = "A valid variable name\ncannot start with a number.";
var message = "This isn\'t the right way to do this.";
```

How to declare Boolean variables and assign values to them

```
var isValid = false;                   // Boolean value is false
```

Description

- To assign values to string variables, you can use the + and += operators, just as you use them with numeric variables.

- To *concatenate* two or more strings, you can use the + operator.

- Within an expression, a *string literal* is enclosed in quotation marks.

- *Escape sequences* can be used to insert special characters within a string like a return character that starts a new line or a quotation mark.

- If you use a plus sign in an expression and both values are strings, JavaScript concatenates them. But if one value is a number and one is a string, JavaScript converts the number to a string and concatenates the strings.

Figure 2-10   How to work with string and Boolean variables

How to use the parseInt and parseFloat methods

The parseInt and parseFloat methods are used to convert strings to numbers. The parseInt method converts a string to an integer, and the parseFloat method converts a string to a decimal value. These methods are needed because the values that are returned by the prompt method and the values that the user enters into text boxes are treated as strings.

The use of these methods is illustrated by the first group of examples in figure 2-11. For this group, assume that the default value in the prompt method isn't changed by the user. As a result, the first statement in this group stores 12345.6789 as a string in a variable named entryA. Then, the third statement in this group converts the string to an integer value of 12345.

Note that the object name isn't coded before the method name in these examples. That's okay because window is the global object of JavaScript. Note too that the parseInt method doesn't round the value. It just removes, or truncates, any decimal portion of the string value.

The last four statements in the first group of examples show what happens when the parseInt or parseFloat method is used to convert a value that isn't a number. In that case, both of these methods return the value NaN, which stands for "Not a Number".

Note, however, that these methods can convert values that consist of one or more numeric characters followed by one or more nonnumeric characters. In that case, these methods simply drop the nonnumeric characters. For example, if a string contains the value "72.5%", the parseFloat method will convert it to a decimal value of 72.5.

The second group of examples in this figure shows how to get the same results by coding the parse methods as the parameters of the alert methods. For instance, the third statement in this group uses the parseInt method as the parameter of the alert method. Embedding one method within another like this can be referred to as *object chaining*, and you'll learn more about that in the next chapter.

Note in the first set of examples that the entryA, entryB, and entryC variables are all changed by the parse methods. For instance, entryA becomes the number 12345 and entryC becomes NaN. In contrast, the entries aren't changed by the statements in the second set of examples. That's because the parsed values aren't assigned to the variables; they're just displayed by the alert statements.

The parseInt and parseFloat methods of the window object

Method	Description
parseInt(*string*)	Converts the string that's passed to it to an integer data type and returns that value. If it can't convert the string to an integer, it returns NaN.
parseFloat(*string*)	Converts the string that's passed to it to a decimal data type and returns that value. If it can't convert the string to a decimal value, it returns NaN.

Examples that use the parseInt and parseFloat methods

```
var entryA = prompt("Enter any value", 12345.6789);
alert(entryA);                              // displays 12345.6789
entryA = parseInt(entryA);
alert(entryA);                              // displays 12345

var entryB = prompt("Enter any value", 12345.6789);
alert(entryB);                              // displays 12345.6789
entryB = parseFloat(entryB);
alert(entryB);                              // displays 12345.6789

var entryC = prompt("Enter any value", "Hello");
alert(entryC);                              // displays Hello
entryC = parseInt(entryC);
alert(entryC);                              // displays NaN
```

The same examples with the parse methods embedded in the alert method

```
var entryA = prompt("Enter any value", 12345.6789);
alert(entryA);                              // displays 12345.6789
alert(parseInt(entryA));                    // displays 12345

var entryB = prompt("Enter any value", 12345.6789);
alert(entryB);                              // displays 12345.6789
alert(parseFloat(entryB));                  // displays 12345.6789

var entryC = prompt("Enter any value", "Hello");
alert(entryC);                              // displays Hello
alert(parseInt(entryC));                    // displays NaN
```

Description

- The window object provides parseInt and parseFloat methods that let you convert string values to integer or decimal numbers.

- When you use the prompt method or a text box to get numeric data that you're going to use in calculations, you need to use either the parseInt or parseFloat method to convert the string data to numeric data.

- *NaN* is a value that means "Not a Number". It is returned by the parseInt and parseFloat methods when the value that's being parsed isn't a number.

- When working with methods, you can embed one method in the parameter of another. This is sometimes referred to as *object chaining*. In the second group of examples above, the parse methods are coded as the parameters for the alert methods.

Figure 2-11   How to use the parseInt and parseFloat methods

How to code control statements

Like all programming languages, JavaScript provides *control statements* that let you control how information is processed in an application. These statements include if statements as well as looping statements. Before you can learn how to use these statements, though, you need to learn how to code conditional expressions, so we'll start there.

How to code conditional expressions

Figure 2-12 shows you how to code *conditional expressions* that use the six *relational operators*. A conditional expression returns a value of true or false based on the result of a comparison between two expressions. If, for example, the value of lastName in the first expression in the first table is "Harrison", the expression will return false. Or, if the value of rate in the last expression is 10, the expression will return true (because 10 / 100 is .1 and .1 is greater than or equal to 0.1).

In addition to using the relational operators to code a conditional expression, you can use the global isNaN method. This method determines whether a string value is a valid numeric value, as illustrated by the next set of examples. To use this method, you pass a parameter that represents the string value that should be tested. Then, this method returns true if the value can't be converted to a number or false if it can be converted.

To code a *compound conditional expression*, you use the *logical operators* shown in the second table in this figure to combine two conditional expressions. If you use the AND operator, the compound expression returns true if both expressions are true. If you use the OR operator, the compound expression returns true if either expression is true. If you use the NOT operator, the value returned by the expression is reversed. For instance, !isNaN returns true if the parameter is a number, so isNaN(10) returns false, but !isNaN(10) returns true.

Note that the logical operators in this figure are shown in their order of precedence. That is the order in which the operators are evaluated if more than one logical operator is used in a compound expression. This means that NOT operators are evaluated before AND operators, which are evaluated before OR operators. Although this is normally what you want, you can override this order by using parentheses.

In most cases, the conditional expressions that you use are relatively simple so coding them isn't much of a problem. In the rest of this chapter, you'll see some of the types of conditional expressions that are commonly used.

The relational operators

Operator	Description	Example
==	Equal	`lastName == "Harris"` `testScore == 10`
!=	Not equal	`firstName != "Ray"` `months != 0`
<	Less than	`age < 18`
<=	Less than or equal	`investment <= 0`
>	Greater than	`testScore > 100`
>=	Greater than or equal	`rate / 100 >= 0.1`

The syntax of the global isNaN method

```
isNaN(expression)
```

Examples of the isNaN method

```
isNaN("Harris") // Returns true since "Harris" is not a number
isNaN("123.45") // Returns false since "123.45" can be converted to a number
```

The logical operators in order of precedence

Operator	Description	Example
!	NOT	`!isNaN(age)`
&&	AND	`age > 17 && score < 70`
||	OR	`isNaN(rate) || rate < 0`

How the logical operators work

- Both tests with the AND operator must be true for the overall test to be true.
- At least one test with the OR operator must be true for the overall test to be true.
- The NOT operator switches the result of the expression to the other Boolean value. For example, if an expression is true, the NOT operator converts it to false.
- To override the order of precedence when two or more logical operators are used in a conditional expression, you can use parentheses.

Description

- A *conditional expression* uses the *relational operators* to compare the results of two expressions.
- A *compound conditional expression* joins two or more conditional expressions using the *logical operators.*
- The isNaN method tests whether a string can be converted to a number. It returns true if the string is not a number and false if the string is a number.

Note

- Confusing the assignment operator (=) with the equality operator (==) is a common programming error.

Figure 2-12   How to code conditional expressions

How to code if statements

If you've programmed in other languages, you won't have any trouble using JavaScript if statements. Just study figure 2-13 to get the syntax and see how the conditions are coded. But if you're new to programming, let's take it slower.

An *if statement* lets you control the execution of statements based on the results of conditional expressions. In a syntax summary like the one in this figure, the brackets [ ] indicate a portion of the syntax that is optional. As a result, this summary means that each if statement must start with an *if clause*. Then, it can have one or more *else if clauses*, but they are optional. Last, it can have an *else clause*, but that clause is also optional.

To code the if clause, you code the keyword *if* followed by a conditional expression in parentheses and a block of one or more statements inside braces. If the conditional expression is true, this block of code will be executed and any remaining clauses in the if statement will be skipped over. If the conditional expression is false, the next clause that follows will be executed.

To code an else if clause, you code the keywords *else if* followed by a conditional expression in parentheses and a block of one or more statements inside braces. If the conditional expression is true, its block of code will be executed and any remaining clauses in the if statement will be skipped over. This will continue until one of the else if expressions is true or they all are false.

To code an else clause, you code the keyword *else* followed by a block of one or more statements inside braces. This code will only be executed if all the conditional expressions in the if and else if clauses are false. If those expressions are false and there isn't an else clause, the if statement won't execute any code.

The first example in this figure shows an if statement with an else clause. If the value of the age variable is greater than or equal to 18, the first message will be displayed. Otherwise, the second message will be displayed.

The second example shows an if statement with two else if clauses and an else clause. If the rate is not a number, the first message is displayed. If the rate is less than zero, the second message is displayed. If the rate is greater than 12, the third message is displayed. Otherwise, the message in the else clause is displayed.

The third example shows an if statement with a compound conditional expression that tests whether the value of the userEntry variable is not a number or whether the value is less than or equal to zero. If either expression is true, a message is displayed. If both expressions are false, nothing is done because this if statement doesn't have else if clauses or an else clause.

The fourth set of examples shows two ways to test whether a Boolean variable is true. Here, both statements are evaluated the same way. That's because a condition that is coded as just a Boolean variable is tested to see whether the variable is equal to true. In practice, this condition is usually coded the way it is in the second statement, with just the name of the variable.

The fifth set of examples is similar. It shows three ways to test whether a Boolean variable is false. Here again, the last statement illustrates the way this condition is usually coded: !isValid.

The syntax of the if statement

```
if ( condition-1 ) { statements }
[ else if ( condition-2 ) { statements }
  ...
  else if ( condition-n ) { statements } ]
[ else { statements } ]
```

An if statement with an else clause

```
if ( age >= 18 ) {
    alert ("You may vote.");
} else {
    alert ("You are not old enough to vote.");
}
```

An if statement with else if and else clauses

```
if ( isNaN(rate) ) {
    alert ("You did not provide a number for the rate.");
} else if ( rate < 0 ) {
    alert ("The rate may not be less than zero.");
} else if ( rate > 12 ) {
    alert ("The rate may not be greater than 12.");
} else {
    alert ("The rate is: " + rate + ".");
}
```

An if statement with a compound conditional expression

```
if ( isNaN(userEntry) || userEntry <= 0 ) {
    alert ("Please enter a valid number greater than zero.");
}
```

Two ways to test whether a Boolean variable is true

```
if ( isValid == true ) { }
if ( isValid ) { }                 // same as isValid == true
```

Three ways to test whether a Boolean variable is false

```
if ( isValid == false ) { }
if ( !isValid == true ) { }
if ( !isValid ) { }                // same as !isValid == true
```

Description

- An *if statement* always has one *if clause*. It can also have one or more *else if clauses* and one *else clause* at the end.

- The statements in a clause are executed when its condition is true. Otherwise, control passes to the next clause. If none of the conditions in the preceding clauses are true, the statements in the else clause are executed.

- If necessary, you can code one if statement within the if, else if, or else clause of another if statement. This is referred to as *nesting if statements*.

Figure 2-13   How to code if statements

How to code while and do-while loops

Figure 2-14 starts by presenting the syntax of the *while statement* that is used to create *while loops*. This statement executes the block of code that's in the loop while its conditional expression is true.

The example that follows this syntax shows how a while loop can be used to add the numbers 1 through 5. Before the while statement starts, a variable named sumOfNumbers is set to zero, a variable named numberOfLoops is set to 5, and a variable named counter is set to 1. Then, the condition for the while statement says that the while loop should be repeated as long as the counter value is less than or equal to the numberOfLoops value.

Within the while loop, the first statement adds the counter value to the sumOfNumbers variable. Then, the counter is increased by 1. As a result, this loop is executed five times, one time each for the counter values 1, 2, 3, 4, and 5. The loop ends when the counter is no longer less than or equal to 5, which is when the counter value equals 6.

This example is followed by the syntax for the *do-while statement* that is used to create *do-while loops*. This is like the while statement, but its condition is tested at the end of the loop instead of at the start. As a result, the statements in the loop are always executed at least once. This statement is illustrated by the example that follows the syntax, which gets the same result as the while statement.

In general, you use the do-while statement when you want to execute the statements in the loop at least once, and you use the while statement for other types of loops. Coded correctly, though, you can get the same results with both statements.

The last example in this figure shows another example of a while loop. This loop keeps going while the user entry is a valid number (!NaN). Within the loop, the number that's entered is added to a variable named total, a variable named count is incremented by 1, and the prompt method is used to get another number from the user. The loop ends when the user clicks the Cancel button, which returns a value that isn't a number (a null value). Then, the next two statements calculate the average of the numbers and display that average.

Incidentally, if !NaN is confusing too you, that's because combining two negatives is always confusing. Rather than think about it too much, just accept that !NaN means the number is valid and NaN means the number isn't valid.

The syntax of a while loop

```
while ( condition ) { statements }
```

A while loop that adds the numbers from 1 through 5

```
var sumOfNumbers = 0;
var numberOfLoops = 5;
var counter = 1;
while (counter <= numberOfLoops) {
    sumOfNumbers += counter;     // adds counter to sumOfNumbers
    counter++;                   // adds 1 to counter
}
alert(sumOfNumbers);             // displays 15
```

The syntax of a do-while loop

```
do { statements } while ( condition );
```

A while loop that adds the numbers from 1 through 5

```
var sumOfNumbers = 0;
var numberOfLoops = 5;
var counter = 1;
do {
    sumOfNumbers += counter;     // adds counter to sumOfNumbers
    counter++;                   // adds 1 to counter
}
while (counter <= numberOfLoops);
alert(sumOfNumbers);             // displays 15
```

A while loop that finds the average of a series of numbers

```
var total = 0, count = 0, number;
number = parseFloat( prompt("Enter a number:") );
while ( !isNaN(number) ) {
    total += number;
    count++;
    number = parseFloat(
        prompt("Enter another number or click Cancel to stop:") );
}
var average = total / count;
alert("The average is: " + average);
```

Description

- The *while statement* creates a *while loop* that contains a block of code that is executed while its condition is true. This condition is tested at the beginning of the loop, and the loop is skipped if the condition is false.

- The *do-while statement* creates a *do-while* loop that contains a block of code that is executed while its condition is true. However, its condition is tested at the end of the loop instead of the beginning, so the code in the loop will always be executed at least once.

Figure 2-14   How to code while and do-while loops

How to code for loops

Figure 2-15 shows how to use the *for statement* to create *for loops*. This type of loop is easier to code when the progress of the loop depends on a value that is incremented each time through the loop. Within the parentheses of a for statement, you initialize a *counter* (or *index*) variable that will be used within the loop. Then, you code a condition that determines when the loop will end. Last, you code an expression that specifies how the counter should be incremented.

The first example in this figure shows how this works. Here, the first statement in the parentheses of the for statement declares a variable named counter and initializes it to 1. Then, the condition in the parentheses determines that the loop will continue as long as counter is less than or equal to the value in numberOfLoops, and the expression that follows increments the counter by 1 each time through the loop. Within the loop, the value of the counter variable is added to the variable named sumOfNumbers.

If you compare this example to the first two examples in figure 2-14, you can see that all three get the same results. But with the for statement, you don't have to initialize the counter before the statement, and you don't have to increment the counter within the statement.

The next example shows a more realistic use of a for loop. This loop calculates the future value of an investment amount ($10,000) at a specific interest rate (7.0%) for a specific number of years (10). This time, *i* is used as the name for the counter variable, which is a common coding practice, and the loop continues as long as this index is less than or equal to the number of years. In other words, the statement in the loop is executed once for each of the 10 years.

Within the loop, the += operator is used to add the interest for the year

```
futureValue * annualRate / 100
```

to the futureValue variable. Note here that the annualRate needs to be divided by 100 for this calculation to work right (7.0 / 100 = .07). Note too in the statements after this example, that this statement could be coded in more than one way and still get the same results.

In both of the examples in this figure, the counter is incremented by 1 each time through the loop, which is usually the way this statement is coded. However, you can also increment or decrement the counter by other amounts. That just depends on what you're trying to do. To increment by 2, for example, you could code the increment expression as:

```
i = i + 2
```

The syntax of a for statement

```
for ( counterInitialization; condition; incrementExpression ) {
    statements
}
```

A for loop that adds the numbers from 1 through 5

```
var sumOfNumbers = 0;
var numberOfLoops = 5;
for ( counter=1; counter <= numberOfLoops; counter++ ) {
    sumOfNumbers += counter;      // adds counter to sumOfNumbers
}
alert(sumOfNumbers);              // displays 15
```

A for loop that calculates the future value of an investment

```
var investment = 10000;
var annualRate = 7.0;
var years = 10;
var futureValue = investment;
for ( i = 1; i <= years; i++ ) {
    futureValue += futureValue * annualRate / 100;
}
alert (futureValue);             // displays 19672
```

Other ways that the future value calculation could be coded

```
futureValue = futureValue + (futureValue * annualRate / 100);

futureValue = futureValue * (1 + (annualRate / 100))
```

Description

- The *for statement* is used when you need to increment or decrement a counter that determines how many times the *for loop* is executed.

- Within the parentheses of a for statement, you code an expression that initializes a *counter* (or *index*) variable, a conditional expression that determines when the loop ends, and an increment expression that indicates how the counter should be incremented or decremented each time through the loop.

- The variable name *i* is commonly used for the counter in a for loop.

Figure 2-15   How to code for loops

Two illustrative applications

You have now learned enough about JavaScript to develop simple applications of your own. These aren't realistic applications because they get the user entries from prompt statements instead of from controls on a form. However, these applications will get you started using the methods and control statements of JavaScript.

The Miles Per Gallon application

Figure 2-16 presents a simple application that issues two prompt statements that let the user enter the number of miles driven and the number of gallons of gasoline used. Then, the application calculates miles per gallon and issues an alert statement to display the result in a third dialog box.

Because this application uses prompt methods to get the input and an alert method to display the output, the HTML for this application is trivial. It contains one h1 element that is displayed after the JavaScript finishes executing. (As I said before, this application is unrealistic.)

In the JavaScript, you can see how the user's entries are stored in variables named miles and gallons and then parsed into decimal values. After that, miles is divided by gallons, and the result is saved in a variable named mpg. Then, the value in that variable is parsed into an integer so any decimal places are removed. Last, an alert statement displays the result that's shown in the third dialog box. When the user clicks on the OK button in that box, the JavaScript ends and the page with its one heading is displayed in the browser.

Can you guess what will happen if the user enters invalid data in one of the prompt dialog boxes? Then, the parse method will return NaN instead of a number, and the calculation won't work. Instead, the last alert statement will display:

```
Miles per gallon = NaN
```

Unlike other languages, though, the JavaScript will run to completion instead of crashing when the calculation can't be done, so the web page will be displayed.

Incidentally, the dialog boxes in this figure are Firefox boxes, and you can ignore the Firefox checkbox and message that are displayed in those boxes. When you use other browsers, the dialog boxes will work the same but have different appearances.

The dialog boxes for the Calculate MPG application

The first prompt dialog box

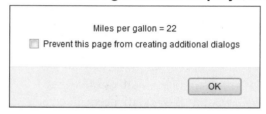

The second prompt dialog box

The alert dialog box that displays the result

The HTML and JavaScript for the application

```
<!doctype html>
<html>
<head>
    <title>The Calculate MPG Application</title>
    <script>
        alert("The Calculate MPG application");
        var miles = prompt("Enter miles driven");
        miles = parseFloat(miles);
        var gallons = prompt("Enter gallons of gas used");
        gallons = parseFloat(gallons);
        var mpg = miles/gallons;
        mpg = parseInt(mpg);
        alert("Miles per gallon = " + mpg);
    </script>
</head>
<body>
<section>
    <h1>This page is displayed after the JavaScript is executed</h1>
</section>
</body>
</html>
```

Figure 2-16   The Miles Per Gallon application

The Test Scores application

Figure 2-17 presents a simple application that lets the user enter a series of test scores. Then, when the user enters 999 to end the series, the application displays the average test score.

Unlike the Miles Per Gallon application, this application tests to make sure that each entry is a valid number from 0 through 100 before it is added to the test score total. This is commonly referred to as *data validation*. If an entry isn't valid, the application displays an error message and issues another prompt statement so the user can either enter another score or 999 to end the entries.

If you look at the JavaScript in the script element of the head section of the HTML, you can see that it starts by declaring the three variables that are needed to get the entries. The total variable has a starting value of zero, and it will be used to add the test scores. The entryCount variable has a starting value of 0, and it will be used to count the number of valid test scores. The third variable is entry, and it doesn't have a starting value assigned to it. It will be used to receive the user entries.

After the variables are declared, a do-while loop is used to get the user entries. Because the application has to get at least one user entry, it makes sense to use a do-while loop instead of a while loop.

Within the do-while loop, the prompt method is used to get each user entry. Note that the second parameter is set to 999 so the user can just press the Enter key to end the entries.

Then, each entry is parsed into an integer and checked for validity by an if statement. If the entry is valid, the entry value is added to the total variable and 1 is added to the entryCount variable. Otherwise, an alert method displays an error message and the entry isn't processed.

When the statements in the loop are finished, the condition for the loop is tested. Then, if the entry value is 999, the statement ends. Otherwise, the loop is repeated for the next entry.

When the loop ends, the average test score is calculated and stored in the variable named average. This calculation simply divides the total variable by the entryCount variable. Then, the parseInt method is used to convert a decimal value to an integer. Last, an alert statement displays the average score.

The dialog boxes for the Test Scores application

The prompt dialog box for the next test score

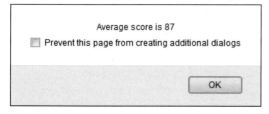

Enter test score
Or enter 999 to end entries

93

☐ Prevent this page from creating additional dialogs

OK   Cancel

The alert dialog box for an entry error

Entry must by a valid number from 0 through 100
Or enter 999 to end entries

☐ Prevent this page from creating additional dialogs

OK

The alert dialog box that displays the result

Average score is 87

☐ Prevent this page from creating additional dialogs

OK

The JavaScript in the head section of the HTML file

```
<script>
    var total = 0;
    var entryCount = 0;
    var entry;
    do {
        entry = prompt("Enter test score\n" +
                    "Or enter 999 to end entries", 999);
        entry = parseInt(entry);
        if (entry >= 0 && entry <= 100) {
            total = total + entry;
            entryCount++; }
        else if (entry != 999){
            alert("Entry must by a valid number from 0 through 100\n" +
                "Or enter 999 to end entries"); }
    }
    while (entry != 999);
    var average = total/entryCount;
    average = parseInt(average);
    alert("Average score is " + average);
</script>
```

Figure 2-17   The Test Scores application

How to find errors in your code

As you enter and test even the simplest of applications, you're likely to have errors in your code. When that happens, the JavaScript may not run at all, or it may run for a short while and then stop. That's why figure 2-18 gives you some ideas for how to find the errors in your code.

How to get error messages with Firefox

When you load a page and the JavaScript doesn't run, the easiest way to find out what's wrong is to display the messages for the errors that the browser has caught. To do that with Firefox, you open the Error Console as shown in this figure. Here, the console shows a message for an error that occurred when the Test Score application was run. It says that the score variable isn't defined. Then, if you click on the link in the Error Console, the JavaScript source code is displayed with the statement that caused the error highlighted.

In this case, the problem is that the variable should be "entry", not "score". Unfortunately, you can't fix the error in the window that contains the source code because that's a browser window. Instead, you need to switch to your text editor or IDE to fix and save the code, and then reload the application in Firefox.

To manage what's shown in the Error Console, you can click on the buttons in its toolbar. For instance, when you first open the Error Console, you may see errors, warnings, and messages that are left over from applications that you tested earlier. Then, to clear the messages, you can click on the Clear button.

Incidentally, the error message that's displayed when you load an application is for the first syntax error that's detected, but there can be other syntax errors in the code. To catch them, you'll have to correct the first error and run the application again.

Common JavaScript errors

This figure also presents some of the coding errors that are commonly made as you write a JavaScript application. If you study this list, you'll have a better idea of what to look for as you try to find an error.

If you're using a good text editor or IDE, you can avoid most of these errors by noting the error markers that are displayed as you enter the code. For instance, Aptana will help you avoid most of these errors, and that can save you many hours of time. If possible, then, be sure that you're using an editor or IDE that does a good job of checking the JavaScript for syntax errors.

The Firefox Error Console with an error description

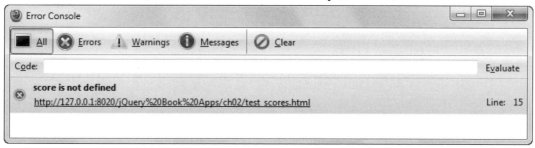

The source code that's displayed when you click on the link

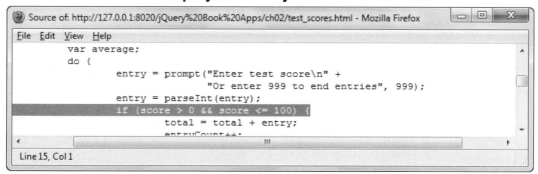

How to display the Firefox Error Console and the source code for an error

- To display the console, use the Tools→Web Developer→Error Console command, or press Ctrl+Shift+J.
- To display the source code for the error, click on the link in the Error Console.

Common syntax errors

- Misspelling keywords, like coding parseInteger instead of parseInt.
- Omitting required parentheses, quotation marks, or braces.
- Not using the same opening and closing quotation mark.
- Omitting the semicolon at the end of a statement.
- Using one equal sign instead of two when testing for equality.
- Misspelling or incorrectly capitalizing an identifier, like defining a variable named salesTax and referring to it later as salestax.

Description

- When the JavaScript engine for Firefox comes to a statement that it can't execute, it displays an error in the Error Console and stops executing the JavaScript.
- The buttons at the top of the Error Console let you display all errors, just fatal errors, just warnings, or just messages. The Clear button removes all errors from the console.
- If you click an error link in the Error Console, Firefox displays the JavaScript statement that caused the error. However, you won't be able to edit the file.

Figure 2-18   How to find errors in your code

Perspective

If you have programming experience, you can now see that JavaScript syntax is similar to other languages like Java and C#. As a result, you should have breezed through this chapter. You may also want to skip the exercises.

On the other hand, if you're new to programming and you understand all of the code in both of the applications in this chapter, you're off to a good start. Otherwise, you need to study the applications until you understand every line of code in each application. You should also do the exercises that follow.

Terms

external JavaScript file
embedded JavaScript
JavaScript statement
syntax
whitespace
identifier
reserved word
keyword
camel casing
comment
comment out
object
method
property
call a method
dot operator (dot)
parameter
window object
global object
primitive data type
number data type
integer
decimal value
floating-point number
string data type
string
empty string
Boolean data type
Boolean value
numeric expression
arithmetic operator
modulus operator

order of precedence
variable
declare a variable
assignment statement
assignment operator
compound assignment operator
numeric literal
concatenate
concatenation operator
string literal
escape sequence
NaN
object chaining
control statement
conditional expression
relational operator
compound conditional expression
logical operator
if statement
if clause
else if clause
else clause
nested if statements
while statement
while loop
do-while statement
do-while loop
for statement
for loop
loop counter or index
data validation

Summary

- The JavaScript for an HTML document page is commonly coded in an *external JavaScript file* that's identified by a script element. However, the JavaScript can also be *embedded* in a script element in the head or body of a document.

- A JavaScript *statement* has a *syntax* that's similar to Java's. Its *identifiers* are case-sensitive and usually coded with either *camel casing* or underscore notation. Its comments can be block or in-line.

- JavaScript provides many *objects* that provide *methods* and *properties* that you can *call* or refer to in your applications. Since the *window object* is the *global object* for JavaScript, you can omit it when referring to its methods or properties.

- JavaScript provides three *primitive data types.* The *number data type* provides for both *integers* and *decimal values.* The *string data type* provides for character (*string*) data. And the *Boolean data type* provides for true and false values. To assign a value to a *variable*, you use an *assignment operator.*

- When you assign a value to a number *variable*, you can use *numeric expressions* that include *arithmetic operators*, variable names, and *numeric literals.*

- When you assign a value to a string variable, you can use *string expressions* that include *concatenation operators*, variable names, and *string literals.* Within a string literal, you can use *escape sequences* to provide special characters.

- When you code a *conditional expression*, you can use *relational operators*, the global isNan method, and *logical operators.*

- An *if statement* always starts with an *if clause.* It can also have one or more *else if clauses* and a concluding *else clause*, but those clauses are optional.

- The *while* and *do-while* statements can be used to loop through a series of statements while a condition is true.

- The *for statement* can be used to loop through a series of statements once for each time a *counter* or *index* is incremented or decremented.

- To help find errors when you test a JavaScript application, you can use the Firefox Error Console.

Before you do the exercises for this book...

If you haven't already done so, you should install the Mozilla Firefox browser and install the downloads for this book as described in appendix A.

Exercise 2-1   Add validation to the MPG application

Add the validation that's described in this exercise, and test the application in Firefox after each step. If the application doesn't run, use the Error Console as shown in figure 2-18 to find your errors.

1. Open your text editor or IDE. Then, open this HTML file:
    `c:\jquery\exercises\ch02\mpg.html`

2. Run the application with valid entries, and note the result. Then, run it with invalid entries like zeros or spaces, and note the result.

3. Add an if statement that validates the miles entry after the statement that parses this entry. This if statement should check if the entry is not a number or if the entry is less than zero. If either of these conditions is true, display an appropriate error message. When you're done, the if statement should be something like this:
    ```
    if (isNaN(miles) || miles <= 0) {
        alert("Miles must be a number greater than zero");
    }
    ```

4. Add an if statement that validates the gallons entry after the statement that parses this entry. This statement should check if the entry is not a number or if the entry is less than zero. If either of these conditions is true, display an appropriate error message. When you're done, the if statement should be similar to the one shown above for the miles entry.

5. Add a do-while loop for each entry that contains the statements that get, parse, and validate the entry. This loop should continue until the entry is valid. To do that, you can use the same conditions in the while clauses that you use in the if clauses. For example, the loop for the gallons entry should be something like this:
    ```
    do {
        // statements for getting, parsing, and validating the entry
    }
    while (isNaN(miles) || miles <= 0);
    ```

Exercise 2-2   Create a Sum of Numbers application

This is a simple application that uses the prompt method to get a user entry that can be from 1 through 100. Then, the application adds all the numbers from 1 through the user's entry and displays the sum of the numbers. If, for example, the user enters 5, the application adds 1, 2, 3, 4, and 5, so it displays 15.

The steps that follow will guide you through the development of this application, and you should test the application in Firefox after each step. If the application doesn't run, use the Error Console as shown in figure 2-18 to find your errors.

1.   Open your text editor or IDE. Then, open this HTML file and review its starting code:

     `c:\jquery\exercises\ch02\sum.html`

2.   Write the code for the prompt method that gets the user entry. It should have a default value of 5 and a prompt message like this: "Enter top number to sum". Then, parse the entry into an integer value.

3.   Declare a variable with a starting value of zero that will hold the sum of the numbers. Then, code a for statement that calculates the sum of the numbers. This statement should use a counter variable with a starting value of 1, it should execute as long as the counter variable is less than or equal to the value of the user entry, and it should increment the count variable by 1 each time through the loop.

4.   Code an alert statement after the for statement that displays the calculated sum.

5.   Add an if statement that validates the user entry. This statement should check if the entry is not a number, if it is less than 1, or if it is greater than 100. If any of these conditions are true, it should display an appropriate error message.

6.   Add a do-while statement that will continue prompting the user for an entry and displaying an error message until the entry is valid.

7.   Improve the display of the result so the message looks like this:

     `Sum of the numbers from 1 through 5 is 15`

     where 5 is the user entry and 15 is the sum. Of course, the numbers 5 and 15 in this example will be replaced by the user's entry and the calculated sum.

3

How to work with objects, functions, and events

In the last chapter, you learned how to code some simple, but unrealistic, applications using the prompt and alert methods. Now, in this chapter, you'll learn how to work with objects, functions, and events. When you finish this chapter, you'll be ready to start developing real-world applications of your own.

How to use objects to work with data **92**
How to use the window and document objects 92
How to use Textbox and Number objects 94
How to use Date and String objects 96
How to use DOM objects to change the text for an element........................98

How to use functions **100**
How to create and call an anonymous function 100
How to create and call a named function...102
When and how to use local and global variables 104

How to handle events..**106**
How to attach an event handler to an event...106
How to use an onload event handler to attach the other event handlers 108

Two illustrative applications..**110**
The Miles Per Gallon application..110
The Email List application 112

Perspective **116**

How to use objects to work with data

In the last chapter, you learned the syntax for using the methods and properties of objects. You were also introduced to some of the methods and properties of the window object. Now, you'll learn how to use the objects, methods, and properties that you need for working with data.

How to use the window and document objects

In chapter 2, you were introduced to the prompt and alert methods of the *window object*. Now, the first table in figure 3-1 presents another method of the window object that can be used to confirm an action.

Then, the second table in this figure summarizes the parseInt and parseFloat methods that you learned about in chapter 2. They are also methods of the window object. These methods are needed because the values that are returned by the prompt method and the values that the user enters into text boxes are treated as strings.

The use of these methods is illustrated by the first group of examples, starting with an example of the confirm method. For the statements after that, assume that the default values in the prompt methods aren't changed by the user. As a result, the second statement in this group stores 12345.6789 as a string in a variable named entryA, and the third statement converts the string to an integer value of 12345. Similarly, the fourth statement stores 12345.6789 as a string in a variable named entryB, and the fifth statement converts the string to a decimal value of 12345.6789.

Note that the object name isn't coded before the method name in these examples. That's okay because window is the *global object* of JavaScript. Note too that the parseInt method doesn't round the value. It just removes, or truncates, any decimal portion of the string.

In contrast to the window object, the *document object* is the highest object in the DOM structure. It represents the document, and you do need to code the object name (document) and the dot when you use one of its methods.

The second group of examples in this figure shows how to use two of the methods of the document object. The first is the getElementById method. It requires one parameter, which is the id for an element in the HTML document. When it is executed, it returns an object that represents that HTML element. In this example, this object is stored in a variable named rateBox.

In contrast, the write and writeln methods can be used in the body of an HTML document to write a string into the HTML document. You saw how this works in figure 2-2 of the previous chapter.

Another method of the window object that displays a dialog box

Method	Description
confirm(*string*)	Displays a dialog box that contains the string in the parameter, an OK button, and a Cancel button. If the user clicks OK, true is returned. If the user clicks Cancel, false is returned.

Two methods of the window object for working with numbers

Method	Description
parseInt(*string*)	Converts the string that's passed to it to an integer data type and returns that value. If it can't convert the string to an integer, it returns NaN.
parseFloat(*string*)	Converts the string that's passed to it to a decimal data type and returns that value. If it can't convert the string to a decimal value, it returns NaN.

Three methods of the document object

Method	Description
getElementById(*id*)	Gets the HTML element that has the id that's passed to it and returns that element.
write(*string*)	Writes the string that's passed to it into the document.
writeln(*string*)	Writes the string and advances to a new line.

Examples of window methods

```
confirm("Are you sure you want to delete it?");

var entryA = prompt("Enter any value", 12345.6789);
entryA = parseInt(entryA);                        // entryA = 12345

var entryB = prompt("Enter any value", 12345.6789);
entryB = parseFloat(entryB);                      // entryB = 12345.6789
```

Examples of document methods

```
// returns the object for the HTML element
var rateBox = document.getElementById("rate");

// writes a line into the document
document.writeln("Today is " + today.toDateString());
```

Description

- The *window object* is the *global object*, and JavaScript lets you omit the object name and dot operator when referring to the window object.

- The *document object* is the object that lets you work with the Document Object Model (DOM) that represents all of the HTML elements of the page.

- Data in a text box is treated as a string. Before you can use it in a calculation, you need to use either the parseInt or parseFloat method to convert it to numeric data.

- *NaN* is a value that means "Not a Number". It is returned by the parseInt and parseFloat methods when the value that's being parsed isn't a number.

- The getElementById method is commonly used to get the object for an HTML element.

Figure 3-1   How to use the window and document objects

How to use Textbox and Number objects

The Textbox object is one of the DOM objects. It represents a text box in the web page that is used to get input from the user or display output to the user. The first two tables in figure 3-2 summarize one of its methods and two of its properties. Then, this figure shows the HTML code for two text boxes that have "first_name" and "sales_amount" as their ids. These text boxes will be used by the examples that follow.

The first group of examples in this figure shows two ways to get the value from the text box with "first_name" as its id. To do that with two statements, the first statement uses the getElementById method of the document object to get the Textbox object for that text box. Then, the second statement uses the value property of the Textbox object to get the value that the user entered into the text box.

In practice, though, you would do that with just one statement by using *object chaining*, or just *chaining*. In that case, a single statement first uses the getElementById method to get the Textbox object, and then uses the value property of that object to get the value from the text box. In other words, you combine the use of the two methods into a single statement.

The second group of examples takes chaining to a third level. Without chaining, it takes three statements to get a valid number from a text box. First, the getDocumentById method gets the Textbox object for the text box with sales_amount as its id. Second, the value property of the Textbox object gets the value that the user entered into the text box. Third, the parseFloat method of the window object converts the string value to a decimal number. If the user entry is a valid number, this stores the number in the salesAmount variable, so it becomes a Number object.

With chaining, though, this requires only one statement. Although this may at first seem more complicated than using three statements, you'll soon see the value of chaining a series of related methods and properties in a single statement.

The third table in this figure summarizes the toFixed method of a Number object. When a user enters a valid number in a text box and the parseInt or parseFloat method is used to parse it before it is stored in a variable, the variable becomes a Number object. Then, you can use the toFixed method of that Number object to round the number to a specific number of decimal places.

This is illustrated by the first statement in the third group of examples. This statement takes chaining to a fourth level by adding the toFixed method to the chain. As a result, the number that's stored in the salesAmount variable is rounded to two decimal places.

The last two statements in this group present two more examples of chaining. The first one shows how to assign a value to a text box. In this case, the value is an empty string, which in effect clears the text box of any data. The second statement shows how to move the focus to a text box.

One method of the Textbox object

Method	Description
`focus()`	Moves the cursor into the text box, but doesn't return anything.

Two properties of the Textbox object

Property	Description
`value`	A string that represents the contents of the text box.
`disabled`	A Boolean value that controls whether the text box is disabled.

One method of the Number object

Method	Description
`toFixed(digits)`	Returns a string representation of the number after it has been rounded to the number of decimal places in the parameter.

HTML tags that define two text boxes

```
<input type="text" id="first_name">
<input type="text" id="sales_amount">
```

How to use the value property to get the value from a text box

Without chaining

```
var firstName = document.getElementById("first_name");
firstName = firstName.value;
```

With chaining

```
var firstName = document.getElementById("first_name").value;
```

How to use the parseFloat method to get a number value from a text box

Without chaining

```
var salesAmount = document.getElementById("sales_amount");
salesAmount = salesAmount.value;
salesAmount = parseFloat(salesAmount);
```

With chaining

```
var salesAmount = parseFloat(document.getElementById("sales_amount").value);
```

Other examples of chaining

```
var salesAmount =
    parseFloat(document.getElementById("sales_amount").value).toFixed(2);

document.getElementById("first_name").value = "";  // clear a text box

document.getElementById("first_name").focus();     // move focus to a text box
```

Description

- When you use the getElementById method to get a text box, the method returns a Textbox object. Then, you can use its value property to get the value in the box.

- When you declare a numeric variable, a Number object is created. Then, you can use the Number methods with the variable.

Figure 3-2   How to use Textbox and Number objects

How to use Date and String objects

When you store a numeric or string value in a variable, it is automatically converted to a Number or String object. This lets you use the properties and methods of the Number and String objects without having to explicitly create the objects.

However, there isn't a primitive data type for dates. As a result, you need to create a Date object before you can use its methods. To do that, you can use the syntax shown in figure 3-3. When you create a Date object, it is initialized with the current date and time, which is the date and time on the user's computer.

After you create a Date object, you can use the methods in this figure to work with it. These methods are illustrated by the first group of examples, assuming that the date is March 9, 2012. Here, the toDateString method converts the date to a string. The getFullYear method gets the four-digit year from the date. The getDate method gets the day of the month. And the getMonth method gets the month, counting from 0, not 1. As a result, the getMonth method returns 2 for March, not 3.

This figure also presents one property and four methods of a String object. Then, the last group of examples presents some statements that show how these properties work. For example, the second statement uses the toUpperCase method to convert a string to uppercase, and the third statement uses the length property to get the number of characters in a string.

The last two statements show how the indexOf and substr methods of a String object can be used to extract a substring from a string. Here, the indexOf method is used to get the position (index) of the first space in the string, counting from zero. Since the space is in the fourth position, this method returns 3. Then, the substr method gets the substring that starts at the first position and has a length of 3. As a result, this method returns "Ray".

Incidentally, JavaScript provides many more methods and properties for Date and String objects, but these will get you started. Later, if an application requires other Date or String properties or methods, we'll fully explain how they work.

The syntax for creating a JavaScript object and assigning it to a variable

```
var variableName = new ObjectType();
```

A statement that creates a Date object

```
var today = new Date();
```

A few of the methods of a Date object

Method	Description
`toDateString()`	Returns a string with the formatted date.
`getFullYear()`	Returns the four-digit year from the date.
`getDate()`	Returns the day of the month from the date.
`getMonth()`	Returns the month number from the date. The months are numbered starting with zero. January is 0 and December is 11.

One property of a String object

Method	Description
`length`	Returns the number of characters in the string.

A few of the methods of a String object

Method	Description
`indexOf(search,position)`	Searches for the first occurrence of the search string starting at the position specified or zero if position is omitted. If found, it returns the position of the first character, counting from 0. If not found, it returns -1.
`substr(start,length)`	Returns the substring that starts at the specified position (counting from zero) and contains the specified number of characters.
`toLowerCase()`	Returns a new string with the letters converted to lowercase.
`toUpperCase()`	Returns a new string with the letters converted to uppercase.

Examples that use a Date object

```
var today = new Date();           // creates Date object with current date
alert ( today.toDateString() );   // displays Fri Mar 09 2012 on 3/9/2012
alert ( today.getFullYear() );    // displays 2012
alert ( today.getDate() );        // displays 9
alert ( today.getMonth() );       // displays 2, not 3 for March
```

Examples that use a String object

```
var name = "Ray Harris";
var nameUpper = name.toUpperCase();     // nameUpper = RAY HARRIS
var nameLength = name.length;           // nameLength = 10
var index = name.indexOf(" ");          // index = 3
var firstName = name.substr(0, index);  // firstName = Ray
```

Description

- To create a Date object and assign it to a variable, use the syntax shown above. Then, you can use the Date methods with the variable.

- When you declare a string variable, a String object is automatically created. Then, you can use the String methods with the variable.

Figure 3-3   How to use Date and String objects

How to use DOM objects to change the text for an element

As a browser loads an HTML page, it builds a *Document Object Model* (*DOM*) that contains *nodes* that represent all of the HTML elements and attributes for the page. This is illustrated by the HTML page and diagram in figure 3-4.

The DOM starts with one node for the html element and follows the nesting down to the lowest levels. In this example, those are the nodes for the label, input, and span elements. Besides the *element nodes* that are represented by ovals in this diagram, the DOM includes *text nodes* that hold the data for the HTML elements. In this diagram, these text nodes are rectangles. For instance, the first text node contains the text for the title element in the head section: "Join Email List". The one to the right of that contains the text for the h1 element in the body: "Please join our email list". And so on.

The DOM also contains other types of nodes like *attribute nodes* and *comment nodes*. For simplicity, though, these nodes aren't included in the diagram in this figure.

To modify the contents of a text node with JavaScript, you can use the syntax shown in the summary in this figure. This syntax is illustrated by the example that follows it:

```
document.getElementById(
    "email_address_error").firstChild.nodeValue = "New contents";
```

Here, the getElementById method is used to get the object for the HTML element with email_address_error as the value of its id attribute. Then, the firstChild property gets the first dependent node of the HTML element (the text node), and the nodeValue property refers to the value of the text node. Last, the statement assigns a new value to that node.

If this is confusing, just accept the fact that firstChild.nodeValue represents the value of the text for an HTML element. You'll see this illustrated more fully in the application at the end of this chapter.

The code for a web page

```
<!DOCTYPE html>
<html>
<head>
    <title>Join Email List</title>
</head>
<body>
    <h1>Please join our email list</h1>
    <form id="email_form" name="email_form"
        action="join.html" method="get">
        <label for="email_address">Email Address:</label>
        <input type="text" id="email_address">
        <span id="email_address_error">*</span><br>
        <label> </label>
        <input type="button" id="join_list" value="Join our List">
    </form>
</body>
</html>
```

The DOM for the web page

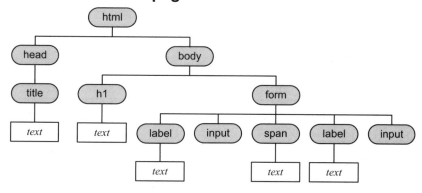

The syntax for changing the text node for an element

```
elementObject.firstChild.nodeValue = "The text for the element";
```

An example that puts a message in the span element

```
document.getElementById("email_address_error").firstChild.nodeValue =
    "This entry is required";
```

Description

- The *DOM (Document Object Model)* is a hierarchical collection of *nodes* in the web browser's memory that represents the current web page.
- The DOM for a web page is built as the page is loaded by the web browser.
- JavaScript can modify the web page in the browser by modifying the DOM. Whenever the DOM is changed, the web browser displays the results of the change.
- To modify the text for an HTML element like an h1, label, or span element, you can use the firstChild property to get the first descendent node for the element and then the nodeValue property to access the text for that node.

Figure 3-4   How to use the DOM to change the text for an element

How to use functions

When you develop JavaScript applications, you need to handle events like a user clicking on a button. To do that, you need to code and call functions that handle the events. As you will see, you can also use functions in other ways.

How to create and call an anonymous function

A *function* is a block of statements that can receive *parameters* and return a value by issuing a *return statement*. Once you've defined a function, you can call it from other portions of your JavaScript code. In figure 3-5, you can see how to create and call one type of JavaScript function, called an *anonymous function*.

To start an anonymous function, you code the keyword *var* followed by the name of the variable that will store the function. Then, you code an assignment operator, the keyword *function*, a list of parameters in parentheses, and a block of code in braces. The parentheses are required even if the function has no parameters.

When functions are coded this way, they are referred to as anonymous functions because technically they aren't named. Instead, they are stored in variables.

To *call* an anonymous function, you code the name of the variable that the function is stored in, followed by the parameters in parentheses. Then, the function uses the data that's passed to it in the parameters as it executes its block of code. Here again, the parentheses are required even if the function has no parameters.

The first example in this figure creates a function that's stored in a variable named showYear. This function doesn't require any parameters and doesn't return a value. When executed, this function displays a dialog box that shows the current year.

The second example creates a function that's stored in a variable named $. This function takes one parameter, which is the name of the id attribute of an HTML element. This function returns an object that represents the HTML element. In this example, the call statement gets the object for the HTML text box with "email_address1" as its id, and then uses the value property of that object to get the value that the user entered.

The third example in this figure creates a function named calculateTax that requires two parameters and returns a value. It calculates sales tax, rounds it to two decimal places, and returns that rounded value to the statement that called it.

To call this function, the statement passes two variables named subtotal and taxRate. In this case, the variable names for these values are the same as the parameter names in the function, but that isn't necessary. What is required is that the calling statement must pass parameters with the same data types and in the same sequence as the parameters in the function.

Incidentally, some programmers treat *parameter* and *argument* as synonyms. Others use *parameter* to refer to a parameter in a function and *argument* to refer to a parameter that is passed to the function. For simplicity in this book, we use *parameter* for both purposes.

The syntax for an anonymous function

```
var variableName = function(parameters) {
    // statements that run when the function is executed
}
```

An anonymous function with no parameters that doesn't return a value

```
var showYear = function() {
    var today = new Date();
    alert( "The year is " + today.getFullYear() );
}
```

How to call the function

```
showYear();
```

An anonymous function with one parameter that returns a DOM element

```
var $ = function (id) {
    return document.getElementById(id);
}
```

How to call the function

```
var emailAddress1 = $("email_address1").value;
```

An anonymous function with two parameters that returns a value

```
var calculateTax = function ( subtotal, taxRate ) {
    var tax = subtotal * taxRate;
    tax = parseFloat( tax.toFixed(2) );
    return tax;
}
```

How to call the function

```
var subtotal = 85.00;
var taxRate = 0.05;
var salesTax = calculateTax( subtotal, taxRate );   // calls the function
alert(salesTax);                                    // displays 4.25
```

Description

- A *function* is a block of code that can be *called* by other statements in the program. When the function ends, the program continues with the statement after the calling statement.

- A function can require that one or more *parameters* be passed to it when the function is called. In the calling statement, these parameters can also be referred to as *arguments*.

- To return a value to the statement that called it, a function uses a *return statement*. When the return statement is executed, the function returns the specified value and ends.

- An *anonymous function* is one that is coded as shown above. Technically, the function has no name, it is stored in a variable, and it is referred to by the variable name.

- In the JavaScript for an application, an anonymous function must be coded before any statements that call it. Otherwise, an error will occur.

Figure 3-5   How to create and call an anonymous function

How to create and call a named function

Since anonymous functions are commonly used to handle the events that occur in JavaScript applications, you'll use them most of the time. However, you should know that JavaScript also lets you code *named functions*.

Figure 3-6 shows you how to create and call a named function. It uses the same examples as the previous figure but with named functions instead of anonymous functions. As the syntax shows, a named function isn't stored in a variable, and its name is coded after the keyword *function* and before the parameters.

As in the previous figure, the showYear function doesn't have any parameters and doesn't return a value. Also, the calculateTax function requires two parameters and returns the sales tax value rounded to two decimal places. In these examples, using named functions is just another way to get the same results as the anonymous functions.

The one benefit of using a named function is that it can be coded before or after any statements that call it. In contrast, an anonymous function must be coded before any statements that call it. This is a minor difference, though, that won't cause any problems as long as you're aware of it.

The syntax for a named function

```
function functionName (parameters) {
    // statements that run when the function is executed
}
```

A named function with no parameters that doesn't return a value

```
function() showYear {
    var today = new Date();
    alert( "The year is " + today.getFullYear() );
}
```

How to call the function

```
showYear();
```

A named function with two parameters that returns a value

```
function calculateTax ( subtotal, taxRate ) {
    var tax = subtotal * taxRate;
    tax = parseFloat( tax.toFixed(2) );
    return tax;
}
```

How to call the function

```
var subtotal = 85.00;
var taxRate = 0.05;
var salesTax = calculateTax( subtotal, taxRate );   // calls the function
alert(salesTax);                                     // displays 4.25
```

Description

- A *named function* is one that is coded as shown above. This is just another way to code functions.

- In contrast to an anonymous function, a named function doesn't have to be coded before any statements that call it.

Figure 3-6   How to create and call a named function

When and how to use local and global variables

Scope in a programming language refers to the visibility of variables and functions. That is, it tells you where in your program you are allowed to use the variables and functions that you've defined.

When you use JavaScript, *local variables* are variables that are defined within functions. They have *local scope*, which means that they can only be used within the functions that define them.

In contrast, *global variables* are variables that are defined outside of functions. These variables have *global scope*, so they can be used by any function without passing them to the function as parameters.

The first example in figure 3-7 illustrates the use of a local variable. Here, the calculateTax function creates a variable named tax and returns that variable to the calling statement. Then, that statement can store the variable in another variable. Note, however, that a statement outside of the function can't refer to the variable named tax without causing an error. That's because it has local scope.

In contrast, the second example first creates a global variable named tax. Then, the function calculates the sales tax and stores the result in that global variable. As a result, the function doesn't have to return the tax variable. Instead, a statement outside of the function can refer to the variable because it is a global.

Although it may seem easier to use global variables than to pass data to a function and return data from it, global variables often create problems. That's because any function can modify a global variable, and it's all too easy to misspell a variable name or modify the wrong variable, especially in large applications. That in turn can create debugging problems.

In contrast, the use of local variables reduces the likelihood of naming conflicts. For instance, two different functions can use the same names for local variables without causing conflicts. That of course means fewer errors and debugging problems. With just a few exceptions, then, all of the code in your applications should be in functions so all of the variables are local.

To complicate the use of variables, the JavaScript engine assumes that a variable is global if you accidentally omit the var keyword when you declare it. This is illustrated by the third example in this figure. Here, the var keyword is missing before the first assignment statement so tax is assumed to be a global variable.

This is a weakness of JavaScript that you need to be aware of because it can lead to coding errors. If, for example, you misspell the name of a variable that you've already declared when you code an assignment statement, it will be treated as a new global variable. With this in mind, be sure to include the var keyword when you declare new variables and always declare a variable before you refer to it in your code.

A function that uses a local variable named tax

```
var calculateTax = function ( subtotal, taxRate ) {
    var tax = subtotal * taxRate;    // tax is a local variable
    tax = parseFloat( tax.toFixed(2) );
    return tax;
}
```

Referring to a local variable from outside the function causes an error

```
alert("Tax is " + tax);              // causes error
```

A function that uses a global variable named tax

```
var tax;                             // tax is a global variable
var calculateTax = function ( subtotal, taxRate ) {
    tax = subtotal * taxRate;
    tax = parseFloat( tax.toFixed(2) );
}
```

Referring to a global variablefrom outside the function doesn't cause an error

```
alert("Tax is " + tax);              // will not cause error
```

A function that inadvertently uses a global variable named tax

```
var calculateTax = function ( subtotal, taxRate ) {
    tax = subtotal * taxRate;  // no var keyword so tax is treated as global
    tax = parseFloat( tax.toFixed(2) );
}
```

Referring to the tax variable
from outside the function doesn't cause an error...but it should!

```
alert("Tax is " + tax);              // will not cause error
```

Best coding practices

- Use local variables whenever possible.
- Always use the var keyword to declare a new variable before the variable is referred to by other statements.

Discussion

- The *scope* of a variable or function determines what code has access to it.
- Variables that are created inside a function are *local variables*, and local variables can only be referred to by the code within the function.
- Variables created outside of functions are *global variables*, and the code in all functions have access to all global variables.
- If you forget to code the var keyword in a variable declaration, the JavaScript engine assumes that the variable is global. This can cause debugging problems.
- In general, it's better to pass local variables from one function to another as parameters than it is to use global variables. That will make your code easier to understand with less chance for errors.

Figure 3-7   When and how to use local and global variables

How to handle events

JavaScript applications commonly respond to user actions like clicking on a button. These actions are called *events*, and the anonymous functions that handle the events are called *event handlers*. To make that happen, you have to *attach* the functions to the events.

How to attach an event handler to an event

The table in figure 3-8 summarizes some of the events that are commonly handled by JavaScript applications. For instance, the load event of the window object occurs when the browser finishes loading the HTML for a page and building the DOM for it. The click event of a button object occurs when the user clicks on the button. And the mouseover action of an element like a heading or link occurs when the user holds (hovers) the mouse over the element.

After this table, you can see the syntax for attaching a function to an event. To do that, you code the object name, a dot, and the event name preceded by the word *on*. Then, you code an equals sign followed by the name of the variable for the anonymous function that's going to handle the event.

The first example in this figure is an anonymous function that can be used as an event handler. This function is stored in a variable named joinList, and all it does is display a message. In an actual application, though, you would code the statements that properly handle the event in the braces for the function.

The second example shows a JavaScript statement that attaches the joinList function to the click event of a button that has "submit_button" as its id. To do that, this statement first uses the getElementById method to get the object for the button. This is followed by the dot operator and the event name preceded by *on* (onclick). Then, the result is set equal to the variable name (joinList) for the function that will be used as the event handler.

Note here that you don't code the parentheses after the name of the variable that's used for the function, as in figure 3-5. That's because you're attaching the event handler, not calling it. As a result, the function will be called when the event is fired. In contrast, if you were to put parentheses after joinList, the function would be called right away, and the function wouldn't be assigned to the event.

The third example is like the second example. It attaches the joinList event handler to the double-click event of a text box that has text_box_1 as its id. This means that the same event handler will be used for two different events. Here again, you don't code the parentheses when you attach the function.

Common events

Object	Event	Occurs when...
window	load	The document has been loaded into the browser.
button	click	The button is clicked.
control or link	focus	The control or link receives the focus.
	blur	The control or link loses the focus.
control	change	The user changes the value in the control.
	select	The user selects text in a text box or text area.
element	click	The user clicks on the element.
	dblclick	The user double-clicks on the element.
	mouseover	The user moves the mouse over the element.
	mousein	The user moves the mouse into the element.
	mouseout	The user moves the mouse out of the element.

The syntax for attaching an event handler

```
objectVariable.oneventName = eventHandlerName;
```

An event handler named joinList

```
var joinList = function() {
    alert("The statements for the function go here");
}
```

How to attach the event handler to the click event of a button

```
document.getElementById("submit_button").onclick = joinList;
```

How to attach the event handler to the double-click event of a text box

```
document.getElementById("text_box_1").ondblclick = joinList;
```

Description

- An *event handler* is a function that's executed when an *event* occurs, so it "handles" the event. As a result, you code an event handler just like any other function.

- To *attach* an event handler to an event, you must first specify the object and the event that triggers the event handler. Then, you assign the event handler function to that event.

- When you code the event for an event handler, you precede the event name with *on*. So, for example, onclick is used for the click event.

- When you attach an event handler to an event, you don't code the parentheses after the variable name for the function.

Figure 3-8   How to attach an event handler to an event

How to use an onload event handler to attach the other event handlers

When do you attach an event handler like the one in the previous figure? You attach it after all the HTML has been loaded into a user's browser and the DOM has been built. To do that, you code an event handler for the load event of the window object as shown in figure 3-9. This gives you a complete picture of how event handlers are set up and used.

In the HTML for this example, you can see a label, a text box, a label that contains one space, and a button. This simple application is supposed to display a message when the button is clicked or when the user changes the value in the text box.

In the JavaScript code, you can see three anonymous functions. The first one is stored in a variable named $. This function uses the getElementById method of the document object to get an element object when the id of an HTML element is passed to it. This is a common function because it makes it easy to get an element object without coding the getElementById method every time. As a result, you'll see it often, and you can think of it as the standard $ function.

The second function is the event handler for the click event of the button, and the third function is the event handler for the change event of the text box. Both of these functions just display a message.

The fourth function is the event handler for the onload event. It is used to attach the other event handlers to the click and change events. Note that this function starts with

```
window.onload
```

so it is executed after the page is loaded and the DOM has been built.

Within this function are the two statements that attach the other event handlers. The first one attaches the joinList handler to the click event of the button. The second one attaches the changeValue handler to the change event of the text box. Both of these statements use the $ function to get the object that the event applies to.

Incidentally, the event handler for the window.onload event can do more than assign functions to events. In fact, it can do whatever needs to be done after the DOM is loaded. You'll see this illustrated throughout this book.

The web browser after the Email Address has been changed

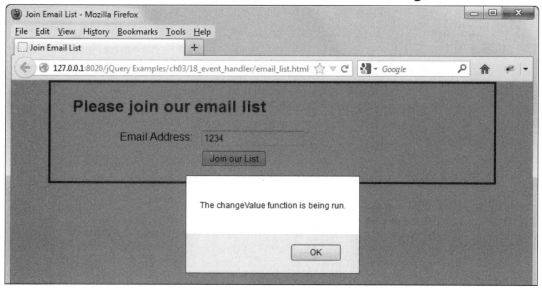

The HTML

```
<h1>Please join our email list</h1>
<label for="email_address">Email Address:</label>
<input type="text" id="email_address" name="email_address"><br>

<label> </label>
<input type="button" id="join_list" value="Join our List"><br>
```

The JavaScript

```
// the $ function
var $ = function (id) {
    return document.getElementById(id);
}
// the event handler for the click event of the button
var joinList = function () {
    alert("The joinList function is being run.");
}
// the event handler for the onchange event of the text box
var changeValue = function () {
    alert("The changeValue function is being run.");
}
// the event handler for the onload event that attaches two event handlers
window.onload = function () {
    $("join_list").onclick = joinList;          // attaches 1st handler
    $("email_address").onchange = changeValue;  // attaches 2nd handler
}
```

Description

- The event handler for the onload event of the window object can be used to attach the event handlers for other events after the DOM has been built.

Figure 3-9   How to use the onload event handler to attach the other event handlers

Two illustrative applications

You have now learned enough about JavaScript to develop applications of your own. To give you a better idea of how to do that, this chapter ends by presenting two JavaScript applications.

The Miles Per Gallon application

Figure 3-10 presents an application that lets the user enter the number of miles driven and the number of gallons of gasoline used into text boxes. Then, when the user clicks on the Calculate MPG button, this application calculates miles per gallon, rounds it to one decimal place, and displays it in the third text box.

To keep this simple, all of the JavaScript code is embedded in the script element of the HTML document. That way, you can see both the HTML and JavaScript in one file. Although CSS is used to format the controls and shade the Miles Per Gallon text box, the CSS isn't shown because it's irrelevant to the operation of this application.

The JavaScript code for this application follows the structure of the example in the previous figure. First, the $ function is used to get the objects that the application needs. Second, the calculateMpg function is used as the event handler. Third, the event handler for the onload event is used to attach the calculateMpg handler to the click event of the Calculate MPG button. Besides attaching this event handler, the onload event handler moves the focus to the first text box on the page.

In the calculateMpg function, the user entries are parsed into the miles and gallons variables. Then, an if statement tests whether either entry is invalid because it isn't a number. If so, an error message is displayed. Otherwise, the two statements in the else clause calculate miles per gallon, round the result to one decimal place, and store the result in the value property of the text box with "mpg" as its id.

If you study the JavaScript code in this application, you can see that all of the code is within the three functions. As a result, there aren't any global variables. This is typical of a JavaScript application.

You should also note the sequence of the functions. Here, the first function is the $ function. The second function is the calculateMpg function, which calls the $ function several times. And the third function is the event handler for the load event, which attaches the calculateMpg function. In short, each function only refers to functions that precede it in the code. This is a logical sequence that makes your code easier to read and understand.

When the code is executed, the onload event handler is executed first, and it attaches the event handler for the click event of the Calculate MPG button. Then, the browser waits until that event occurs. When it does, the calculateMpg function is executed and the user entries are validated.

The Miles Per Gallon application in a browser

```
Calculate Miles Per Gallon

        Miles Driven:  2021
   Gallons of Gas Used:  55.3
     Miles Per Gallon  36.5

                    Calculate MPG
```

The HTML and JavaScript for the application

```html
<!DOCTYPE html>
<html>
<head>
    <title>Calculate MPG</title>
    <link rel="stylesheet" href="mpg.css">
    <script>
        var $ = function (id) {
            return document.getElementById(id);
        }
        var calculateMpg = function () {
            var miles = parseFloat($("miles").value);
            var gallons = parseFloat($("gallons").value);
            if (isNaN(miles) || isNaN(gallons)) {
                alert("Both entries must be numeric");
            }
            else {
                var mpg = miles / gallons;
                $("mpg").value = mpg.toFixed(1);
            }
        }
        window.onload = function () {
            $("calculate").onclick = calculateMpg;
            $("miles").focus();
        }
    </script>
</head>
<body>
    <section>
        <h1>Calculate Miles Per Gallon</h1>
        <label for="miles">Miles Driven:</label>
        <input type="text" id="miles"><br>
        <label for="gallons">Gallons of Gas Used:</label>
        <input type="text" id="gallons"><br>
        <label for="mpg">Miles Per Gallon</label>
        <input type="text" id="mpg" disabled><br>
        <label> </label>
        <input type="button" id="calculate" value="Calculate MPG">
    </section>
</body>
</html>
```

Figure 3-10   The Miles Per Gallon application

The Email List application

Figure 3-11 presents an Email List application like the one that you were introduced to in chapter 1. In this application, the user enters the data for three text boxes and clicks the Join our List button. Then, the JavaScript application checks the data for validity. If any entry is invalid, this application displays an error message to the right of the entry. If all entries are valid, the data is submitted to the server for server-side processing.

The data validation that's done in this application is typical of the client-side validation that's done for any form before its data is submitted to the server for processing. This application also illustrates DOM scripting because it changes the text that's displayed by the span elements of the HTML.

In the head section of the HTML, you can see that a link element is used to include a CSS file for this page. You can also see a script element that includes an external JavaScript file for this page. Here again, the CSS isn't shown because it's irrelevant to the operation of the application.

In the body of the HTML, you can see the form, label, and input elements for this page. You can also see that the first three input elements are followed by span elements that include asterisks. Since the CSS for this page applies the color red to the text in span elements, the asterisks are red when the page is displayed. Then, since the JavaScript stores the error messages in the span elements, the error messages are also red.

You might also notice the id attributes for the form and the text boxes: email_form, email_address1, email_address2, and first_name. These are the ids that will be passed to the $ function in the JavaScript.

Note too that the values for the name attributes are the same as the values for the id attributes. The name attributes for the text boxes are used by the server-side code to get the user entries that are passed to it.

The Email List application in a web browser

Please join our email list

Email Address:	zak@yahoo.com
Re-enter Email Address:	zak@yahoo This entry must equal first entry.
First Name	This field is required.
	Join our List

The HTML file for the page

```html
<!DOCTYPE html>
<html>
<head>
    <title>Join Email List</title>
    <link rel="stylesheet" href="email_list.css">
    <script src="email_list.js"></script>
</head>
<body>
    <section>
        <h1>Please join our email list</h1>
        <form id="email_form" name="email_form"
            action="join.html" method="get">
            <label for="email_address1">Email Address:</label>
            <input type="text" id="email_address1 name="email_address1">
            <span id="email_address1_error">*</span><br>

            <label for="email_address2">Re-enter Email Address:</label>
            <input type="text" id="email_address2" name="email_address2">
            <span id="email_address2_error">*</span><br>

            <label for="first_name">First Name</label>
            <input type="text" id="first_name" name="first_name">
            <span id="first_name_error">*</span><br>

            <label> </label>
            <input type="button" id="join_list" value="Join our List">
        </form>
    </section>
</body>
</html>
```

Figure 3-11   The HTML for the Email List application

Figure 3-12 shows one way that the JavaScript for this application can be coded. Here, the onload event handler attaches the joinList function to the click event of the button with join_list as its id. The onload event handler also moves the focus to the first text box.

When the joinList function is called, its first two statements use the $ function to store the entries for the first two text boxes in variables named emailAddress1 and emailAddress2. Then, the third statement sets a Boolean variable named isValid to true. The three if statements that follow will change this variable to false if any of entries are invalid.

Each of the three if statements that follow checks one user entry for validity. If an error is detected, the statement sets the text in the span element for the field to an appropriate error message. To do that, it uses the firstChild and nodeValue properties of the span element, as shown in figure 3-4. An if statement that detects an invalid entry also sets the isValid variable to false. However, if the entry is valid, the else clause of the statement sets the text in the span element to an empty string so nothing is displayed.

After the three entries are checked for validity, a fourth if statement tests the isValid variable to see whether it's true or false. If it's true, that means that none of the preceding if statements have set it to false, which means that all of the entries are valid. As a result, the if clause uses the submit method of the form object to send the data to the server. Although this method hasn't been presented yet, you'll learn more about it in the chapter on forms and data validation.

On the other hand, if isValid is false, nothing is done because the if statement doesn't have an else clause. Instead, the application waits for the user to correct the entries and click again on the Join our List button.

If you study this code, you can see that the second if statement checks the second entry for two types of validity. First, it checks to make sure an entry has been made. Second, if an entry has been made, it checks to make sure that the first email address entry is equal to the second email address entry.

Here again, all of the code for this application is in functions so there are no global variables. Also, the functions are coded in a sequence that's easy to read because the called functions always precede the function calls.

You might notice, however, that this code doesn't provide all of the validity checking that you might want. In particular, it doesn't test whether the entries in the first two text boxes are valid email addresses. In the chapter on forms and data validation, though, you'll learn how to provide that type of data validation.

The JavaScript for the Email List application with one if statement

```javascript
var $ = function (id) {
    return document.getElementById(id);
}
var joinList = function () {
    var emailAddress1 = $("email_address1").value;
    var emailAddress2 = $("email_address2").value;
    var isValid = true;

    // validate the first entry
    if (emailAddress1 == "") {
        $("email_address1_error").firstChild.nodeValue =
            "This field is required.";
        isValid = false;
    } else {
        $("email_address1_error").firstChild.nodeValue = "";
    }

    // validate the second entry
    if (emailAddress2 == "") {
        $("email_address2_error").firstChild.nodeValue =
            "This field is required.";
        isValid = false;
    } else if (emailAddress1 !== emailAddress2) {
        $("email_address2_error").firstChild.nodeValue =
            "This entry must equal first entry.";
        isValid = false;
    } else {
        $("email_address2_error").firstChild.nodeValue = "";
    }

    // validate the third entry
    if ($("first_name").value == "") {
        $("first_name_error").firstChild.nodeValue =
            "This field is required.";
        isValid = false;
    } else {
        $("first_name_error").firstChild.nodeValue = "";
    }

    if (isValid) {
        // use the submit method of the form object to submit the form
        $("email_form").submit();
    }
}
window.onload = function () {
    $("join_list").onclick = joinList;
    $("email_address1").focus();
}
```

Figure 3-12   The JavaScript for the Email List application

Perspective

In this chapter, you've seen the way real-world JavaScript applications use objects and respond to events. Now, if you understand everything in this chapter, you should be ready to start developing applications of your own.

Terms

window object	parameter
global object	argument
document object	return statement
object chaining	anonymous function
chaining	named function
DOM (Document Object Model)	scope
DOM node	local variable
element node	local scope
text node	global variable
attribute node	global scope
comment node	event
function	event handler
call a function	attach an event handler

Summary

- The *document object* provides methods and properties that let you work with the *Document Object Model*, or *DOM*.

- The Textbox, Number, Date, and String objects provide methods and properties for text boxes, number data types, dates, and string data types. When working with the methods and properties of these objects, you often use *chaining*.

- The DOM is built when a page is loaded into a browser. It includes *element nodes* that represent the elements in an HTML document and *text nodes* that represent the text within those elements. To access the text for an element, you can refer to the nodeValue property of the firstChild property of the element.

- A *function* consists of a block of code that is executed when the function is *called*. The function can require one or more *parameters* that are passed to it by the calling statement.

- An *anonymous function* is stored in a variable, and a *named function* is given a name but not stored in a variable.

- *Local variables* are defined within a function and can only be accessed by statements within the function. *Global variables* are defined outside of all functions and can be accessed by any of the other code.

- An *event handler* is a function that is called when an *event* like clicking on a button occurs. To make this work, the function must be *attached* to the event.

Exercise 3-1   Enhance the MPG application

In this exercise, you'll enhance the MPG application in several ways.

Test the application

1. Open your text editor or IDE, and open this HTML file:

   `c:\jquery\exercises\ch03\mpg\index.html`

   Then, review the code to see that it's the same as in figure 3-10.

2. Run and test this application with valid data to see how it works. When you click the Calculate MPG button, the correct result should be displayed.

3. Now, test the data validation routine. Note that one error message is displayed no matter which entry is invalid.

Enhance the data validation

4. Enhance the if statement so it provides a different error message for each text box and for each type of error:
   - Miles must be numeric
   - Miles must be greater than zero
   - Gallons must be numeric
   - Gallons must be greater than zero

   The if statement should include one if clause that tests for the first condition, followed by three if else clauses that test for the next three conditions. Then, test this change.

Add a Clear Entries button

5. Add a Clear Entries button below the Calculate MPG button. To do that, copy the HTML for the label and input elements for the Calculate button, and paste it after the input element for the Calculate button. Then, modify the HTML for the Clear Entries button so it has a unique id and the appropriate value attribute.

6. Add the JavaScript code for an anonymous function that's stored in a variable named clear. This function should clear the text boxes by using the $ function to get a Textbox object for each text box and then setting the value property of the text box to an empty string. Then, add a statement in the onload event handler that attaches the clear function to the click event of the Clear Entries button like this:

   `$("clear").onclick = clear;`

   Now, test this enhancement.

7. Add a statement to the onload event handler that attaches the clear function to the double-click event of the miles text box. Then, test this change.

Exercise 3-2   Develop a Future Value application

This exercise will guide you through the development of a new application called the Future Value application. The interface for this application follows:

Be sure to test this application after each of the steps in this exercise.

1. Open your text editor or IDE, and open the HTML and JavaScript files in this folder:

    `c:\jquery\exercises\ch03\future_value\`

    Run the HTML file to see that it provides all the code for the user interface. Then, note that the JavaScript file only has the $ function that's commonly used to get the objects for elements with specific ids.

2. Add a calculateClick function that will be used as the event handler for the click event of the Calculate button. Within this function, code three variables that get the values from the first three text boxes by using the $ function. Convert the first two values to decimals and the third value to an integer. Then, code a for loop like the one in the second example of figure 2-15 that calculates the future value of an investment. When the loop ends, use the toFixed method to remove the decimal places from the future value and put that value in the Future Value text box.

    Code an onload event handler for the window object that attaches the calculateClick function to the click event of the Calculate button.

3. Add an if statement that tests just that the first entry is a valid number greater than zero. If the entry isn't valid, use the alert method to display an appropriate error message. Finish this if statement with an else clause that contains the code that you used for calculating and displaying the future value in step 2.

4. Enhance the if statement so it checks the other two entries for validity. Here again, each entry should be a number greater than zero and the alert method should be used to display appropriate error messages.

5. Add any finishing touches to this application, like moving the focus to the first text box when the application starts. This is now a working application that you developed by coding and testing a limited number of statements in each step.

4

How to test and debug a JavaScript application

As you build a JavaScript application, you need to test it to make sure that it performs as expected. Then, if there are any problems, you need to debug your application to correct those problems. This chapter shows you how to do both.

An introduction to testing and debugging **120**
Typical test phases for a JavaScript application 120
The three types of errors that can occur 120
Common JavaScript errors 122
How top-down coding and testing can simplify debugging 124
How to debug with Firebug **126**
How to enable Firebug and find errors 126
How to use breakpoints and step through code 128
Other debugging methods **130**
When and how to get error messages with other browsers 130
A simple way to trace the execution of your JavaScript code 132
When and how to view the source code 134
When and how to validate the HTML.. 136
Perspective **138**

An introduction
to testing and debugging

When you *test* an application, you run it to make sure that it works correctly. As you test the application, you try every possible combination of input data and user actions to be certain that the application works in every case. In other words, the goal of testing is to make an application fail.

When you *debug* an application, you fix the errors (*bugs*) that you discover during testing. Each time you fix a bug, you test again to make sure that the change that you made didn't affect any other aspect of the application.

Typical test phases for a JavaScript application

When you test an application, you typically do so in phases, like the three that are summarized in figure 4-1.

In the first phase, as you test the user interface, you should visually check the controls to make sure they're displayed properly with the correct text. Then, you should make sure that all the keys and controls work correctly.

In the second phase, you should test the application with valid data. To start, you can enter data that you would expect a user to enter. Before you're done, though, you should enter valid data that tests all of the limits of the application.

In the third phase, you go all out to make the application fail by testing every combination of invalid data and user action that you can think of. That should include random actions like pressing the Enter key or clicking the mouse at the wrong time.

The three types of errors that can occur

As you test an application, three types of errors can occur. *Syntax errors* violate the rules for coding JavaScript statements. These errors are detected by the JavaScript engine as a page is loaded into the browser. As you learned in chapter 1, some syntax errors are also detected by IDEs like Aptana. Syntax errors are the easiest to fix, because web browsers and IDEs provide error messages that help you do that.

A *runtime error* occurs after a page has been loaded and the application is running. Then, when a statement can't be executed, the JavaScript engine throws an *exception* that stops the execution of the application.

Logic errors are errors in the logic of the coding: an arithmetic expression that delivers the wrong result, using the wrong relational operator in a comparison, and so on. To illustrate, the Calculate MPG application in this figure has a logic error. Here, you can see that the second entry is empty and the result of the calculation is NaN, but the calculation shouldn't be done at all if one of the entries is empty. Could it be a problem with the if statement?

The Calculate MPG application with a logic error

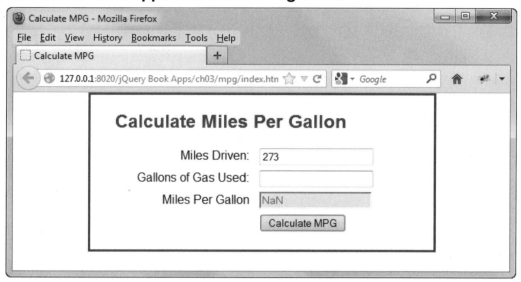

The goal of testing

- To find all errors before the application is put into production.

The goal of debugging

- To fix all errors before the application is put into production.

Three test phases

- Check the user interface to make sure that it works correctly.
- Test the application with valid input data to make sure the results are correct.
- Test the application with invalid data or unexpected user actions. Try everything you can think of to make the application fail.

The three types of errors that can occur

- *Syntax errors* violate the rules for how JavaScript statements must be written. These errors are caught by the JavaScript engine as a page is loaded into the web browser.
- *Runtime errors* occur after a page is loaded and the application is being run. When a runtime error occurs, the JavaScript engine throws an *exception* that stops the execution of the application.
- *Logic errors* are statements that don't cause syntax or runtime errors, but produce the wrong results.

Description

- To *test* a JavaScript application, you run it to make sure that it works properly no matter what data you enter or what events you initiate.
- When you *debug* an application, you find and fix all of the errors (*bugs*) that you find when you test the application.

Figure 4-1   An introduction to testing and debugging

Common JavaScript errors

Figure 4-2 presents some of the coding errors that are commonly made as you write a JavaScript application. If you did the exercises for the last chapter, you've probably experienced some of these errors already. Now, if you study this figure, you'll have a better idea of what to watch out for.

If you're using a good text editor or IDE, you can avoid most of these errors by noting the error markers that are displayed as you enter the code. For instance, Aptana will help you avoid most of the errors in the first two groups in this figure. However, it won't help you avoid the errors in the third group.

The fourth group in this figure addresses the problem with floating-point arithmetic that was mentioned in chapter 2. In brief, JavaScript uses the IEEE 754 standard for floating-point numbers, and this standard can introduce inexact results, even for simple calculations. Although these results are extremely close to the exact results, they can cause problems, especially in comparisons. For instance, the number 7.495 is not equal to 7.495000000000001.

To get around this problem, you can round the result as shown by the examples. Here, the first statement rounds the salesTax value to two decimal places by using the toFixed method of the number. In this case, the result is stored as a string because the toFixed method returns a string. In contrast, the second statement gets the rounded result and then uses the parseFloat method to store it as a number. Which approach you use depends on whether you need the result to be a string or a number.

The last group in this figure illustrates the type of problem that can occur when JavaScript assumes that a variable is global. This problem was introduced in chapter 3. In this example, the salesTax variable is declared properly by using the var keyword. But the next statement misspells salesTax as salestax when it tries to assign a rounded and parsed value to salesTax. As a result, salestax is treated as a global variable, and the rounded and parsed value goes into salestax, not salesTax, which of course causes a bug.

Needless to say, that type of bug can be difficult to find. But now that you're aware of errors like this, you'll be better prepared to debug them.

Common syntax errors

- Misspelling keywords, like coding getElementByID instead of getElementById.
- Omitting required parentheses, quotation marks, or braces.
- Not using the same opening and closing quotation mark.
- Omitting the semicolon at the end of a statement.
- Misspelling or incorrectly capitalizing an identifier, like defining a variable named salesTax and referring to it later as salestax.

Problems with HTML references

- Referring to an attribute value or other HTML component incorrectly, like referring to an id as salesTax when the id is sales_tax.

Problems with data and comparisons

- Not testing to make sure that a user entry is the right data type before processing it.
- Not using the parseInt or parseFloat method to convert a user entry into a numeric value before processing it.
- Using one equal sign instead of two when testing for equality.

Problems with floating-point arithmetic

- The number data type in JavaScript uses floating-point numbers, and that can lead to arithmetic results that are imprecise. For example,

```
var salesAmount = 74.95;
salesTax = salesAmount * .1;                 // result is 7.495000000000001
```

- One way to fix this potential problem is to round the result to the right number of decimal places and then convert it back to a floating-point number:

```
salesTax = salesTax.toFixed(2)               // result is 7.50 as a string
salesTax = parseFloat(salesTax.toFixed(2));  // result is 7.50 as a number
```

Problems with undeclared variables that are treated as global variables

- If you assign a value to a variable that hasn't been declared, the JavaScript engine treats it as a global variable. This can happen when you misspell a variable name, as in this example:

```
var calculateTax = function (subtotal, taxRate) {
    var salesTax = subtotal * taxRate;            // salesTax is local
    salestax = parseFloat(salesTax.toFixed(2));   // salestax is global
    return salesTax;           // salesTax isn't rounded but salestax is
}
```

Description

- When the JavaScript engine in a browser comes to a JavaScript statement that it can't execute, it throws an error and skips the rest of the JavaScript statements.

Figure 4-2   Common JavaScript errors

How top-down coding and testing can simplify debugging

One way to simplify debugging is to code and test just a small portion of code at a time. This can be referred to as *top-down coding and testing* or just *top-down testing*. The implication is that you test the most important operations first and work your way down to the least important operations and the finishing touches.

This is illustrated by the example in figure 4-3. Here, the first testing phase consists of 15 lines of code that provide an event handler for the click event of the Calculate button. However, that event handler doesn't do any data validation. It just calculates the future value of the investment amount, which is the essence of this application.

Then, phase 2 adds to this code by doing the data validation for just the first entry. Phase 3 adds the data validation for the other two entries. And phase 4 adds finishing touches like moving the focus to the first text box when the application starts.

The result is that you're testing a small amount of code at a time. That makes debugging easy because you know that any errors were introduced by the lines of code that you've just added. This also makes developing an application more enjoyable because you're making continuous progress without the frustration of complex debugging problems.

The user interface for a Future Value application

Future Value Calculator

Investment Amount: `1375000`

Annual Interest Rate: `5.5`

Number of Years: `7`

Future Value: `2000184`

`Calculate`

Testing phase 1: No data validation

```
var $ = function (id) {
    return document.getElementById(id);
}
var calculateClick = function () {
    var investment = parseFloat( $("investment").value );
    var annualRate = parseFloat( $("rate").value );
    var years = parseInt( $("years").value );
    for ( i = 1; i <= years; i++ ) {
        investment += investment * annualRate / 100;
    }
    $("future_value").value = investment.toFixed();
}
window.onload = function () {
    $("calculate").onclick = calculateClick;
}
```

Testing phase 2: Add data validation for just the first entry

```
if (isNaN(investment) || investment <= 0) {
    alert("Investment must be a number and greater than zero.");
}
else {
    // the future value calculation from phase 1
}
```

Testing phase 3: Add data validation for the other entries

```
// Add data validation for the other entries
```

Testing phase 4: Add the finishing touches

```
// Add finishing touches like moving the focus to the first text box
```

Discussion

- When you use *top-down coding and testing*, you start by coding and testing a small portion of code. Then, you build on that base by adding the code for an operation or two at a time and testing after each addition.

- Top-down testing simplifies debugging because you know that the errors are caused by the code that you've just added. As a result, it's relatively easy to find the errors.

Figure 4-3   How top-down coding and testing can simplify debugging

How to debug with Firebug

In chapter 2, you were introduced to the Firefox Error Console as a way to find syntax errors. Besides that, though, Firefox offers a Firebug extension that works better than the Error Console. Firebug also offers some excellent debugging features for more complicated applications.

Since Firebug is relatively easy to use, the topics that follow don't present the procedures for using all of its features. Instead, these topics present just the skills that you're going to use the most. Then, if you decide that you want to use some of the other features, you can experiment with them on your own.

How to enable Firebug and find errors

Firebug is a free Firefox extension that provides some excellent debugging capabilities. After Firebug is installed, as shown in appendix A, you will see the Firebug icon in the Firefox toolbar, as shown in figure 4-4. Then, you can click this icon or press the F12 key to open and close Firebug.

One of the primary uses of Firebug is to get error messages like those displayed by the Error Console, but to do that in a more efficient way. For instance, to get an error message, you can just open Firebug and click on the Console tab to display the Console panel. That should display the first error that was detected when the page was loaded. Then, you can click on the link to switch to the Script panel with the JavaScript code for the error statement highlighted.

In some cases, you may need to enable the Console and Script panels before you can use them. If a panel isn't enabled, it will contain a link that you can use to enable it. Or, you can select the Enable command from the list that drops down from the tab for the panel.

Because Firebug works so well, we recommend that you install it right away and start using it to find errors. Whenever you test a JavaScript application and nothing happens, just click on the Firebug icon and look in the Console panel to see if an error has been caught. If it has, go on from there. Otherwise, you have a more serious debugging problem.

Incidentally, the error message that's displayed when you load an application is for the first syntax error that's detected, but there can be other syntax errors in the code. To catch them, you have to correct the first error and run the application again. You should also know that the JavaScript engine won't run the application until all of the syntax errors have been corrected. As a result, you won't discover the runtime errors until the syntax errors have been fixed.

In the next figure, you'll learn how to use the Script panel for debugging. But before you leave this figure, note that Firebug provides four panels besides the Console and Script panels. Here's a brief description of each.

The first two tabs to the right of the Console tab access the HTML and CSS panels that show the HTML and CSS for a page. If there is more than one CSS file for a page, you can switch to a different file by using the drop-down list of file names in the toolbar for the CSS panel.

The last two tabs access the DOM and Net panels. The DOM panel shows the objects, properties, and methods in the DOM in an expandable tree view

Firebug with an open Console panel that shows an error

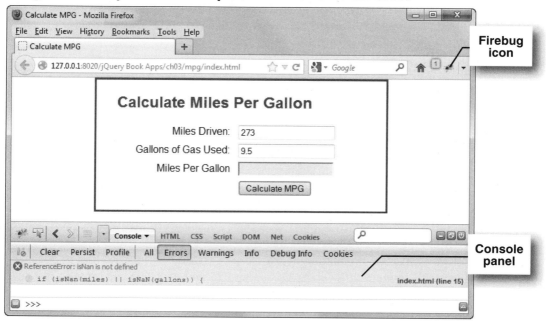

The Script panel after the link in the Console panel has been clicked

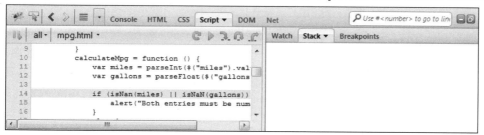

How to open or close Firebug

- Click the Firebug icon or press F12.

How to find the JavaScript statement that caused an error

- Open the Console panel by clicking on the Console tab. Then, if necessary, click on the Errors button. That will display an error message like the one above along with the line of code that caused the error.

- Click on the line of code in the Console panel or click on the line marker to the right of the line of code. That will open the Script panel with the portion of JavaScript code that contains the statement displayed and the statement highlighted.

Description

- *Firebug* is a free Firefox extension that provides some excellent debugging features.

- One of the uses of the Console panel is to display error messages like those that are displayed by the Error Console, but to do that in a more efficient way.

Figure 4-4   How to enable Firebug and find errors

that starts with the global object. The Net panel displays information about each request sent to the web browser. That includes download times, the server used, the HTTP request headers, the HTTP response headers, the HTTP response entity body, and local caching information.

How to use breakpoints and step through code

A *breakpoint* is a point in your code at which the execution of your application will be stopped. Then, you can examine the contents of variables to see if your code is executing as expected. You can also *step through* the execution of the code from that point on. These techniques can help you solve difficult debugging problems.

Figure 4-5 shows you how to set breakpoints, step through the code, and view the contents of variables in the Watch pane. In this example, you can see that a breakpoint has been set on line 5 of the Email List application.

When you run your application, it will stop at the first breakpoint that it encounters and display a yellow triangle on top of that breakpoint. While your code is stopped, you can hover your mouse over an object's name in the Script panel to display the current value of that object.

At a breakpoint, you can also view the current variables in the Watch pane on the right side of the panel. Those are the variables that are used by the function that is being executed. You can also see the values of other variables and expressions by clicking "New watch expression…" and typing the variable name or expression that you want to watch.

To step through the execution of an application after a breakpoint is reached, you can use the Step Into, Step Over, and Step Out buttons. If you repeatedly click the Step Into button, you will execute the code one line at a time and the next line to be executed will be marked by the yellow triangle. After each line of code is executed, you can use the Watch pane to observe any changes in the variables.

As you step through an application, you can click the Step Over button if you want to execute a called function without taking the time to step through it. Or, you can click the Step Out button to step out of a function that you don't want to step through. When you want to return to normal execution, you can click the Continue button. Then, the application will run until the next breakpoint is reached.

These are powerful debugging features that can help you find the causes of serious debugging problems. Stepping through an application is also a good way to understand how the code in an existing application works. If, for example, you step through the if statements in the Email List application, you'll get a better idea of how they work.

A breakpoint in the Firebug Script tab

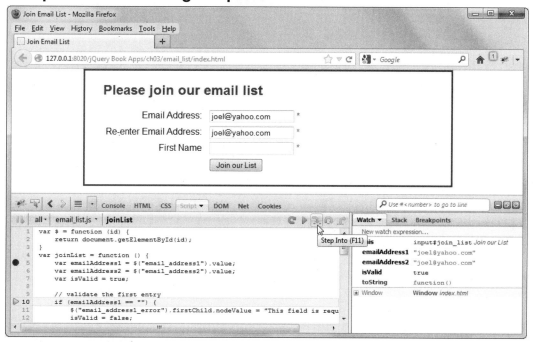

How to set or remove a breakpoint in the Script panel

- To set a breakpoint, click in the bar to the left of a statement.
- To remove a breakpoint, click on the red breakpoint marker.

How to step through the JavaScript code in the Script panel

- Click the Step Into button or press F11 to step through the code one line at a time.
- Click the Step Over button to run any called functions without stepping through them.
- Click the Step Out button to execute the rest of a function without stepping through it.
- Click the Continue button to resume normal execution.

How to view the current data values at each step

- Hover the mouse cursor over a variable name in the Script panel.
- View the current variables in the Watch pane to the right of the Script panel.
- Click "New watch expression..." in the Watch pane and type the variable name or expression that you want to watch.

Description

- You can set a *breakpoint* on any line except a blank line. When the JavaScript engine encounters a breakpoint, it stops before executing the statement with the breakpoint.
- A red circle in the Script panel marks each breakpoint, and a yellow triangle marks the next statement to be executed as you *step through* your code.

Figure 4-5   How to use breakpoints and step through your code

Other debugging methods

Because Firebug is an excellent debugging tool, you should use it for most of your debugging. Here, though, are four other debugging methods that you may occasionally find useful.

When and how to get error messages with other browsers

All modern browsers detect JavaScript errors and provide tools like the Firefox Error Console and Firebug to help fix them. However, if you use Firefox and Firebug to debug all your JavaScript applications, you shouldn't need to use the tools provided by other browsers. That's because an application that works on Firefox should work on all of the other browsers, with one possible exception.

The exception is Internet Explorer, which creates most of the cross-browser compatibility problems that you may encounter. Occasionally, then, you may need to debug an application on IE after you've tested it on Firefox and the other browsers. That's why figure 4-6 shows how to access the IE tools for debugging.

As this figure shows, the Developer Tools for the current version of IE work much like Firebug with similar panels. If you experiment with these tools, you'll see that you can go from the Console panel to the error statement in the Script panel just as you can with Firebug. You can also set breakpoints and step through statements in much the same way.

Internet Explorer with a Console panel that shows an error

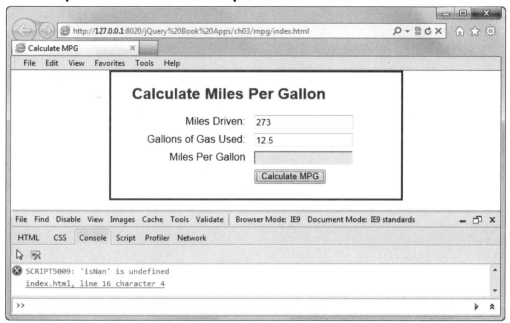

How to display the Developer Tools on the current version of IE

- Use the Tools→Developer Tools command, or press F12.

How to display an error message with older versions of IE

- Double-click on the error icon in the lower left corner of the browser to view the IE message box. Then, if necessary, click the Show Details button to view the entire message.

Description

- All modern browsers offer debugging tools like the Firefox Error Console and Firebug. However, if you debug a JavaScript application on Firefox, it should run on all modern browsers so you shouldn't need their debugging tools.
- The one exception is IE, which still presents some compatibility problems. As a result, you may sometimes need to do further debugging when you test an application on IE.
- The current version of IE provides debugging tools that are similar to those for Firebug. To access them, you can use the methods above.
- Older versions of IE offer a message box that you can access using the method above. This message box is somewhat similar to the Error Console of Firefox that's shown in figure 2-18, but it's not as easy to use.

Figure 4-6   When and how to get error messages with other browsers

A simple way to trace the execution of your JavaScript code

When you trace the execution of an application, you determine the sequence in which the statements in the application are executed. A simply way to do that is to add alert statements to your code that display messages or variable values at key points in the code.

This is illustrated by the example in figure 4-7. Here, the first alert statement that's highlighted lets you know that the $ function has been started. The second alert statement lets you know that the calculateMpg function has been started. The third alert statement displays the user entries for miles and gallons to make sure the two statements that precede it have worked correctly. The fourth alert statement lets you know that the else clause of the if statement has been started. And the fifth alert statement lets you know that the onload function has been started.

When you use this technique, you usually start by adding just a few alert statements to the code. Then, if that doesn't help you solve the problem, you can add more. Often, this is all you need for solving simple debugging problems, and this is quicker than setting breakpoints and stepping through the code with Firebug.

JavaScript with five alert statements that trace the execution of the code

```javascript
var $ = function (id) {
    alert("$ function has started");
    return document.getElementById(id);
}
calculateMpg = function () {
    alert("calculateMpg function has started");
    var miles = parseInt($("miles").value);
    var gallons = parseFloat($("gallons").value);
    alert("miles = " + miles +
            "\ngallons = " +  gallons);

    if (isNaN(miles) || isNaN(gallons)) {
        alert("Both entries must be numeric");
    }
    else {
        alert("The data is valid and the calculation is next");
        var mpg = miles / gallons;
        $("mpg").value = mpg.toFixed(1);
    }
}
window.onload = function () {
    alert("onload function has started");
    $("calculate").onclick = calculateMpg;
    $("miles").focus();
}
```

The alert dialog boxes are displayed as the JavaScript is executed

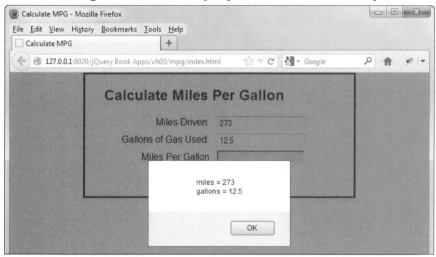

Description

- A simple way to *trace* the execution of a JavaScript application is to insert alert statements at key points in the code.

- The alert dialog boxes can display messages that indicate what portion of the code is being executed or display the values of variables.

- For simple debugging problems, this trace method is all that you'll need for solving them.

Figure 4-7   A simple way to trace the execution of your JavaScript code

When and how to view the source code

Occasionally, when nothing seems to be working right as you test an application, you may want to view the source code for the application. That will at least confirm that you're testing the right files.

To view the HTML source code, you use one of the techniques shown in figure 4-8. When the HTML is displayed in Firefox, you can also display the code for an external CSS or JavaScript file by clicking on the link in the HTML code.

Be aware, however, that the HTML source code is the code that is initially loaded into the browser, so it doesn't reflect any changes made to the DOM by the JavaScript. In this figure, for example, the JavaScript code has changed the text in the span elements after the text boxes. If you look at the HTML source code, though, you can see that the span elements still contain asterisks. In other words, the HTML source code doesn't reflect any changes made to the DOM by DOM scripting.

The Email List application after JavaScript has changed the span elements

Please join our email list

Email Address:	zak@yahoo.org
Re-enter Email Address:	z This entry must equal first entry.
First Name	This field is required.

[Join our List]

The HTML source code for the browser display

Source of: http://127.0.0.1:8020/jQuery%20Book%20Apps/ch02/email_list/email_list.html - Mozilla Firefox

File   Edit   View   Help

```html
<!doctype html>
<html>
<head>
        <title>Join Email List</title>
        <link rel="stylesheet" href="email_list.css">
        <script src="http://html5shiv.googlecode.com/svn/trunk/html5.js"></script>
        <script src="email_list.js"></script>
</head>
<body>
    <section>
        <h1>Please join our email list</h1>
        <form id="email_form" name="email_form" action="join.html" method="get">
                <label for="email_address1">Email Address:</label>
                <input type="text" id="email_address1" name="email_address1">
                <span id="email_address1_error">*</span><br>

                <label for="email_address2">Re-enter Email Address:</label>
                <input type="text" id="email_address2" name="email_address2">
                <span id="email_address2_error">*</span><br>

                <label for="first_name">First Name</label>
                <input type="text" id="first_name" name="first_name">
                <span id="first_name_error">*</span><br>

                <label> </label>
                <input type="button" id="join_list" value="Join our List"><br>
        </form>
    </section>
</body>
</html>
```

How to view the source code for a web page

- If it's available, use a menu command like View→Source or View→Page Source.
- You can also right-click on the page and select a command like Source, View Source, or View Page Source.

Description

- When you're debugging, you may occasionally want to display the HTML that's in the browser, just to see if something unexpected has happened.
- If you're using Firefox, you can click on the link in a link or script element to display the source code for the CSS or JavaScript in another window.
- Note, however, that changes to the DOM don't change the HTML that is loaded into the browser. It only changes the DOM, which in turn causes the display to be changed.

Figure 4-8   How to view the source code for a web page

When and how to validate the HTML

When you test a JavaScript application, you are not only testing the JavaScript code, but also the HTML. Then, if you suspect that there might be a problem with the HTML, it's worth taking the time to *validate* the HTML code. To do that, you can use the technique in figure 4-9.

In fact, we recommend that you validate the HTML for all of the pages in an application. Of course, this isn't necessary when you're doing exercises or developing applications for a class, but this may help you fix a problem that is affecting your JavaScript.

The home page for the W3C validator

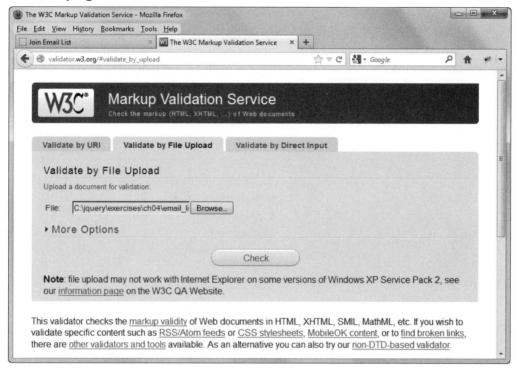

How to use the W3C Markup Validation Service

- Go to the URL that follows, identify the file to be validated, and click the Check button:

  http://validator.w3.org/

How to validate an HTML file from Aptana

- Select the file. Then, select the Commands→HTML→Validate Syntax (W3C) command.

Description

- Occasionally, an error in the HTML for a page will affect the operation of the JavaScript for that page. If you suspect that could be happening, it never hurts to *validate* the HTML for the page.

- To validate the HTML for a page, you can use a program or web site for that purpose. One of the most popular web sites is the W3C Markup Validation Service.

- When you use the W3C Markup Validation Service, if the file you want to validate has already been uploaded to a web server, you can validate it by entering its URL on the Validate by URI tab. If the file you want to validate hasn't been uploaded to a web server, you can validate it by locating it on the Validate by File Upload tab.

- If you're using Aptana, you can validate an HTML file by using the command above. However, you may get slightly different results because Aptana uses the HTML Tidy validator and W3 uses its own validator.

Figure 4-9   How to validate an HTML file

Perspective

All too often, JavaScript applications are put into production before they have been thoroughly tested and debugged. In the early days of JavaScript programming, that was understandable because the tools for testing and debugging were limited. Today, however, Firefox and Firebug provide all the tools that you need for thoroughly debugging an application before you put it into production.

Terms

test	top-down coding and testing
debug	top-down testing
bug	Firebug
syntax error	breakpoint
runtime error	step through code
exception	trace
logic error	validate the HTML

Summary

- When you *test* an application, you try to make it fail. When you *debug* an application, you fix all of the problems that you discover during testing.

- When you write the code for a JavaScript application, you are likely to introduce three types of errors: *syntax errors*, *runtime errors*, and *logic errors*.

- *Top-down coding and testing* simplifies debugging because you build an application by coding and testing a small number of statements at a time.

- *Firebug* is a Firefox extension that provides some excellent debugging features. You can use its Console panel to display error messages. Then, you can click on the link in a message to go to the error statement in the Script panel.

- In Firebug's Script panel, you can set *breakpoints* that stop the execution of code when the application is run. Then, you can *step through* the code starting from a breakpoint and view the changes in the variables at each step.

- Although all modern browsers provide debugging tools like Firebug's, you shouldn't need them if you test and debug first on Firefox. The one exception is IE, so you may occasionally want to use its debugging tools.

- An easy way to *trace* the execution of an application is to insert alert statements at key points in the JavaScript code. After you debug the application, you delete these statements.

- As you're debugging an application, you may occasionally want to view the source code that's in the browser or *validate* the HTML for the page.

Exercise 4-1   Use Firebug's debugging features

In this exercise, you'll use Firebug to find a syntax error, set a breakpoint, and step through the Email List application.

1. If you haven't already done so, install Firebug as shown in appendix A.

2. Open this html file for the Email List application:
   `c:\jquery\exercises\ch04\email_list\index.html`

3. Run the application, enter valid values in just the first two text boxes, and click on the Join our List button. Then, note that nothing happens.

4. Open Firebug and use the Console panel to display the error that caused the problem, as shown in figure 4-4. (You may need to enable the panel first.) Use the link for the error to find and fix the code. Then, test the application again.

5. In Firebug, switch to the Script panel. Then, if necessary, enable the panel and use the drop-down list in the toolbar to display the code for the email_list.js file.

6. Set a breakpoint on the first statement in the joinList function, as shown in figure 4-5. Then, with valid values in just the first two text boxes, click the Join our List button. The application should stop at the breakpoint.

7. Use the Step Into button or F11 to step through the application. At each step, notice the values that are displayed in the Watch pane. Also, hover the mouse over a variable in the Script tab to see what its value is.

8. Experiment with the Step Over and Step Out buttons as you step through the application. When you're through experimenting, remove the breakpoint.

Exercise 4-2   Use the other debugging methods

In this exercise, you'll use the other debugging methods that you learned in this chapter.

1. Open this html file, and notice that it includes the alert statements for tracing the execution of this application that are shown in figure 4-7:
   `c:\jquery\exercises\ch04\mpg\index.html`

2. Run the application, and note the three dialog boxes that are displayed for the statements in the load event handler.

3. When the application stops, enter valid data for the text boxes and click on the Calculate button. As the event handler for the click event of that button runs, note how the alert dialog boxes provide information that lets you know what is happening.

4. Remove the alert statements used for tracing, and run the application again to make sure you've removed them all.

5. Use one of the methods in figure 4-8 to display the source code for the page. Then, use one of the methods in figure 4-9 to validate the HTML for the page.

5

How to work with arrays

In this chapter, you'll learn how to use arrays. This is another of the essential JavaScript skills. The concept of arrays is also important for jQuery users because jQuery often creates and operates upon arrays.

How to create and use an array **142**
How to create an array and refer to its elements 142
How to add and delete array elements 144
How to use for loops to work with arrays 146
How to use for-in loops to work with arrays 148
How to use the methods of an Array object 150
An enhanced Email List application **152**
The user interface and HTML 152
The JavaScript 154
Perspective **156**

How to create and use an array

In the topics that follow, you'll learn the basic skills for creating and using arrays. These skills are important not only because arrays have many common uses, but also because you often have to use arrays when you're DOM scripting.

How to create an array and refer to its elements

An *array* is an object that contains one or more items called *elements*. Each of these elements can be a primitive data type or an object. For instance, you can store numbers, strings, and Date objects in the same array. The *length* of an array indicates the number of elements that it contains.

Figure 5-1 shows two ways to create an array. When you use the first method, you use the *new* keyword followed by the Array object name to create an array with the number of elements that is indicated by the length parameter. This length must be a whole number that is greater than or equal to zero. If you don't specify the length, the array will be empty.

When you use the second method, you just code a set of brackets. This gives you the same result that you get with the first method and no parameter, an empty array.

Next, this figure shows you how to create a new array and assign values to its elements in a single statement. In this case, you code the values in a list that's separated by commas. For instance, the first group of examples shows a statement that creates an array named rates that contains four numeric values and a statement that creates an array named names that contains three strings.

Note, however, that when you create an array with the new keyword, the array list must not be a single number. Otherwise, it will be treated as the length of the array, not a value in the array.

To refer to the elements in an array, you use an *index* that ranges from zero to one less than the number of elements in an array. In an array with 12 elements, for example, the index values range from 0 to 11. This is the reason the getMonth method of a Date object numbers the months from 0 to 11 instead of 1 to 12. Then, the return value of the getMonth method can be used as an index for an array of month names.

To use an index, you code it within brackets after the name of the array. In this figure, all of the examples use literal values for the indexes, but an index can also be a variable that contains an index value. If you try to access an element that hasn't been assigned a value, the value of undefined will be returned.

The last group of examples in this figure shows how to assign values to an empty array. To do that, you refer to the elements by using indexes, and you assign values to those elements.

The syntax for creating an array

Using the new keyword with the Array object name
```
var arrayName = new Array(length);
```

Using the brackets literal
```
var arrayName = [];
```

The syntax for creating an array and assigning values in one statement

Using the new keyword with the Array object name
```
var arrayName = new Array(arrayList);
```

Using the brackets literal
```
var arrayName = [arrayList];
```

How to create an array and assign values in one statement
```
var rates = new Array(14.95, 12.95, 11.95, 9.95);
var names = ["Ted Lewis", "Sue Jones", "Ray Thomas"];
```

The syntax for referring to an element of an array
```
arrayName[index]
```

Code that refers to the elements in an array
```
rates[2]        // Refers to the third element in the rates array
names[1]        // Refers to the second element in the names array
```

How to assign values to an array by accessing each element

How to assign rates to an array that starts with four undefined elements
```
var rates = new Array(4);
rates[0] = 14.95;
rates[1] = 12.95;
rates[2] = 11.95;
rates[3] = 9.95;
```

How to assign strings to an array that starts with no elements
```
var names = [];
names[0] = "Ted Lewis";
names[1] = "Sue Jones";
names[2] = "Ray Thomas";
```

Description

- An *array* can store one or more *elements*. The *length* of an array is the number of elements in the array.

- One way to create an array is to use the new keyword, the name of the object (Array), and a set of parentheses that contains a length parameter. If you don't specify a length, the array doesn't contain any elements. If you specify a length, each element is set to undefined.

- The other way to create an array is to code a set of brackets with or without a list of elements.

- To refer to the elements in an array, you use an *index* where 0 is the first element, 1 is the second element, and so on.

Figure 5-1   How to create an array and refer to its elements

How to add and delete array elements

Figure 5-2 presents one property and one operator that you can use as you work with arrays. The length property returns the number of elements in an array. The delete operator can be used to delete the value of an element in an array.

To add an element to the end of an array, you can use the length property of the array as the index of the new element. Since this property will always be 1 more than the highest index used in the array, this adds the new element at the end of the array as illustrated in the first example.

To add an element at a specific index, you use its index to refer to the element and assign a value to it. If you use an index that's greater than the length of the array, the elements that you skipped over will be created and assigned the value of undefined. This is illustrated in the second example.

The third example shows how to delete the value of an element in an array. To do that, you use the delete operator. When you use this operator, the element is left in the array with an undefined value so the length of the array remains the same.

One property and one operator for an array

Property	Description
length	The number of elements in an array.

Operator	Description
delete	Deletes the contents of an element and sets the element to undefined, but doesn't remove the element from the array.

How to add an element to the end of an array

```
var numbers = [1, 2, 3, 4];        // array is 1, 2, 3, 4
numbers[numbers.length] = 5;       // array is 1, 2, 3, 4, 5
```

How to add an element at a specific index

```
var numbers = [1, 2, 3, 4];        // array is 1, 2, 3, 4
numbers[6] = 7;                    // array is 1, 2, 3, 4, undefined, undefined, 7
```

How to delete a number at a specific index

```
var numbers = [1, 2, 3, 4];        // array is 1, 2, 3, 4
delete numbers[2];                 // array is 1, 2, undefined, 4
```

Description

- One way to add an element to the end of an array is to use the length property as the index.

- If you add an element at a specific index that isn't the next one in sequence, undefined elements are added to the array between the new element and the end of the original array.

Figure 5-2   How to add and delete array elements

How to use for loops to work with arrays

For loops are commonly used to process one array element at a time by incrementing an index variable. Figure 5-3 shows how this works.

The first example in this figure shows how to create an array and fill it with the numbers 1 through 10. First, the code creates an empty array named numbers. Then, an index variable named i is used to loop through the first ten elements of the array by using values that range from 0 to 9. In the body of this loop, one is added to the value in i and the result is stored in the element. As a result, the element at index 0 stores a 1, the element at index 1 stores a 2, and so on.

Next, this example displays the values in the array. First, it creates an empty string named numbersString. Then, it uses a for loop to access the elements in the array. In the for loop, the length property of the array is used to control how many times the loop executes. This allows the same code to work with arrays of different lengths. Inside the for loop, the value in the element and a space are concatenated to the end of numbersString. Finally, numbersString is displayed, which shows the ten numbers that were stored in the array.

The second example in this figure shows how you can calculate the sum and average of an array of totals. First, the code creates an array named totals that stores four total values. Then, it creates a variable named sum that is initialized to zero. Next, it uses a for loop to access each of the elements in the totals array and add it to the sum. This is different from the previous example, which didn't add the numbers together. Finally, it calculates the average by dividing the sum by the length of the array.

After that, this example displays the totals, the sum, and the average. First, it creates an empty string named totalsString. Then, it uses a for loop to concatenate the value of each element and a new line character to totalsString. Finally, it displays a message containing totalsString, the sum, and the average.

Code that puts the numbers 1 through 10 into an array

```
var numbers = [];
for (var i = 0; i < 10; i++) {
    numbers[i] = i + 1;
}
```

Code that displays the numbers array created above

```
var numbersString = "";
for (var i = 0; i < numbers.length; i++) {
    numbersString += numbers[i] + " ";
}
alert (numbersString);
```

The message that's displayed

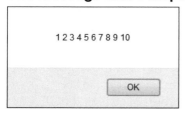

Code that computes the sum and average of an array of totals

```
var totals = [141.95, 212.95, 411, 10.95];
var sum = 0;
for (var i = 0; i < totals.length; i++) {
    sum += totals[i];
}
var average = sum / totals.length;
```

Code that displays the totals array, the sum, and the average

```
var totalsString = "";
for (var i = 0; i < totals.length; i++) {
    totalsString += totals[i] + "\n";
}
alert ("The totals are:\n" + totalsString + "\n" +
    "Sum: " + sum.toFixed(2) + "\n" + "Average: " + average.toFixed(2) );
```

The message that's displayed

```
The totals are:
141.95
212.95
411
10.95

Sum: 776.85
Average: 194.21
```

Description

- When you use a for loop to work with an array, you can use the counter for the loop as the index for the array.

Figure 5-3   How to use for loops to work with arrays

How to use for-in loops to work with arrays

In contrast to a for loop, a *for-in loop* makes it easier to work with an array. Figure 5-4 shows how this type of loop works.

As the syntax at the top of this figure shows, the for-in loop doesn't require separate expressions that initialize, test, and increment an index counter like a for loop does. Instead, you declare a variable that will be used to refer to the index of each element in the array. Then, within the loop, you can use this variable to access each element in the array.

The first example in this figure stores the numbers 1 through 10 in an array and creates an empty string named numbersString. Then, it uses a for-in loop to concatenate each number in the array and a space to the string. Last, it displays the numbers in a message box.

The second example shows the difference in the ways that for loops and for-in loops handle the undefined elements in an array. In short, a for loop processes the undefined elements, but a for-in loop skips over them. You can see this difference in the messages that are displayed for each of the loops in this example.

The syntax of a for-in loop

```
for (var elementIndex in arrayName) {
    // statements that access the elements
}
```

A for-in loop that displays the numbers array in a message box

```
var numbers = [1, 2, 3, 4, 5, 6, 7, 8, 9, 10];
var numbersString = "";
for (var index in numbers) {          // The start of the for-in loop
    numbersString += numbers[index] + " ";
}
alert(numbersString);
```

The message that's displayed

Code that shows the difference between for and for-in loops

```
var names = ["Mike", "Anne", "Ray"];
names[4] = "Joel";               // Array is Mike, Anne, Ray, undefined, Joel
names[names.length] = "Pren";    // Pren is added to the array
delete names[2];                 // Ray is deleted from the array

var namesString1 = "The elements displayed by the for loop:\n\n";
for (var i = 0; i < names.length; i++) {
    namesString1 += names[i] + "\n"; }    // Includes undefined elements

var namesString2 = "The elements displayed by the for-in loop:\n\n";
for (var i in names) {
    namesString2 += names[i] + "\n"; }    // Omits undefined elements

alert (namesString1);
alert (namesString2);
```

The messages that are created by the for and the for-in loops

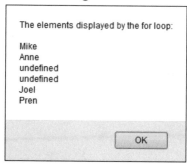
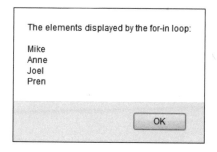

Description

- You can use a *for-in statement* to create a *for-in loop* that accesses only those elements in an array that are defined.

Figure 5-4   How to use for-in loops to work with arrays

How to use the methods of an Array object

Like a number, string, or date, an array is a JavaScript object. In figure 5-5, you can see just a few of the many methods that JavaScript provides for working with Array objects.

The first two methods, push and pop, are used to add elements to and remove elements from the end of an array. This lets you use an array as a stack in which the last element added to it is the first element removed (last-in, first-out). In this case, the oldest element is at the start of the array.

The next two methods, unshift and shift, are used to add elements to and remove elements from the start of an array. These methods also let you use an array as a stack in which the last element added to it is the first element removed. In this case, though, the oldest element is at the end of the array.

If you combine the unshift and pop methods, you can use an array as a queue in which the first element added is the first element removed (first-in, first out). In this case, the oldest element is at the end of the array. You can also use push and shift to use an array as a first-in, first-out queue. In this case, though, the oldest element is at the start of the array.

When you use the pop or shift method, it actually removes the element from the array and reduces the length property of the array by 1. In contrast, when you use the delete operator that you learned about earlier, the element isn't removed. Its value is just set to undefined.

The join and toString methods let you create a single string that contains the elements in the array. They differ mainly in how they handle the separator string. These methods will use an empty string for any undefined elements, both those that aren't defined and those that were set equal to undefined.

The examples in this figure show how these methods work. Here, the first example uses the push and pop methods to add and remove elements. The second example uses the unshift and shift methods to do the same. And the third example shows how the join and toString methods work. Note that the results of the join methods used by the first two examples don't include any undefined elements. That's because the pop and shift methods used by these examples remove the elements.

Four of the methods of an Array object

Methods	Description
push(*elements_list*)	Adds one or more elements to the end of the array, and returns the new length of the array.
pop()	Removes the last element in the array, decrements the length, and returns the element that it removed.
unshift(*elements_list*)	Adds one or more elements to the beginning of the array, and returns the new length of the array.
shift()	Removes the first element in the array, decrements the array length, and returns the element that it removed.
join(*separator*)	When no parameter is passed, this method converts all the elements of the array to strings and concatenates them separated by commas. To change the separator, you can pass this method a string literal.
toString()	Same as the join method without any parameter passed to it.

How to use the push and pop methods to add and remove elements

```
var names = ["Mike", "Anne", "Joel"];
names.push("Ray", "Pren");          // names is Mike, Anne, Joel, Ray, Pren
var removedName = names.pop();      // removedName is Pren
alert (names.join());               // displays Mike,Anne,Joel,Ray
```

How to use the unshift and shift methods to add and remove elements

```
var names = ["Mike", "Anne", "Joel"];
names.unshift("Ray", "Pren");       // names is Ray, Pren, Mike, Anne, Joel
removedName = names.shift();        // removedName is Ray
alert (names.join());               // displays Pren,Mike,Anne,Joel
```

How to use the join and toString methods

```
var names = ["Mike", "Anne", "Joel", "Ray"];
alert (names.join());               // displays Mike,Anne,Joel,Ray
alert (names.join(", "));           // displays Mike, Anne, Joel, Ray
alert (names.toString());           // displays Mike,Anne,Joel,Ray
```

Description

- The push and pop methods are commonly used to add elements to and remove elements from the end of an array.

Figure 5-5   How to use the methods of an Array object

An enhanced Email List application

Now, to show you how an array can be used in a simple application, the next two figures present an enhanced version of the Email List application that you studied in chapter 3.

The user interface and HTML

Figure 5-6 shows the interface for this application. It's like the earlier version, but with one extra text box that is used to get the state code. This field is required and the code must be valid. In this example, since cc isn't a valid state code, a message is displayed to the right of that text box.

In the HTML for this application, the only addition is the highlighted code. This is the code for the label, text box, and span element for the state code entry. As you can see, the id for the text box is "state_code" and the id for the span element is "state_code_error".

The enhanced Email List application in a web browser

Please join our email list

Email Address:	zak@yahoo.com
Re-enter Email Address:	zak@yahoo	This entry must equal first entry.
First Name:	Zak
State Code:	cc	State code is invalid.

[Join our List]

The HTML file for the page

```
<body>
    <section>
        <h1>Please join our email list</h1>
        <form id="email_form" name="email_form"
            action="join.html" method="get">

            <label for="email_address1">Email Address:</label>
            <input type="text" id="email_address1 name="email_address1">
            <span id="email_address1_error">*</span><br>

            <label for="email_address2">Re-enter Email Address:</label>
            <input type="text" id="email_address2" name="email_address2">
            <span id="email_address2_error">*</span><br>

            <label for="first_name">First Name</label>
            <input type="text" id="first_name" name="first_name">
            <span id="first_name_error">*</span><br>

            <label for="state_code">State Code:</label>
            <input type="text" id="state_code" name="state_code">
            <span id="state_code_error">*</span><br>

            <label> </label>
            <input type="button" id="join_list" value="Join our List">
        </form>
    </section>
</body>
```

Note

- This code is the same as it was in the earlier versions except for the highlighted code that defines the text box for the state code.

Figure 5-6   The HTML for the enhanced Email List application

The JavaScript

Figure 5-7 presents the JavaScript code for this application. It is like the code for the earlier version, but with the addition of the code for validating the state code entry. In this case, an anonymous function is used to look up the state code that the user enters. This function is right after the standard $ function, and that adheres to the principle that all functions should appear before the statements that call them.

If you look at the stateCodeLookup function, you can see that it has a single parameter that receives the state code entered by the user. Then, its first statement creates an array that contains the valid state codes for the application. Here, only eight codes are included in the array, but the statement could include all 50 codes.

After the array is created, the function uses the toUpperCase method to convert the code that's passed to the function to uppercase in case the user entered the code in lowercase. That way, when the code is compared to an element in the states array, both values will be uppercase, even if the user entered the code in lowercase.

Next, this function uses a for loop to compare the user entry to each element in the states array. However, if the user entry is equal to one of the elements, the if statement within the loop issues the return statement with a true value and the loop and function ends. Otherwise, if the for loop ends without an equal comparison, the statement after the loop returns false and the function ends.

Now, look at the code in the joinList function that is used to validate the state code entry. It starts by getting the user entry and saving it in a variable named stateCode. Then, it passes this variable to the stateCodeLookup function as the condition in an if statement:

```
(!stateCodeLookup(stateCode))
```

Because this condition starts with the not operator (!), it means that the condition is true if the function returns false, which means the state code is invalid. As a result, the if clause puts the error message into the span element for the text box. Otherwise, the else clause sets the span element to an empty string.

Could the statements in the stateCodeLookup function be embedded in the joinList event handler instead of being treated as a separate function? Yes, but putting the code in a separate function simplifies the code in the event handler and makes the application easier to debug.

The JavaScript for the enhanced Email List application

```javascript
var $ = function (id) {
    return document.getElementById(id);
}
var stateCodeLookup = function (stateCode) {
    var states = ["CA", "WA", "OR", "NV", "NM", "AZ", "WY", "MT"];
    stateCode = stateCode.toUpperCase();
    for (var i = 0; i < states.length; i++) {
        if (states[i] == stateCode) {
            return true;
        }
    }
    return false;
}
var joinList = function () {
    var emailAddress1 = $("email_address1").value;
    var emailAddress2 = $("email_address2").value;
    var isValid = true;

    // same code as before for validating the first three entries

    // validate the state code entry
    var stateCode = $("state_code").value;
    if (!stateCodeLookup(stateCode)) {          // calls stateCodeLookup
        $("state_code_error").firstChild.nodeValue =
            "State code is invalid.";
        isValid = false;
    }
    else {
        $("state_code_error").firstChild.nodeValue = "";
    }

    // submit the form if all entries are valid
    if (isValid) {
        $("email_form").submit();
    }
}
window.onload = function () {
    $("join_list").onclick = joinList;
    $("email_address1").focus();
}
```

Figure 5-7   The JavaScript for the enhanced Email List application

Perspective

Loops and arrays are an important part of many JavaScript applications. Because you also use arrays when you use jQuery, the concepts that you've learned in this chapter apply there too. As you will see, though, jQuery makes it a lot easier to work with arrays.

Terms

array	array index
array element	for-in statement
array length	for-in loop

Summary

- An *array* consists of *elements* that can be referred to by an *index*. To process each element in an array, you can use a *for-in statement*.

- In JavaScript, each array is an Array object that provides methods for working with the array. These include the push and pop methods that let you add elements to and remove elements from an array.

Exercise 5-1   Use a for-in loop with an array

1. Use your text editor to open the index.html and email_list.js files that are in this folder:

   ```
   c:\jquery\exercises\ch05\email_list
   ```

2. Test the application to see how it works, and review the code.

3. In the JavaScript file, comment out the for loop that determines whether a state code entry is valid. Then, replace it with a for-in loop that gets the same result, and test this change.

4. Just for fun, use the push method of the states array to add "UT" for Utah to that array. You can code that statement right after the declaration for the array. Then, test to see whether the lookup works for that state code.

6

How to script the DOM with JavaScript

At this point, you have all of the JavaScript skills that you need for some serious DOM scripting. You just need to learn how to use some of the properties and methods that are provided by the DOM specifications, as well as some special skills for working with links and images.

DOM scripting properties and methods **158**
DOM scripting concepts..158
The Node interface 160
The Document and Element interfaces 162

The FAQs application..**164**
The user interface, HTML, and CSS...164
The JavaScript..166
Another way the FAQs application could be coded 168

Two critical issues for JavaScript applications..............**170**
Usability..170
Accessibility..170
The FAQs application with improved accessibility.......................172

DOM scripting skills for links and images **174**
How to cancel the default action of an event..............................174
How to preload images 176

The Image Swap application **178**
The HTML and CSS...178
The JavaScript..180

How to use timers..**182**
How to use a one-time timer...182
How to use an interval timer 184

The Slide Show application..**186**
The HTML and CSS...186
The JavaScript..188

Perspective **190**

DOM scripting properties and methods

In chapter 3, you were introduced to DOM scripting by using two properties to put a message into a span element. Now, you'll learn other properties and methods that you can use for DOM scripting. These properties and methods are defined by the *DOM Core specification* that is implemented by all current browsers.

DOM scripting concepts

Before you learn the properties and methods of the DOM Core specification, figure 6-1 presents the DOM scripting concepts that you should understand before using them. First, as you may recall from chapter 3, the *Document Object Model*, or *DOM*, is built as an HTML page is loaded into the browser. It contains *nodes* that represent all of the HTML elements and attributes for the page. This is illustrated by the HTML and diagram in this figure.

Besides the *element nodes* that are represented by ovals in this diagram, the DOM includes *text nodes* that hold the data for the HTML elements. In this diagram, these text nodes are rectangles. For instance, the first text node contains the text for the title element in the head section: "Join Email List". The one to the right of that contains the text for the h1 element in the body: "Please join our email list". And so on.

For simplicity, this diagram only includes the element and text nodes, but the DOM also contains *attribute nodes*, and each attribute node can have a text node that holds the attribute value. Also, if the HTML includes comments, the DOM will include *comment nodes*.

If you study the table in this figure, you can see that an element node can have element, text, and comment nodes as child nodes. An attribute node can have a text node as a child node. And a text node can't have a child node. Curiously, even though an attribute node is attached to an element node, it isn't considered to be a child node of the element node.

The properties and methods for working with DOM nodes are defined by a specification called an *interface*. In the topics that follow, you'll learn how to work with the properties and methods of the Node, Document, and Element interfaces.

As you work with these interfaces, you'll come across terms like *parent*, *child*, *sibling*, and *descendant*. These terms are used just as they are in a family tree. In the diagram in this figure, for example, the form element is the parent of the label, input, and span elements, and the label, input, and span elements are children of the form element. The label, input, and span elements are also siblings (brothers and sisters) because they have the same parent. Similarly, the h1 and form elements are children of the body element, and the h1, form, label, input, and span elements are all descendants of the body element.

You should also be able to see these relationships in the HTML for a web page. In the HTML in this figure, for example, the indentation clearly shows the children and descendants for each element.

The code for a web page

```
<!DOCTYPE html>
<html>
<head>
    <title>Join Email List</title>
</head>
<body>
    <h1>Please join our email list</h1>
    <form id="email_form" name="email_form" action="join.html" method="get">
        <label for="email_address">Email Address:</label>
        <input type="text" id="email_address">
        <span id="email_error">*</span><br>
    </form>
</body>
</html>
```

The DOM for the web page

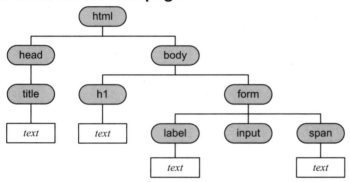

The DOM nodes that you commonly use

Type	Description
Document	Root node of the DOM. It can only have one Element node as a child node.
Element	An element in the web page. It can have Element, Text, and Comment nodes as child nodes.
Attr	An attribute of an element. Although it is attached to an Element node, it isn't considered a child node. It can have a Text node as a child node.
Text	The text for an element or attribute. It can't have a child node.

Description

- The *DOM (Document Object Model)* is a hierarchical collection of *nodes* in the web browser's memory that represents the current web page.
- The DOM for a web page is built as the page is loaded by the web browser.
- JavaScript can modify the web page in the browser by modifying the DOM. Whenever the DOM is changed, the web browser displays the results of the change.
- To modify the DOM, you can use the properties and methods that are defined by the *DOM Core specification.*

Figure 6-1   DOM scripting concepts

The Node interface

Figure 6-2 describes six properties that you can use for working with nodes. These properties are defined by the Node interface. All the examples in this figure assume the use of the standard $ method that gets an element by id.

The first example shows how to use the firstChild and nodeValue properties to get the text of an HTML element. In this case, this statement will store an asterisk (*) in the variable named errorText if the statement is run before the node is changed. That's because this node is set to the asterisk by the HTML.

If you refer back to the diagram in the previous figure, you can see that the firstChild property is needed to get the text node for the span element. Then, the nodeValue property gets the text from that text node.

The second example shows how to use the firstChild and nodeValue properties to put text into the text node of an HTML element. This is how the Email List application puts the error messages in the span elements that follow the text boxes.

The third example shows how to use three properties of the input element with "email_address" as its id to set the text for the span element that follows it to an empty string. First, the nextElementSibling property gets the span element that is the next sibling of the input element. Then, the firstChild and nodeValue properties get the text.

Some of the properties of the Node interface

Property	Description
`nodeValue`	For a Text, Comment, or Attribute node, this property returns the text that's stored in the node. Otherwise, it returns a null value.
`parentNode`	Returns the parent node of the current node if one exists. Otherwise, this property returns a null value.
`childNodes`	Returns an array of Node objects representing the child nodes of the current node.
`firstChild`	Returns a Node object for the first child node. If this node doesn't have child nodes, this property returns a null value.
`lastChild`	Returns a Node object for the last child node. If this node doesn't have child nodes, this property returns a null value.
`nextElementSibling`	Returns a Node object for the next sibling. If this node doesn't have a sibling element that follows it, this property returns a null value.

HTML that contains element and text nodes

```
<body>
    <h1>Please join our email list</h1>
    <form id="email_form" name="email_form" action="join.html" method="get">
        <label for="email_address">Email Address:</label>
        <input type="text" id="email_address">
        <span id="email_error">*</span><br>
        <label> </label>
        <input type="button" id="join_list" value="Join our List">
    </form>
</body>
```

How to get the text of an HTML element with "email_error" as its id

```
var errorText = $("email_error").firstChild.nodeValue;
```

How to set the text of an HTML element with "email_error" as its id

```
$("email_error").firstChild.nodeValue = "Entry is invalid.";
```

How to set the text for the span tag to an empty string without using its id

```
$("email_address").nextElementSibling.firstChild.nodeValue = "";
```

Description

- An *interface* describes the properties and methods for an object.
- When DOM scripting, you often use the properties of the Node interface. Some of the most useful ones are summarized in the table above.
- In the examples above, the $ sign calls the standard $ function that uses the getElementById method to get the element that has the id that's passed to it as the parameter.

Figure 6-2   The properties of the Node interface

The Document and Element interfaces

The first table in figure 6-3 summarizes three methods that are in both the Document and Element interfaces. All three of these methods return arrays. For instance, the getElementsByTagName method returns an array that contains all of the Element nodes with the specified tag name.

If these methods are used with the document object, they get all of the elements in the document. This is illustrated by the first example that gets all of the <a> elements in the document and puts them in an array named links.

If these methods are used with an element as the object, they get all of the elements that are descendants of that element. For instance, the first statement in the second example gets the element with "image_list" as its id. Then, the second statements gets an array of all of the li elements that are descendants of the image_list element.

The second table in this figure summarizes some of the methods of the Element interface that work with attributes. For instance, the third example in this figure uses the hasAttribute method to find out whether an element has a class attribute. Then, if it does, it uses the getAttribute method to get the value of that attribute.

The fourth example shows how to use the setAttribute method to set an attribute. Here, the second statement sets the class attribute to "open". When this method is used, if the class doesn't already exist, the method creates it. Then, the last example in this figure uses the removeAttribute method to remove the class attribute.

Common methods of the Document and Element interfaces

Method	Description
`getElementsByTagName(tagName)`	Returns an array of all Element objects descended from the document or element that have a tag that matches the specified tag.
`getElementsByName(name)`	Returns an array of all Element objects descended from the document or element that have a name attribute that matches the specified name.
`getElementsByClassName(classNames)`	Returns an array of all Element objects descended from the document or element that have a class attribute with a name or names that match the parameter. The classNames parameter can be a single name or a space-separated list of class names.

Common methods of the Element interface

Method	Description
`hasAttribute(name)`	Returns true if the Element has the attribute specified in name.
`getAttribute(name)`	Returns the value of the attribute specified in name or an empty string if an attribute of that name isn't set.
`setAttribute(name, value)`	Sets the attribute specified in name to the specified value. If the attribute doesn't already exist, it creates the attribute too.
`removeAttribute(name)`	Removes the attribute specified in name.

How to create an array of all <a> tags in a document

```
var links = document.getElementsByTagName("a");
```

How to create an array of all li tags within a ul element (image_list)

```
var list = document.getElementById("image_list");
var items = list.getElementsByTagName("li");
```

How to test for and get an attribute

```
var list = document.getElementById("image_list");
if ( list.hasAttribute("class") ) {
    var classAttribute = list.getAttribute("class"));
}
```

How to set an attribute

```
var image = document.getElementById("div");
image.setAttribute("class", "open");
```

How to remove an attribute

```
var list = document.getElementById("image_list");
list.removeAttribute("class");
```

Description

- The methods of the Document and Element interfaces let you get arrays of elements.

- The methods of the Element interface also let you work with attributes.

Figure 6-3   The methods of the Document and Element interfaces

The FAQs application

Now, you'll see how the properties and methods of the Node, Document, and Element interfaces are used in a typical DOM scripting application. We call this application the FAQs (Frequently Asked Questions) application.

The user interface, HTML, and CSS

Figure 6-4 presents the user interface for the FAQs application. If the user clicks on a heading with a plus sign before it, the text below it is displayed and the plus sign is changed to a minus sign. Similarly, if the user clicks on a heading with a minus sign before it, the text below it is hidden and the minus sign is changed to a plus sign.

In the HTML, you can see that each of the questions is coded in an h2 element that is followed by a div element that contains the answer. Note that each of these h2 elements has a class attribute of "plus" and each div element has a class of "closed". As the user clicks on the headings, these classes are changed by the DOM scripting.

In the CSS, you can see that the h2 elements in the "plus" class have a background property that includes an image named plus.png. This image is displayed just once (no-repeat) to the left of the element and it is vertically centered. Similarly, the h2 elements in the "minus" class have a background property that uses an image named minus.png.

You can also see that the div elements in the "closed" class have a display property that hides them. But the div elements in the "open" class have a display property that displays them as block elements.

Because the HTML sets the starting classes for the h2 elements to "plus" and the classes for the div elements to "closed", the user interface starts with plus signs in the headings and the div elements closed. Now, all the JavaScript has to do is reverse these classes each time the user clicks on a heading.

The FAQs application in a browser

> ### jQuery FAQs
> + **What is jQuery?**
> − **Why is jQuery becoming so popular?**
>   Three reasons:
>   - It's free.
>   - It lets you get more done in less time.
>   - All of its functions are cross-browser compatible.
>
> + **Which is harder to learn: jQuery or JavaScript?**

The HTML

```
<section id="faqs">
    <h1>jQuery FAQs</h1>
    <h2 class="plus">What is jQuery?</h2>
    <div class="closed">
        <p>jQuery is a library of the JavaScript functions that you're most
            likely to need as you develop web sites.
        </p>
    </div>
    <h2 class="plus">Why is jQuery becoming so popular?</h2>
    <div class="closed">
        <p>Three reasons:</p>
        <ul>
            <li>It's free.</li>
            <li>It lets you get more done in less time.</li>
            <li>All of its functions cross-browser compatible.</li>
        </ul>
    </div>
    <h2 class="plus">Which is harder to learn: jQuery or JavaScript?</h2>
    <div class="closed">
        <p>For most functions, jQuery is significantly easier to learn and
            use than JavaScript. But remember: jQuery is JavaScript.
        </p>
    </div>
</section>
```

The CSS

```
h2 {
    padding: .25em 0 .25em 25px;
    cursor: pointer; }
h2.plus {
    background: url(images/plus.png) no-repeat left center; }
h2.minus {
    background: url(images/minus.png) no-repeat left center; }
div.closed {
    display: none; }
div.open {
    display: block; }
```

Figure 6-4   The HTML and CSS for the FAQs application

The JavaScript

Figure 6-5 shows the JavaScript for this application. Here, the event handler for the onload function creates and attaches the event handlers for each of the h2 elements. To do that, its first statement gets the object for the section element that has "faqs" as its id. The second statement uses the getElementsByTagName method to get an array of the h2 elements within that section. This array is stored in a variable named h2Elements.

This is followed by a for statement that creates and attaches the event handlers for the h2 elements. Its loop is executed once for each element in the h2Elements array. The first statement in this loop assigns the current h2 element in the array to the h2Node variable. Then, the code for creating and attaching the event handler for each h2 element starts.

To start, a function is created for the click event of the object in the h2Node variable. Unlike the functions you've seen up to this point that handle events, this function is coded within the function for the onload event handler. This is the standard way to code event handlers for DOM scripting.

The first statement within this function declares a new variable named h2 and assigns it the *this* keyword. This is the critical statement in this function, because the this keyword refers to that specific h2 object in the DOM. As a result, one event handler is created for each h2 element in the DOM.

Without this statement, the loop would create just one event handler and attach it to each h2 element. If, for example, you assigned h2Node to the h2 variable instead of the this keyword, clicking on any heading would open and close the div element for the last heading. That's because the statements in the event handler would be replaced each time through the loop, ending up with the statements for the last heading.

After that, the code is quite straightforward. The first if statement tests whether the h2 element has a class attribute with a value of "plus". If so, it changes that to "minus". If not, it changes it to "plus". That provides for the change in signs each time a heading is clicked.

Then, the second if statement uses similar coding to change the class for a division each time the heading before it is clicked. To refer to the div element that follows a heading, though, the statements use the nextElementSibling property.

Now that you've reviewed this code, you should note that it will work for any number of heading and division elements that are defined by the HTML. You should also note that a division can contain whatever HTML elements the application requires, including img and <a> elements.

The JavaScript for the FAQs application

```
var $ = function (id) {
    return document.getElementById(id);
}
window.onload = function () {
    var faqs = $("faqs");
    var h2Elements = faqs.getElementsByTagName("h2");

    var h2Node;
    for (var i = 0; i < h2Elements.length; i++ ) {
        h2Node = h2Elements[i];

        // Attach event handler
        h2Node.onclick = function () {

            var h2 = this;          // h2 is the current h2Node object

            if (h2.getAttribute("class") == "plus") {
                h2.setAttribute("class", "minus");
            }
            else {
                h2.setAttribute("class", "plus");
            }
            if (h2.nextElementSibling.getAttribute("class") == "closed") {
                h2.nextElementSibling.setAttribute("class", "open");
            }
            else {
                h2.nextElementSibling.setAttribute("class", "closed");
            }
        }
    }
}
```

Notes

- The first two statements in the onload event handler create an array of the h2 elements in the section with "faqs" as its id.

- The for loop is executed once for each of the h2 elements. It attaches an event handler to the onclick event of each h2 element.

- In the code that attaches the event handler to each h2 element, the *this* keyword refers to the current h2 element. As a result, the statements that follow apply to the h2 element that is currently being processed by the loop. This is critical to the operation of this program.

Figure 6-5   The JavaScript for the FAQs application

Another way the FAQs application could be coded

As you develop a JavaScript application, your first goal is to get it to work right. But after you've done that, it's worth taking the time to review your code to see whether it can be improved. In many cases, you'll find that the code can be simplified or improved in a way that will make it easier to maintain, enhance, and reuse.

One way to improve the code for the FAQs application is to eliminate the need for coding the starting class attributes in the HTML. That will make the application easier to reuse because the HTML will be simplified. That will also simplify the JavaScript code.

This is illustrated by the code in figure 6-6. Here, the class attributes have been removed from the h2 and div elements in the HTML. Then, the CSS has been modified so h2 elements start with a plus sign in the background, and the div elements start by being hidden. This CSS also changes the background for an h2 element to a minus sign when it has a class attribute of "minus", and it displays a div element when it has a class attribute of "open".

This works because the h2.minus and div.open selectors are more specific than the h2 and div selectors. As a result, their rules override the rules for the h2 and div elements. Now, all the JavaScript has to do is add or remove the classes when the headings are clicked.

You can see how this works in the JavaScript. If an h2 element has a class attribute, the attribute is removed. Otherwise, it is added by the setAttribute method and set to a value of "minus". If a div element has a class attribute, the attribute is removed. Otherwise, it is added with a value of "open".

Is this a better way to code this application? No doubt about it.

The HTML

```
<section id="faqs">
    <h1>jQuery FAQs</h1>
    <h2>What is jQuery?</h2>
    <div>
        // contents
    </div>
    <h2>Why is jQuery becoming so popular?</h2>
    <div>
        // contents
    </div>
    <h2>Which is harder to learn: jQuery or JavaScript?</h2>
    <div>
        // contents
    </div>
</section>
```

The CSS

```
h2 {
    padding: .25em 0 .25em 25px;
    cursor: pointer;
    background: url(images/plus.png) no-repeat left center; }
h2.minus {
    background: url(images/minus.png) no-repeat left center; }
div {
    display: none; }
div.open {
    display: inline;
}
```

The JavaScript for attaching the event handlers

```
// Attach event handler
h2Node.onclick = function () {
    var h2 = this;           // h2 is the current h2Node object
    if (h2.hasAttribute("class")) {
        h2.removeAttribute("class");
    }
    else {
        h2.setAttribute("class", "minus");
    }
    if (h2.nextElementSibling.hasAttribute("class")) {
        h2.nextElementSibling.removeAttribute("class");
    }
    else {
        h2.nextElementSibling.setAttribute("class", "open");
    }
}
```

Description

- After you get an application working correctly, it's always good to ask whether the code can be improved in a way that makes it easier to maintain, enhance, and reuse.

- When the FAQs application is coded as it is in this figure, you don't need to set class attributes for the h2 and div elements in the HTML, which makes it easier to reuse this code for other web pages.

Figure 6-6   Another way the FAQs application could be coded

Two critical issues
for JavaScript applications

In chapter 1, you were introduced to the issue of cross-browser compatibility. Now, figure 6-7 presents two other issues. Throughout this book, we'll refer back to these issues as new applications are introduced.

Usability

Usability refers to how easy it is to use a web site, and usability is what web site users want the most. They want to find what they're looking for as quickly and easily as possible. And when they find it, they want to extract the information or do the task as quickly and easily as possible.

Although there are many components to the usability of a web site, some of the most important have to do with navigation. In brief, the navigation should be obvious. For instance, underlined text should always be a link that a user can click on, and a button should always be clickable. The users shouldn't have to guess about what is clickable and where the clicks will take them.

If you look at the FAQs application in this figure, you can see that the navigation is pretty good. Here, the headings that are clickable are preceded by a plus or minus sign, which is a common convention that indicates a clickable item. Also, the CSS changes the mouse pointer to a hand pointer when the pointer hovers over the heading, which lets the user know that the item is clickable.

That should be good enough, but you could improve this by highlighting the heading when the mouse hovers over it. That way, the user can be sure that the heading is clickable. It would also be nice to highlight the heading when the heading has the focus, but a heading can't receive the focus.

Accessibility

Accessibility refers to the qualities that make a web site accessible to as many users as possible, especially disabled users. For instance, visually-impaired users may not be able to read text that's in images so you need to provide other alternatives for them. Similarly, users with motor disabilities may not be able to use the mouse, so you need to make sure that all of the content and features of your web site can be accessed through the keyboard.

To a large extent, this means that you should develop your applications so the content of your web site is still usable if images aren't used and JavaScript is disabled. That doesn't mean you shouldn't use JavaScript. It just means that you should make your JavaScript as accessible as possible or provide other alternatives for users who can't use the JavaScript features.

To illustrate, the FAQs application in this figure needs to be improved so it can be used by the motor-disabled. This is summarized by the four points that are listed in this figure. To provide those features, though, you need to make the headings links, as you'll see in the next figure.

The FAQs application

> ### jQuery FAQs
> ✢ **What is jQuery?**
> ✢ **Why is jQuery becoming so popular?**
> ✢ **Which is harder to learn: jQuery or JavaScript?**

Navigation guidelines for usability

- Underlined text is always a link.
- A small symbol in front of a text phrase is clickable.
- Images that are close to short text phrases are clickable.
- Buttons should look like buttons and should always be clickable.

How the usability of this application can be improved

- Highlight the heading when it has the focus or when the mouse hovers over it.

Guidelines for accessibility

- For the visually-impaired, all of the essential information should be presented in text that's easy to read because some users may not be able to read the text that's in images.
- For the motor-impaired, all of the essential content and features should be accessible with the keyboard because some users may not be able to use a mouse.

How the accessibility of this application can be improved

- Make the headings links so the user can use the Tab key to move from one to the next.
- Move the cursor to the first heading when the page is loaded.
- Highlight the heading when it has the focus or the mouse is hovered over it.
- Let the user activate the click event of a heading by pressing the Enter key when the heading has the focus.

Description

- *Usability* refers to how easy it is to use a web site, and usability is a critical requirement for an effective web site.
- *Accessibility* refers to the qualities that make a web page accessible to users, especially disabled users.
- When you develop an interesting JavaScript application, be sure that it also meets the best standards for usability and accessibility.

Figure 6-7   Two critical issues for JavaScript applications

The FAQs application with improved accessibility

Figure 6-8 shows how easy it is to improve the accessibility of the FAQs application. First, <a> elements are coded within the h2 elements in the HTML so the heading content will be treated as a link. This means that the user can use the Tab key to move to the next link and the Shift+Tab key to move to the previous link.

Second, the CSS provides two rule sets: one for all <a> elements and one for <a> elements that either have the focus or the mouse hovering over them. In the first rule set, the color of the links is changed to black and the underlines are removed. In the second rule set, the color of the links is changed to blue. This color change clearly shows which link has the focus or the mouse hovering over it. Although the hover pseudo-class can be used with h2 elements, the focus pseudo-class only applies to links.

Third, the last JavaScript statement in the onload event handler moves the focus to the first <a> element in the HTML. To make that work, the first link has "first_link" as its id attribute, and the JavaScript gets the object for that link.

The user interface at the top of this figure shows how these changes improve the accessibility. Here, the user pressed the Enter key when the mouse was on the first link to display the text below it. Then, the user pressed the Tab key to move to the second link. Because it's a link, this heading (actually, the link) has a dotted border around it to indicate that it has the focus. Because of the CSS, this link is also highlighted in blue.

If you're using a mouse, this application still works the way that it did before. In other words, adding the accessibility features doesn't change the experience for the mouse user. Often, in fact, improving the accessibility also improves the usability.

The FAQs application with improved accessibility

jQuery FAQs

− **What is jQuery?**

jQuery is a library of the JavaScript functions that you're most likely to need as
you develop web sites.

+ **Why is jQuery becoming so popular?**

+ **Which is harder to learn: jQuery or JavaScript?**

The HTML

```html
<section id="faqs">
    <h1>jQuery FAQs</h1>
    <h2><a href="#" id="first_link">What is jQuery?</a></h2>
    <div>
        ...
    </div>
    <h2><a href="#">Why is jQuery becoming so popular?</a></h2>
    <div>
        ...
    </div>
    <h2><a href="#">Which is harder to learn: jQuery or JavaScript?</a></h2>
    <div>
        ...
    </div>
</section>
```

The CSS

```css
a {
    color: black;
    text-decoration: none;
}
a:focus, a:hover { color: blue; }
```

The JavaScript

```javascript
window.onload = function () {
    var faqs = $("faqs");
    var h2Elements = faqs.getElementsByTagName("h2");
    var h2Node;
    for (var i = 0; i < h2Elements.length; i++ ) {
        h2Node = h2Elements[i];
        // Attach event handler
        h2Node.onclick = function () {
            var h2 = this;          // h2 is the current headingNode object
            // same as before
        }
    }
    $("first_link").focus();            // move the focus to the first link
}
```

Figure 6-8   The FAQs application with improved accessibility

DOM scripting skills for links and images

Next, you'll learn two DOM scripting skills for working with links and images.

How to cancel the default action of an event

The table in figure 6-9 presents some of the common *default actions* for the click event of HTML elements. For instance, the default action for clicking on a link is to load the page or go to the placeholder that's specified by the href attribute of the link. Similarly, the default action for clicking on a submit or reset button in a form is to submit or reset the data in the form.

For some applications, though, you don't want the default actions to occur. Then, you need to cancel those actions. Unfortunately, this introduces a browser-compatibility problem, because older versions of IE work differently than DOM-compliant browsers like Firefox, Safari, Opera, and Chrome.

The first example in this figure shows how easy it is to cancel a default action in a DOM-compliant browser. In these browsers, an event object is created whenever an event occurs, and this object is automatically passed to the event handler. This object contains information about the event and provides a method that lets you control the behavior of the event.

To access this event, you code a parameter in the function for the event handler as shown in the first example. In this case, evt is used as the parameter name, and it will receive the event object when the handler is called. Then, to cancel the default action, you use the preventDefault method of the event object that the parameter represents.

With older versions of IE, though, you need to use the code in the second example. To get the event object, you use the window.event property instead of getting the object as a parameter. Then, you set the returnValue property of the event object to false to prevent the default action from occurring.

To make your applications compatible with both types of browsers, you combine the two techniques as shown in the third example. Here, the function has a parameter that will receive the event object in a DOM-compliant browser. Then, the first if statement in the function tests the evt parameter to see if it's undefined. If so, the browser is IE, so this code assigns the event object in the window.event property to the evt parameter. Otherwise, the browser is DOM-compliant, so the evt parameter already contains the event object.

Then, the second if statement tests the evt parameter to see if it provides a preventDefault method. If so, this code calls the preventDefault method. If not, this code sets the returnValue property to false.

From a practical point of view, you just copy and paste this code into any event handler that requires the cancellation of default actions. You'll see this illustrated in the applications that follow.

Common default actions for the click event

Tag	Default action for the click event
`a`	Load the page or go to the placeholder in the href attribute.
`input`	Submit the form if the type attribute is set to submit.
`input`	Reset the form if the type attribute is set to reset.
`button`	Submit the form if the type attribute is set to submit.
`button`	Reset the form if the type attribute is set to reset.

DOM-compliant code that cancels the default action

```
var eventHandler = function (evt) {
    evt.preventDefault();
}
```

IE code that cancels the default action

```
var eventHandler = function () {
    var evt = window.event;
    evt.returnValue = false;
}
```

Browser-compatible code that cancels the default action

```
var eventHandler = function (evt) {
    // If the event object is not sent, get it
    if (!evt) { evt = window.event; }       // for IE

    // Cancel the default action
    if (evt.preventDefault) {
        evt.preventDefault();               // for most browsers
    }
    else {
        evt.returnValue = false;            // for IE
    }
}
```

Description

- In some JavaScript applications, you need to cancel the *default action* of an event.

- All browsers except older IE browsers pass an event object to the first parameter of the event handler, but IE stores the event object in the global window.event property.

- All browsers except older IE browsers provide a preventDefault method for the event object. When called, this method prevents the default action of the event from occurring.

- In contrast, older IE browsers provide a property named returnValue in the event object. When set to false, this property prevents the default action of the event from occurring.

Figure 6-9   How to cancel the default action of an event

How to preload images

In DOM scripting applications that load an image in response to a user event, the image isn't downloaded until the JavaScript code changes the src attribute of the img element that will display the changed image. For large images or slow connections, this can cause a delay while the browser loads the image.

To solve this problem, your application can download the images before the user event occurs. This is known as *preloading images*. Although this may result in a longer delay when the page is initially loaded, the user won't encounter any delays when using the application.

Figure 6-10 shows how to preload an image. First, you use the new keyword to create an Image object and store it in a variable. This creates an empty image object. Then, you set the src property to the URL of the image that you want to preload. This causes the web browser to preload the image.

The example in this figure shows how to preload the images for all the links on a page. This assumes that the href attribute in each link contains the location of each image that needs to be preloaded. First, the getElementsByTagName method is used to get an array of all the links, and this array is stored in a variable named links. Then, a for loop is used to process each link in the array.

Within the loop, the first statement copies the current link into the link variable, and the second statement creates a new Image object. Then, the third statement sets the src property of the Image object to the href property of the link. This preloads the image. As a result, all of the images will be preloaded when the loop finishes.

How to create and preload an Image object

How to create an Image object

```
var image = new Image();
```

How to preload an image in an Image object

```
image.src = "image_name.jpg";
```

How to preload all images referenced by the href attributes of <a> tags

```
var links = document.getElementsByTagName("a");
var i, link, image;
for ( i = 0; i < links.length; i++ ) {
    link = links[i];
    image = new Image();
    image.src = link.href;
}
```

Description

- When an application *preloads images*, it loads all of the images that it's going to need when the page loads, and it stores these images in the web browser's cache for future use.

- If the images aren't preloaded, they are retrieved from the server as needed. In some cases, that can cause a noticeable delay.

- When you use the new keyword to create an Image object, the object is empty. Then, when you set the src attribute of this object, the web browser preloads the image identified by that attribute.

Figure 6-10   How to preload images

The Image Swap application

Figure 6-11 illustrates an *image swap* application, which is a common type of JavaScript application. Here, the main image is swapped whenever the user clicks on one of the small (thumbnail) images. In this example, the user has clicked on the sixth thumbnail so the larger version of that image is displayed. In this application, the caption above the large image is also changed as part of the image swap, but that isn't always done in image swaps.

The HTML and CSS

In the HTML for this application, img elements are used to display the six thumbnail images. However, these elements are coded within <a> elements so the images are clickable and they can receive the focus. In the <a> elements, the href attributes identify the images to be swapped when the links are clicked and the title attributes provide the text for the related captions. In this case, both the <a> elements and the img elements are coded within a ul element.

After the ul element, you can see the h2 element for the caption and the img element for the main image on the page. The contents of the h2 element provides the caption for the first image, and the src attribute of the img element provides the location for the first image. That way, when the application first starts, the first caption and image are displayed.

The three ids that are used by the JavaScript are highlighted here. First, the id of the first <a> element is set to "first_link" so the JavaScript can set the focus for that link. Second, the id of the h2 element is set to "caption" so the JavaScript can change the caption. And third, the id of the main img element is set to "image" so the JavaScript can change the image.

For the motor-impaired, this HTML provides accessibility by coding the img elements for the thumbnails within <a> elements. That way, the user can access the thumbnail links by clicking on the Tab key, and the user can swap the image by pressing the Enter key when a thumbnail has the focus, which starts the onclick event handler.

Of note in the CSS for this page is the rule set for the li elements. As this figure shows, their display properties are set to inline so the thumbnail images go from left to right instead of from top to bottom. Also, the padding to the right of each item is set to 10 pixels to provide space between the thumbnail images.

The user interface for the Image Swap application

The HTML

```
<section>
    <h1>Ram Tap Combined Test</h1>
    <ul id="image_list">
        <li><a href="images/h1.jpg" title="James Allison: 1-1"
            id="first_link">
            <img src="thumbnails/t1.jpg" alt=""></a></li>
        <li><a href="images/h2.jpg" title="James Allison: 1-2">
            <img src="thumbnails/t2.jpg" alt=""></a></li>
        <li><a href="images/h3.jpg" title="James Allison: 1-3">
            <img src="thumbnails/t3.jpg" alt=""></a></li>
        <li><a href="images/h4.jpg" title="James Allison: 1-4">
            <img src="thumbnails/t4.jpg" alt=""></a></li>
        <li><a href="images/h5.jpg" title="James Allison: 1-5">
            <img src="thumbnails/t5.jpg" alt=""></a></li>
        <li><a href="images/h6.jpg" title="James Allison: 1-6">
            <img src="thumbnails/t6.jpg" alt=""></a></li>
    </ul>
    <h2 id="caption">James Allison 1-1</h2>
    <p><img src="images/h1.jpg" alt="" id="image"></p>
</section>
```

The CSS for the li elements

```
li {
    padding-right: 10px;
    display: inline;
}
```

Figure 6-11   The user interface, HTML, and CSS for the Image Swap application

The JavaScript

Figure 6-12 presents the JavaScript for this application. In the onload event handler, the first three statements get the objects for the ul element (image_list), the h2 element for the caption, and the img element that displays the swaps. These objects are for the nodes in the DOM. Then, the fourth statement creates an array of the <a> elements within the image list and saves it in a variable named imageLinks. The code then processes each of the links in the array.

In the for loop for each element, an event handler is created for the click event of each link. Note here that the function that creates each event handler has an evt parameter that will receive the event object for each link in a DOM-compliant browser. Note too that the first statement in this function uses the this keyword so a different event handler is applied to each link.

After that, the first statement changes the src attribute in the image node to the href attribute of the link. Then, the next statement changes the value of the first child of the caption node to the title attribute of the link. Later, when the application is run and the user clicks on a thumbnail, these statements will change the DOM so the image and caption are immediately changed in the display.

This event handler ends by cancelling the default action of the event for the link using the code in figure 6-9. Since the default event is to display the file identified by the href attribute, cancelling this action is essential. Otherwise, clicking on the link would display the image that's specified by the href attribute in a new browser window or tab.

After the function for the event handler ends, the images that are swapped are preloaded using statements like those in figure 6-10. Then, the focus is moved to the first link in the user interface.

The JavaScript for the Image Swap application

```
$ = function (id) {
    return document.getElementById(id);
}
window.onload = function () {
    var listNode = $("image_list");        // the ul element
    var captionNode = $("caption");        // the h2 element
    var imageNode = $("image");            // the main img element

    var imageLinks = listNode.getElementsByTagName("a");

    // Process image links
    var i, linkNode, image;
    for ( i = 0; i < imageLinks.length; i++ ) {
        linkNode = imageLinks[i];

        // Attach event handler
        linkNode.onclick = function (evt) {
            var link = this;                   // link is the linkNode
            imageNode.src = link.getAttribute("href");
            captionNode.firstChild.nodeValue = link.getAttribute("title");

            // Cancel the default action of the event
            if (!evt) evt = window.event;
            if ( evt.preventDefault ) {
                evt.preventDefault();          // DOM compliant code
            }
            else {
                evt.returnValue = false;
            }
        }
        // Preload image
        image = new Image();
        image.src = linkNode.getAttribute("href");
    }
    $("first_link").focus();
}
```

Figure 6-12   The JavaScript for the Image Swap application

How to use timers

Timers let you execute functions after a specified period of time. These timers are provided by web browsers, and they are often used in DOM scripting applications like slide shows. Here, you'll learn about the two types of timers.

How to use a one-time timer

The first type of timer calls its function only once. To create this type of timer, you use the global setTimeout method that's shown in figure 6-13. Its first parameter is the function that the timer calls. Its second parameter is the number of milliseconds to wait before calling the function.

When you use the setTimeout method to create a timer, this method returns a reference to the timer that's created. Then, if necessary, you can use this reference to cancel the timer. To do that, you pass this reference to the clearTimeout method.

The examples in this figure use a one-time timer to hide a message in a heading at the top of the page after a delay of five seconds. It does that by setting the class attribute of the heading to "closed". That hides the heading because the CSS for this class sets the display property to none.

In the first example of JavaScript code, the onload event hander creates a timer that calls the hideMessage function after a delay of 5 seconds (5000 milliseconds). In the hideMessage function, the setAttribute method is used to set the class attribute for the heading to "closed". After that, the hideMessage function uses the clearTimeout method to cancel the timer. That isn't necessary, but it's okay to do since the timer won't be used again.

In the second example of JavaScript code, the function that's called is embedded in the first parameter of the setTimeout method. Look closely to see how this is coded. After the left parentheses of the setTimeout method, the entire function is coded followed by a comma. Then, the second parameter is coded as 5000. Although this is more complicated than the coding in the first example, you'll often see parameters with embedded functions like this. This also avoids the need for the global timer variable that the first example requires.

Two methods for working with a timer that calls a function once

```
setTimeout( function, delayTime )        // creates a timer
clearTimeout ( timer )                   // cancels a timer
```

The FAQs application with a first heading that is hidden after 5 seconds

> **Still under construction!**
>
> **jQuery FAQs**
>   ✦ What is jQuery?

The HTML for the heading

```
<h1 id="startup_message">Still under construction!</h1>
```

The CSS for the heading when the class attribute is "closed"

```
#startup_message.closed { display: none; }
```

How to use a named one-time timer to hide the first heading

```
// declare a global variable so it can be accessed by the function
var timer;                               // declare the timer variable

// create a timer that calls the hideMessage function once
window.onload = function () {
    timer = setTimeout(hideMessage, 5000);
}
// create the function that the timer calls
// when the class attribute is set to closed, the css hides the element
var hideMessage = function () {
    $("startup_message").setAttribute("class", "closed");
    clearTimeout(timer);
}
```

How to embed the timer function in the first parameter of the setTimeout method

```
window.onload = function () {
    var timer = setTimeout(
        function () {                     // the start of the first parameter
            $("startup_message").setAttribute("class", "closed");
            clearTimeout(timer);
        },
        5000);                            // the second parameter
}
```

Description

- The setTimeout method creates a timer that calls the specified function once after the specified delay in milliseconds. This method returns a reference to the new timer that can be used to cancel the timer.

- The clearTimeout method cancels the timer that was created with the setTimeout method.

- When you embed a timer function, you avoid the need for global variables.

Figure 6-13   How to use a one-time timer

How to use an interval timer

The second type of timer calls its function repeatedly. To create this type of timer, you use the global setInterval method shown in figure 6-14. Its first parameter is the function to be called. Its second parameter is the time interval between function calls. To cancel this type of timer, you pass the timer to the clearInterval method.

The example in this figure shows how to use an interval timer to create a counter that is incremented every second. This timer is coded within the onload event handler.

Before the timer is created, a counter variable is declared with a starting value of zero. Then, the setInterval method is used to create a timer. Here, the first parameter is the function that updates the counter variable and displays the updated counter value on the web page. The second parameter sets the interval to 1000 milliseconds, so the web page is updated every second.

When you use the setInterval method to create a timer, the timer waits for the specified interval to pass before calling the function the first time. So, if you want the function to be called immediately, you need to call the function before you create the timer.

Once you create an interval timer, you can't modify it. However, you can cancel the old timer and create a new one that works the way you want it to. This has the same effect as modifying the original timer.

Two methods for working with a timer that calls a function repeatedly

```
setInterval( function, intervalTime )     // creates a timer
clearInterval ( timer )                   // cancels a timer
```

The FAQs application with a counter at the bottom

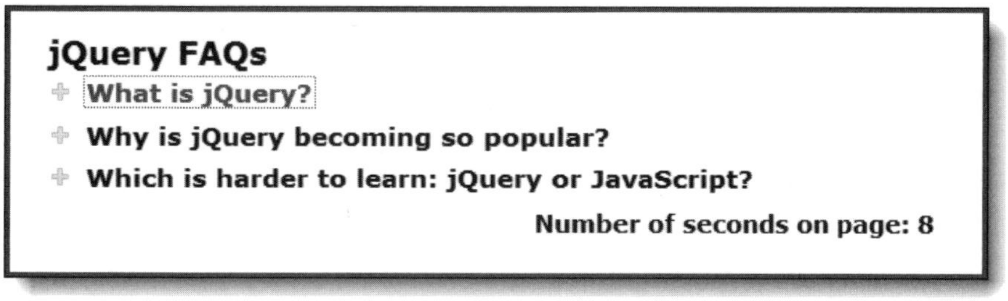

jQuery FAQs

✢ What is jQuery?

✢ Why is jQuery becoming so popular?

✢ Which is harder to learn: jQuery or JavaScript?

Number of seconds on page: 8

The HTML for the counter

```
<h3>Number of seconds on page: <span id="counter">0</span></h3>
```

The JavaScript for the interval timer that updates the counter

```
window.onload = function () {
    // create a timer that calls a function every second
    var counter = 0;
    var timer = setInterval(
        function () {                          // the start of the first parameter
            counter++;
            document.getElementById("counter").firstChild.nodeValue
                = counter;
        },
        1000 );                               // the second parameter
}
```

Description

- The setInterval method creates a timer that calls a function each time the specified interval in milliseconds has passed.

- The setInterval method returns a reference to the new timer that can be used by the clearInterval method to cancel the timer.

- Although you can't modify an interval timer, you can cancel it and create a new one that works the way you want it to.

Figure 6-14   How to use an interval timer

The Slide Show application

Figure 6-15 illustrates a Slide Show application that requires the use of an interval timer. When the user starts this application, it displays a new caption and image every two seconds.

The HTML and CSS

If you look at the HTML, you can see that five <a> elements are coded within a ul element. The href attribute for each <a> element provides the location for one of the images in the slide show. The title attribute provides the caption for the slide.

After the unordered list, the h2 element is the element that will display the caption for each slide. Its contents provide the caption for the first slide. It is followed by the img element that will display the image for each slide. Its src attribute provides the location of the first slide. That way, the first caption and slide are displayed when the application starts.

To keep this application simple, no controls are provided for stopping the slide show or moving through the slides manually. As a result, this slide show doesn't meet the best standards for usability or accessibility.

Of note in the CSS is the rule set for the ul element that contains the list. Since the purpose of this list is to provide the captions and images for the slide show, the list shouldn't be displayed. That's why its display property is set to none.

The Slide Show application with the third image displayed

The HTML

```
<section>
    <h1>Fishing Slide Show</h1>
    <ul id="image_list">
        <li><a href="images/casting1.jpg"
            title="Casting on the Upper Kings"></a></li>
        <li><a href="images/casting2.jpg"
            title="Casting on the Lower Kings"></a></li>
        <li><a href="images/catchrelease.jpg"
            title="Catch and Release on the Big Horn"></a></li>
        <li><a href="images/fish.jpg"
            title="Catching on the South Fork"></a></li>
        <li><a href="images/lures.jpg"
            title="The Lures for Catching"></a></li>
    </ul>
    <h2 id="caption">Casting on the Upper Kings</h2>
    <p><img src="images/casting1.jpg" alt="Casting 1" id="image"></p>
</section>
```

The CSS for the ul element

```
ul { display: none; }
```

Figure 6-15   The user interface, HTML, and CSS for the Slide Show application

The JavaScript

Figure 6-16 presents the JavaScript for this application. Here, you can see that the onload event handler starts by declaring variables that contain the nodes for the ul element, the h2 element for the caption, and the img element for the slide show. Then, the getElementsByTagName method is used to create an array named links that contains one object for each <a> element in the ul element.

Each of these links is processed by the for loop that follows. All this loop does, however, is preload the images and set the title property of each image to the title property of the current link. Then, the image object is added to the imageCache array so it can be used later.

At this point, the onload event handler starts the slide show. To do that, it creates an interval timer with a function that's embedded in the first parameter and 2000 (2 seconds) as the second parameter. It is the embedded function that displays the next slide when the interval time is up.

Within this function, the variable named imageCounter determines which slide in the imageCache array will be displayed next. The first statement in this function adds one to the imageCounter, and then uses the modulus operator (%) to get the remainder when the imageCounter property is divided by the length of the imageCache array. This means the imageCounter property will range from 0 through one less than the length of the array.

If, for example, the imageCache array contains 5 images, the counter values will range from 0 through 4 (1%5=1; 2%5=2; 3%5=3; 4%5=4, 5%5 = 0; 6%5=1, and so on). So, if the imageCounter value is used as the index of the imageCache array, the function will loop through the elements of the array and the index will never be larger than 4.

After the value of the imageCounter variable is set, the second statement in this function uses the imageCounter as the index for the imageCache array and stores that image object in the image variable. The third statement sets the src attribute of the img node to the src attribute of the image object. The last statement sets the text for the caption node to the title attribute of the image object. As soon as these changes are made to the DOM, the image and caption are changed in the browser display.

You might notice that this code doesn't set up any event handlers for user events. Instead, the slide show is driven by the interval timer, which issues timer events. Then, after each time interval passes, the function in the first parameter is executed again, which changes the src attribute of the img element in the DOM and the text of the h2 element.

The JavaScript for the Slide Show application

```javascript
var $ = function (id) {
    return document.getElementById(id);
}
window.onload = function () {
    var listNode = $("image_list");      // the ul element
    var captionNode = $("caption");      // the h2 element for the caption
    var imageNode = $("image");          // the img element for the show

    var links = listNode.getElementsByTagName("a");

    // Process image links
    var i, linkNode, image;
    var imageCache = [];
    for ( i = 0; i < links.length; i++ ) {
        linkNode = links[i];

        // Preload image and copy title properties
        image = new Image();
        image.src = linkNode.getAttribute("href");
        image.title = linkNode.getAttribute("title");
        imageCache.push(image);
    }

    // Start slide show
    var imageCounter = 0;
    var  timer = setInterval(
        function () {
            imageCounter = (imageCounter + 1) % imageCache.length;
            image = imageCache[imageCounter];
            imageNode.src = image.src;
            captionNode.firstChild.nodeValue = image.title;
        },
        2000);
}
```

Figure 6-16   The JavaScript for the Slide Show application

Perspective

Now that you've completed this chapter, you should know how to use JavaScript for some common DOM scripting applications like image swaps and slide shows. If some of this has been confusing, that's because this is both complicated and difficult.

The good news is that jQuery makes it much easier to develop DOM scripting applications like the ones you've just seen. Even better, you now have all the JavaScript skills that you need for using jQuery, and those skills will make it easier for you to learn jQuery.

Terms

DOM (Document Object Model)	interface
DOM node	usability
element node	accessibility
text node	default action
attribute node	preloading an image
comment node	image swap
DOM Core specification	timer

Summary

- The *Document Object Model*, or *DOM*, is built when a page is loaded into a browser. It consists of various types of *nodes*.

- In the DOM, *element nodes* represent the elements in an HTML document and *text nodes* represent the text within those elements. The DOM can also contain *attribute nodes* with text nodes that store the attribute values as well as *comment nodes*.

- JavaScript provides properties and methods for the objects of the DOM that are described in the *DOM Core Specification*. These include the properties and methods that are described by the Node, Document, and Element *interfaces*.

- *Usability* refers to how easy a web page is to use. *Accessibility* refers to how accessible a web page is to its users, especially disabled users.

- For some JavaScript applications, you need to cancel the *default action* of an event, like clicking on a link or a button.

- For applications like *image swaps* and slide shows, it's good to *preload* the images. That way, the page may take longer to load, but the image changes will take place immediately.

- Browsers provide two different types of *timers*. A one-time timer executes a function just once after the specified interval of time. An interval timer executes a function each time the specified interval passes.

Exercise 6-1   Experiment with the FAQs application

In section 2 of this book, you'll learn how to use jQuery to script the DOM. Since that's easier than using JavaScript for DOM scripting, you don't need to practice DOM scripting in JavaScript right now. However, you should understand how the JavaScript applications in this chapter work. To help you with that, you can start by experimenting with the FAQs application.

1. Use your text editor or IDE to open the index.html and faqs.js files that are in this folder:

    `c:\jquery\exercises\ch06\faqs`

2. Test the application to see how it works, and review the code.

3. Comment out the first statement in the headingNode.onclick function like this:

    `// var h2 = this;`

    Then, add this statement right after it:

    `var h2 = headingNode;`

4. Test the program and note that all three headings have the same event handler attached to it. As a result, clicking on any one of the headings affects only the third heading and its division. This demonstrates the importance of using the this keyword to refer to the current instance of the heading node.

5. Undo the changes you made in step 3 and test again. Then, experiment with any of the code that you don't fully understand.

Exercise 6-2   Review the other chapter applications

If you have any questions about how any of the applications in this chapter work, you'll find them all in this folder:

    `c:\jquery\exercises\ch06\`

That way, you can test them, modify them, and experiment with them until you completely understand how they work. Besides the complete applications presented in this chapter, you'll find another one in a folder named faqs_timers that uses the timers shown in figures 6-13 and 6-14.

Exercise 6-3   Develop a Book List application

If you want a challenge, this exercise provides the HTML and CSS for the user interface that follows. Then, you develop the JavaScript that makes it work.

This will be a serious test of your JavaScript and DOM scripting skills. So don't get frustrated, and keep in mind that an application like this is much easier to develop with jQuery.

Murach products
- **Books for web developers**
  - Murach's HTML5 and CSS3
  - Murach's JavaScript and DOM Scripting
  - Murach's PHP and MySQL
  - Murach's MySQL
- **Books for Java developers**
- **Books for .NET developers**

Development guidelines

1. You'll find the HTML, CSS, and image files for this application in this folder:
    `c:\jquery\exercises\ch06\book_list\`
    You'll also find a JavaScript file named book_list.js that contains just the code for the standard $ function. You can add your code to this file.

2. This application works like the FAQs application you saw in this chapter, except that a list of book links is displayed below each heading. If the user clicks on one of these links, an image for the book is displayed to the right of the list. In addition, anytime the user clicks on a heading with a plus or minus sign before it, the image should no longer be displayed.

3. The HTML for the links of this application is like the HTML for the Image Swap application. However, the links for this application don't require the title attribute since no caption is displayed for the image.

4. The images that are referred to by the href attributes of the links in this application should be preloaded. To do that, you can loop through all the links in the section element. Also, be sure to cancel the default actions of the links.

5. Feel free to copy and paste code from any of the applications that are available to you. That's the most efficient way to build a new application.

Note: If you set the src attribute of the img element to an empty string so no image is displayed when the application starts and when the user clicks on a heading, a placeholder will be displayed for this element in Internet Explorer. To avoid that, you can set the style attribute of the img element so the display property is set to "none". Then, you can set this property to "block" when you want to display an image. In the next section, you'll learn other ways to set CSS properties using jQuery.

Section 2

jQuery essentials

Now that you have the JavaScript skills that you need for using jQuery, you're ready to learn jQuery. So, in chapter 7, you'll learn a working subset of jQuery that will get you off to a fast start. And in chapter 8, you'll learn how to use the jQuery effects and animations that can bring a web page to life.

Then, in chapter 9, you'll learn how to use the DOM manipulation and traversal methods for advanced DOM scripting. In chapter 10, you'll learn how to use the jQuery features for working with forms. And in chapter 11, you'll learn how to use the many jQuery plugins that can quickly improve your productivity, and you'll also learn how to create your own plugins.

When you complete this section, you'll have all the jQuery skills that you need for developing professional web pages. You can also go on to any of the three sections that follow because they are written as independent modules. If, for example, you want to learn how to use Ajax next, skip to section 4.

7

Get off to a fast start with jQuery

In this chapter, you'll quickly see how jQuery makes JavaScript programming easier. Then, you'll learn a working subset of jQuery that will get you off to a fast start. Along the way, you'll study four complete applications that will show you how to apply jQuery.

Introduction to jQuery **196**
What jQuery is..196
How to include jQuery in your web pages 196
How jQuery can simplify JavaScript development 198
How jQuery can affect testing and debugging...198
How jQuery UI and plugins can simplify JavaScript development 200

The basics of jQuery programming...............................**202**
How to code jQuery selectors.. 202
How to call jQuery methods.. 204
How to use jQuery event methods... 206

The Email List application in jQuery **208**
The user interface and HTML.. 208
The jQuery..210

A working subset of selectors, methods, and event methods..**212**
The most useful selectors 212
The most useful methods...214
The most useful event methods 216
Other event methods that you should be aware of.....................................218

Three illustrative applications.......................................**220**
The FAQs application in jQuery...220
The Image Swap application in jQuery...222
The Image Rollover application in jQuery 226

Perspective **228**

Introduction to jQuery

In this introduction, you'll learn what jQuery is, how to include it in your applications, and how jQuery, jQuery UI, and plugins can simplify JavaScript development.

What jQuery is

As figure 7-1 summarizes, *jQuery* is a free, open-source, JavaScript library that provides dozens of methods for common web features that make JavaScript programming easier. Beyond that, the jQuery functions are coded and tested for cross-browser compatibility, so they will work in all browsers.

Those are two of the reasons why jQuery is used by more than half of the 10,000 most-visited web sites today. And that's why jQuery is commonly used by professional web developers. In fact, you can think of jQuery as one of the four technologies that every web developer should know how to use: HTML, CSS, JavaScript, and jQuery. But don't forget that jQuery is actually JavaScript.

How to include jQuery in your web pages

If you go to the web site that's shown in this figure, you'll find a download button that lets you download the single file that contains the jQuery core library. By default, the version that's downloaded is a compressed version that today is around 32KB. As a result, this version loads quickly into browsers, which is another reason why developers like jQuery.

The other version is uncompressed and currently about 247KB. If you download this version, you can study the JavaScript code that's used in the library. But beware, this code is extremely complicated.

Once you've downloaded the compressed version of the core library, you can include it in a web page by coding a script element like the first one in this figure. Then, if you store the file on your own computer or a local web server, you'll be able to develop jQuery applications without being connected to the Internet. For production applications, though, you'll need to deploy the file to your Internet web server.

In this script element, the file name includes the version number, but you can use whatever file name you want. However, if the file name doesn't include the version number, it's easy to lose track of which version you're using.

The other way to include the jQuery library in your web applications and the one we recommend is to get the file from a *Content Delivery Network* (*CDN*). A CDN is a web server that hosts open-source software, and the Google, Microsoft, and jQuery web sites are CDNs for getting the jQuery libraries. In the second example in this figure, the script element uses the jQuery CDN with a URL that gets version 1.8.3 of jQuery, and that's the way all of the applications in this book include the jQuery library.

The benefit to using a CDN is that you don't have to download the jQuery file. The disadvantage is that you have to be connected to the Internet to use a CDN.

The jQuery web site at www.jQuery.com

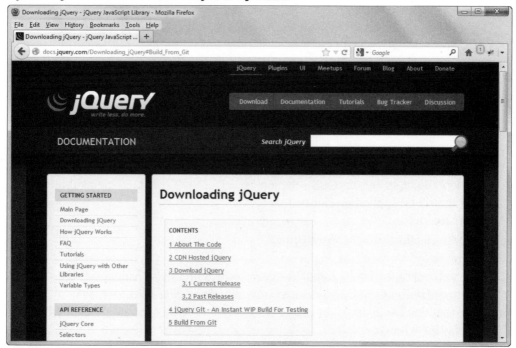

What jQuery offers

- Dozens of methods that make it easier to add JavaScript features to your web pages
- Methods that are tested for cross-browser compatibility

How to include the jQuery file after you've downloaded it to your computer

```
<script src="jquery-1.8.3.min.js"></script>
```

How to include the jQuery file from a Content Delivery Network (CDN)

```
<script src="http://code.jquery.com/jquery-1.8.3.min.js"></script>
```

Description

- *jQuery* is a free, open-source, JavaScript library that provides methods that make JavaScript programming easier. Today, jQuery is used by more than 50% of the 10,000 most-visited web sites, and its popularity is growing rapidly.
- The jQuery download comes in two versions. One version (min) is a compressed version that is relatively small and loads fast. The other version is uncompressed so you can use it to study the JavaScript code in the library.
- If you include the jQuery file from a *Content Delivery Network* (*CDN*), you don't have to provide it from your own server, but then you can't work offline. All of the applications in this book get version 1.8.3 this way, which is the current version at this writing.
- If you download the jQuery file to your system, you can change the filename so it's simpler, but then you may lose track of what version you're using.

Figure 7-1   What jQuery is and how to include it in your applications

How jQuery can simplify JavaScript development

To show you how jQuery can simplify JavaScript development, figure 7-2 shows both the JavaScript and the jQuery for the FAQs application that you learned how to develop in chapter 6. If you're like most people who are learning JavaScript, you probably found the JavaScript code for this application both complicated and confusing. That's because it is.

In contrast, the jQuery code takes less than half as many lines of code. You'll also find that it is much easier to understand once you learn how to use the JQuery selectors, methods, and event methods. And you'll start learning those skills right after this introduction.

Incidentally, jQuery uses CSS selectors to select the HTML elements that the methods should be applied to. For instance,

```
$("#faqs h2")
```

is a jQuery selector for the CSS selector

```
#faqs h2
```

which selects all of the h2 elements in the element with "faqs" as its id. In fact, jQuery supports all of the CSS selectors including the CSS3 selectors, even in browsers that don't support all of the CSS3 selectors. This is another reason why developers like jQuery.

How jQuery can affect testing and debugging

When you use jQuery to develop applications, you can use the same testing and debugging skills that you learned in chapter 4. Remember, though, that a call to a jQuery method is a call to the jQuery file that you specify in a script element in the head section of the HTML. In other words, when your code executes a jQuery method, it is the JavaScript in the jQuery file that does the processing.

Then, if the jQuery code can't be executed, the display in Firebug or in the error console of the browser will point to a statement in the jQuery file. This can happen, for example, because a faulty parameter is passed to a jQuery method. Unfortunately, the information in Firebug or the error console doesn't tell you which statement in your code caused the problem. Instead, you have to use the other debugging techniques to find the bug and fix it.

In most cases, though, Firebug and the error console of the browser do provide information that helps you find and fix the bug. So this is a minor problem that is more than compensated for by the benefits that you get from using jQuery.

The user interface for the FAQs application

jQuery FAQs

+ **What is jQuery?**

− **Why is jQuery becoming so popular?**
  Three reasons:
  - It's free.
  - It lets you get more done in less time.
  - All of its functions are cross-browser compatible.

+ **Which is harder to learn: jQuery or JavaScript?**

The JavaScript for the application

```javascript
var $ = function (id) {
    return document.getElementById(id);
}
window.onload = function () {
    var faqs = $("faqs");
    var h2Elements = faqs.getElementsByTagName("h2");
    var h2Node;
    for (var i = 0; i < h2Elements.length; i++ ) {
        h2Node = h2Elements[i];
        // Attach event handler
        h2Node.onclick = function () {
            var h2 = this;           // h2 is the current h2Node object
            if (h2.getAttribute("class") == "plus") {
                h2.setAttribute("class", "minus");
            }
            else {
                h2.setAttribute("class", "plus");
            }
            if (h2.nextElementSibling.getAttribute("class") == "closed") {
                h2.nextElementSibling.setAttribute("class", "open");
            }
            else {
                h2.nextElementSibling.setAttribute("class", "closed");
            }
        }
    }
}
```

The jQuery for the application

```javascript
$(document).ready(function() {
    $("#faqs h2").toggle(
        function() {
            $(this).addClass("minus");
            $(this).next().show();
        },
        function() {
            $(this).removeClass("minus");
            $(this).next().hide();
        }
    );   // end toggle
});  // end ready
```

Figure 7-2   How jQuery can simplify JavaScript development

How jQuery UI and plugins can simplify JavaScript development

Besides the core jQuery library, jQuery provides the *jQuery UI* (User Interface) library. The functions in this library use the core jQuery library to build advanced features that can be created with just a few lines of code. These features include themes, effects, widgets, and mouse interactions.

For instance, the browser display in figure 7-3 shows the FAQs application as a jQuery UI widget known as an accordion. To implement this widget, you just need the three lines of JavaScript code that are highlighted, and that also applies the formatting that's shown.

To use jQuery UI, you include a jQuery UI library file in your web pages in much the same way that you include the jQuery core library. You also include a jQuery UI CSS file that provides the themes for jQuery UI. In section 3, you'll learn how to do that, and you'll learn how to use the features of jQuery UI.

Because jQuery UI can make JavaScript development even easier than it is when using jQuery, it makes sense to use jQuery UI whenever it provides an effect, widget, or mouse interaction that you need. Keep in mind, though, that jQuery UI is limited, so you'll still need jQuery for most of your web applications. As a result, you should think of jQuery UI as an add-on that you should learn how to use after you master jQuery.

Besides jQuery UI, the jQuery web site provides access to dozens of *plugins* that have been developed for jQuery. These plugins provide higher-level functions like data validation and drop-down menus that require minimal coding for their implementation. To facilitate the development of plugins, jQuery provides specifications that help standardize the way that plugins are implemented. Plugins are one more reason why developers like jQuery.

Like jQuery UI, plugins are libraries that make use of the core jQuery library. In fact, you can think of jQuery UI as a plugin. To use a plugin, you use a script element to include the plugin file in a web page, and you code that script element after the script element for the jQuery core library. In chapter 11, you'll learn how to get the most from plugins, and you'll also learn how to create your own plugins.

In practice, it makes sense to look first for a plugin that implements a feature that you want to add to a web page. If you can find one, you may be able to do in a few hours what would otherwise take a few days. Next, if you can't find a suitable plugin, it makes sense to see whether jQuery UI can facilitate the implementation of the feature. Finally, if neither a plugin nor jQuery UI can help you implement a feature, you have to use jQuery to develop it. That's why you need to master all of the jQuery skills in this section.

The FAQs application as a jQuery UI accordion

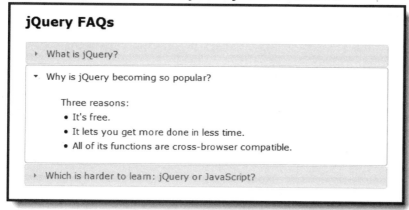

The HTML for a jQuery UI accordion

```
<div id="accordion">
  <h3><a href="#">What is jQuery?</a></h3>
  <div> <!-- panel contents --> </div>
  <h3><a href="#">Why is jQuery becoming so popular?</a></h3>
  <div> <!-- panel contents --> </div>
  <h3><a href="#">Which is harder to learn: jQuery or JavaScript?</a></h3>
  <div> <!-- panel contents --> </div>
</div>
```

The JavaScript code for the jQuery UI accordion

```
<script>
    $(document).ready(function() {
        $("#accordion").accordion();
    });
</script>
```

Some typical plugin functions

- Data validation
- Slide shows
- Carousels

Description

- *jQuery UI* is a free, open-source, JavaScript library that provides higher-level effects, widgets, and mouse interactions that can be customized by using themes. In section 3, you'll learn how to use jQuery UI.

- A *plugin* is a JavaScript library that provides functions that work in conjunction with jQuery to make it easier to add features to your web applications. In chapter 11, you'll learn how to use some of the most useful plugins, and you'll also learn how to create your own plugins.

- In general, if you can find a plugin or jQuery UI feature that does what you want it to do, you should use it. Often, though, you won't be able to find what you want so you'll need to develop the feature with just the core jQuery library.

Figure 7-3   How jQuery UI and plugins can simplify JavaScript development

The basics of jQuery programming

In the next three figures, you're going to learn the basics of jQuery programming. Then, you'll study an application that uses these skills. That will show you how jQuery simplifies JavaScript programming.

How to code jQuery selectors

When you use jQuery, you start by selecting the element or elements that you want to apply a jQuery method to. To do that, you can use jQuery *selectors* as shown in figure 7-4.

To code a jQuery selector, you start by coding the dollar sign ($) followed by set of parentheses that contains a set of quotation marks. Then, within the quotation marks, you code the CSS selector for the element or elements that you want to select. This is shown by the syntax summary at the top of this figure.

The HTML and the examples that follow show how easy it is to select one or more elements with jQuery. For instance, the first selector in the first group of examples selects all <p> elements within the entire document. The second selector selects the element with "faqs" as its id. And the third selector selects all elements with "plus" as the value of its class attribute.

In the second group of examples, you can see how other types of CSS selectors are coded with jQuery. Here, you can see how descendants, adjacent siblings, general siblings, and children are coded. For instance, the first selector gets all <p> elements that are descendants of the element with "faqs" as its id. That includes all of the <p> elements in the HTML in this figure.

In contrast, the second selector gets the div elements that are adjacent siblings to the h2 elements, which includes all of the div elements. The third selector gets all <p> elements that are siblings of ul elements, which selects the one <p> element in the second div element. And the fourth selector gets all ul elements that are children of div elements, which selects the ul element in the second div element.

The third group of examples shows how to code multiple selectors. To do that, you separate them with commas, just as you do with CSS.

The syntax for a jQuery selector

```
$("selector")
```

The HTML for the elements that are selected by the examples

```
<section id="faqs">
    <h1>jQuery FAQs</h1>
    <h2 class="plus">What is jQuery?</h2>
    <div>
        <p>jQuery is a library of the JavaScript functions that you're most
            likely to need as you develop web sites.
        </p>
    </div>
    <h2 class="plus">Why is jQuery becoming so popular?</h2>
    <div>
        <p>Three reasons:</p>
        <ul>
            <li>It's free.</li>
            <li>It lets you get more done in less time.</li>
            <li>All of its functions cross-browser compatible.</li>
        </ul>
    </div>
</section>
```

How to select elements by element, id, and class

By element type: All <p> elements in the entire document
```
$("p")
```

By id: The element with "faqs" as its id
```
$("#faqs")
```

By class: All elements with "plus" as a class
```
$(".plus")
```

How to select elements by relationship

Descendants: All <p> elements that are descendants of the section element
```
$("#faqs p");
```

Adjacent siblings: All div elements that are adjacent siblings of h2 elements
```
$("h2 + div")
```

General siblings: All <p> elements that are siblings of ul elements
```
$("ul ~ p")
```

Children: All ul elements that are children of div elements
```
$("div > ul")
```

How to code multiple selectors

```
$("#faqs li, div p")
$("p + ul, div ~ p")
```

Description

- When you use jQuery, the dollar sign ($) is used to refer to the jQuery library. Then, you can code *selectors* by using the CSS syntax within quotation marks within parentheses.

Figure 7-4   How to code jQuery selectors

How to call jQuery methods

Once you've selected the element or elements that you want to apply a *method* to, you call the method using the syntax shown at the top of figure 7-5. This is the same way that you call a method of any object. You code the selector that gets the element or elements, the dot, the method name, and any parameters within parentheses.

To get you started with jQuery, the table in this figure summarizes some of the jQuery methods that you'll use the most. For instance, the val method without a parameter gets the value from a selected text box or other form control, and the val method with a parameter sets the value in a selected text box or other form control. The first two examples after the table show how this works.

Similarly, the text method without a parameter can be used to get the text of a selected element, and the text method with a parameter can be used to set the text of a selected element. Methods like these are often referred to as *getter* and *setter* methods. Here, third example illustrates the setter version of the text method, which sets the text of an element to "Email address is required".

The fifth method in the table is the next method, which is used to get the next (or adjacent) sibling of an element. This method is often followed by another method. To do that, you use *object chaining*, which works just as it does with JavaScript. This is illustrated by the fourth example. Here, the next method gets the next sibling after the element that has been selected, and the text method sets the text for that sibling.

The last two methods in the table are the submit and focus methods, which are just like the JavaScript submit and focus methods. The submit method submits the data for a selected form to the server, and the focus method moves the focus to the selected form control or link.

In a moment, you'll see how these selectors and methods work in an application. But first, you need to learn how to set up the event handlers for an application.

The syntax for calling a jQuery method

```
$("selector").methodName(parameters)
```

Some common jQuery methods

Method	Description
val()	Get the value of a text box or other form control.
val(value)	Set the value of a text box or other form control.
text()	Get the text of an element.
text(value)	Set the text of an element.
next([type])	Get the next sibling of an element or the next sibling of a specified type if the parameter is coded.
submit()	Submit the selected form.
focus()	Move the focus to the selected form control or link.

Examples

How to get the value from a text box
```
var gallons = $("#gallons").val();
```

How to set the value for an input element
```
$("#gallons").val("");
```

How to set the text in an element
```
$("#email_address_error").text("Email address is required");
```

How to set the text for the next sibling with object chaining
```
$("#last_name").next().text("Last name is required");
```

How to submit a form
```
$("#join_list").submit();
```

How to move the focus to a form control or link
```
$("#email_address").focus();
```

Description

- To call a jQuery *method*, you code a selector, the dot operator, the method name, and any parameters within parentheses. Then, that method is applied to the element or elements that are selected by the selector.

- When you use *object chaining* with jQuery, you code one method after the other. This works because each method returns the appropriate object.

- If the selector for a method selects more than one element, jQuery applies the method to all of the elements so you don't have to code a loop to do that.

Figure 7-5   How to call jQuery methods

How to use jQuery event methods

When you use jQuery, you use *event methods* to attach event handlers to events. To do that, you use the syntax shown at the top of figure 7-6. First, you code the selector for the element that will initiate the event like a button that will be clicked. Then, you code the name of the event method that represents the event that you want to use. Last, you code a function that will be the event handler for the event within parentheses.

In the table in this figure, the two event methods that you'll use the most are summarized. The ready event is the jQuery alternative to the JavaScript load event, except that it works better. Unlike the load event, the ready event is triggered as soon as the DOM is built, even if other elements like images are still being loaded into the browser. This means that the user can start using the web page faster.

Because the DOM usually has to be built before you can use JavaScript or jQuery, you'll probably use the ready event method in every JavaScript application that you develop. The examples in this figure show two ways to do that. In the long form, you use document as the selector for the web page followed by the dot, the method name (ready), and the function for the event handler.

In the short form, you can omit the selector and event method name and just code the function in parentheses after the dollar sign. Although this form is often used by professional developers, all of the examples in this book use the long form. That way, it's clear where the ready event handler starts.

The next example in this figure shows an event handler for the click event of all h2 elements. This is coded just like the event handler for the ready event except h2 is used as the selector and click is used as the name of the event method.

The last example in this figure shows how you code an event handler within the ready event handler. Note here that the closing brace, parenthesis, and semicolon for each event handler is critical. As you can guess, it's easy to omit one of these marks or get them out of sequence so this is a frequent source of errors. That's why professional programmers often code inline comments after the ending marks for each event handler to identify which event handler the marks are for.

The syntax for a jQuery event method

```
$(selector).eventMethodName(function() {
    // the statements of the event handler
});
```

Two common jQuery event methods

Event method	Description
ready(handler)	The event handler runs when the DOM is ready.
click(handler)	The event handler runs when the selected element is clicked.

Two ways to code an event handler for the jQuery ready event

The long way

```
$(document).ready(function() {
    alert("The DOM is ready");
});
```

The short way

```
$(function(){                    // (document).ready is assumed
    alert("The DOM is ready");
});
```

An event handler for the click event of all h2 elements

```
$("h2").click(function() {
    alert("This heading has been clicked");
});
```

The click event handler within the ready event handler

```
$(document).ready(function() {
    $("h2").click(function() {
        alert("This heading has been clicked");
    }); // end of click event handler
}); // end of ready event handler
```

Description

- To code a jQuery event handler, you code a selector, the dot operator, the name of the jQuery *event method*, and an anonymous function that handles the event within parentheses.

- The event handler for the ready event will run any methods that it contains as soon as the DOM is ready, even if the browser is loading images and other content for the page. This works better than the JavaScript onload event, which doesn't occur until all of the content for the page is loaded.

- In this book, the ready event is always coded the long way that's shown above. In practice, though, many programmers use the short way.

- When coding one event handler within another, the use of the closing braces, parentheses, and semicolons is critical. To help get this right, many programmers code inline comments after these punctuation marks to identify the ends of the handlers.

Figure 7-6   How to use jQuery event methods

The Email List application in jQuery

With that as background, you're ready to see how jQuery can be used in the Email List application that you studied in section 1. That will show you how jQuery can simplify coding.

The user interface and HTML

To refresh your memory, figure 7-7 presents the user interface and HTML for the Email List application. To use the application, the user enters text into the first three text boxes and clicks on the Join our List button. Then, the JavaScript validates the entries and displays appropriate error messages if errors are found. If no errors are found, the data in the form is submitted to the web server for processing.

In the HTML, note first the script element that loads jQuery. It is followed by the script element that identifies the file that holds the JavaScript for this application. That sequence is essential because the JavaScript file is going to use the jQuery file.

Also note that the span elements are adjacent siblings to the input elements for the text boxes. The starting text for each of these span elements is an asterisk that indicates that the text box entry is required. Later, if the JavaScript finds errors in the entries, it displays error messages in these span elements.

The user interface for the Email List application

Please join our email list

Email Address:	zak@yahoo.com
Re-enter Email Address:	zak@yahoo	This entry must equal first entry.
First Name		This field is required.
	Join our List

The HTML

```html
<!DOCTYPE html>
<html>
<head>
    <meta charset="UTF-8">
    <title>Join Email List</title>
    <link rel="stylesheet" href="email_list.css">
    <script src="http://html5shiv.googlecode.com/svn/trunk/html5.js">
    </script>
    <script src="http://code.jquery.com/jquery-latest.min.js"></script>
    <script src="email_list.js"></script>
</head>
<body>
    <section>
        <h1>Please join our email list</h1>
        <form id="email_form" name="email_form"
            action="join.html" method="get">
            <label for="email_address1">Email Address:</label>
            <input type="text" id="email_address1">
            <span>*</span><br>

            <label for="email_address2">Re-enter Email Address:</label>
            <input type="text" id="email_address2">
            <span>*</span><br>

            <label for="first_name">First Name:</label>
            <input type="text" id="first_name">
            <span>*</span><br>

            <label> </label>
            <input type="button" id="join_list" value="Join our List">
        </form>
    </section>
</body>
</html>
```

Figure 7-7   The user interface and HTML for the Email List application

The jQuery

Figure 7-8 presents the jQuery for this application. This is the code in the email_list.js file that's included by the HTML. Here, all of the jQuery is highlighted. The rest of the code is JavaScript code.

To start, you can see that an event handler for the click event of the Join our List button is coded within the event handler for the ready event. Then, if you look at the last three lines of code, you can see the ending punctuation marks for these handlers. Within the click event handler, the first two statements show how jQuery selectors and the val method can be used to get the values from text boxes.

In the first if statement, you can see how an error message is displayed if the user doesn't enter an email address in the first text box. Here, the next method gets the adjacent sibling for the text box, which is the span element, and then the text method puts an error message in that span element. This changes the DOM, and as soon as it is changed, the error message is displayed in the browser.

The next, text, and val methods are used in similar ways in the next two if statements. Then, the fourth if statement tests to see whether the isValid variable is still true. If it is, the submit method of the form is issued, which sends the data to the web server.

That ends the event handler for the click event of the Join our List button. But that handler is followed by one more statement. It moves the focus to the first text box, the one with "email_address1" as its id.

As you review this code, note that it doesn't require the standard $ function that gets an element object when the element's id is passed to it. Instead, the $ sign is used to start a jQuery selector that gets elements by their ids. This simplifies the coding.

Although this jQuery code illustrates how jQuery can simplify a data validation application, it doesn't begin to show the power of jQuery. For that, you need to learn more selectors, methods, and event methods, and then see how they can be used in other types of applications. You'll do that next.

The jQuery for the Email List application (email_list.js)

```javascript
$(document).ready(function() {
    $("#join_list").click(function() {
        var emailAddress1 = $("#email_address1").val();
        var emailAddress2 = $("#email_address2").val();
        var isValid = true;

        // validate the first email address
        if (emailAddress1 == "") {
            $("#email_address1").next().text("This field is required.");
            isValid = false;
        } else {
            $("#email_address1").next().text("");
        }

        // validate the second email address
        if (emailAddress2 == "") {
            $("#email_address2").next().text("This field is required.");
            isValid = false;
        } else if (emailAddress1 != emailAddress2) {
            $("#email_address2").next().text(
                "This entry must equal first entry.");
            isValid = false;
        } else {
            $("#email_address2").next().text("");
        }

        // validate the first name entry
        if ($("#first_name").val() == "") {
            $("#first_name").next().text("This field is required.");
            isValid = false;
        }
        else {
            $("#first_name").next().text("");
        }

        // submit the form if all entries are valid
        if (isValid) {
            $("#email_form").submit();
        }
    }); // end click
    $("#email_address1").focus();
}); // end ready
```

Figure 7-8   The jQuery for the Email List application

A working subset of selectors, methods, and event methods

The next three figures present a working subset of the most useful jQuery selectors, methods, and event methods. This is a lot to take in, but once you understand them, you'll be able to write practical jQuery applications of your own.

The most useful selectors

In figure 7-4, you were introduced to the basic selectors that you can use with jQuery. Now, figure 7-9 presents the other selectors that you're most likely to use in your jQuery applications. The only selectors of significance that are missing are ones that you'll learn about in later chapters, like the animate selector that you use with animations and the form control selectors that you use with forms.

If this summary seems daunting, just read the list and realize that these selectors let you select just about any element that you need to select. Then, make sure that you understand the examples in this figure. Later, when you need to make a specific type of selection for an application, you can refer back to this summary and to figure 7-4.

To illustrate the use of these selectors, the first example shows a selector that gets the li elements that are the first children of their parent elements. If the HTML contains more than one list, this selects the first li element of each list. The second example shows how to get the even tr (row) elements in an HTML table.

The third example shows how to use the :eq selector to get a specific element within an array of elements. If, for example, there are four <p> elements that are descendants of the "faqs" element, :eq(2) will return the third <p> element because the index values start with zero.

The last example shows a selector that gets all input elements with type attributes that have "text" as the value. In other words, this selector gets all text boxes. Note, however, that you can also get the text boxes by using this selector:

```
$("input[type=text]")
```

This just shows that you can often select the elements that you want in more than one way.

A summary of the most useful jQuery selectors

Selector	Selects
[attribute]	All elements with the named attribute.
[attribute=value]	All elements with the named attribute and value.
:contains(text)	All elements that contain the specified text.
:empty	All elements with no children including text nodes.
:eq(n)	The element at index n within the selected set.
:even	All elements with an even index within the selected set.
:first	The first element within the set.
:first-child	All elements that are first children of their parent elements.
:gt(n)	All elements within the selected set that have an index greater than n.
:has(selector)	All elements that contain the element specified by the selector.
:header	All elements that are headers (h1, h2, ...).
:hidden	All elements that are hidden.
:last	The last element within the selected set.
:last-child	All elements that are the last children of their parent elements.
:lt(n)	All elements within the selected set that have an index less than n.
:not(selector)	All elements that aren't selected by the selector.
:nth-child	All elements that are the nth children of their parent elements.
:odd	All elements with an odd index within the selected set.
:only-child	All elements that are the only children of their parent elements.
:parent	All elements that are parents of other elements, including text nodes.
:text	All input elements with the type attribute set to "text".
:visible	All elements that are visible.

Examples

How to select the li elements that are the first child of their parent element
```
$("li:first-child")
```

How to select the even tr elements of a table
```
$("table > tr:even")          // numbering starts at 0, so first tag is even
```

How to select the third descendant <p> element of an element
```
$("#faqs p:eq(2)")            // numbering starts at 0
```

How to select all input elements with "text" as the type attribute
```
$(":text")
```

Description

- Figure 7-4 and the table above summarize the selectors that you are most likely to need.
- Not included are six attribute selectors that let you select attributes with attribute values that contain specific substrings.
- In chapter 8, you'll learn about a selector that's used with animation, and in chapter 10, you'll learn about other selectors that are used for form controls.

Figure 7-9   The most useful selectors

The most useful methods

The table in figure 7-10 represents a collection of methods that are taken from several jQuery categories. For instance, the prev and next methods are DOM traversal methods. The attr, css, addClass, removeClass, and toggleClass methods are DOM manipulation methods. The hide and show methods are effect methods. And the each method is a miscellaneous method.

These are some of the most useful jQuery methods, and they will get you off to a fast start with jQuery. Then, you'll add methods to your repertoire as you read the rest of the chapters in this section. For instance, you'll learn how to use the other effect methods in chapter 8, and you'll learn how to use the other DOM transversal and manipulation methods in chapter 9.

Here again, if this table seems daunting, just read through these methods to see what's available. Then, study the examples to see how they can be used. Later, when you need a specific method for an application, you can refer back to this summary.

In the first example, the attr method is used to get the src attribute of an element with "image" as its id. The second example uses the attr method to add a src attribute to the selected element with the value that's stored in the variable named imageSource. If the element already has an src attribute, this method changes its value. The third example uses the css method to change the color property of the selected elements to blue.

In the fourth example, the addClass method is used to add a class to all of the h2 elements within the element that has "faqs" as its id. That's similar to what you've done using JavaScript.

In the last example, the each method is used to perform a function for each element in an array. In this case, the array contains all of the <a> elements within the element with "image_list" as its id, and the each method loops through these elements. As you will see, this simplifies the handling of the elements in the array.

A summary of the most useful jQuery methods

Method	Description
next([*selector*])	Get the next sibling of an element or the first sibling of a specified type if the parameter is coded.
prev([*selector*])	Get the previous sibling of an element or the previous sibling of a specified type if the parameter is coded.
attr(*attributeName*)	Get the value of the specified attribute.
attr(*attributeName, value*)	Set the value of the specified attribute.
css(*propertyName*)	Get the value of the specified property.
css(*propertyName, value*)	Set the value of the specified property.
addClass(*className*)	Add one or more classes to an element and, if necessary, create the class. If you use more than one class as the parameter, separate them with spaces.
removeClass([*className*])	Remove one or more classes. If you use more than one class as the parameter, separate them with spaces.
toggleClass(*className*)	If the class is present, remove it. Otherwise, add it.
hide([*duration*])	Hide the selected element. The duration parameter can be "slow", "fast", or a number giving the time in milliseconds. By default, the duration is 400 milliseconds, "slow" is 600 milliseconds, and "fast" is 200 milliseconds.
show([*duration*])	Show the selected element. The duration parameter is the same as for the hide method.
each(*function*)	Run the function for each element in an array.

Get the value of the src attribute of an image

```
$("#image").attr("src");
```

Set the value of the src attribute of an image to the value of a variable

```
$("#image").attr("src", imageSource);
```

Set the value of the color property of the h2 elements to blue

```
$("h2").css("color", "blue");
```

Add a class to the h2 descendants of the "faqs" element

```
$("#faqs h2").addClass("minus");
```

Run a function for each <a> element within an "image_list" element

```
$("#image_list a").each(function() {
    // the statements of the function
});
```

Description

- The table above presents a powerful set of jQuery methods. This table adds to the methods that were presented in figure 7-5.

- In the chapters that follow, you'll learn how to use other methods, including those for effects (chapter 8), DOM scripting and traversal (chapter 9), forms (chapter 10), and Ajax and JSON (chapter 14).

Figure 7-10   The most useful methods

The most useful event methods

Figure 7-11 summarizes the most useful event methods, and this summary includes the ready and click methods that were introduced in figure 7-6. As you can see, most of these event methods provide for a single event handler that runs when the event occurs. Those event methods work like the ready and click methods, but with different events.

This is illustrated by the first example, which works just like the click event method, except that it handles the double-click event. Of note here is the use of the this keyword within the handler. Here, it is coded as a jQuery selector, and it refers to the text box that has been double-clicked. This is similar to the way the this keyword works with JavaScript. Note that it isn't enclosed within quotation marks, even though it's a selector. What this function does is use the val method to set the value of the double-clicked text box to an empty string.

In contrast, the toggle and hover event methods provide for two event handlers. For instance, the hover event method provides one event handler for when the mouse pointer moves into an element and another handler for when the mouse pointer moves out of an element. This is illustrated by the second example in this figure. Note here that the first function is the first parameter of the hover method, and it is followed by a comma. Then, the second function is the second parameter of the hover method. To end the parameters, the last line of code consists of a right parenthesis followed by a semicolon.

Similarly, the toggle event method provides for two event handlers. The first event handler runs the first time the element is clicked and every other time thereafter. This is referred to as the even event handler, because the counting starts with zero. In contrast, the second event handler is referred to as the odd event handler, because it runs on odd clicks of the element, counting from zero. The result is that this event method lets you alternate event handlers each time the element is clicked. This makes it much easier to develop an application that requires this functionality.

Note, however, that the toggle method is deprecated in version 1.8 of jQuery and will be removed in version 1.9. As a result, you should replace this method in existing applications with other methods. Nevertheless, this method is used in a few of the examples in this book because it has been so widely used in existing applications.

The hover and toggle methods are typical of jQuery coding, which often requires the use of one or more functions within another function. That's why you need to code the functions in a way that helps you keep the punctuation straight. It also helps to code inline comments that mark the ends of functions and methods.

In these examples, note that when a selector gets more than one element, the event method sets up the event handler for each of the selected elements. This makes it much easier to set up event handlers with jQuery than it is with JavaScript.

A summary of the most useful jQuery event methods

Event method	Description
ready(*handler*)	The handler runs when the DOM is ready.
unload(*handler*)	The handler runs when the user closes the browser window.
error(*handler*)	The handler runs when a JavaScript error occurs.
click(*handler*)	The handler runs when the selected element is clicked.
toggle(*handlerEven, handlerOdd*)	The first handler runs on even clicks of the element, starting with 0. The second handler runs on odd clicks of the element. Note, however, that this event method is deprecated in version 1.8 and will be removed in version 1.9, so you need to stop using it.
dblclick(*handler*)	The handler runs when the selected element is double-clicked.
mouseenter(*handler*)	The handler runs when the mouse pointer enters the selected element.
mouseover(*handler*)	The handler runs when the mouse pointer moves over the selected element.
mouseout(*handler*)	The handler runs when the mouse pointer moves out of the selected element.
hover(*handlerIn, handlerOut*)	The first event handler runs when the mouse pointer moves into an element. The second event handler runs when the mouse pointer moves out.

A handler for the double-click event of all text boxes that clears the clicked box

```
$(":text").dblclick(function () {
    $(this).val("");
});
```

A handler for the hover event of each img element within a list

```
$("#image_list img").hover(
    function() {
        alert("The mouse pointer has moved into an img element");
    },
    function() {
        alert("The mouse pointer has moved out of an img element);
    }
);  // end hover
```

Description

- The table above presents the event methods that you'll use the most. Not included are: keydown, keypress, keyup, mousedown, mouseup, mouseleave, and mousemove.

Figure 7-11   The most useful event methods

Other event methods that you should be aware of

For most applications, you'll use the event methods that have already been presented. You'll also code the function or functions for the event handlers as the parameters of the event methods.

Sometimes, though, you'll want to attach event handlers in other ways, remove an event handler, or trigger an event that starts an event handler. Then, you can use the methods that are presented in the table in figure 7-12.

When you use the first two methods in this table, you usually store the function for the event handler in a variable, as illustrated by the first example after the table. Then, you can use the name of the variable as the second parameter of the event method.

To illustrate, the second example shows how to use the bind method to attach an event handler to the click event of an element with "clear" as its id. Note, however, that the bind method is also used when you use the shortcut method to attach an event handler to an event. It's just done behind the scene so you may not be aware of it.

One of the benefits of storing an event handler in a variable is that you can attach the handler to more than one event. That's illustrated by the third example. There, two statements are used to apply the clearClick event handler to the click event of a button with "clear" as its id as well as the dblclick event of all text boxes.

For some applications, you may want to remove an event handler when some condition occurs. To do that, you can use the unbind method, as illustrated by the fourth example in this figure.

Or, if you want to remove an event handler after it runs just one time, you can use the one event method. This is illustrated by the fifth example.

If you want to initiate an event from your jQuery code, you can use the trigger method in either the long or short form, as illustrated by the sixth set of examples. Both of those examples trigger the click event of the element with "clear" as its id, which in turn causes the clearClick event handler to be run.

That provides another way to run the same event handler for two different events. All you have to do is trigger the event for one event handler from another event handler. That's illustrated by the last example in this figure. There, the event handler for the double-click event of all text boxes triggers the click event of the element with "clear" as its id, and that starts the clearClick event handler.

Other event methods that you should be aware of

Event method	Description
bind(*event, handler*)	Attach an event handler to an event.
unbind(*event, handler*)	Remove an event handler from an event.
one(*event, handler*)	Attach an event handler and remove it after it runs one time.
trigger(*event*)	Trigger the event for the selected element.

How to store an event handler in a variable

```
var clearClick = function () {
    // the statements for the event handler
}
```

How to attach an event handler to an event

With the bind method

```
$("#clear").bind(click, clearClick);
```

With the shortcut method

```
$("#clear").click(clearClick);
```

How to attach an event handler to two different events

```
$("#clear").click(clearClick);
$(":text").dblclick(clearClick);
```

How to remove an event handler from an event

```
$("#clear").unbind("click", clearClick);
```

How to attach and remove an event handler so it runs only once

```
$("#clear").one("click", confirmClick);
```

How to trigger an event

With the trigger method

```
$("#clear").trigger("click");
```

With the shortcut method

```
$("#clear").click();
```

How to use the shortcut method to trigger an event from an event handler

```
$(":text").dblclick(function () {
    $("#clear").click();       // triggers the click event of the clear button
}
```

Description

- When you store an event handler in a variable, you can use the bind method to attach it to more than one event.

- When you use the shortcut method to attach an event handler to an event, you're actually using the bind method.

- The submit and focus methods are actually event methods. When you use the shortcut method to trigger them, they trigger the submit and focus events.

Figure 7-12   Other event methods that you should be aware of

Three illustrative applications

Now, to help you see how the selectors, methods, and event methods work in actual applications, this chapter presents three typical JavaScript applications.

The FAQs application in jQuery

Figure 7-13 presents the FAQs application that you studied in chapter 6, but this time it uses jQuery. When this applications starts, the div elements after the h2 elements are hidden by the CSS, and the h2 elements are preceded by a plus sign. Then, if the user clicks on an h2 element, the div element below it is displayed and the plus sign is changed to a minus sign. And if the user clicks on the heading again, the process is reversed.

The jQuery code for this application consists of a toggle event method that's within the ready method. This toggle event method sets up the event handlers for every h2 element within the section that has "faqs" as its id:

```
$("#faqs h2").toggle
```

Remember that the parameters for the toggle event method are two functions, separated by a comma. So that's what's coded within the parentheses for this method. In both of these functions, the this keyword is used, and it refers to the current h2 element because that's the object of the toggle method.

In the first function (parameter) for this method, the first statement uses the addClass method to add a class attribute to the h2 element with "minus" as the value. The CSS for this application (not shown) uses this class to change the background image for the element from a plus sign to a minus sign. Then, the second statement chains the next and show methods to display the hidden div element that is an adjacent sibling to the h2 element.

The second function for this method works the same way, but in reverse. There, the first statement uses the removeClass method to remove the "minus" class that was added the first time the heading was clicked. The second statement uses the next and hide methods to hide the adjacent div element.

This application begins to show the power of jQuery. Here, it takes just 12 lines of code to set up the event handlers for alternating clicks of as many h2 elements as there are in the "faqs" section. If you compare this code with the JavaScript code for this application in figure 7-2, you can get a better idea of how much this simplifies this application. In fact, since JavaScript doesn't provide for show and hide methods, the JavaScript has to use a class and CSS to hide and close the div elements.

Remember, though, that the toggle event method is deprecated in jQuery 1.8 and will be removed in jQuery 1.9. So the focus here should be on how you code jQuery methods and functions, not the toggle method. When you use jQuery, you can usually get the result you want in more than one way, and figure 8-2 in the next chapter shows an even simpler way to code the FAQs application.

The FAQs application in a browser

jQuery FAQs

+ **What is jQuery?**

− **Why is jQuery becoming so popular?**
    Three reasons:
    • It's free.
    • It lets you get more done in less time.
    • All of its functions are cross-browser compatible.

+ **Which is harder to learn: jQuery or JavaScript?**

The HTML

```html
<section id="faqs">
    <h1>jQuery FAQs</h1>
    <h2>What is jQuery?</h2>
    <div>
        <p>jQuery is a library of the JavaScript functions that you're most
            likely to need as you develop web sites.
        </p>
    </div>
    <h2>Why is jQuery becoming so popular?</h2>
    <div>
        <p>Three reasons:</p>
        <ul>
            <li>It's free.</li>
            <li>It lets you get more done in less time.</li>
            <li>All of its functions are cross-browser compatible.</li>
        </ul>
    </div>
    <h2>Which is harder to learn: jQuery or JavaScript?</h2>
    <div>
        <p>For most functions, jQuery is significantly easier to learn and
            use than JavaScript. But remember: jQuery is JavaScript.
        </p>
    </div>
</section>
```

The jQuery

```javascript
$(document).ready(function() {
    $("#faqs h2").toggle(
        function() {
            $(this).addClass("minus");
            $(this).next().show();
        },
        function() {
            $(this).removeClass("minus");
            $(this).next().hide();
        }
    );  // end toggle
});  // end ready
```

Figure 7-13   The FAQs application in jQuery

The Image Swap application in jQuery

Figure 7-14 presents another application that shows the power of jQuery. It is the Image Swap application that you studied in chapter 6. In short, when the user clicks on one of the thumbnail images at the top of the browser window, the caption and image below the thumbnails are changed.

In the HTML for this application, img elements are used to display the six thumbnail images. However, these elements are coded within <a> elements so the images are clickable and they can receive the focus. In the <a> elements, the href attributes identify the images to be swapped when the links are clicked, and the title attributes provide the text for the related captions. In this case, both the <a> elements and the img elements are coded within a ul element.

After the ul element, you can see the h2 element for the caption and the img element for the main image on the page. The ids of these elements are highlighted because the jQuery will use those ids as it swaps captions and images into them.

For the motor-impaired, this HTML provides accessibility by coding the img elements for the thumbnails within <a> elements. That way, the user can access the thumbnail links by clicking on the Tab key, and the user can swap the image by pressing the Enter key when a thumbnail has the focus, which starts the click event.

Of note in the CSS for this page is the rule set for the li elements. Their display properties are set to inline so the images go from left to right instead of from top to bottom. Also, the padding on the right of each item is set to 10 pixels to provide space between the images.

The user interface for the Image Swap application

The HTML

```
<section>
    <h1>Ram Tap Combined Test</h1>
    <ul id="image_list">
        <li><a href="images/h1.jpg" title="James Allison: 1-1">
            <img src="thumbnails/t1.jpg" alt=""></a></li>
        <li><a href="images/h2.jpg" title="James Allison: 1-2">
            <img src="thumbnails/t2.jpg" alt=""></a></li>
        <li><a href="images/h3.jpg" title="James Allison: 1-3">
            <img src="thumbnails/t3.jpg" alt=""></a></li>
        <li><a href="images/h4.jpg" title="James Allison: 1-4">
            <img src="thumbnails/t4.jpg" alt=""></a></li>
        <li><a href="images/h5.jpg" title="James Allison: 1-5">
            <img src="thumbnails/t5.jpg" alt=""></a></li>
        <li><a href="images/h6.jpg" title="James Allison: 1-6">
            <img src="thumbnails/t6.jpg" alt=""></a></li>
    </ul>
    <h2 id="caption">James Allison 1-1</h2>
    <p><img src="images/h1.jpg" alt="" id="image"></p>
</section>
```

The CSS for the li elements

```
li {
    padding-right: 10px;
    display: inline;
}
```

Figure 7-14   The user interface, HTML, and CSS for the Image Swap application

Figure 7-15 presents the JavaScript and jQuery for this application. Within the ready event handler, the each method is used to run a function for each <a> element in the unordered list. This function preloads the images that will be swapped so they are in the browser when the user starts using the application. If an application uses many images, this can make the application run faster.

Within the function for each <a> element, the first statement creates a new Image object. Then, the second statement uses the this keyword and the attr method to set the src attribute of the Image object to the value of the href attribute in the <a> element. As soon as that's done, the image is loaded into the browser.

The each method is followed by a click event method that sets up the event handlers for the click events of the <a> elements that contain the thumbnail images. Note here that evt is coded as the parameter for the click event method, which receives the event object when the event occurs. This object will be used later to cancel the default action of each link.

The first two statements in this event handler swap the image in the main portion of the browser window. The first statement uses the this keyword and attr method to get the value of the href attribute of the <a> element. This value gives the location of the image to be swapped. Then, the second statement sets the src attribute of the main img element to this value. As soon as that's done, the image is swapped in the browser.

The next two statements work similarly. They swap the caption of the image in the main portion of the browser window. This time, the caption is taken from the title attribute of the <a> element.

The last statement in the click event handler uses the preventDefault method of the evt object that is passed to the event handler to cancel the default action of the link. This is a jQuery method that is cross-browser compatible, which simplifies the JavaScript code. It is executed in place of the preventDefault method of the browser when you include the jQuery library. If the default isn't cancelled, clicking on the link will display the image that's referred to by the href attribute in a new window or tab, and that isn't what you want.

After the click event handler, the last statement in the ready method moves the focus to the first thumbnail image. That will make it easier for the users to tab to the thumbnails that they want to swap. To identify the first <a> element in the thumbnails, the :first-child selector is used twice: first to get the first li element of the unordered list, then to get the first <a> element of the li element.

The JavaScript

```
$(document).ready(function() {
    // preload images
    $("#image_list a").each(function() {
        var swappedImage = new Image();
        swappedImage.src = $(this).attr("href");
    });

    // set up event handlers for links
    $("#image_list a").click(function(evt) {
        // swap image
        var imageURL = $(this).attr("href");
        $("#image").attr("src", imageURL);

        //swap caption
        var caption = $(this).attr("title");
        $("#caption").text(caption);

        // cancel the default action of the link
        evt.preventDefault();   // jQuery cross-browser method
    }); // end click

    // move focus to first thumbnail
    $("li:first-child a:first-child").focus();
}); // end ready
```

Description

- When you attach an event handler to a link, you often need to cancel the default action of the link, which is to open the page or image that's identified by its href attribute.

- To cancel the default action of a link, you can use the jQuery preventDefault method of the event object that is passed to the event handler. The jQuery version of this method is cross-browser compatible.

- To get the event object that's passed to a method, you need to code a parameter for the event handler function. You can use whatever name you want for this parameter, like evt or event. Then, you must use that name whenever you refer to the event object.

- When you use jQuery to work with images that aren't included in the HTML, preloading the images can improve the performance of the application because the user doesn't have to wait for a new image to be loaded into the browser.

- To preload an image, you create a new Image object and assign the URL for the image to the Image object's src attribute. As soon as that's done, the image is loaded into the browser.

Figure 7-15   The JavaScript for the Image Swap application

The Image Rollover application in jQuery

Figure 7-16 presents another application that shows the power of jQuery. In short, when the user hovers the mouse pointer over one of the starting images, it is replaced by another image. And when the user moves the mouse pointer out of the image, the original image is again displayed.

In the HTML for this application, img elements are coded within the li elements of an unordered list. In these img elements, the src attribute identifies the image that is displayed when the application is loaded into the browser, and the id attribute identifies the image that should be displayed when the mouse hovers over the img element.

In the JavaScript for this application, the hover event method is used to set up the event handlers. But note that this event method is coded within an each method that performs a function for each occurrence of an img element within the ul element that has "image_rollovers" as its id:

```
$("#image_rollovers img").each
```

The function for the each method starts by using the this keyword and the attr method to get the values of the src and id attributes of each image and storing them in variables named oldURL and newURL. Remember that these attributes hold the values that locate each starting image and its rollover image. If you look at the HTML, you can see that these images are jpg files that are stored in an images folder. For instance, the rollover image specified by the first id attribute is:

```
images/h4.jpg
```

The next two statements preload the rollover images by creating a new Image object for each one and assigning the value of the newURL variable to its src attribute. As soon as the src attribute is set, the browser loads the image. Although preloading isn't essential, it can improve the user experience because the users won't have to wait for a rollover image to be loaded.

At this point, the hover event method is used to set up the event handlers for each image. Remember that this event method has two event handlers as its parameters. The first event handler is run when the mouse pointer moves into the element, and the second one is run when the mouse pointer moves out of the image. Here, the this keyword is used so the hover event applies to each img element.

In the function for the first event handler, you can see that the this keyword and the attr method are used to set the src attribute of the image to the value of the newURL variable. That causes the rollover image to be displayed. The function for the second event handler reverses this process by restoring the src attribute of the image to the value of the oldURL variable.

Of course, there's more than one way to code an application like this. For instance, you could implement this application by using the mouseover and mouseout event methods instead of the hover event method. Then, you would code the first function of the hover event as the mouseover event handler and the second function as the mouseout event handler.

Three images with the middle image rolled over

The HTML

```
<section>
    <h1>Ram Tap Combined Test</h1>
    <ul id="image_rollovers">
        <li><img src="images/h1.jpg" alt="" id="images/h4.jpg"></li>
        <li><img src="images/h2.jpg" alt="" id="images/h5.jpg"></li>
        <li><img src="images/h3.jpg" alt="" id="images/h6.jpg"></li>
    </ul>
</section>
```

The JavaScript

```
$(document).ready(function() {
    $("#image_rollovers img").each(function() {
        var oldURL = $(this).attr("src");          // gets the src attribute
        var newURL = $(this).attr("id");           // gets the id attribute

        // preload images
        var rolloverImage = new Image();
        rolloverImage.src = newURL;

        // set up event handlers
        $(this).hover(
            function() {
                $(this).attr("src", newURL);       // sets the src attribute
            },
            function() {
                $(this).attr("src", oldURL);       // sets the src attribute
            }
        );   // end hover
    }); // end each
}); // end ready
```

Figure 7-16   The Image Rollover application in jQuery

Perspective

To get you off to a fast start, this chapter has presented a working subset of the most useful jQuery selectors, methods, and event methods. That should give you some idea of what you have to work with when you use jQuery. And you'll add to those selectors and methods as you read other chapters in this book.

The trick of course is being able to apply the right selectors, methods, and event methods to the application that you're trying to develop. To get good at that, it helps to review many different types of jQuery applications. That's why this chapter has presented four applications, and that's why you'll see many more before you complete this book.

Terms

jQuery	method
CDN (Content Delivery Network)	getter method
jQuery UI	setter method
plugin	object chaining
selector	event method

Summary

- *jQuery* is a JavaScript library that provides methods that make JavaScript programming easier. These methods have been tested for cross-browser compatibility.

- *jQuery UI* and *plugins* are JavaScript libraries that use the jQuery library to build higher-level features.

- To use jQuery, you code a script element in the head section that includes the file for the jQuery core library. This file can be downloaded and stored on your computer or server, or you can access it through a *Content Delivery Network (CDN)*.

- When you code statements that use jQuery, you use *selectors* that are like those for CSS. You also use a dot syntax that consists of the selector for one or more elements, the dot, and the name of the *method* that should be executed.

- To set up event handlers in jQuery, you use *event methods*. Most of these methods have one parameter that is the event handler that will be run when the event occurs. But some event methods like the toggle method take two event handler parameters.

Exercise 7-1   Add a Clear button to the Email List application

In this exercise, you'll add a Clear button to the Email List application of figures 7-7 and 7-8. That will force you to create and attach another event handler.

1. Use your text editor to open the index.html and email_list.js files in this folder:

    `c:\jquery\exercises\ch07\email_list\`

2. Run the application to refresh your memory about how it works. Note that a Clear button has been added below the Join our List button, but the button doesn't work.

3. Add an event handler for the click event of the Clear button that clears all of the text boxes by setting them to an empty string (""). This can be done in one statement. To select just the text boxes, you use a selector like the last one in figure 7-9. To set the values to empty strings, you use the val method like the second example in figure 7-5. Now, test this change.

4. This event handler should also put the asterisks back in the span elements that are displayed to the right of the text boxes to show that entries are required. That requires just one statement that uses the next and the text methods.

5. Add one more statement to this event handler that moves the focus to the first text box. Then, test this change.

6. Add another event handler to this application for the double-click event of any text box. This event handler should do the same thing that the event handler for the click event of the Clear button does. The easiest way to do that is to trigger the click event of the Clear button from the handler for the double-click event, as in the last example in figure 7-12.

7. Comment out the line of code that you just used to trigger the click event of the Clear button. Then, add a statement to the double-click event handler that only clears the text from the text box that the user double-clicks in. To do that, you'll have to use the this keyword, as in the first example in figure 7-11.

Exercise 7-2   Use different event methods for the Image Rollover application

This exercise asks you to modify the Image Rollover application of figure 7-16 so it uses different events for the event handlers.

1. Use your text editor to open the HTML and JavaScript files that are in this folder:

    `c:\jquery\exercises\ch07\image_rollover\`

2. Run the application to refresh your memory about how it works.

3. Comment out the hover method in the JavaScript, and rewrite the code so it uses the mouseover and mouseout event methods to implement this application. That should take about five minutes.

Exercise 7-3   Develop a Book List application

In this exercise, you'll start with the HTML and CSS for the user interface that follows. Then, you'll develop the jQuery code that makes it work.

Murach products

⊕ **Books for web developers**

⊖ **Books for Java developers**
  - Murach's Java Programming
  - Murach's Java Servlets and JSP
  - Murach's Oracle SQL and PL/SQL

⊕ **Books for .NET developers**

Development guidelines

1. You'll find the HTML, CSS, and image files for this application in this folder:
    `c:\jquery\exercises\ch07\book_list\`
    You'll also find an empty JavaScript file named book_list.js. You can add your code to this file.

2. This application works like the FAQs application you saw in this chapter, except that a list of book links is displayed below each heading. If the user clicks on one of these links, an image for the book is displayed to the right of the list. In addition, anytime the user clicks on a heading with a plus or minus sign before it, the image should no longer be displayed.

3. The HTML for the links of this application is like the HTML for the Image Swap application. However, the links for this application don't require the title attribute since no caption is displayed for the image.

4. The images that are referred to by the href attributes of the links in this application should be preloaded. To do that, you can loop through all the links in the section element. Also, be sure to cancel the default actions of the links.

5. Feel free to copy and paste code from any of the applications that are available to you. That's the most efficient way to build a new application.

IE note: If you set the src attribute of the img element to an empty string so no image is displayed when the application starts and when the user clicks on a heading, a placeholder will be displayed for this element in Internet Explorer. To avoid that, you can set the style attribute of the img element so the display property is set to "none". Then, you can set this property to "block" when you want to display an image. In chapter 9, you'll learn an easier way to set CSS properties using jQuery.

8

How to use effects and animations

Now that you know the basics of using jQuery, this chapter presents the methods for effects and animations. Many developers like these jQuery methods the best because effects and animations are fun to develop and can add interest to a page. As you study these methods, though, remember that the primary goal of a web site is usability, so make sure that your effects and animations don't detract from that goal.

Keep in mind too that it may be difficult to understand how some of these methods work until you see them in action. To help you with that, we've included most of the examples in this chapter in the downloadables for this chapter. So, you may want to run these examples as you progress through this chapter to see how they work.

How to use effects...**232**
The jQuery methods for effects...232
The FAQs application with jQuery effects................................234

A Slide Show application with effects...........................**236**
The user interface, HTML, and CSS...236
Two ways to code the jQuery..238
How to stop and start a slide show 240

How to use animation **242**
How to use the basic syntax of the animate method...................242
How to chain animate methods 244
How to use the delay and stop methods.....................................246
How to use easings with effects and animations......................248
How to use the advanced animate syntax
and the methods for working with queues...................................250

A Carousel application with animation **252**
The user interface, HTML, and CSS...252
The jQuery 254

Perspective **256**

How to use effects

This chapter starts by presenting the basic methods for effects that are provided by jQuery. After you learn how to use them, you'll learn how to use what the jQuery documentation refers to as custom effects. In practice, though, any illusion of movement on a web page can be referred to as *animation*, so you can think of all the examples in this chapter as animation.

The jQuery methods for effects

Figure 8-1 summarizes the jQuery methods for *effects*. These include the show and hide methods that were presented in chapter 7.

For all of the methods except the fadeTo method, the primary parameter is the duration parameter that determines how long the effect will take. If, for example, the duration parameter for the fadeOut method is 5000, the selected element or elements will be faded out over 5 seconds (5000 milliseconds). If the duration parameter is omitted, the effect takes place immediately so there is no animation.

In contrast, the fadeTo method not only requires the duration parameter but also an opacity parameter. The opacity parameter must be a value from 0 through 1, where 1 is the full (normal) opacity and 0 is invisible.

The examples in this figure show how these methods work. Here, the first example uses the fadeOut method to fade out a heading over 5 seconds. Then, the second example chains the fadeOut and slideDown methods to first fade out the heading over five seconds and then redisplay it by increasing its height over one second so it appears to slide down. As you will see, chaining is commonly used with effects to get the desired animation.

The next example shows how fadeTo methods can be chained. Here, the heading is first faded to an opacity of .2 over 5 seconds. Then, the heading is faded to an opacity of 1 over 1 second. This has the effect of the heading almost fading away completely and then being restored to its full opacity.

The last example shows how a *callback function* can be used with any of these methods. To use a callback function, you code a function as the last parameter of the method. Then, that function is called after the method finishes.

In this example, the fadeTo method is used to fade a heading to .2 opacity. Then, the callback function fades the heading back to full opacity. Note in the callback function that the this keyword is used to refer to the heading that's selected for the first fadeTo method. As you will see, though, the callback method often selects other elements for its operations.

Please note that the last two examples in this figure get the same result. However, chaining is the better way to get this result.

Note too that the toggle method in the table in this figure is different from the toggle event method, which is deprecated and will be removed in jQuery 1.9. In fact, one of the reasons why the toggle event method will be removed and the toggle method retained is to eliminate confusion between the two.

Before I go on, you may be interested to know that when you specify a duration with the hide or show method, the effect is implemented by changing the

The basic methods for jQuery effects

Method	Description
show()	Display the selected elements from the upper left to the lower right.
hide()	Hide the selected elements from the lower right to the upper left.
toggle()	Display or hide the selected elements. This method isn't deprecated.
slideDown()	Display the selected elements with a sliding motion.
slideUp()	Hide the selected elements with a sliding motion.
slideToggle()	Display or hide the selected elements with a sliding motion.
fadeIn()	Display the selected elements by fading them in to opaque.
fadeOut()	Hide the selected elements by fading them out to transparent.
fadeToggle()	Display or hide the selected elements by fading them in or out.
fadeTo()	Adjust the opacity property of the selected elements to the opacity set by the second parameter. With this method, the duration parameter must be specified.

The basic syntax for all of the methods except the fadeTo method

```
methodName([duration][, callback])
```

The basic syntax for the fadeTo method

```
fadeTo(duration, opacity[, callback])
```

HTML for a heading that is animated after the web page is loaded

```
<h1 id="startup_message">Temporarily under construction!</h1>
```

jQuery that fades the heading out over 5 seconds

```
$("#startup_message").fadeOut(5000);
```

jQuery that uses chaining to fade the heading out and slide it back down

```
$("#startup_message").fadeOut(5000).slideDown(1000);
```

Chaining with fadeTo methods

```
$("#startup_message").fadeTo(5000, .2).fadeTo(1000, 1);
```

jQuery with a callback function that gets the same result as the chaining

```
$("#startup_message").fadeTo(5000, .2,
    function() {                      // start callback function
        $(this).fadeTo(1000, 1);
    }                                 // end callback function
);
```

Description

- The duration parameter can be "slow", "fast", or a number giving the time in milliseconds. By default, the duration is 400 milliseconds, "slow" is 600 milliseconds, and "fast" is 200 milliseconds.

- The callback parameter is for a function that is called after the effect has finished. If more than one element is selected, the *callback function* is run once for each element.

- Chaining is commonly used with effects. This works because each effect method returns the object that it performed the effect on.

Figure 8-1   The jQuery methods for effects

height, width, and opacity properties of the elements. To show an element, for example, its height, width, and opacity are increased so it appears to grow from its upper left corner. Conversely, to hide an element, its height, width, and opacity are decreased so it appears to shrink from its lower right corner.

The FAQs application with jQuery effects

Remember the FAQs application from the last chapter? That application used the show and hide methods without duration parameters to show and hide the answers to the questions in h2 elements. Now, figure 8-2 shows two ways that you can apply animation to that application.

In the first example, slideDown and fadeOut methods are used with duration parameters to add animation to the application. This is just like the code for the application in chapter 7 but with the show and hide methods replaced by the new methods.

Note here that the toggle event method is used for the h2 headings so the first function is done on the even clicks for a heading, and the second one is done for the odd clicks. Since the counting starts with zero, this works the way you want it to with the answers displayed on the first click, hidden on the second click, and so on. Remember, though, that the toggle event method will be removed in jQuery 1.9.

That's why the second example shows another way to get the same results. Here, the click method is used for the h2 headings. Then, within the function for the click event, the toggleClass method is used to toggle the "minus" class on each click and the slideToggle method is used to toggle the slideOut and slideIn methods on each click. This works just like the example with the toggle event method, except the slideUp method is used instead of the fadeOut method. It also requires fewer lines of code.

The FAQs application as the text for a heading is displayed

jQuery FAQs

✛ **What is jQuery?**

– **Why is jQuery becoming so popular?**
Three reasons:
- It's free.
- It lets you get more done in less time

✛ **Which is harder to learn: jQuery or JavaScript?**

The HTML

```
<section id="faqs">
    <h1>jQuery FAQs</h1>
    <h2>What is jQuery?</h2>
    <div>
        <!-- div content -->
    </div>
    <h2>Why is jQuery becoming so popular?</h2>
    <div>
        <!-- div content -->
    </div>
    <h2>Which is harder to learn: jQuery or JavaScript?</h2>
    <div>
        <!-- div content -->
    </div>
</section>
```

The jQuery with slideDown and fadeOut methods

```
$(document).ready(function() {
    $("#faqs h2").toggle(
        function() {
            $(this).addClass("minus");
            $(this).next().slideDown(1000);
        },
        function() {
            $(this).removeClass("minus");
            $(this).next().fadeOut(1000);
        }
    );  // end toggle
});  // end ready
```

The jQuery with toggleClass and slideToggle methods

```
$(document).ready(function() {
    $("#faqs h2").click(
        function() {
            $(this).toggleClass("minus");
            $(this).next().slideToggle(1000);
        }
    );  // end click
});  // end ready
```

Figure 8-2   The FAQs application with jQuery effects

A Slide Show application with effects

To give you a better idea of how effects can be used, you will now review two different ways that a Slide Show application can be coded.

The user interface, HTML, and CSS

In figure 8-3, the screen capture shows the third slide in a slide show as it is being faded in. In the div element in the HTML, you can see that five img elements provide the slides for the show, and each of these has an alt attribute that provides the caption that is shown above the slide.

In the HTML, note that an h2 element is used for the caption, an img element is used for the slide show, and the div element that follows contains the img elements for the slides. The id attributes for these elements are "caption", "slide", and "slides", and the "caption" and "slide" elements contain the caption and slide for the first slide in the series.

In the CSS that's shown for this application, you can see that the height of the images is set to 250 pixels. In practice, all of the images for a slide show would usually be the same size, but setting the height for all of them ensures that the heights will be the same, even if the widths aren't.

Note too that the CSS sets the display property of all of the img elements in the div element named "slides" to "none". This means that those img elements will be loaded into the browser when the page is loaded, but they won't be displayed. Instead, they will be displayed one at a time as they're moved into the "slide" img element by the JQuery.

A Slide Show application with fading out and fading in

Fishing Slide Show

Catch and Release on the Big Horn

The HTML for the slide show

```
<section>
    <h1>Fishing Slide Show</h1>
    <h2 id="caption">Casting on the Upper Kings</h2>
    <img id="slide" src="images/casting1.jpg" alt="">
    <div id="slides">
        <img src="images/casting1.jpg" alt="Casting on the Upper Kings">
        <img src="images/casting2.jpg" alt="Casting on the Lower Kings">
        <img src="images/catchrelease.jpg"
             alt="Catch and Release on the Big Horn">
        <img src="images/fish.jpg" alt="Catching on the South Fork">
        <img src="images/lures.jpg" alt="The Lures for Catching">
    </div>
</section>
```

The critical CSS for the slide show

```
img {
    height: 250px;
}
#slides img {
    display: none;
}
```

Description

- The images in the "slides" div element will be used in the slide show.
- The caption for each image will come from its alt attribute.

Figure 8-3   The HTML and CSS for a slide show

Two ways to code the jQuery

It should be obvious by now that most jQuery applications can be coded in many different ways. In fact, the biggest problem when learning jQuery is figuring out how to apply jQuery to get the result that you want. That's why this book frequently shows more than one way to get a result, and that's why figure 8-4 shows two ways to code the Slide Show application.

In the first example, the code starts by creating an array of Image objects that store the src and alt attributes of the five img elements in the "slides" division of the HTML. That's done by using the each method to process each of the five elements. Within the processing loop, the attr method is used to get the src and alt attributes from each img element and store them in the src and title properties of each Image object. Then, the Image object is added to the array.

After the array has been created, the setInterval method is used to perform its function (the first parameter) every 3000 milliseconds (the second parameter). Within that function, the first statement selects the caption and fades it out over 1000 milliseconds. Then, the second statement selects the slide and fades it out. But note that this statement includes a callback function.

Within the callback function, the first statement gets a new value for the imageCounter variable, which was initially set to zero. To do that, it increases the counter value by 1 and uses the modulus operator to get the remainder that's left when the counter is divided by the length of the array. For the second slide in the show, that means the counter is increased to 1 and divided by 5 so the remainder is 1. For the fifth slide, the counter is increased to 5 and divided by 5 so the remainder is 0. Since this remainder is assigned back to the imageCounter variable, this means that variable will range from 0 to 4 as the slide show progresses.

Once the imageCounter value is set, the rest is easy. First, the nextImage variable is set to the next image in the array. Second, the src attribute for the "slide" img element is set to the src property of the next image object in the array, and that slide is faded in. Last, the text for the caption is set to the title property of the next image object in the array, and that caption is faded in.

In the second example, the code starts by setting the nextSlide variable to the first img element in the "slides" division. Then, the function for the setInterval timer fades out the starting slide and caption, just as it did in the first example. However, the code in the callback function for the fadeOut method is completely different.

It starts by testing whether the next img element in the "slides" division has a length of zero. If so, that means that there isn't a next slide, and the nextSlide variable is set to the first img element in that division. Otherwise, the next slide is set to the next img element in the "slides" division.

Once the next slide is established, the code sets variables for the next slide's src and alt attributes. Then, it uses the first variable to set the src attribute for the img element that is displaying the slide show and fades it in, and it uses the second variable to set the text for the next caption and fades that in.

This shows just two of the ways that an application like this can be coded, and you'll see a few more in subsequent chapters. When you develop any appli-

One way to code the jQuery

```
$(document).ready(function() {
    // create an array of the slide images
    var image, imageCache = [];
    $("#slides img").each(function() {
        image = new Image();
        image.src = $(this).attr("src");
        image.title = $(this).attr("alt");
        imageCache.push( image );
    });
    // start slide show
    var imageCounter = 0;
    var nextImage;
    var  timer = setInterval(
        function () {
            $("#caption").fadeOut(1000);
            $("#slide").fadeOut(1000,
                function() {
                    imageCounter = (imageCounter + 1) % imageCache.length;
                    nextImage = imageCache[imageCounter];
                    $("#slide").attr("src", nextImage.src).fadeIn(1000);
                    $("#caption").text(nextImage.title).fadeIn(1000);
                }
            );
        },
    3000);
})
```

Another way to code the jQuery

```
$(document).ready(function() {
    var nextSlide = $("#slides img:first-child");
    var nextCaption;
    var nextSlideSource;
    // start slide show
    setInterval(
        function () {
            $("#caption").fadeOut(1000);
            $("#slide").fadeOut(1000,
                function () {
                    if (nextSlide.next().length == 0) {
                        nextSlide = $("#slides img:first-child");
                    }
                    else {
                        nextSlide = nextSlide.next();
                    }
                    nextSlideSource = nextSlide.attr("src");
                    nextCaption = nextSlide.attr("alt");
                    $("#slide").attr("src", nextSlideSource).fadeIn(1000);
                    $("#caption").text(nextCaption).fadeIn(1000);
                }
            )
        },
    3000);
})
```

Figure 8-4   Two ways to code the jQuery for the slide show

cation, one of the goals is to write code that is easy to read, maintain, and reuse in other web pages. The other is to write code that's efficient. Judging by those goals, the second example in this figure is better because its code is relatively straightforward, and it doesn't require an array of Image objects.

Regardless of how you code this application, though, you'll notice that when you run it, the captions and slides are faded out almost simultaneously, not one after the other. That's because the effects for two different elements run as soon as they're started. In this case, that means that one effect is started a few milliseconds after the other, so the fade out and in for the caption runs at almost the same time that the fade out and fade in for the slide runs.

How to stop and start a slide show

To improve the usability of a slide show, you usually provide some way for the user to stop and restart the show. Figure 8-5 shows one way to do that. It stops on the current slide when the user clicks on it, and it restarts when the user clicks on it again.

First, this code sets up an anonymous function for running the slide show and stores it in a variable named runSlideShow. If you look at the code in this function, you can see that it's the same as the code in the second example in the previous figure.

Second, this function is followed by a statement that creates a timer variable that calls the runSlideShow function every 3 seconds. Note, however, that this must be coded after the runSlideShow function because that function is an anonymous function. If this statement is coded before the function, the JavaScript engine will throw an error.

Third, the last event handler uses the click event method to cancel and restore the timer on alternate clicks of the current slide. When a slide is clicked and the timer isn't null, the function uses the clearInterval method to cancel the timer and thus stop the slide show. Otherwise, the timer is created again so the show restarts.

You'll also notice that the slide show stops on a full image, not one that is fading out or fading in. That's because the timer for the slide show isn't cancelled until the current interval ends. Also, the slide show restarts with the next image in sequence. That's because the values of the nextSlide, nextCaption, and nextSlideSource variables are retained, even though the timer has been cancelled.

Of course, there are many other ways that you can stop and restart a slide show. For instance, you could provide a stop/start button that works the same way that clicking on a slide works. You could also add next and previous buttons that would let the user manually move from one slide to the next while the slide show is stopped. Now that you know the basic code for running, stopping, and starting a slide show, you should be able to add these enhancements on your own.

The jQuery for stopping and restarting a slide show

```
$(document).ready(function() {
    var nextSlide = $("#slides img:first-child");
    var nextCaption;
    var nextSlideSource;

    // the function for running the slide show
    var runSlideShow = function() {
        $("#caption").fadeOut(1000);
        $("#slide").fadeOut(1000,
            function () {
                if (nextSlide.next().length == 0) {
                    nextSlide = $("#slides img:first-child");
                }
                else {
                    nextSlide = nextSlide.next();
                }
                nextSlideSource = nextSlide.attr("src");
                nextCaption = nextSlide.attr("alt");
                $("#slide").attr("src", nextSlideSource).fadeIn(1000);
                $("#caption").text(nextCaption).fadeIn(1000);
            }
        )
    }

    // start slide show
    var timer1 = setInterval(runSlideShow, 3000);

    // starting and stopping the slide show
    $("#slide").click(function() {
        if (timer1 != null) {
            clearInterval(timer1);
            timer1 = null;
        }
        else {
            timer1 = setInterval(runSlideShow, 3000);
        }
    });
})
```

Description

- With this code, the user can stop a slide show by clicking on a slide and restart the slide show by clicking on it again.

- So the code for the slide show doesn't have to be repeated, it is coded in an anonymous function and stored in the variable named runSlideShow.

- Because the runSlideShow function is an anonymous function, it must come before the setInterval method that calls it. Otherwise, the JavaScript engine will throw an error.

Figure 8-5   How to stop and start a slide show

How to use animation

Now that you know how to use the basic jQuery effects, you'll learn how to use what the jQuery web site refers to as custom effects. We refer to these custom effects as animation, and that starts with the animate method.

How to use the basic syntax of the animate method

Figure 8-6 presents the basic syntax of the animate method. Here, the first parameter is a *properties map* that's coded in braces. This map consists of name/value pairs. For instance, the first example in this figure sets the fontSize property to 275%, the opacity property to 1, and the left property to 0. Then, the second parameter is the duration for the animation, which in the first example is 2 seconds.

When the animate method is executed, it modifies the selected element or elements by changing their properties to the ones in the properties map over the duration specified. This gives the illusion of animation.

If you look at the starting CSS for the heading that is animated in the examples, you can see that the heading starts with its font size at 75% of the browser default, its opacity at .2 (faded out), and its left position at -175 pixels, which is 175 pixels to the left of its normal position. Then, when the animate method in the first example is run, the heading's font size is increased to 275%, its opacity is increased to 1, and its position is moved to zero, which is its normal position. Since this is done over 2 seconds, the result is an interesting animation, with the heading moving to the right and increasing in size and opacity.

Incidentally, to make this work correctly, the position property for the heading must be set to relative. That means that the settings for the left and top properties are relative to the position the element would be in with normal flow. That position has left and top properties of 0.

The second example is like the first one, but it includes a callback function. Here, the callback function selects the h2 headings on the page and then uses the next, fadeIn, and fadeOut methods to fade in and out the div elements that follow the h2 headings. The one difference in the properties map is that the left property is set to "+=175" which moves the heading 175 pixels to the right of where it started. This gets the same results as the properties map in the first example.

When you code the properties map for a function, you must obey the rules that are summarized in this figure. For instance, you either use camel casing for the property names, like fontSize instead of font-size, or you code the property names in quotation marks. You code numeric values as numbers or decimal values, but otherwise you code the values in quotation marks. And when you code a numeric value for a property like left, pixels are assumed, unless you specify the unit of measurement and enclose the entire value in quotation marks.

For some properties, like width, height, and opacity, you can use "show", "hide", or "toggle" as the property values. If, for example, you code "hide" for the width or opacity value, it is decreased to zero. If you code "show", the width is increased to its normal width or the opacity is increased to 1. And if you code "toggle", the values toggle between the show and hide values.

The basic syntax for the animate method

```
animate({properties}[, duration][, callback])
```

An animated heading that is moving into the "faqs" section

```
jQuery FAQs
        ✤ What is jQuery?
        ✤ Why is jQuery becoming so popular?
        ✤ Which is harder to learn: jQuery or JavaScript?
```

The CSS for the h1 heading

```
#faqs h1 {
    position: relative;
    left: -175px;
    font-size: 75%;
    opacity: .2;
}
```

An animate method for the h1 heading without a callback function

```
$("#faqs h1").animate(
    { fontSize: "275%", opacity: 1, left: 0 },    // the properties map
    2000
);  // end animate
```

An animate method for the h1 heading with a callback function

```
$("#faqs h1").animate(
    { fontSize: "275%", opacity: 1, left: "+=175" },
    2000,
    function() {
        $("#faqs h2").next().fadeIn(1000).fadeOut(1000);
    }
);  // end animate
```

Description

- When the animate method is run, the CSS properties for the selected elements are changed to the properties in the *properties map* that is coded as the first parameter of the method. The animation is done in a phased transition based on the duration parameter.

- To specify a property name in the properties map, you can use camel casing instead of the CSS hyphenation (as above) or you can enclose the property name in quotation marks.

- To specify a non-numeric property value, enclose the value in quotation marks.

- To specify a numeric property value, just code the value. For measurements, pixels are assumed. You can also use the += and -= operators with numeric values, but these expressions must be enclosed in quotation marks.

- For some properties, like width, height, and opacity, you can use "show", "hide", or "toggle" as the property values. These will show, hide, or toggle the element by setting the property appropriately.

- Although color transitions aren't handled properly by jQuery, they are by jQuery UI.

Figure 8-6   How to use the basic syntax of the animate method

Last, you should be aware that jQuery animation doesn't work right with colors. How, for example, do you change a color from orange to black over time? However, jQuery UI does provide for color animations, and you'll learn about that in section 3.

How to chain animate methods

To chain animations, you use the same technique that you use for chaining effects or any other methods. You code a dot operator after the first animate method and then code the second animate method.

This is illustrated by the first example in figure 8-7, which chains two animate methods in the click event handler for a heading. Here, the indentation and alignment of the code is meant to show that the two animate methods are chained. The first method increases the font size and opacity and moves the heading 275 pixels to the right. Then, the second method reduces the font size and moves the heading 275 pixels to the left so it's back where it started.

When you chain effects or animations for a selected element, they are placed in the *queue* for that element. Then, the effects and animations are run in sequence. This makes it easy for you to create some interesting animations.

Note, however, that animations that are coded separately are also placed in queues. This is illustrated by the second example in this figure. Here, the first statement is for one animate method that is applied to the heading (this). The second statement is for another animate method that is applied to the same heading (this). Then, when the user clicks the heading, these animations are placed in a queue and run in succession just as though they were chained, so the result is the same as for the chained methods in the first example.

Now, what happens if you click on the heading two or three times in quick succession? Either way, the animate methods are put in the queue for the heading so they will run two or three times in a row.

In contrast, the third example uses a callback function for the first animate method to provide the second animate method. Then, if the user clicks on the heading just once, it works the same as the other two examples. But if the user clicks on it twice in succession, the second click will queue the second animate method so it runs right after the first. But this may mean that the second animate method will start before the callback method of the first animate method is finished.

As you will see, the concept of queuing is important for some applications, especially when you want to stop the methods in the queue from running. Remember too that there is a separate queue for each element. That's why the fading in and fading out of the caption and slide show in the Slide Show application are almost simultaneous.

A heading with two animations started by its click event

Chained animations

```
$("#faqs h1").click(function() {
    $(this).animate(
            { fontSize: "650%", opacity: 1, left: "+=275" }, 2000 )
        .animate(
            { fontSize: "175%", left: "-=275" }, 1000 )
});     // end click
```

Queued animations

```
$("#faqs h1").click(function() {
    $(this).animate(
        { fontSize: "650%", opacity: 1, left: "+=275" }, 2000 );
    $(this).animate(
        { fontSize: "175%", left: "-=275" }, 1000 );
});     // end click
```

An animation with a second animation in its callback function

```
$("#faqs h1").click(function() {
    $(this).animate(
        { fontSize: "650%", opacity: 1, left: "+=275" },
        2000,
        function() {
            $(this).animate(
                { fontSize: "175%", left: "-=275" }, 1000
            )
        }
    )} // end function
);      // end click
```

Description

- When you chain the effects and animations for an element, they are placed in a *queue* for that element and run in sequence, not at the same time.

- When separate effects and animations are started for an element, they are also placed in a queue for that element and run in sequence.

- When you use a callback function with an animate method, the callback function is run after the animation is finished.

- In some cases, a problem will occur if the user starts a second animation for an element before the callback function for the first animation has finished.

Figure 8-7   How to chain animate methods

How to use the delay and stop methods

Figure 8-8 shows how to use the delay and stop methods for effects and animations. As the first example shows, the delay method delays the start of the next animation in the queue for the number of milliseconds that are specified. Here, the fadeOut effect of the selected heading is delayed for five seconds.

In contrast, the stop method stops the animations in the queue for the selected element. This is illustrated by the second example. Here, the animation is for the hover event of the <a> elements in the HTML. This animation moves an <a> element down 15 pixels when the mouse pointer moves into the element, and it moves it back to its starting location when the mouse pointer moves out of the element.

But what if the user swipes the mouse pointer back and forth over the <a> elements several times in succession? As you've just learned, this will queue multiple animations for each <a> element that will run in succession. This will cause a bouncing effect after the user stops using the mouse, and that's not what you want.

To fix this, the developer can use the stop method as shown in this figure. As the summary shows, this method stops the current animation for the selected elements. In addition, when the first parameter is set to true, the queues for the elements are cleared. As a result, all of the animations for an element in the example are stopped and the queue is cleared before another animation is added to the queue. This stops the bouncing of the <a> elements, which makes the application easier to use.

The second parameter for the stop method causes the current animation to be completed immediately. For example, suppose an element is being faded in when the stop method is executed. In that case, the element is left at its current opacity. If that's not what you want, you can code true for the second parameter so the end result of the animation is displayed. In the case of the fadeIn method, that means that the element is displayed with an opacity of 1.

The delay and stop methods

Method	Description
delay(*duration*)	Delay the start of the next animation in the queue.
stop([*clearQueue*][,*jumpToEnd*])	Stop the current animation for the selected element. The two parameters are Boolean with false default values. If set to true, the first parameter clears the queue so no additional animations are run. The second parameter causes the current animation to be completed immediately.

HTML for a heading that is displayed when the web page is loaded

```
<h1 id="startup_message">Temporarily under construction!</h1>
```

jQuery that fades the heading out after 5 seconds

```
$("#startup_message").delay(5000).fadeOut(1000);
```

Thumbnail images with queues that are still running

The HTML for the thumbnail images

```
<ul id="image_list">
    <li><a href="images/h1.jpg" title="James Allison: 1-1"
        <img src="thumbnails/t1.jpg" alt=""></a></li>
    // four more li elements that contain thumbnail images
    <li><a href="images/h6.jpg" title="James Allison: 1-6">
        <img src="thumbnails/t6.jpg" alt=""></a></li>
</ul>
```

The CSS for the <a> elements

```
a { position: relative; }
```

The stop method stops the queued animations before starting a new one

```
$("#image_list a").hover(
    function(evt) { $(this).stop(true).animate({ top: 15 }, "fast"); },
    function(evt) { $(this).stop(true).animate({ top: 0 }, "fast"); }
);  // end hover
```

Description

- The delay method in the example works as an alternative to the use of a one-time timer.

- If you use the stop method as shown in the example above, you can stop the current animation for each <a> element and clear the queue. This will stop the bouncing effect that occurs when the user moves the mouse pointer rapidly back and forth over the thumbnails.

Figure 8-8   How to use the delay and stop methods

How to use easings with effects and animations

Figure 8-9 shows how to use easings with effects and animations. An *easing* determines the way an animation is performed. For instance, an animation can start slowly and pick up speed as it goes. Or, an animation can start or end with a little bounce.

Right now, jQuery only provides two easings: linear and swing. As you might guess, the linear easing moves an animation at a uniform speed, but the swing easing varies the speed in a way that is more interesting. Fortunately, swing is the default, so you don't need to change that.

If you want to use other easings, you need to use a plugin or jQuery UI. Both provide many different easings that you can experiment with. To show you how to use the jQuery UI easings, this figure provides the basic skills that you need, but you'll learn more about easings in section 3.

To use the jQuery UI easings, you start by coding a script element for jQuery UI. In the example in this figure, this script element gets jQuery UI from the Google CDN. Note that this script element must be coded after the script element for jQuery because jQuery UI uses jQuery.

Then, to use one of the easings that jQuery UI provides, you code the easing parameter for an effect or animation. The location of this parameter in each type of statement is shown in the syntax summaries at the top of this figure.

To code this parameter, of course, you need to know the names of the easings that you want to use. Perhaps the best way to find out what's available is to go to the URL that's specified at the bottom of this figure. This page of the jQuery UI web site not only gives you the names of the easings, but also lets you run a demonstration of each one. That will help you select the easings that you want to use for each type of animation.

The syntax for using easing with effects and animations

The syntax for all of the basic methods except the fadeTo method

```
methodName([duration][, easing][, callback])
```

The syntax for the fadeTo method

```
fadeTo(duration, opacity[, easing][, callback])
```

The syntax for the basic animate method

```
animate({properties}[, duration][, easing][, callback])
```

A script element for getting the jQuery UI library from the Google CDN

```
<!-- the script element for jquery ui must come after the one for jquery -->
<script
    src="https://ajax.googleapis.com/ajax/libs/jqueryui/1.8.16/jquery-ui.js">
</script>
```

Two easings used by the FAQs application

```
$("#faqs h2").toggle(
    function() {
        $(this).toggleClass("minus");
        $(this).next().slideDown(1000, "easeOutBounce");
    },
    function() {
        $(this).toggleClass("minus");
        $(this).next().slideUp(1000, "easeInBounce");
    }
);  // end toggle
```

Two easings for an animated heading

```
$("#faqs h1").click(function() {
    $(this).animate(
        { fontSize: "650%", opacity: 1, left: "+=275" }, 2000, "easeInExpo" )
    .animate(
        { fontSize: "175%", left: "-=275" }, 1000, "easeOutExpo" );
});  // end click
```

Description

- *Easing* refers to the way an animation is performed. jQuery provides only two easings: swing and linear. Swing is the default, and it's the animation that you usually want.

- Plugins, including jQuery UI, provide many other types of easings.

- To use an easing, you code a script element for the plugin library or jQuery UI. Then, you code the easing parameter for a method with the name of any easing that the plugin or jQuery UI supports.

- In chapter 11, you'll learn more about plugins, and in chapters 12 and 13, you'll learn more about jQuery UI.

- For a full list and demonstration of all the jQuery UI easings, you can go to:
  http://jqueryui.com/effect/#easing

Figure 8-9   How to use easings with effects and animations

How to use the advanced animate syntax and the methods for working with queues

At this point, you've probably already learned all of the methods and skills that you're going to want to use for your effects and animations. But in case you are trying to build applications that require more control over the queues, figure 8-10 presents the advanced syntax of the animate method and the methods for working with queues.

When you use the advanced syntax of the animate method, you code two parameters within braces and separated by a comma. In the first set of braces, you code the properties map, just as you do in the basic syntax. In the second set of braces, you code one or more of the options that are summarized in the first table in this figure.

The first example in this figure shows how this works with three options: duration, specialEasing, and complete. Here, the duration option is like the duration parameter in the basic syntax, and the complete option is like the callback parameter in the basic syntax. However, the special easing parameter lets you specify a different easing for each property that is being animated.

Although the use of special easings may be more than you need, you should know that you can also use them with the basic syntax. That is illustrated by the second example in this figure. Here, you just code each property and its easing within brackets within the properties map.

The step option of the advanced animate method lets you run a function after each step of the animation. This makes you realize that an animation is actually broken down into small steps that give the illusion of continuous progress. If, for example, you code the step option with a function that displays an alert message after each step of the first example, you'll see how many steps the animation is broken down into.

The queue option of the advanced animate method lets you execute an animation immediately without placing it in the queue. You can also use the methods in the second table in this figure to work with the animations in a queue. But as I said at the start of this topic, you may never find the need for the advanced animate syntax or the methods for working with queues.

The advanced syntax for the animate method

```
animate({properties}, {options})
```

The options for the advanced syntax

Option	Description
duration	A string or number that specifies the duration of the animation.
easing	A string that specifies an easing function.
complete	A callback function that runs when the animation is complete.
step	A function to call after each step that the animation is broken down into.
queue	A Boolean value. If true, the animation will be placed in the queue. If false, the animation will start immediately.
specialEasing	A map of one or more of the properties in the properties map with their corresponding easings.

The methods for working with animation queues

Method	Description
queue([name])	Get the queue for the selected element.
queue([name], newQueue)	Replace the queue for the selected element with a new queue.
queue([name], callback)	Adds a new function (callback) to the end of the queue for the selected element.
dequeue([name])	Run the next item in the queue for the selected element.
clearQueue([name])	Remove all items that haven't yet been run from the queue.

An animate method that uses the advanced syntax

```
$("#faqs h1").animate(
    { fontSize: "650%", opacity: 1, left: "+=175" },
    { duration: 2000,
      specialEasing: { fontSize: "easeInExpo", left: "easeOutExpo" },
      complete: function() {
          $("#faqs h2").next().fadeIn(1000).fadeOut(1000); }
    }
);  // end animate
```

How to provide easings by property with the basic syntax

```
$("#faqs h1").animate(
    { fontSize: ["650%", "easeInExpo"],
      opacity: [1, "swing"],
      left: ["+=275", "easeOutExpo"] }, 2000
);  // end animate
```

Description

- The specialEasing option of the advanced syntax of the animate method lets you specify easings by property, as shown by the first example. However, you can also do that with the basic syntax as shown by the second example.

- The name parameter in the methods for working with queues isn't needed for the default queue (fx). It's only needed for custom queues that you create.

Figure 8-10　How to use the advanced animate syntax and the methods for queues

A Carousel application with animation

This chapter ends by presenting a common application called a Carousel application. It makes use of a simple animate method, but the setup for using that method is extensive.

The user interface, HTML, and CSS

Figure 8-11 presents the user interface, HTML, and CSS for the Carousel application. Because carousels are so common, you've most likely used one on more than one web site. If you click on the button to the right of the three books in the carousel shown here, the books slide left and three more are shown. If you click on the button to the left of the books, the books slide right to the previous three books.

In the HTML, you can see that three div elements are coded within a div element for the entire carousel. The first of these div elements contains the left button; the second contains all nine of the books that will be used in the carousel; and the third contains the right button.

Within the second div element, you can see a ul element that contains 9 li elements. Then, within each li element, there is an img element for each book within an <a> element. That means that the user can click on each book to go to the page for that book. In this example, the values of all of the href attributes are coded as "newpage.html", but these values would refer to the actual pages for the books in a real-world application.

In the critical CSS for this application, you can see that the width of the middle div element (id is "display_panel") is set to 300 pixels, which is the width of three books. Also, its overflow property is set to hidden, which means that anything that goes beyond 300 pixels (the other books) will be hidden.

Next, the CSS for the ul element (id is "image_list") sets the position property to relative, which means that any settings for the top or left properties will be relative to the normal position of this element. As you'll see in the jQuery for this application, the books that are displayed in the carousel are determined by the value of the left property. The CSS for this element also sets the width to 900 pixels, and the list-style to "none", which removes the bullets from the list items. The left property for this ul element illustrates one of the browser incompatibilities. With IE, this property must be set to 0. With other browsers, 0 is assumed.

Then, the CSS for the list items floats them to the left. This means that the items in the ul element will be displayed horizontally, but the 900 pixel width (100 pixels for each item) will exceed the width of its div container by 600 pixels. Remember, though, that this overflow will be hidden.

The last CSS rule set sets the width of the img elements within the li items to 95 pixels. That means that there should be 5 pixels to the right of each image within each of the li items. If you run this application in both IE and Firefox, though, you'll see that you get less padding with IE than you do with Firefox.

Since there are nine images in total and each li item is set to a width of 100 pixels, nine images require 900 pixels and that's the width that the ul element has

A Carousel application

The HTML for the application

```html
<section>
    <h1>View our Books</h1>
    <div id="carousel">
        <div id="left_button" class="button_panel">
            <img src="images/left.jpg" alt=""></div>
        <div id="display_panel">
            <ul id="image_list">
                <li><a href="newpage.html">
                    <img src="images/book1.jpg" alt=""></a></li>
                <li><a href="newpage.html">
                    <img src="images/book2.jpg" alt=""></a></li>
                // 5 more li elements that contain images
                <li><a href="newpage.html">
                    <img src="images/book8.jpg" alt=""></a></li>
                <li><a href="newpage.html">
                    <img src="images/book9.jpg" alt=""></a></li>
            </ul>
        </div>
        <div id="right_button" class="button_panel">
            <img src="images/right.jpg" alt=""></div>
    </div>
</section>
```

The critical CSS for the application

```css
#display_panel {
    width: 300px;
    overflow: hidden;
    float: left;
    height: 125px; }
#image_list {
    position: relative;
    left: 0px;              // this is required for IE, not for Firefox
    width: 900px;
    list-style: none; }
#image_list li {
    float: left;
    width: 100px; }
#image_list li img {
    width: 95px; }
```

Figure 8-11   The HTML and CSS for the Carousel application

been set to. For this application to work properly, of course, the widths of the div, ul, and li elements have to be properly coordinated.

The jQuery

If you look at the jQuery code for this application in figure 8-12, you can see that it consists of two event handlers: one for the right button, and one for the left. You can also see that the last line in each event handler uses the animate method to move the left property of the slider variable to the value of the variable named newLeftProperty. Since the first line of code in the ready event handler sets the slider variable to the ul element, this means that the ul element is moved right or left based on the value in the newLeftProperty variable.

The trick, then, is setting the value of the newLeftProperty variable each time the right or left button is clicked. That's what the rest of the code in each event handler does. As you study this code, keep in mind that the ul element must move to the left to display the images in the li elements, so the left property will either be zero (the starting position) or a negative number.

Now, look at the event handler for the right button. There, the first statement gets the value of the current left property by using the css method. Then, it uses the parseInt method to convert that value to an integer. The first time the button is clicked, for example, the value will be zero.

The if/else statement that follows sets the value of the newLeftProperty variable that's used by the animate method. If the current value of the left property (which is either 0 or a negative number) minus 300 (which is the width of three images) is less than or equal to -900, the new left property is set to zero. Then, the animate method will slide the images all the way back to the right so the first three images will be displayed. Otherwise, 300 is subtracted from the new left property so the animate method will move the slider three images to the left.

The click event handler for the left button works similarly. After it gets the value of the current left property, it uses an if/else statement to set the new left property. This time, if the current property is less than zero, the new left property is increased by 300. This means that the animate method will move the slider three images to the right. Otherwise, the new left property is set to zero, so the slider is moved all the way to its starting position.

The jQuery for the Carousel application

```
$(document).ready(function() {
    var slider = $("#image_list");   // slider = ul element
    var leftProperty, newleftProperty;

    // the click event handler for the right button
    $("#right_button").click(function() {

        // get value of current left property
        leftProperty = parseInt(slider.css("left"));

        // determine new value of left property
        if (leftProperty - 300 <= -900) {
            newLeftProperty = 0; }
        else {
            newLeftProperty = leftProperty - 300; }

        // use the animate method to change the left property
        slider.animate( {left: newLeftProperty}, 1000);

    }); // end click

    // the click event handler for the left button
    $("#left_button").click(function() {

        // get value of current left property
        leftProperty = parseInt(slider.css("left"));

        // determine new value of left property
        if (leftProperty < 0) {
            newLeftProperty = leftProperty + 300;
        }
        else {
            newLeftProperty = 0;
        }

        // use the animate method to change the left property
        slider.animate( {left: newLeftProperty}, 1000);

    }); // end click
}); // end ready
```

Description

- To get the value of the left property of the ul element, the css method is used.
- The value of the left property for the ul element will range from 0 to -600.

Figure 8-12   The jQuery for the Carousel application

Perspective

Now that you've completed this chapter, you should be able to add some of the common animations to your web pages, like a slide show or a carousel. In the next chapter, though, you'll learn how to use the jQuery methods for DOM scripting that are often used in combination with effects and animations. So, when you complete that chapter, you'll be able to develop more sophisticated animations.

Terms

effect
animation
callback function
properties map
queue
easing

Summary

- jQuery provides methods for *effects*, like fading in and fading out, that let you add *animation* to your web pages.

- The jQuery animate method lets you change the CSS properties for an element over a specific duration. This lets you create interesting animations.

- To get the animation that you want, you often chain one effect after another. This places the effects in a *queue* so the effects are executed in sequence.

- If a user starts an effect for an element several times in quick succession, the effects are placed in a queue for that element. In some cases in which a user is likely to do that, you may want to use the stop method to stop the effects and clear the queue.

- *Easings* refer to the ways that effects and animations are executed over time. Although jQuery provides for only two easings, linear and swing, jQuery UI provides for many more.

Exercise 8-1   Experiment with animation

In this exercise, you'll experiment with effects, animations, and easings.

Review the application

1. Use your text editor to open the HTML, CSS, and JavaScript files in this folder:

   `c:\jquery\exercises\ch08\animation\`

2. Run the application to see how it works. Note how the top-level heading is animated into view from off the page. Then, click on the FAQ headings to see what happens.

Experiment with the effects for the FAQ headings

3. In the jQuery code, change the effects for the FAQ headings so the answers fade in and fade out of view when the headings are clicked.

4. Now, change the effects for the FAQ headings so the answers slide down and slide up when the headings are clicked.

5. Experiment with the durations and effects to see which ones you think are best for usability.

Experiment with the h1 heading

6. Check the CSS for the h1 heading to see that it starts with its left property at minus 175 pixels. Then, check the jQuery code to see that it moves the left property 375 pixels to the right and then 200 pixels to the left, which means the left property ends at zero pixels.

7. Restart the application and note the animation as the h1 heading moves from off the page into its proper location. Then, click the heading to see that the animation is repeated, which moves the heading farther to the right. Click on it again to see that it's repeated, which moves the heading still farther.

8. Restart the application. Then, click on the top-level heading twice in rapid succession. This should run the animations twice in a row, which shows that the animations are queued.

9. Fix the animation for the top-level heading so it always returns to its proper location above the FAQs at the end of the animation. That way, it won't move across the page. To do that, set its ending left property to zero pixels.

Add jQuery UI easings to the application

10. Note that there's a script element for jQuery UI in the HTML for the page. Then, add the easings shown in figure 8-9 to the effects and animations. Does that improve them?

11. After you run the application to see how those easings work, click on the link at the bottom of the page to go to a demonstration of the jQuery UI easings. Note that this opens a new page or tab in your browser. Then, try some of the other easings to see how you like them.

Exercise 8-2   Modify the Slide Show application

This is a simple exercise that has you experiment with the effects that can be used with the slide show in figure 8-3. It uses the second block of jQuery code that's shown in figure 8-4.

1. Use your text editor to open the HTML, CSS, and JavaScript files in this folder:

   `c:\jquery\exercises\ch08\slide_show\`

   Then, run the application to see how it works.

2. Modify the jQuery so the caption and the image slide up and then back down as the show moves from one slide to the next. Then, test to see how you like this.

3. Modify the jQuery so the caption is hidden by the hide method and displayed by the show method, both over an interval of one second. Also, increase the time for displaying and hiding the slide to two seconds, and increase the interval for the timer to five seconds. Then, test these changes.

4. If you're curious, experiment with effects, durations, and easings until you get the slide show to work in a way that you like.

Exercise 8-3   Modify the Carousel application

This is a simple exercise that will test whether you understand the code for the Carousel application in figures 8-11 and 8-12.

1. Use your text editor to open the HTML, CSS, and JavaScript files in this folder:

   `c:\jquery\exercises\ch08\carousel\`

2. The way it is now, nothing happens if you click on the left button when the first three books are displayed. Change this so the last three books are displayed when you click on the left button while the first three books are visible.

3. Modify the jQuery code so the carousel moves one book at a time when you click on one of the buttons instead of three books at a time. Now, what happens when you click on the right button when the last three books are displayed?

4. Modify the CSS and jQuery code so only one book is displayed. Otherwise, the application should work the same way.

9

How to use
the DOM manipulation
and traversal methods

In chapter 7, you learned a few of the methods for scripting the DOM. Now, this chapter presents most of the other methods for DOM manipulation and DOM traversal. Once you master all of these methods, you'll be able to get your DOM scripting applications to work just the way you want them to.

The DOM manipulation methods **260**
The methods for working with attributes 260
The methods for DOM replacement 262
The methods for DOM insertion and cloning 264
The methods for DOM wrapping and removal 266
The TOC application **268**
The user interface and HTML..268
The jQuery 270
The methods for working with styles and positioning ...272
The methods for working with styles 272
The methods for positioning elements..274
The enhanced TOC application..276
The DOM traversal methods...**278**
The tree traversal methods 278
The filtering methods.. 280
A Slide Show application that uses DOM traversal methods.....................282
Perspective **284**

The DOM manipulation methods

In the next four figures, you'll learn how to use the methods for *DOM manipulation*, except the ones for working with styles and positioning. Then, after you review an application that uses DOM manipulation, you'll learn the methods for working with styles and positioning.

The methods for working with attributes

The first table in figure 9-1 presents the methods for working with attributes. You were introduced to the first two methods in chapter 7. These methods get and set the value of the attribute you name. You can also set the value of multiple attributes with a single method by using a map to provide name/value pairs.

For instance, the first attribute example sets the src attribute of an img element with "image" as its id to a value of "book1.jpg". That will change the image that is displayed in the element. In contrast, the second example uses a map to set the values of both the src and alt attributes with a single method. This map, which is coded within braces, is like the properties maps that you used with the animate method in chapter 8.

Finally, you can set the value of a named attribute to the result of a function. If you use a function with the attr method, you should know that two parameters are passed to the function. The first parameter is an index that indicates which element in the set of selected elements is being processed. The second parameter is the old value of the attribute. You should also know that because the function is executed once for each selected element, you can use the this keyword within the function to refer to the current element. This works just like the each method that you learned about in chapter 7.

This is illustrated by the third example, which uses a function as the second parameter to provide the values that the href attributes for the selected <a> elements should be set to. To generate these values, the first statement in the function concatenates the index value of the <a> element plus 1 to the literal "#heading". Because the index values of the elements start with zero, that means that the href values that are returned to the attr method will be "#heading1", "#heading2", and so on.

You can use the last method in this table to remove an attribute from selected elements. To specify the attribute you want to remove, you code its name. This is illustrated by the fourth example, which removes the id attribute from each h2 element within an element that has "faqs" as its id.

The second table in this figure summarizes the methods for working with class attributes, and you were introduced to some of these in chapter 7. As a result, you shouldn't have any trouble using them. Here again, though, you can use a function to supply the values that are required by some of these methods, and these functions receive an index and the old class value.

The first class attribute example shows how you can use the hasClass method to test whether an element has a specific class. The second example shows how you can add a "minus" class to an element. And the third example shows how you can remove a "minus" class.

The methods for working with attributes

Method	Description
`attr(name)`	Gets the value of the named attribute.
`attr(name, value)`	Sets the value of the named attribute.
`attr(map)`	Sets the value of multiple attributes specified by the name/value pairs in the attribute map.
`attr(name, function)`	Sets the value of the named attribute to the value returned by the function.
`removeAttr(name)`	Removes the named attribute.

The methods for working with class attributes

Method	Description
`hasClass(name)`	Returns true if the named class is present.
`addClass(name)`	Adds the named class.
`addClass(function)`	Adds the class specified by the value returned by the function.
`removeClass(name)`	Removes the named class.
`removeClass(function)`	Removes the class specified by the value returned by the function.
`toggleClass(name)`	If the named class is present, remove it. Otherwise, add it.
`toggleClass(function)`	If the class specified by the value returned by the function is present, remove it. Otherwise, add it.

Attribute examples

Set the value of the src attribute of an image to the value of a variable
```
$("#image").attr("src", "book1.jpg");
```

Use a map to set the values of two attributes
```
$("#image").attr( {"src": "book1.jpg", "alt": "Book 1" } );
```

Use a function to set the value of the href attribute of each <a> element
```
$("aside a").attr("href", function(index) {
    var href = "#heading" + (index + 1);
    return href;
    });
```

Remove the id attribute from all h2 elements within the "faqs" element
```
$("#faqs h2").removeAttr("id");
```

Class attribute examples

Test whether an element has a "closed" value in its class attribute
```
if ($("#faqs").hasClass("closed")) { ... }
```

Add a class to the h2 descendants of the "faqs" element
```
$("#faqs h2").addClass("minus");
```

Remove the "minus" class from the class attribute of the h2 descendants
```
$("#faqs h2").removeClass("minus");
```

Figure 9-1   The methods for working with attributes

The methods for DOM replacement

Figure 9-2 summarizes the methods for DOM replacement, and you should already know how to use the val and text methods to work with the values in a control or the text within an element. Note, however, that like many of the methods you saw in the previous figure, you can use the value returned by a function to specify the value or text.

The examples in this figure show you how to use the other methods for DOM replacement. The first example shows how to use the html method to get the HTML that's within an aside element, and the second shows how to put HTML into an aside element. In this case, an h2 element is placed within the aside element.

The third example uses the replaceWith method to replace all elements with "old" as a class with empty h2 elements. Here, the selector gets the elements that are replaced and the parameter supplies the elements that will replace them.

In contrast, the fourth example uses the replaceAll method to get the same result. This time, the h2 element is where the selector normally is and the parameter specifies the target elements that will be replaced.

The methods for DOM replacement

Method	Description
`val()`	Gets the value of the first selected control on a form.
`val(value)`	Sets the value of the first selected control on a form.
`val(function)`	Sets the value of the first selected control on a form to the value returned by the function.
`text()`	Gets the combined text contents of all selected elements including their descendants.
`text(textString)`	Sets the contents of each selected element to the specified text.
`text(function)`	Sets the contents of each selected element to the text returned by the function.
`html()`	Gets the HTML contents of the first selected element.
`html(htmlString)`	Sets the HTML contents of the first selected element to the specified HTML string.
`html(function)`	Sets the HTML contents of the first selected element to the HTML string returned by the function.
`replaceWith(content)`	Replaces each selected element with the specified content. This could be an HTML string, a DOM element, or a jQuery object.
`replaceAll(target)`	Replaces each target element with the selected elements. This is the reverse of how the replaceWith method is coded.

Examples

Display all of the HTML in the aside element
```
alert($("aside").html());
```

Put an h2 element into an aside element
```
$("aside").html("<h2>Table of contents</h2>");
```

Replace all elements that have a class named "old" with an h2 element
```
$(".old").replaceWith("<h2></h2>");
```

Replace all elements that have a class named "old" with an h2 element
```
$("<h2></h2>").replaceAll(".old");
```

Description

- In chapter 7, you learned how to use the val and text methods to get and set values and text. Note, however, that you can also use functions to supply the values and text.

- If you use a function with the val, text, or html method, the function receives two parameters. The first is the index of the current element in the set, and the second is the old value, text, or html of the element.

- The replaceWith and replaceAll methods provide two different ways to replace one set of elements with another set.

Figure 9-2   The methods for DOM replacement

The methods for DOM insertion and cloning

Figure 9-3 summarizes the methods for inserting content into the DOM. For instance, the prepend method inserts content at the start of an element, and the append method inserts content at the end of an element. In contrast, the before method inserts content before an element, and the after method inserts content after an element. The critical distinction is that the prepend and append methods insert content within an element, while the before and after methods insert content before and after an element.

This is illustrated by the first two examples. In the first example, an h2 element is inserted within an aside element. In the second example, an <a> element is inserted after the last <p> element in an article.

The prependTo, appendTo, insertBefore, and insertAfter methods reverse the coding sequence by specifying the target elements in their parameters. This is illustrated by the third example in this figure. Here, all of the <a> elements in an article element are inserted after the h2 elements in an aside element. But note that the <a> elements will be removed from the article element. In other words, the elements are moved, not copied.

If you don't want the <a> elements removed from the article element, you need to clone them before you insert them after the h2 element. This is illustrated by the fourth example. Note that chaining is used in this example. This works because the clone method returns the objects that were just cloned.

The methods for DOM insertion and cloning

Method	Description
prepend(*content*)	Inserts the specified content at the start of each selected element.
prepend(*function*)	Inserts the content returned by the function at the start of each selected element.
prependTo(*target*)	Inserts all of the selected elements at the start of each target element.
append(*content*)	Inserts the specified content at the end of each selected element.
append(*function*)	Inserts the content returned by the function at the end of each selected element.
appendTo(*target*)	Inserts all of the selected elements at the end of each target element.
before(*content*)	Inserts the specified content before each selected element.
before(*function*)	Inserts the content returned by the function before each selected element.
insertBefore(*target*)	Inserts all of the selected elements before each target element.
after(*content*)	Inserts the specified content after each selected element.
after(*function*)	Inserts the content returned by the function after each selected element.
insertAfter(*target*)	Inserts all of the selected elements after each target element.
clone([*withEvents*])	Creates a copy of the selected elements. The parameter is a Boolean that indicates if the event handlers are also copied.

Examples

Insert an h2 element at the end of an aside element
```
$("aside").append("<h2>Table of contents</h2>");
```

Insert an <a> element after the last <p> element in an article
```
$("article p:last").after("<a href='#top'>Back to top</a>");
```

Insert the <a> elements in an article after the h2 elements in an aside
```
("article a").insertAfter($("aside h2"));
```

Clone the <a> elements and insert them after the h2 element in an aside element
```
("article a").clone().insertAfter($("aside h2"));
```

Description

- The prepend and append methods insert the content at the start or end of the selected elements, but within the elements.

- The before and after methods insert the content before or after the selected elements, not within the selected elements.

- If you use a function with the prepend or append method, it receives the index of the current element in the set and the old HTML for the element. If you use a function with the before or after method, it receives just the index of the current element.

- If you want to copy an element before you insert it somewhere else in the document, you need to use the clone method. Otherwise, the element is moved from its old location to its new one.

Figure 9-3   The methods for DOM insertion and cloning

The methods for DOM wrapping and removal

Figure 9-4 presents the methods for wrapping and removing DOM elements. For instance, the first example wraps all <a> elements within <h2> elements, like this:

```
<h2><a id="heading1">The text for the a element</a></h2>
```

The second example wraps just the text of an h1 element with an <a> element, like this:

```
<h1><a id="top">The text for the h1 element</a></h1>
```

The third example removes the first <a> element in an article.

The methods for DOM wrapping and removal

Method	Description
wrap(*element*)	Wraps the specified element around each selected element.
wrap(*function*)	Wraps the element returned by the function around each selected element.
wrapAll(*element*)	Wraps the specified element around all of the selected elements.
wrapInner(*element*)	Wraps the specified element around the content of each selected element.
wrapInner(*function*)	Wraps the element returned by the function around the content of each selected element.
empty()	Removes all of the child nodes of the selected elements.
remove([*selector*])	Removes the selected elements from the DOM. If a selector is specified, it filters the selected elements.
unwrap()	Removes the parents of the selected elements.

Examples

Wrap all <a> elements in h2 elements
```
$("a").wrap("<h2></h2>");
```

Wrap the h1 text in an <a> element
```
$("article h1").wrapInner("<a id='top'></a>");
```

Remove the first <a> element in an article
```
$("article a:first").remove();
```

Description

- The DOM elements for wrapping let you wrap elements like <a> elements around other elements or text that you want to treat in a different way.
- If you use a function with the wrap or wrapInner method, it receives a single parameter with the index of the current element in the set.
- The DOM elements for removal and unwrapping let you remove or unwrap elements.

Figure 9-4   The methods for DOM wrapping and removal

The TOC application

If you're wondering how or why you will use the methods that you've just learned, you will now review an application that should give you some ideas.

The user interface and HTML

Figure 9-5 presents the user interface for a TOC (table of contents) application. It provides a series of links in the sidebar for the page that let the user jump to any of the seven topics in the article. It also provides a "Back to top" link after each topic that lets the user return to the top of the page.

In the HTML for this page, you can see that HTML5 aside and article elements are used to structure the page. But note that the aside element is empty. That means that the jQuery will provide all of the content for the aside.

In the article element, you can see that each topic consists of an h2 element followed by one or more paragraphs. But note that the last paragraph in each topic isn't followed by a "Back to top" link. That means that the jQuery will also have to provide for those links.

After the HTML, you can see the effect that the DOM scripting in this application will have on the HTML. Although the HTML isn't actually changed (the DOM is), this shows the changes that have to be made to the DOM.

First, an <a> element has been wrapped around the text in the h1 element. The id in this element is "top", which means that another <a> element can link to it by using "#top" as its href attribute. In other words, the <a> element within the h1 element is a placeholder that other <a> elements can link to. That's the way HTML works, so the jQuery just has to set up the id and href attributes for the <a> elements.

Second, all of the code in the aside element has been generated by the jQuery. That consists of one h2 element followed by one <a> element for each topic in the article. Note that the text for each <a> element is the same as the text for each h2 element in the article. Note too that the href attributes in these <a> elements are "#heading1", "heading2", and so forth.

Third, an <a> element has been wrapped around the text in each h2 element in the article. Note here that the id attributes in these <a> elements are "heading1", "heading2", and so on. That means that each link in the aside will jump to the corresponding heading in the article when the user clicks on it.

Last, an <a> element has been inserted after the last paragraph for each topic in the article. Each of these has its id set to "#top". That means that clicking on one of these links will jump to the top of the page, because the id for the <a> element within the h1 element is "top".

The user interface for the TOC application

> # 7 reasons why trainers like our books
>
> **Table of contents**   **Modular book organization**
> Modular book organization
> Top-down chapter design   In the first section or two of all our books, we present the core content
>   for the book, which includes a complete subset of usable skills. After the
> Paired-pages format   core content, each section of the book is designed as an independent
>   module. This means that these sections don't have to be taught in
> Performance on the job   sequence. As a result, you can customize your courses by assigning just
>   those sections that you want to teach.
> More practice in less time
>   Whenever possible, each of the chapters is also designed as an
> Complete, real-world applications independent module. When this is true, you can assign just those chapters
>   that are right for your courses. This approach also makes the chapters
> Complete instructor's materials better for on-the-job reference later on.
>
>   Back to top
>
>   **Top-down chapter design**
>   Unlike many competing books and products, most chapters in our books
>   have a unique top-down design that moves from the simple to complex. This

The HTML

```
<body>
    <h1>7 reasons why trainers like our books</h1>
    <aside></aside>
    <article>
        <h2>Modular book organization</h2>
        <p>In the first section or two of all our books, ... </p>
        <p>Whenever possible, each of the chapters is also ... </p>
        <h2>Top-down chapter design</h2>
        <p>Unlike many competing books and products, ... </p>
        <!-- The other h2 headings and paragraphs for the article -->
    </article>
</body>
```

How the jQuery will modify the DOM

```
<h1><a id="top">7 reasons why trainers like our books</a></h1>
<aside>
    <h2>Table of contents</h2>
    <a href="#heading1">Modular book organization</a>
    <a href="#heading2">Top-down chapter design</a>
    <!-- The rest of the a elements for the headings -->
</aside>
<article>
    <h2><a id="heading1">Modular book organization</a></h2>
    <p>In the first section or two of all our books, ... </p>
    <p>Whenever possible, each of the chapters is also ... </p>
    <a href="#top">Back to top</a>
    <h2><a id="heading2">Top-down chapter design puts</a></h2>
    <p>Unlike many competing books and products, ... </p>
    <a href="#top">Back to top</a>
    <!-- The other paragraphs and h2 headings -->
</article>
```

Figure 9-5   The user interface and HTML for the TOC application

The jQuery

When you develop an application like this, you need to plan what has to be done and what sequence it needs to be done in. This is illustrated by the simple plan at the start of figure 9-6. This plan is reflected by the comments in the jQuery for this application.

First, the jQuery uses an append method to add the "Table of contents" heading to the aside. Second, the jQuery uses a wrapInner method to wrap an <a> element around the text for each h2 element in the article.

Third, the jQuery adds id attributes to those <a> elements. To do that, it uses an each method to process each <a> element within the article. In the function for this each method, the parameter named index will receive the index value for each of the <a> elements, starting with zero. Then, the index plus 1 is concatenated to the word "heading" and stored in a variable named id. Last, the attr method is used to set the id attribute of each <a> element (this) to the value of the id variable. As a result, the id values will be "heading1", "heading2", and so on.

Fourth, all the <a> elements in the article are cloned and inserted after the h2 element in the aside. This creates all of the links that are needed. But fifth, the id attributes of the <a> elements in the aside are removed because they aren't needed. Besides that, the duplicate ids would cause errors.

Sixth, the href attributes that are needed are added to those <a> elements. This time, a function is used as the second parameter in an attr method to set the values of these href attributes. An each method could have been used to get the same result, but this shows that jQuery provides many ways to get jobs done.

At this point, the links will work, but there's no way for the user to get back to the top of the page other than clicking on the Back button or scrolling. To fix that, the seventh block of code wraps an <a> element around the text in the h1 element with "top" as its id.

Then, the last block of code uses three statements to add "Back to top" links after the last paragraph for each topic. Here, the first statement adds the links before all of the h2 elements. However, that puts a link before the first h2 element, which isn't needed, and it doesn't put a link after the last paragraph, which is needed. To fix that, the second statement removes the first link in the article, and the third statement adds a link after the last paragraph in the article.

This is a useful application because it will work with any article that consists of h2 headings and paragraphs. On the other hand, it only does what can be done by HTML itself. Worse, this application won't work in browsers that don't have JavaScript enabled. What's most important, though, is that this application should give you an early indication of what you can do when you script the DOM with jQuery.

The jQuery plan

- Add the h2 element for the "Table of contents" heading to the aside.
- Wrap the text of the h2 elements in the article with <a> elements.
- Add the correct id attributes to the <a> elements in the article.
- Clone the <a> elements in the article and insert them after the h2 element in the aside.
- Remove the id attributes from the <a> elements in the aside.
- Add the correct href attributes to the <a> elements in the aside.
- Wrap an <a> element with "top" as its id around the text in the h1 element.
- Insert <a> elements that go to the h1 element at the end of each topic.

The jQuery

```
$(document).ready(function() {
    // add h2 heading to the aside
    $("aside").append("<h2>Table of contents</h2>");

    // wrap h2 text in article in <a> tags
    $("article h2").wrapInner("<a></a>");

    // add ids to the a tags
    $("article a").each (function(index) {
        var id = "heading" + (index + 1);
        $(this).attr("id", id);
    });

    // clone the <a> tags in the article and insert them into the aside
    $("article a").clone().insertAfter($("aside h2"));

    // remove the id attributes from the <a> tags in the aside
    $("aside a").removeAttr("id");

    // add the href attributes to the <a> tags in the aside
    $("aside a").attr("href", function(index) {
        var href = "#heading" + (index + 1);
        return href;
    });

    // wrap an <a> tag around the h1 text
    $("h1").wrapInner("<a id='top'></a>");

    // insert "back to top" <a> tags after each topic
    $("article h2").before("<a href='#top'>Back to top</a>");
    $("article a:first").remove();
    $("article p:last").after("<a href='#top'>Back to top</a>");
})
```

Description

- Because the functions of the jQuery methods often overlap, you can code this application in many different ways and still get the same results.

Figure 9-6   The jQuery for the TOC application

The methods for working with styles and positioning

The next two topics present the jQuery methods for working with styles and positioning. Then, you'll see how some of these methods can be used to enhance the TOC application that you just studied.

The methods for working with styles

Figure 9-7 presents the DOM manipulation methods for working with styles. Like the attr method, the css method lets you get and set CSS properties. You can also use a map to set more than one property with a single method, and you can use a function to set the value of a property. The first two examples in this figure show how to set one or more than one property with the css method.

The various height and width methods let you get and set the heights and widths of elements. These methods vary by whether they include margins, padding, and borders in their measurements. For instance, the third example in this figure uses the height method to get the height of an article element, which doesn't include padding, margins, or borders.

The methods for working with styles

Method	Description
css(*name*)	Gets the value of the named property.
css(*name*, *value*)	Sets the value of the named property.
css(*map*)	Sets the values of multiple properties specified by the name/value pairs in the properties map.
css(*name*, *function*)	Sets the value of the named property to the value returned by the function.
height()	Gets the height of the first selected element. This height doesn't include padding, margins, or borders.
height(*value*)	Sets the height of the first selected element.
innerHeight()	Gets the height of the first selected element including padding but not margins or borders.
outerHeight([*includeMargin*])	Gets the height of the first selected element including padding and borders. If the parameter is set to true, it also includes margins.
width()	Gets the width of the first selected element. This width doesn't include padding, margins, or borders.
width(*value*)	Sets the width of the first selected element.
innerWidth()	Gets the width of the first selected element including padding but not margins or borders.
outerWidth([*includeMargin*])	Gets the width of the first selected element including padding and borders. If the parameter is set to true, it also includes margins.

Examples

Set the CSS color property for all h2 elements to blue
```
$("h2").css("color", "blue");
```

Use a map to set two CSS properties for all h2 elements
```
$("h2").css( { "color": "blue", "font-size": "150%" } );
```

Get the height of an article element
```
var height = $("article").height();
```

Description

- These properties make it easy to get and set the properties for an element and also to get and set the height and width of an element.

- When you get a height or width value, it is returned as a number and pixels are assumed.

- When you specify a number for a height or width value, pixels are assumed. If you want to include the unit of measurement, enclose the value in quotation marks.

- If you use a function with the css method, it receives a parameter with the index of the current element in the set and a parameter with the old property value.

Figure 9-7   The methods for working with styles

The methods for positioning elements

Figure 9-8 presents the methods for positioning elements. Here, the offset method gets the coordinates for the offset position of an element relative to the document window. In contrast, the position method gets the coordinates relative to the parent element (its containing element). These coordinates are returned in an object with top and left properties that give the distances from the top and left of the document or parent element.

For instance, the first example gets the top coordinate for an article element relative to the document. In contrast, the second example creates a new coordinates object and assigns it to a variable named asideCoordinates like this:

```
var asideCoordinates = new Object();
```

This is the JavaScript way to create a new, general-purpose object. Then, the next two statements assign values to the top and left properties of the object. Last, the offset method is used to set the top and left coordinates for the aside element to the ones in the object.

Similarly, you can use the scroll methods to get and set the top and left positions of the vertical and horizontal scroll bars. For instance, the third example uses the scrollTop method to set the top of the vertical scroll bar for the window to zero. This means that the scroll bar will be at the top of the window.

The methods for positioning elements

Method	Description
offset()	Gets the coordinates of the first selected element and returns them in an object with top and left properties. These coordinates are relative to the document.
offset(*coordinates*)	Sets the coordinates of the first selected element relative to the document. The parameter is an object with top and left properties.
position()	Gets the coordinates of the first selected element and returns them in an object with top and left properties. These coordinates are relative to the parent element.
scrollTop()	Gets the position of the vertical scroll bar for the first selected element.
scrollTop(*value*)	Sets the position of the vertical scroll bar for the first selected element.
scrollLeft()	Gets the position of the horizontal scroll bar for the first selected element.
scrollLeft(*value*)	Sets the position of the horizontal scroll bar for the first selected element.

Examples

Get the top offset for an article element
```
var offsetTop = $("article").offset().top;
```

Set the offset coordinates for an aside element
```
var asideCoordinates = new Object();
asideCoordinates.top = 200;
asideCoordinates.left = 100;
$("aside").offset(asideCoordinates);
```

Move the scroll bar for the window to the top
```
$(window).scrollTop(0);
```

Description

- The scroll methods apply to window objects, elements with the overflow CSS property set to scroll, and elements with the overflow property set to auto if the height of the elements are smaller than their contents.

- The scrollTop method returns the number of pixels that are hidden from view above the scrollable area. If the scroll bar is at the top or if the element isn't scrollable, this number is 0.

- The scrollLeft method returns the number of pixels that are hidden from view to the left of the scrollable area. If the scroll bar is all the way to the left or if the element isn't scrollable, this number is 0.

Figure 9-8   The methods for positioning elements

The enhanced TOC application

To show you how these methods can be put into use, figure 9-9 presents an enhanced version of the TOC application along with the jQuery code for the enhancements. This application works like the earlier application but with two enhancements.

First, the heading of the selected topic is enlarged and changed to blue when the user clicks on the link for it so it's easy to tell which heading has been selected. Second, the table of contents moves to the left of the selected heading each time the user clicks a link. That way, the table of contents is always visible, and the users can easily select the next topics that they're interested in. That means that the "Back to top" links aren't needed, although one could be added at the bottom of the TOC.

The jQuery code for these enhancements is in the event handler for the click event of an <a> element in the aside. The default action for the click event of each of these links is to jump to the related heading in the article. But this event handler will add to that default action.

The first block of code in this event handler gets the href attribute from the <a> element that was clicked in the aside, and it assigns it to a variable named "id". To do that, it uses the this keyword to refer to the <a> element that has been clicked. If, for example, the third link in the table of contents was clicked, the id will be "#heading3".

The second block of code uses that id to get the heading in the article. For instance, "#heading3" is a selector that gets the element with "heading3" as its id. Then, the css method is used to set two properties for the selected heading.

The third block of code moves the aside element so it is to the left of the selected heading. The first three statements in this block get the top offset of the selected heading, the height of the aside, and the height of the article. Then, it uses those values to determine what the offset for the table of contents should be.

If the offset for the selected heading plus the height of the aside is less than or equal to the height of the article, the aside is given the same offset as the selected heading. That means that the top of the aside will align with the heading in the article. Otherwise, the offset for the aside is set to the article height minus the aside height, which means the aside will be located at the bottom of the page, but not past the bottom of the page.

The last statement in this block uses the css method to set the top property of the aside to the value specified by that offset. That's what moves the aside up and down the page.

For this to work, the position property for the body should be set to relative, and the position property for the aside should be set to either relative or absolute. Then, the TOC will be positioned within the aside based on the setting for the CSS top property. However, that location will vary slightly based on whether relative or absolute positioning is used for the aside.

Please note that this application will work the same whether you use the position method or the offset method to get the top offset. Note too that this application will work whether the HTML for the links is generated by jQuery, as in figure 9-6, or whether the links are entered manually into the HTML.

The TOC application with the TOC moving to the selected topic

7 reasons why trainers like our books

Modular book organization

In the first section or two of all our books, we present the core content for the book, which includes a complete subset of usable skills. After the core content, each section of the book is designed as an independent module. This means that these sections don't have to be taught in sequence. As a result, you can customize your courses by assigning just those sections that you want to teach.

Whenever possible, each of the chapters is also designed as an independent module. When this is true, you can assign just those chapters that are right for your courses. This approach also makes the chapters better for on-the-job reference later on.

Table of contents

Modular book organization

Top-down chapter design

Paired-pages format

Performance on the job

More practice in less time

Complete, real-world applications

Complete instructor's materials

Top-down chapter design

Unlike many competing books and products, most chapters in our books have a unique top-down design that moves from the simple to complex. This makes it easier for trainees to learn. It also means that you can present the topics at the start of a chapter to make sure everyone understands the essential details, without presenting all of the topics in a chapter. Then, your trainees can learn the other topics on their own or as they're needed on the job.

Paired-pages format

If you page through one of our books, you'll see that all of the information

The position property for the aside must be either relative or absolute

```
body  { position: relative; }
aside { position: absolute; }
```

The jQuery event handler that has been added to the application

```
// change the CSS for the selected topic and move the TOC
$("aside a").click (function() {
    // derive the id of the selected h2 element from the <a> tag
    id = $(this).attr("href");    // get value of href attribute in <a> tag

    // change the styles for the selected heading
    $(id).css({ "color": "blue", "font-size": "150%" });

    // move the aside so it is next to the selected heading
    var h2Offset = $(id).offset().top;          // get top offset of the h2
    var asideHeight = $("aside").height();      // get height of aside
    var articleHeight = $("article").height();  // get height of article
    if ((h2Offset + asideHeight) <= articleHeight) {
        asideOffset = h2Offset;}
    else {
        asideOffset = articleHeight - asideHeight; }
    $("aside").css("top", asideOffset);
});
```

Description

- This application changes the color and size of the heading for the selected topic so it's easy to tell which topic has been selected.

- This application also moves the table of contents next to the selected topic so it's easy to select the next topic. Since the TOC moves, "Back to top" links aren't required.

Figure 9-9   The enhanced TOC application

The DOM traversal methods

The next two figures in this chapter present the *DOM traversal* methods. These methods make it easier to get any of the elements in the DOM that you want to work with.

The tree traversal methods

If you study the table in figure 9-10, you can see that jQuery provides a comprehensive set of methods for traversing (traveling through) the DOM tree. Those methods make it relatively easy to select the siblings, children, parents, and ancestors of another element. For instance, the first example selects the first <p> sibling before the element with "last_heading" as its id. The second example selects the parent of the element with "faqs" as its id.

This set of methods includes a find method that lets you get the descendants of the selected elements that match the specified selector. For instance, the third example in this figure uses the find method to get the span elements within the <p> elements within an article element. Often, though, the find method gets a result that could also be done with a normal selector.

The tree traversal methods

Method	Description
siblings([*selector*])	Gets the siblings of each selected element, optionally filtered by a selector.
next([*selector*])	Gets the first sibling that follows each selected element, optionally filtered by a selector.
nextAll([*selector*])	Gets all siblings that follow each selected element, optionally filtered by a selector.
nextUntil(*selector*)	Gets all siblings that follow each selected element, up to but not including the element specified by the selector.
prev([*selector*])	Gets the first sibling that precedes each selected element, optionally filtered by a selector.
prevAll([*selector*])	Gets all siblings that precede each selected element, optionally filtered by a selector.
prevUntil(*selector*)	Gets all siblings that precede each selected element, up to but not including the element specified by the selector.
children([*selector*])	Gets the children of each selected element, optionally filtered by a selector.
parents([*selector*])	Gets the ancestors of each selected element, optionally filtered by a selector.
parentsUntil(*selector*)	Gets the ancestors of each selected element, up to but not including the element specified by the selector.
parent([*selector*])	Gets the parent of each selected element, optionally filtered by a selector.
offsetParent()	Gets the closest ancestor that is positioned.
closest(*selector*[, *context*])	Gets the first element that matches the specified selector, beginning at the current element and going up the DOM tree. If the context parameter is specified, it specifies a DOM element within which the selected element must be found.
find(*selector*)	Gets the descendants of each selected element after it has been filtered by the specified selector.

Examples

Get the previous paragraph sibling of an element
```
var previousParagraph = $("#last_heading").prev("p");
```

Get the parent of an element
```
var parent = $("#faqs").parent();
```

Get all span elements within <p> elements with an article element
```
$("article p").find("span").css("color", "red");
```

Description

- The tree traversal methods help you select the siblings, children, parents, and ancestors of selected elements in the DOM.

Figure 9-10   The tree traversal methods

The filtering methods

To enhance the tree traversal methods, the DOM traversal methods also include filtering methods. These are summarized in the table in figure 9-11. For instance, the first example in this figure shows how to use the filter method to select only the h2 elements that are in the "best" class. And the second example shows how to use the not method to select all <p> elements except the ones in the "first" class.

The third example shows how to use the slice method to select all of the images in the element with "slides" as its id from the second image through the last one. To do that, it uses an index value of 1, which gets the second image since the indexes start with zero.

In many cases, these filtering methods duplicate the results that you can get with normal selectors and with the find method. For instance,

```
$("h2.best")
```

selects the same elements as

```
$("h2").filter(".best")
```

In some cases, though, the filtering methods can get results that you can't get with a normal selector.

The other benefit of the filtering methods is that they facilitate chaining. This is illustrated by the last example in this figure. Here, the methods are coded over several lines, but the methods could be coded in a single line.

In the first line of methods, the first method is used to filter the set of images in the element with "slides" as its id so it contains just the first image. Then, that image is faded out. In the second line, the next method is used to get the first sibling of the first image, which is the second image. Then, that image is faded in.

At that point, the only object in the set is the second image. Because of that, the method that follows in the chain will be executed on that image. For example, if the method that follows is the appendTo method shown in this example, this method will move the second image to the end of the other images. In this case, though, you want to move the first image to the end of the images so it will be displayed again after the last image in the original set of images is displayed. To accomplish that, the end method is executed before the appendTo method. This returns the set of selected elements to it previous state, which is the set that contains just the first image. You'll see how this works in a slide show in the next figure.

The filtering methods

Method	Description
filter(*selector*)	Reduces the set of selected elements to those that match the selector.
filter(*function*)	Reduces the set of selected elements to those that pass the function's test.
not(*selector*)	Removes the elements specified by the selector from the set of selected elements.
not(*elements*)	Removes the specified elements from the set of selected elements.
not(*function*)	Removes the elements that pass the function's test from the set of selected elements.
has(*selector*)	Reduces the set of selected elements to those that have a descendant that matches the selector.
eq(*index*)	Reduces the set of selected elements to the one at the specified index.
first()	Reduces the set of selected elements to the first one in the set.
last()	Reduces the set of selected elements to the last one in the set.
slice(*start*[, *end*])	Reduces the set of selected elements to the those within the range of indexes that are specified by the parameters.
end()	Returns the set of selected elements to its previous state.

Examples

Change a property for the h2 elements that are in the "best" class
```
$("h2").filter(".best").css("color", "red");
```

Change a property for all <p> elements except the ones in the "first" class
```
$("p").not(".first").css("text-indent", "1.5em");
```

Hide all images in the "slides" element except for the one with index 0
```
$("#slides img").slice(1).hide();
```

Work with the images in a set
```
$("#slides img")
    .first().fadeOut(1000)      // fade out first img element in set
    .next().fadeIn(1000)        // fade in the next element in set
    .end()                      // return to first element in set
    .appendTo("#slides");       // append first element to end of set
```

Description

- Many of the filtering methods duplicate functions that can be done with selectors.

- The benefit of using the filtering methods is that they facilitate chaining. In particular, the end method lets you return the object in the chain to the original selection.

- If you use a function with the filter or not method, it receives a parameter with the index of the current element in the set.

Figure 9-11   The filtering methods

A Slide Show application
that uses DOM traversal methods

Figure 9-12 shows how the DOM traversal methods can be used in a slide show. Here, the slides are img elements that are in a div element with "slides" as its id. Then, the jQuery fades these images out and in to create a slide show.

For this code to work, the position property for the images must be set to absolute by the CSS. Otherwise, the image that fades in will appear briefly to the right of the faded out image before it moves to the left. That's because the fadeIn method starts slightly before the fadeOut method is finished.

To show that the jQuery can be written in more ways than one, this figure presents two ways to run the slide show. In the first example, the first statement uses a slice method to hide all of the images except the first one. Next, the first statement in the setInterval function uses the first method to get the first image. Then, that image is faded out and the next image is faded in.

The key to this code is the end method that follows. It returns the chaining object to the first image after the next method has set it to the second image. Then, the appendTo method moves the first image to the end of the images. At that point, there's a new first image and the chain of methods can start again with that image.

In the second example, the images stay where they are in the DOM, and the eq method is used to select the images that are faded in and faded out. For instance, the first method in the setInterval method fades out the image with an index that's equal to the value of the slideIndex variable. Since this variable starts at 0, this application starts by fading out the first image in the "slides" division.

Then, an if statement is used to determine which slide is faded in. If the slideIndex variable is less than the topIndex value for the slides, which is one less than the length of the images, the next image is faded in and the slide index is increased by 1. Otherwise, the image with an index value of zero is faded in and the slide index is set back to 0. In this way, the slide show cycles through as many images as there are in the "slides" division.

A Slide Show application

The HTML

```
<section>
    <h1>Current Books Slide Show</h1>
    <div id="slides">
        <img src="images/book1.jpg" alt="HTML5 and CSS3">
        <img src="images/book2.jpg" alt="PHP and MySQL">
        <!-- more images -->
    </div>
</section>
```

The critical CSS

```
#slides img { position: absolute; }
```

One way to write the jQuery code

```
$(document).ready(function() {
    $("#slides img").slice(1).hide();
    setInterval(function(){
        $("#slides img").first().fadeOut(1000)    // fade out 1st image
        .next().fadeIn(1000)                       // fade in next image
        .end()                                     // return object to 1st image
        .appendTo("#slides");                      // move 1st image to last
    }, 3000);
});
```

Another way to write the jQuery code

```
$(document).ready(function() {
    $("#slides img").slice(1).hide();
    var slideIndex = 0, topIndex = $("#slides img").length - 1;
    setInterval(function(){
        $("#slides img").eq(slideIndex).fadeOut(1000);
        if (slideIndex < topIndex) {
            $("#slides img").eq(slideIndex).next().fadeIn(1000);
            slideIndex++ }
        else {
            $("#slides img").eq(0).fadeIn(1000);
            slideIndex = 0; }
    }, 3000);
});
```

Figure 9-12   A Slide Show application that uses DOM traversal methods

Perspective

As you have seen, the DOM manipulation and traversal methods let you select elements and script the DOM in a variety of ways. The trick of course is using them to get the results that you want. However, if you can plan the scripting operations that need to be done for an application, this chapter provides the methods that you need for doing them.

Terms

DOM manipulation   DOM traversal

Summary

- The *DOM manipulation* methods let you get and set attribute values. They also let you replace, insert, copy, wrap, and remove DOM elements.
- The *DOM traversal* methods let you get the siblings, children, parents, ancestors, and descendants of selected elements. They also let you filter a set of elements so you can get just the elements that you want.
- The end method facilitates the chaining of methods because it returns the chaining object to the one that was used at the start of the chain.

Exercise 9-1   Modify the TOC application

In this exercise, you'll change the TOC application that's presented in figures 9-5, 9-6, and 9-9. That will force you to use the DOM manipulation and DOM traversal methods. When you're through, the application should look like this:

7 reasons why trainers like our books

Modular book organization

In the first section or two of all our books, we present the core content for the book, which includes a complete subset of usable skills. After the core content, each section of the book is designed as an independent module. This means that these sections don't have to be taught in sequence. As a result, you can customize your courses by assigning just those sections that you want to teach.

Whenever possible, each of the chapters is also designed as an independent module. When this is true, you can assign just those chapters that are right for your courses. This approach also makes the chapters better for on-the-job reference later on.

Table of contents
Modular book organization
Top-down chapter design
Paired-pages format
Performance on the job
More practice in less time
Complete, real-world applications
Complete instructor's materials

Back to top

Top-down chapter design

Unlike many competing books and products, most chapters in our books have a unique top-down design that moves from the simple to complex. This makes it easier for trainees to learn. It also means that you can present the topics at the start of a chapter to make sure everyone understands the essential details, without presenting all of the topics in a chapter. Then, your trainees can learn the other topics on their own or as they're needed on the job.

Paired-pages format

If you page through one of our books, you'll see that all of the information is presented in "paired pages." In each pair, the right page is a figure that contains the syntax, guidelines, and examples, and the left page is text that contains the perspective and extra explanation.

One benefit of this format is that it lets trainees learn at their own pace.

Review the application

1. Use your text editor to open the HTML file in this folder:
    `c:\jquery\exercises\ch09\toc\`
    Note that this file contains the script element that has the JavaScript for this application.

2. Run the application and click on several of the links in the TOC to see how the navigation works. Note that this application doesn't include "Back to top" links after each topic. Note too that when a topic is selected, its h2 heading in the article is enlarged and changed to blue, but the heading isn't reset to its original CSS values when another topic is selected.

Enhance the application

3. The third block of code in the ready event handler adds ids to the <a> elements that have just been added to the article. Comment out this code. Then, right below it, rewrite the code so it uses a function with the attr method instead of an each event method to set the ids. If you have any trouble with this, look at the code three blocks down that uses a function to set the href attributes in the <a> elements of the aside. When you're done, test this change.

4. Add a "Back to top" <a> element at the end of the aside. When clicked, this link should go to the first heading in the article. Note that there's space between the other links and the "Back to top" link, and you can get that space by inserting a <br> element ahead of the "Back to top" link.

5. Indent all of the paragraphs for each topic except the first one as shown above. To do that, set the text-indent property to 1.5em. If you use a DOM traversal method, you can set the indents with a single statement. Otherwise, it's okay to use two statements to get that result.

6. In the event handler for the click event of the <a> elements in the aside, the first block sets the color and font size for the <a> element in the article that has just been selected. Right after that, write one or more statements that reset all of the other <a> elements in the article to the color black and a font size of 120% since those were the starting values in the CSS. (To select all <a> elements except the one that's currently selected, try using the not method.)

10

How to work with forms and data validation

To create dynamic web pages, you use HTML to create forms that let the user enter data. Then, the user can click on a button to submit the data to a web server for processing. Before the data is submitted, though, the data is usually validated by JavaScript in the browser.

In this chapter, you'll learn how to use jQuery to work with forms, and you'll learn how to use JavaScript for data validation in the browser. You'll also learn how to use a validation plugin to validate the data in forms.

Introduction to forms and controls **288**
How forms work 288
The HTML5 and CSS3 features for working with forms 290

How to use jQuery to work with forms **292**
The jQuery selectors and methods for forms 292
The jQuery event methods for forms..294

A Validation application that uses JavaScript **296**
The user interface and HTML..296
Some of the JavaScript for the application 298

How to use a plugin for data validation **300**
How to use the validation plugin 300
The options and default error messages for the validation plugin 302

**A Validation application
that uses the validation plugin**..**304**
The user interface 304
The HTML.. 306
The CSS 308

Perspective **310**

Introduction to forms and controls

A *form* contains one or more *controls* such as text boxes and buttons. The controls that accept user entries are also known as *fields*. In the two topics that follow, you'll learn how forms work and how to use the HTML5 features for working with forms.

How forms work

Figure 10-1 shows how to create a form that contains three controls: two text boxes and a button. To start, you code the form element. On the opening tag for this element, you code the action and method attributes. The action attribute specifies the file on the web server that will be used to process the data when the form is submitted. The method attribute specifies the HTTP method that will be used for sending the form to the web server.

In the example in this figure, the form will be submitted to the server using the HTTP "get" method when the user clicks the Join our List button. Then, the data in the form will be processed on the server by the code that's in the file named join.php. That file will use PHP as the scripting language.

When you use the get method, the form data is sent as part of the URL for the HTTP request. That means that the data is visible and the page can be bookmarked. This is illustrated by the URL in this figure. Here, the URL is followed by a question mark and name/value pairs separated by ampersands that present the name attributes and field values. In this case, two values are submitted: the email address and first name entries.

When you use the post method, the form data is packaged as part of an HTTP request and isn't visible in the browser. Because of that, the submission is more secure than it is when you use the "get" method, but the resulting page can't be bookmarked.

Within the opening and closing tags of the form element, you code the controls for the form. In this example, the first two input elements are for text boxes that will receive the user's email address and first name. The third input element has "submit" as the value for its type attribute, which means it is a *submit button*. When it is clicked, the data in the form will automatically be submitted to the server.

If the type attribute of an input element is "reset", the button is a *reset button*. When that type of button is clicked, all of the values in the controls of the form will be reset to their starting HTML values.

When a form is submitted to the server, the data in the form is completely validated on the server before the data is processed. Then, if any of the data isn't valid, the form is sent back to the browser with appropriate error messages so the entries can be corrected. This is referred to as *data validation*.

Usually, the form data is validated by the browser too before it is submitted to the server. Note, however, that the browser validation doesn't have to be as thorough as the server-side validation. If the browser validation catches 80 to 90% of the entry errors, it will save many round trips to the server.

A form in a web browser

The HTML for the form

```
<form id="email_form" name="email_form" action="join.php" method="get">
    <label for="email_address">Email Address:</label>
    <input type="text" id="email_address" name="email_address"><br>
    <label for="first_name">First Name:</label>
    <input type="text" id="first_name" name="first_name"><br>
    <label> </label>
    <input type="submit" id="join_list" value="Join our List"><br>
</form>
```

The URL that's sent when the form is submitted with the get method

```
join.php?email_address=judy%40murach.com&first_name=Judy
```

Attributes of the form element

Attribute	Description
name	A name that can be referred to by client-side or server-side code.
action	The URL of the file that will process the data in the form.
method	The HTTP method for submitting the form data. It can be set to either "get" or "post". The default value is "get".

Description

- A *form* contains one or more *controls* (or *fields*) like text boxes, radio buttons, lists, or check boxes that can receive data.

- When you click on a *submit button* for a form (type is "submit"), the form data is sent to the server as part of an HTTP request. When you click on a *reset button* for a form (type is "reset"), the form data is reset to its default values.

- When a form is submitted to the server for processing, the data in the controls is sent along with the HTTP request.

- When you use the get method to submit a form, the URL that requests the file is followed by a question mark and name/value pairs that are separated by ampersands. These pairs contain the name attributes and values of the data that is submitted. When you use the post method, the data is hidden.

- *Data validation* refers to checking the data collected by a form to make sure it is valid, and complete data validation is always done on the server. Then, if any invalid data is detected, the form is returned to the client so the user can correct the entries.

- To save round trips to the server when the data is invalid, some validation is usually done on the client before the data is sent to the server. However, this validation doesn't have to be as thorough as the validation that's done on the server.

Figure 10-1   How forms work

The HTML5 and CSS3 features for working with forms

In case you aren't familiar with HTML5 and CSS3, figure 10-2 summarizes their main features for working with forms. These features are already affecting the way some forms are developed, and they will have a greater effect when they are fully supported by all browsers.

To start, HTML5 provides the new input controls that are summarized in the first table in this figure. In general, these controls are implemented as text boxes, but the type attribute indicates what type of data should be entered in each text box. Some browsers already provide automatic validation for some of these entries, and some browsers may add widgets to help users make a valid entry.

If, for example, you use "email" for the type attribute, some browsers will provide data validation for the email address that's entered. If you use "number" for the type attribute, some browsers will add buttons that let the user increase or decrease the current value. And if you use "date" as the type attribute, some browsers will validate the entry, and Opera will also display a calendar widget the lets the user select a date. At the least, these attributes indicate the type of data that the control is for, and that's good for semantic reasons.

HTML5 also provides new attributes for working with controls, and the most important ones are summarized in the second table in this figure. The autofocus attribute moves the focus to the control when the form is loaded. This means that you don't need to use JavaScript to do that. Also, the placeholder attribute can be used to put starting text in a control to help the user enter the data in the correct format. When the user moves the focus to the control, that text is removed.

In contrast, the required attribute causes the browser to check whether a field is empty before it submits the form for processing. If the field is empty, it displays a message and the form isn't submitted. The browser also highlights all of the other required fields that are empty when the submit button is clicked.

If you code a title attribute for a field, the value of that attribute is displayed when the mouse hovers over the field. It is also displayed at the end of the browser's standard error message for a field.

The pattern attribute provides for data validation through the use of regular expressions. A *regular expression* provides a way to match a user entry against a *pattern* of characters. As a result, regular expressions can be used for validating user entries like credit card numbers, zip codes, dates, or phone numbers. Regular expressions are supported by many programming languages including JavaScript and PHP, and now regular expressions are supported by HTML5. The trick of course is coding the regular expressions that you need, and that can be difficult.

To format required, valid, and invalid fields, you can use the CSS3 pseudo-classes that are listed in this figure. For instance, you can use the :required pseudo-class to format all required fields and the :invalid pseudo-class to format all invalid fields.

For simple forms, you may already be able to get by with just HTML5 validation. For most forms, though, you are going to need JavaScript. One reason for that is the HTML5 features aren't supported by all browsers yet. The other reason is that the HTML5 features don't provide for all of the types of validation that most forms need.

HTML5 controls for input data

Control	Description
email	Gets an email address with validation done by the browser.
url	Gets a URL with validation done by the browser.
tel	Gets a telephone number with no validation done by the current browsers.
number	When supported, gets a numeric entry with min, max, and step attributes, browser validation, and buttons to increase or decrease the entry.
range	When supported, gets a numeric entry with min, max, and step attributes, browser validation, and a slider control.
date	When supported, gets a date entry with min and max attributes and browser validation, and may include a calendar widget.
time	When supported, gets a time entry with min and max attributes and browser validation.

The primary HTML5 attributes for working with forms

Attribute	Description
autofocus	A Boolean attribute that tells the browser to set the focus on the field when the page is loaded.
placeholder	A message in the field that is removed when the control receives the focus.
required	A Boolean attribute that indicates that a value is required for a field. If the field is empty when the form is submitted, the browser displays its default error message.
title	Specifies text that is displayed in a tooltip when the mouse hovers over a field. This text is also displayed after the browser's error message.
pattern	Specifies a regular expression that is used to validate the entry in a field. If the field is invalid when the form is submitted, the browser displays its default error message plus the message in the title attribute for the control.

CSS3 pseudo-classes for required, valid, and invalid fields

`:required`   `:valid`   `:invalid`

Two of the reasons why you need JavaScript for data validation

- The HTML5 features for data validation aren't implemented by all current browsers, and the ones that are implemented aren't always implemented the same way.

- HTML5 is limited in the types of validation it can do. For instance, HTML5 can't check whether a field is equal to another one or look up a state code in a table.

Description

- Eventually, all of the modern browsers will support the HTML5 features for data validation, so HTML5 validation will be adequate for some forms.

- Until then, you need to use JavaScript and jQuery and maybe even a plugin to do an adequate job of client-side validation.

- For a complete description of the HTML5 and CSS3 features for working with forms, please refer to *Murach's HTML5 and CSS3*.

Figure 10-2   The HTML5 and CSS3 features for working with forms

How to use jQuery to work with forms

To make it easier to work with forms, jQuery provides selectors, methods, and event methods that are designed for that purpose. However, as the next two figures show, jQuery doesn't provide specific features for data validation.

The jQuery selectors and methods for forms

The first table in figure 10-3 summarizes the jQuery selectors that you can use with forms. As you can see, these selectors make it easy to select the various types of controls. They also make it easy to select disabled, enabled, checked, and selected controls.

The second table in this figure summarizes the val methods that you are already familiar with. They let you get and set the value in a control. For instance, the first example in this figure gets the entry in the control with "age" as its id. The code also parses this entry into an integer before saving it in the variable named "age".

The third table summarizes the trim method, which is one of the miscellaneous jQuery methods. It is useful because JavaScript doesn't provide its own trim method. In the second example in this figure, you can see how this method is used to trim the entry in the control with "first_name" as its id before the entry is saved in the variable named "firstName". The second statement in this example puts that trimmed entry back into the control.

The third example in this figure shows how to get the value of the checked radio button in a named group. Here the selector starts by selecting all of the input elements with "contact_by" as the name attribute. That includes all the radio buttons in the group, since they all must have the same name. Then, it uses the :checked selector to get the radio button within that group whose checked attribute has a value of true. This works because only one radio button in a named group can be selected. For a radio button, the val method returns the value of the value attribute, so that's what's saved in the variable named radioButton.

The last example shows how to get an array of the selected options in a select list that allows multiple selections. First, an empty array named selectOptions is created. Next, the :selected selector is used to get all of the selected options in a select list with "select_list" as its id. These options are then saved in the selectOptions variable.

Notice in this example that there's a space between the id of the select list and the :selected selector. That's because a select list consists of a select element that contains option elements. So the selector in this example selects all the descendant option elements that are selected.

In contrast, there's no space before the :checked selector in the third example. That's because a group of radio buttons consists of independent input elements with the same name attribute. So the selector in this example selects the radio button that's checked in the group.

The jQuery selectors for form controls

Selector	Selects
:input	All form elements: input, select, textarea, button.
:text	All text boxes: input elements with type equal to "text".
:radio	All radio buttons: input elements with type equal to "radio".
:checkbox	All check boxes: input elements with type equal to "checkbox".
:file	All file upload fields: input elements with type equal to "file".
:password	All password fields: input elements with type equal to "password".
:submit	All submit buttons and button elements: input elements with type equal to "submit" and button elements.
:reset	All reset buttons: input elements with type equal to "reset".
:image	All image buttons: input elements with type equal to "image".
:button	All buttons: button elements and input elements with type equal to "button".
:disabled	All disabled elements: elements that have the disabled attribute.
:enabled	All enabled elements: elements that don't have the disabled attribute.
:checked	All check boxes and radio buttons that are checked.
:selected	All options in select elements that are selected.

The jQuery methods for getting and setting control values

Method	Description
val()	Gets the value of a text box or other form control.
val(*value*)	Sets the value of a text box or other form control.

The jQuery method for trimming an entry

Method	Description
trim()	Removes all spaces at the start and end of the string.

How to get the value of a numeric entry from a text box

```
var age = parseInt($("#age").val());
```

How to trim the value of an entry and put it back into the same text box

```
var firstName = $("#first_name").val().trim();
$("#first_name").val(firstName);
```

How to get the value of the checked radio button in a group

```
var radioButton = $("input[name='contact_by']:checked").val();
```

How to get an array of the selected options from a list

```
var selectOptions = [];
selectOptions = $("#select_list :selected");
```

Description

- jQuery provides special selectors for selecting the controls on a form; the val method for getting and setting the value in a control; and a trim method that can be used to trim a user's entry.

Figure 10-3   The jQuery selectors and methods for forms

The jQuery event methods for forms

The first table in figure 10-4 summarizes the jQuery event methods for working with forms, and you have already been introduced to some of these. For instance, the handler for the focus event method is run when the focus moves to the selected element, and the handler for the change event method is run when the value in the selected element is changed.

The last event method in this table runs when the submit event occurs. That event occurs when the user clicks on a submit button or when the user moves the focus to the submit button and presses the Enter key. But it also occurs when the submit method is used to trigger the event.

The second table in this figure summarizes the jQuery methods for triggering (or starting) events. If, for example, you code the focus method for a text box, the focus is moved to that text box, and the focus event is triggered. However, if a handler hasn't been assigned to that event, that event isn't processed. Please note that the names of these triggering methods are the same as the ones for the event methods.

The examples in this figure show how you can use event methods. In the first example, the change event method is used to create an event handler for the change event of a check box with "contact_me" as its id. Then, the function within this handler checks the value of the check box's attr property to see if the check box is checked. If it is checked, the code turns off the disabled attribute of all of the radio buttons on the form. Otherwise, the code turns on the disabled attribute for all of the radio buttons.

This is useful in an application in which the radio buttons should only be enabled if the check box is checked. If, for example, the user checks the Contact Me box, the radio buttons should be enabled so the user can click the preferred method of contact. Otherwise, the radio buttons should be disabled.

The second example in this figure shows how you can trigger the submit event at the end of an event handler for the click event of an input button with "button" as its type attribute. Here, the function for the event handler starts by validating the code in all of the entries. Then, if all the entries are valid, it uses the submit method to initiate the submit event of the form, and that will send the form to the server. This is the method that you've been using in the Email List application in the earlier chapters.

The other way to provide for data validation is to use a submit button instead of a regular button. Then, you can code an event handler for the submit event of the form. Within that handler, you can test all of the entries for validity. If they are all valid, you can end the handler, so the form will be submitted. But if one or more entries are invalid, you can issue the preventDefault method of the event object for the submit event to cancel the submission of the form. You'll see this illustrated in figure 10-6.

The jQuery event methods for forms

Event method	Description
focus(*handler*)	The handler runs when the focus moves to the selected element.
blur(*handler*)	The handler runs when the focus leaves the selected element.
change(*handler*)	The handler runs when the value in the selected element is changed.
select(*handler*)	The handler runs when the user selects text in a text or textarea box.
submit(*handler*)	The handler runs when a submit button is clicked.

The jQuery methods for triggering events

Event method	Description
focus()	Moves the focus to the selected element and triggers the focus event.
blur()	Removes the focus from the selected element and triggers the blur event.
change()	Triggers the change event.
select()	Triggers the select event.
submit()	Triggers the submit event for a form.

A handler that disables or enables radio buttons when a check box is checked or unchecked

```
$("#contact_me").change(                    // the change event for a check box
    function(){
        if ($("#contact_me").attr("checked")) {
            $(":radio").attr("disabled", false) }    // enables radio buttons
        else {
            $(":radio").attr("disabled", true)}      // disables radio buttons
});
```

A handler that triggers the submit event after some data validation

```
$(document).ready(function() {
    $("#join_list").click(        // join_list is a button, not a submit button
        function() {
            // data validation code
            $("#email_form").submit();
        }  // end function
    );  // end click
});  // end ready
```

Description

- You can use event handlers for the focus, blur, change, and select events to process data as the user works with individual controls.

- You can use an event handler for the click event of a regular button, not a submit button, to validate the data in a form. Then, if the data is valid, you can use the submit method to submit the form. That's the way data validation has been done in the email_list examples.

- You can also use an event handler for the submit event of a form to validate data before it is sent to the server. Then, if any of the data is invalid, you must issue the preventDefault method of the event object to cancel the submission of the data to the server.

Figure 10-4   The jQuery event methods for forms

A Validation application that uses JavaScript

To show you how you can use jQuery to work with forms, you will now study a simple Validation application. As you will see, jQuery makes it easy to access the user entries and display error messages. To test the validity of the user entries, though, you need to use JavaScript.

The user interface and HTML

Figure 10-5 presents the user interface and HTML for a Validation application. To use the form, the user enters data into its nine fields and clicks on the Submit button. Or, if the user wants to start over, she can click on the Reset button to return the fields to their original values.

In the HTML for this form, you can see that the id of the form is "member_form" and the Submit button at the bottom of the form is the "submit" type. This means that it will automatically submit the form to the server when it is clicked. As you will see, though, the JavaScript for this form will validate the entries before the form is actually submitted and cancel the submission if any entries are invalid.

You should also note that the HTML for each field consists of just a label and an input element. Unlike the Email List application that you worked with before, those fields aren't followed by span elements. However, span elements will be added by the JavaScript and will be used to display error messages to the right of the user entries.

You might also notice that HTML5 placeholder attributes are used for fields like the phone number field. These attributes can be used to show the user the entry formats that should be used or to provide other entry hints. As soon as the focus is moved to a field with a placeholder, the placeholder text disappears.

On the other hand, this HTML doesn't use the HTML5 type attributes for email, phone, and date entries. That way, you don't have to worry about getting some unexpected validation messages from the browser, like a message that indicates an invalid email address. Instead, the JavaScript will have complete control of the validation that's done.

The form for a Validation application

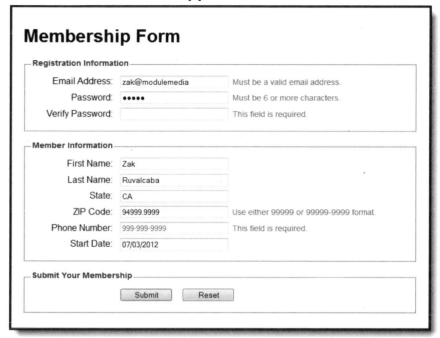

The HTML

```
<form action="register.html" method="get"
    name="member_form" id="member_form">
    <fieldset>
        <legend>Registration Information</legend>
        <label for="email">Email Address:</label>
        <input type="text" id="email" name="email"><br>
        <label for="password">Password:</label>
        <input type="password" id="password" name="password"
            placeholder="At least 6 characters"><br>
        <label for="verify">Verify Password:</label>
        <input type="password" id="verify" name="verify"><br>
    </fieldset>
    <fieldset>
        <legend>Member Information</legend>
        <!-- Four fields are are missing here -->
        <label for="phone">Phone Number:</label>
        <input type="text" id="phone" name="phone"
            placeholder="999-999-9999"><br>
        <label for="start_date">Start Date:</label>
        <input type="text" id="start_date" name="start_date"><br>
    </fieldset>
    <fieldset id="buttons">
        <legend>Submit Your Membership</legend>
        <label> </label>
        <input type="submit" id="submit" name="submit" value="Submit">
        <input type="reset" id="reset" name="reset" value="Reset"><br>
    </fieldset>
</form>
```

Figure 10-5   The user interface and HTML for the Validation application

Some of the JavaScript for the application

Figure 10-6 presents some of the JavaScript for this application. This will give you a better idea of how you can use jQuery for data validation, and why you need JavaScript if you want to do a thorough job of data validation.

The first statement in the ready event handler adds a span element after each input control. To do that, the statement uses the :text selector to select all input elements with type equal to "text" and the :password selector to select all input elements with type equal to "password". Then, the after method that you learned about in chapter 9 inserts a span element after each of the selected fields. These elements will be used to display the error messages.

The next block of code uses a Date object and some string handling to set the start_date field to the current date. That way, the user doesn't have to enter a date if the current date is okay. This type of processing is often done to set the controls in a form to the right starting values. For instance, you can also use JavaScript to set the values and text in drop-down lists.

The rest of the code in this figure is the event handler for the submit event of the form. That event occurs when the user clicks on the submit button or moves the focus to it and presses the Enter key. The code in this event handler contains the validation routines for just three of the nine fields, but that should give you a better idea of how jQuery and JavaScript can be used for data validation.

The validation for the email entry assigns a regular expression to a variable named emailPattern. Later, the test method of this regular expression is used in an else if clause to see whether the user's entry matches the pattern. If it doesn't, the jQuery next and text methods are used to display an error message in the span element for the entry that was created by the first statement in the ready event handler.

The validation for the password entry uses the length property of a string to test whether the length of the entry is less than 6. If it is, an error message is displayed.

The validation for the first name entry uses the jQuery trim method to trim the entry before it is tested to see whether it is equal to an empty string. If you don't use the trim method, an entry of one or more spaces won't be equal to an empty string so the entry will be treated as valid.

After the three blocks of code for validating the fields, you can see a final if statement that is true if the isValid variable is false, which means that one or more fields are invalid. In that case, the preventDefault method of the event object is executed. This object is passed to the function for the submit event handler as a parameter that's stored in the event variable by the first line in this handler. If you don't use the preventDefault method when one or more fields are invalid, the form will be submitted to the server since that's its default action.

If you already know JavaScript, you should understand this code. Otherwise, this shows the need for a complete set of JavaScript skills. If you want to develop them, we of course recommend our JavaScript book. But another alternative for data validation is to use a validation plugin like the one that's presented next.

JavaScript validation

```
$(document).ready(function() {
    // add span element after each input element
    $(":text, :password").after("<span>*</span>");

    // put today's date in the start_date text box
    var today = new Date();
    var month = today.getMonth() + 1;        // Add 1 since months start at 0
    var day = today.getDate();
    var year = today.getFullYear();
    var dateText = ((month < 10) ? "0" + month : month) + "/"; // Pad month
    dateText += ((day < 10) ? "0" + day: day) + "/";          // Pad date
    dateText += year;
    $("#start_date").val(dateText);

    $("#member_form").submit(
        function(event) {
            var isValid = true;

            // validate the email entry with a regular expression
            var emailPattern =
                /\b[A-Za-z0-9._%+-]+@[A-Za-z0-9.-]+\.[A-Za-z]{2,4}\b/;
            var email = $("#email").val();
            if (email == "") {
                $("#email").next().text("This field is required.");
                isValid = false;
            } else if ( !emailPattern.test(email) ) {
                $("#email").next().text("Must be a valid email address.");
                isValid = false;
            } else {
                $("#email").next().text(""); }

            // validate the password entry
            var password = $("#password").val();
            if ( password.length < 6) {
                $("#password").next().text("Must be 6 or more characters.");
                isValid = false;
            } else {
                $("#password").next().text(""); }

            // validate the first name entry
            var firstName = $("#first_name").val().trim();
            if (firstName == "") {
                $("#first_name").next().text("This field is required.");
                isValid = false;
            } else {
                $("#first_name").val(firstName);
                $("#first_name").next().text(""); }

            // prevent the submission of the form if any entries are invalid
            if (isValid == false) { event.preventDefault(); }

        }  // end function
    );  // end submit
});  // end ready
```

Figure 10-6   The JavaScript for validating three entries and submitting the form

How to use a plugin for data validation

If you search for validation plugins, you'll see that there are many of them. Some work with certain types of entries and some work with a wide range of entries. One of the most popular of these plugins is presented next.

How to use the validation plugin

Figure 10-7 introduces the validation plugin that was developed by Jörn Zaefferer, a member of the jQuery team and a lead developer of the jQuery UI team. To download this plugin and to get full documentation and more, you can go to URL that's at the start of this figure.

The rest of this figure shows how to use this plugin for the simple form that's shown at the top of the figure. To start, you code a script element for the validation file. This element must come after the script element for jQuery because it uses jQuery.

In the HTML for the form that will be validated by the plugin, you need to use the name attributes for the input fields. These are highlighted in the HTML in this figure. You also use a submit button to start the processing of the form.

Then, in the JavaScript, you run the validate method of the form. This is one of the methods in the validation plugin. So, when the submit method of the form is activated, usually by the user clicking on the submit button, the validation plugin intervenes and validates the fields of the form.

To specify the validation that should take place, you code a rules map as the first parameter of the validate method, as shown in this figure. For each field that is going to be validated, you code the value of its name attribute in the HTML. Then, you code a set of braces that contains one or more validation options. For instance, the rules for the field that's named email_address specify that the required option is true and the email option is also true. That way, the validation option will first check this field to make sure it's there, and then check it to make sure the entry is a valid email address. You'll learn about the basic validation options that are available in just a minute.

For each validation option, the validation plugin provides a default error message. If you want to change the default messages, though, you can code a second parameter for messages, as shown in this figure. Here, for example, the first set of message options changes the default message for the required option of the email_address field to "Please supply an email address". It also changes the default message for the email option to "This is not a valid email address".

Another way to use this plugin is to embed attributes for the rules and messages in the HTML instead of coding them as parameters of the validate method. Then, you just run the validate method without any parameters. Although this works okay for simple forms, it's usually better to use the technique that's illustrated in this figure. That separates the validation rules from the HTML so the code is easier to maintain and debug, especially for longer, more complicated forms.

The user interface

Email Address:	zak@modulemedia	This is not a valid email address.
First Name:		Please supply a first name.
	Join our List	

The URL for the validation plugin

http://bassistance.de/jquery-plugins/jquery-plugin-validation

The script elements in the head section of the HTML

```html
<script src="http://code.jquery.com/jquery-1.8.3.min.js"></script>
<script src="jquery.validate.min.js"></script>
<script src="email_list.js"></script>
```

The form in the body of the HTML

```html
<form id="email_form" name="email_form" action="join.html" method="post">
    <label for="email_address">Email Address:</label>
    <input type="text" id="email_address" name="email_address"><br>
    <label for="first_name">First Name:</label>
    <input type="text" id="first_name" name="first_name"><br>
    <label> </label>
    <input type="submit" id="join_list" value="Join our List"><br>
</form>
```

The JavaScript (email_list.js) that uses the validate method of the plugin

```javascript
$("#email_form").validate({       // use the id attribute to select the form
    rules: {
        email_address: {          // use name attributes to refer to fields
            required: true,
            email: true },
        first_name: {
            required: true }
    },
    messages: {
        email_address: {          // use name attributes to refer to fields
            required: "Please supply an email address.",
            email: "This is not a valid email address." },
        first_name: {
            required: "Please supply a first name." }
    }
}); // end validate
```

Description

- The validation plugin was written and is maintained by Jörn Zaefferer, a member of the jQuery team and a lead developer on the jQuery UI team.

- One way to use this plugin is to run the validate method for the form and specify the validation rules and messages for the entries as parameters, as shown above.

- Another way to use the validate method of this plugin is to embed attributes for the rules and messages in the HTML. For simple forms, this is easier, but it's harder to maintain and debug.

Figure 10-7   How to use the validation plugin

The options and default error messages for the validation plugin

Now that you have a general idea of how to use the validation plugin, figure 10-8 summarizes the basic options that it provides along with their default error messages. As you can see, this plugin validates email addresses, URLs, dates, numbers, digits, and credit card numbers. It can check to make sure that an entry is within a certain range or that the number of characters in an entry is within a certain range. It can check for valid extensions. And it can check to make sure one entry is equal to another entry.

Unfortunately, that doesn't provide for every type of entry that a form might require, and it doesn't do every validation the way you might want it to. One way to add to this list is to use the additional-methods file that can be downloaded from the validation web site. This file, for example, adds phoneUS and phoneUK options. You'll see this file used in the application at the end of this chapter.

Another option is to write your own methods for this plugin. You can also use some of the customizing options that are presented in the plugin. But the more time you spend going beyond what's readily available, the less valuable the use of this plugin becomes. At some point, then, you're probably better off writing your own data validation code in JavaScript so your forms will work exactly the way you want them to.

Remember, though, that the browser validation doesn't have to perfect. If it catches most of the errors in a form, that may be good enough. Then, the server validation can finish the job.

This figure also shows how the validation plugin adds error messages to your HTML. To do that, it just adds a label element with the class attribute set to "error" after each input element with the text set to the error message. As a result, you can use CSS to specify the formatting for the messages in the "error" class.

The validation options for the validation method of the plugin

Option	Default message
`required: true`	This field is required.
`email: true`	Please enter a valid email address.
`url: true`	Please enter a valid URL.
`date: true`	Please enter a valid date.
`dateISO: true`	Please enter a valid date (ISO).
`number: true`	Please enter a valid number.
`digits: true`	Please enter only digits.
`creditcard: true`	Please enter a valid credit card number.
`equalTo: "selector"`	Please enter the same value again.
`accept: "extension1|` `        extension2|..."`	Please enter a value with a valid extension.
`maxlength: value`	Please enter no more than (value) characters.
`minlength: value`	Please enter at least (value) characters.
`rangelength: [value1, value2]`	Please enter a value between (value1) and (value2) characters long.
`range: [value1, value2]`	Please enter a value between (value1) and (value2).
`max: value`	Please enter a value less than or equal to (value).
`min: value`	Please enter a value greater than or equal to (value).

Examples of options in a validate event handler

```
$("#email_form").validate({
    rules: {
        email_address2: { equalTo: "#email_address1" },
        number: { max: 100 },
        message: { rangelength: [2, 140] },
        upload: { accept: "jpg|gif" }
    }
}); // end validate
```

How the validation plugin adds an error message for a field

The HTML for a text box

```
<input type="text" id="email_address2" name="email_address2"><br>
```

The label that gets added to the DOM if the email address is invalid

```
<input type="text" id="email_address2" name="email_address2">
<label class="error">Please enter a valid email address.</label><br>
```

Description

- The basic options of the validation plugin are adequate for the client-side validation of many forms. The additional-methods file of this plugin also provides some other options, like the phoneUS and phoneUK options for validating phone numbers.

- When the validation method finds an error, it inserts a label element into the DOM right after the input element that has the invalid data. This label displays the error message, and this label is removed from the DOM when the error is corrected. To format the error messages with CSS, you can select labels that have the class attribute set to "error".

Figure 10-8   The options and default error messages for the validation plugin

A Validation application that uses the validation plugin

To give you a better idea of when and how to use the validation plugin, this chapter ends with a Validation application that uses this plugin.

The user interface

Figure 10-9 presents the user interface for this application. Here, you can see that the interface has a few more fields than the one you saw earlier. That will give you a better indication of the strengths and limitations of the validation plugin.

If you look at the expiration date fields near the bottom of the form, you can see that drop-down lists are used for month and year. That way, the user can't enter a month and year in the wrong format. Of course, the user can enter a year and month that are incorrect, but validation code can't catch that type of error.

If you look at the credit card type field, you can see that it uses another drop-down list. Here again, this means that the user can't enter an invalid credit card type. This shows that using check boxes, radio buttons, and drop-down lists usually eliminates the need for validation.

If you refer to the list of options in the previous figure, though, you can see that the validation plugin doesn't provide for all of the validation that this form requires. In particular, it doesn't have an option for state code, zip code, phone number, and requested start date, and the error messages that are displayed for these fields show that.

By using the additional-methods file, as shown in the next two figures, you can provide validation for a US phone number. Remember that you can also customize the error messages as shown in figure 10-7. But you're still left to decide whether the rest of the validation is adequate for your purposes.

The Validation application

Membership Form

Registration Information

Email Address:	zak@modulemedia	Please enter a valid email address.
Password:	••••	Please enter at least 6 characters.
Verify Password:		This field is required.

Member Information

First Name:	Zak	
Last Name:		This field is required.
State:	CAL	Please enter a value between 2 and 2 characters long.
ZIP Code:	9372	Please enter a value between 5 and 10 characters long.
Phone Number:	555-555-55555	Please specify a valid phone number

Payment Information

Requested Start Date:	07/05/2012	
Credit Card Type:	Visa ▾	
Credit Card Number:	1234123412341234	Please enter a valid credit card number.
Expiration Date:	01 ▾ 2012 ▾	

Submit Your Membership

Submit   Reset

Fields that aren't adequately validated by the basic plugin options

- State code, zip code, phone number, and requested start date

Description

- When the user clicks the Submit button, the validation plugin tests the fields in the form for validity based on the options you have set. Then, it displays any error messages to the right of the invalid fields.

- Using just the basic options of the validation plugin, you can do 80% or more of the validation for a form like this. With the additional-methods file, you can do even more.

- In general, you don't need to validate radio buttons, check boxes, and select lists because they only allow valid entries.

- To avoid the need for validating an entry like a state code, you can replace its text box with a drop-down list that includes only the valid codes.

- To avoid the need for validating date entries, you can use drop-down lists for month, day, and year or a jQuery UI calendar widget (see chapter 12).

Figure 10-9   The Validation application with the validation plugin

The HTML

Figure 10-10 presents the HTML for this form. In the head section, you can see the script element for jQuery, followed by one for the validation plugin, followed by one for the additional-methods file, followed by one for the JavaScript file that initiates the processing. This sequence is essential because each file calls methods in the previous file.

In the HTML for the form, a submit button is used to submit the form to the server. That means that the validation plugin has to cancel the default action of the form if it finds errors.

If you look at the code for the individual text fields, you can see that name attributes are coded for all of them. That's because the validation plugin uses those names. You can also see that the fields aren't followed by elements that will display the error messages. That's because the validation plugin will add label elements for the messages whenever they're needed.

The script elements for the validate and additional-methods plugins

```
<script src="http://code.jquery.com/jquery-1.8.3.min.js"></script>
<script src="jquery.validate.min.js"></script>
<script src="additional-methods.min.js"></script>
<script src="member.js"></script>
```

The form element in the body of the HTML

```
<form action="register.html" method="get"
    name="member_form" id="member_form">
    <fieldset>
        <legend>Registration Information</legend>
        <label for="email">Email Address:</label>
        <input type="text" name="email" id="email" autofocus><br>
        <label for="password">Password:</label>
        <input type="password" name="password" id="password"
                placeholder="At least 6 characters"><br>
        <label for="verify">Verify Password:</label>
        <input type="password" name="verify" id="verify"><br>
    </fieldset>
    <fieldset>
        <legend>Member Information</legend>
        <!-- Four fields are missing here -->
        <input type="text" name="phone" id="phone"
                placeholder="999-999-9999"><br>
    </fieldset>
    <fieldset>
        <legend>Payment Information</legend>
        <label for="start_date">Requested Start Date:</label>
        <input type="text" name="start_date" id="start_date"
                placeholder="99/99/9999"><br>
        <label for="payment_type">Payment Type:</label>
        <select name="payment_type" id="payment_type">
            <option value="v">Visa</option>
            <option value="m">Master Card</option>
            <option value="x">American Express</option>
        </select><br>
        <label for="card_number">Credit Card Number:</label>
        <input type="text" name="card_number" id="card_number"><br>
        <select name="expiry_month" id="expiry_month">
            <option value="01">01</option>
            <option value="02">02</option>
            <!-- The rest of the option elements for months -->
        </select>
        <select name="expiry_year" id="expiry_year">
            <option value="2012">2012</option>
            <option value="2013">2013</option>
            <!-- The rest of the option elements for years -->
        </select><br>
    </fieldset>
    <fieldset id="buttons">
        <legend>Submit Your Membership</legend>
        <label> </label>
        <input type="submit" id="submit" value="Submit">
        <input type="reset" id="reset" value="Reset"><br>
    </fieldset>
</form>
```

Figure 10-10   The HTML for the Validation application

The CSS

Figure 10-11 starts by showing the CSS for the labels that are used by the validation error messages. The float property indicates that these labels shouldn't be floated. To understand how this works, you need to remember that the labels that identify the text fields are floated to the left of the text fields. However, you want the error labels to appear to the right of the text fields, and setting the float property to "none" accomplishes that.

The next two properties set the color for the error messages to red and reduce their font size to 87.5% so the long messages will fit into the space provided. Of course, you can set the CSS for these labels any way you want, which lets you control where and how they're displayed.

The jQuery

Figure 10-11 also presents the jQuery for this form. Before the validate method, you can code any setup operations for the form like moving the focus to the first field on the form, setting the starting dates, or loading the options of the drop-down lists.

Then, you code the validate method for the form along with its rules as the first parameter. Here, the phoneUS method is one of the methods in the additional-methods file, and it does a good job of validating a US phone number. Most of the other validation is adequate too, but the validation for the state code and zip code could be improved, especially since the zip code in this application can be either a five- or a nine-digit code.

For most forms, you will also want to provide some custom error messages, as shown in figure 10-7. For instance, you could change the message for the state code from "Please enter a value between 2 and 2 characters long" to something like "Please enter a two-character state code."

The CSS for the error messages of the plugin

```
label.error {
    float: none;
    color: red;
    font-size: 87.5%;
}
```

The jQuery for the Validation application

```
$(document).ready(function() {
    $("#email").focus();

    // other setup processing can go here

    $("#member_form").validate({
        rules: {
            email: {
                required: true,
                email: true
            },
            password: {
                required: true,
                minlength: 6
            },
            verify: {
                required: true,
                equalTo: "#password"
            },
            first_name: {
                required: true
            },
            last_name: {
                required: true
            },
            state: {
                required: true,
                rangelength: [2, 2]
            },
            zip: {
                required: true,
                rangelength: [5, 10]
            },
            phone: {
                required: true,
                phoneUS: true
            },
            start_date: {
                required: true,
                date: true
            },
            card_number: {
                required: true,
                creditcard: true
            }
        }
    }); // end validate
}); // end ready
```

Figure 10-11   The CSS and jQuery for the Validation application

Perspective

At this point, you should be comfortable with the jQuery features for working with forms, and you should understand the differences between writing your own JavaScript code for validation and using a validation plugin. Eventually, you will probably want to learn more about JavaScript so you can write your own data validation code. When that day comes, please remember our JavaScript book.

Terms

form	reset button
control	data validation
field	regular expression
submit button	pattern

Summary

- A *form* contains one or more *controls* like text boxes, radio buttons, or check boxes that can receive data. These controls are also referred to as *fields*. When a form is submitted to the server for processing, the data in the controls is sent along with the HTTP request.

- A *submit button* submits the form data to the server when the button is clicked. A *reset button* resets all the data in the form when it is clicked.

- HTML5 introduces some input controls like the email, url, tel, and date controls that are good semantically because they indicate what types of data the controls are for. HTML5 also introduces some attributes for *data validation*, and CSS3 introduces some pseudo-classes for formatting required, valid, and invalid fields.

- When a form is submitted to the server, the server script should provide complete validation of the data in the form and return the form to the client if any errors are found.

- Before a form is submitted to the server, JavaScript should try to catch 80% or more of the entry errors. That will reduce the number of trips to the server and back that are required to process the form.

- jQuery provides some selectors, methods, and event methods for working with forms, but nothing for data validation. So, to validate the entries that a user makes, many developers use JavaScript features like *regular expressions* and string methods that aren't presented in this book.

- Another way to validate the user entries in a form is to use a validation plugin. That usually makes it easier to add validation to a form, but the validation may not be adequate for all forms.

Exercise 10-1   Validate with JavaScript

Since you already know how to validate some types of fields with JavaScript, most of the code for this exercise is provided for you. However, you will make some enhancements to this code. The form that you will be working with looks like this:

Please join our email list

Email Address:	ed@yahoocom	Must be a valid email address.
Re-enter Email Address:	ed@yaho.com	Must equal first email entry.
First Name:		
Last Name:	Koop	
2-Character State Code:	cal	Use 2-character code.
5-Digit Zip Code:	1234567	Use 99999 format.

[Join our List]   [Reset]

1. Use your text editor to open the HTML and JavaScript files in this folder:
   `c:\jquery\exercises\ch10\email_list_javascript\`

2. In the HTML file, note that span elements aren't coded after each input field. In the JavaScript file, then, add a statement that adds a span element after each input field. The contents of each span element should be an asterisk. To do this, you need to use a statement similar to the first one in figure 10-6.

3. Review the code in the JavaScript file and note that it contains validation routines for the first five fields. Then, test this form by clicking the Join our List button before you enter any data in this form. Oops! The data is submitted even though no entries have been made.

4. To fix this, you must stop the default action of the submit button. To do that, code the preventDefault method of the event object in the if statement at the end of the file, as in figure 10-6. Remember that the name that you use for the event object must be the same as the name of the parameter that's used for the submit event handler. Now, test again with empty fields. This should display "This field is required" to the right of each field except the zip-code field.

5. Enter four spaces in the first-name field and click the Join our List button again. Note that the error message is removed, which means the four spaces have been accepted as a valid entry.

6. Fix this problem by trimming the first-name entry before it is validated, as in the code for the last-name entry. This trimmed value should also be placed in the text box if the entry is valid. Test this enhancement by first entering just four spaces in this field and then by entering four spaces followed by a first name.

7. Add the code for validating the zip-code field by testing to make sure it consists of five characters. To do this, you can copy and modify the code that's used to validate the state-code field. Now, test this change.

Exercise 10-2   Use the validation plugin

This exercise will give you a chance to use the validation plugin that's presented in figures 10-7 through 10-11. You will use this plugin to validate the data in a form that looks like this:

Please join our email list

Email Address:	ed@yahoo.com
Re-enter Email Address:	ed@yaho.com This entry must equal previous entry.
First Name:	Ed
Last Name:	Koop
2-Character State Code:	cal Please enter a 2-character state code.
5-Digit Zip Code:	123456 Please enter a 5-digit zip code.

[Join our List]   [Reset]

1. Use your text editor to open the HTML, CSS, and JavaScript files in this folder:

   `c:\jquery\exercises\ch10\email_list_plugin\`

2. In the index file, note the script element for the validation plugin. Note too that the folder for this application includes that plugin file.

3. In the JavaScript file, add the code for using the validation plugin to edit the six fields in the form above. The validation should be as follows:

   All of the fields are required.

   The first two fields should be valid email addresses, and the second email address should be the same as the first.

   The state code should be a two-character code.

   The zip code should be a five-digit number, so it should be tested both for digits and five characters.

4. Test the validation that's done and note that the messages aren't displayed how or where you want them. To fix that, add the CSS code at the top of figure 10-11 to the CSS file. You may also want to add a margin-left property to the rule set that puts some space before the error messages.

5. Test the validation again and note the default messages that are displayed. Then, replace the default messages with the three custom messages that are shown above. You can use figure 10-7 as a guide for doing that.

6. Note that the validation for the state and zip codes could be improved by using JavaScript to do lookups. But remember that all entries will be thoroughly validated by the server-side code. As a result, client-side validation at this level is usually acceptable.

How to create
and use plugins

One quick way to improve your web development productivity is to use plugins.
As you will see, plugins are available for all of the common web development
tasks, and many of them are easy to use. Often, the use of plugins can save you
many hours of development time, and most plugins are likely to do their tasks
even better than your code might have done them.

In chapter 8, for example, you learned how to use a plugin for easings.
And in chapter 10, you learned how to use a plugin for form validation. Now,
in this chapter, you'll first learn the skills for using any jQuery plugin. Then,
you'll learn how to create your own plugins.

Introduction to plugins **314**
How to find jQuery plugins 314
Some of the most useful plugins..316
How to use any plugin 318

How to use four of the most useful plugins **320**
How to use the Lightbox plugin for images 320
How to use the bxSlider plugin for carousels............................322
How to use the Cycle plugin for slide shows.............................324
How to use the jLayout plugin for two-column layouts 326

How to create your own plugins **328**
The structure of a plugin 328
How to code a plugin that highlights menu items......................330
How to add options to a plugin...332

A web page that uses two plugins..................................**334**
The user interface 334
The script elements..334
The HTML for the elements used by the plugins.......................336
The jQuery for using the plugins...336

Perspective **338**

Introduction to plugins

In this introduction, you'll learn how to find and use plugins. A *plugin* is just a JavaScript application that does one web task or a set of related web tasks. A plugin makes use of the jQuery library, and most plugins can save you many hours of development time.

How to find jQuery plugins

Figure 11-1 starts with a screen capture that shows the results of a Google search for "jquery plugin form validation". Here, you can see the first three items in the search results. In most cases, a Google search is the best way to find what you're looking for. Note, however, that the search entry includes the word *jquery* because there are other types of plugins.

Another way to find the type of plugin that you're looking for is to go to the URLs for the web sites in the table in this figure. The first one is for the jQuery Plugin Repository, which is part of the jQuery web site, and the second one is for a site that is only for jQuery plugins.

In contrast, the next three web sites are repositories for many types of code, including jQuery plugins. As a result, you must search for jQuery plugins to find what you want on these sites.

In most cases, jQuery plugins are free or are available for a small price or donation. Besides that, jQuery plugins can often save you hours of development time and do the jobs better than you would have done them with your own code. For those reasons, it makes sense to look for a plugin whenever you need to add a common function to your web site.

A Google search for validation plugins

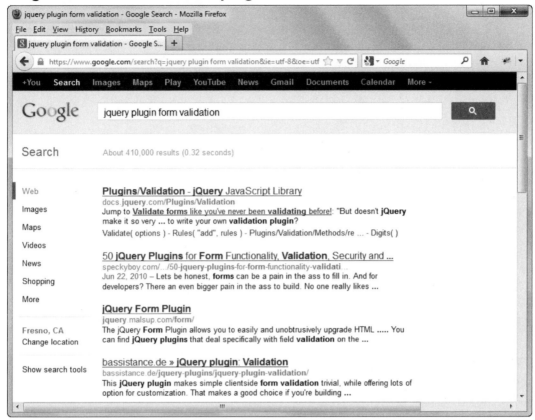

Web sites for finding jQuery plugins

Site name	URL
jQuery Plugin Repository	http://plugins.jquery.com
jQuery Plugins	http://www.jqueryplugins.com
Google Code	http://code.google.com
GitHub	https://github.com
Sourceforge	http://sourceforge.net

Description

- jQuery *plugins* are JavaScript applications that extend the functionality of jQuery. These plugins require the use of the core jQuery library.

- Plugins are available for hundreds of web functions like slide shows, carousels, tabs, menus, text layout, data validation, and mobile application development.

- Some of the web sites that provide jQuery plugins are listed above. Often, though, you can find what you're looking for by doing a Google search.

- In general, if you can find a plugin for doing what you want, that's better than writing the jQuery code yourself.

Figure 11-1   How to find jQuery plugins

Some of the most useful plugins

Figure 11-2 summarizes some of the most useful plugins. These are grouped by type of plugin. In a moment, you'll see examples from the first three groups. In chapter 10, you learned how to use the validation plugin for forms that's in the fourth group. In section 3, you'll learn how to use the jQuery UI plugin that's in the fifth group. And in section 5, you'll learn how to use the jQuery Mobile plugin that's in the sixth group.

Some of the most useful plugins

Plugins for displaying images	
Lightbox	http://lokeshdhakar.com/projects/lightbox2/
Fancybox	http://fancybox.net
ThickBox	http://jquery.com/demo/thickbox
ColorBox	http://www.jacklmoore.com/colorbox
Shadowbox.js	http://www.shadowbox-js.com
Plugins for slide shows, carousels, and galleries	
bxSlider	http://bxslider.com
Malsup jQuery Cycle	http://jquery.malsup.com/cycle
jCarousel	http://sorgalla.com/jcarousel
Nivo Slider	http://nivo.dev7studios.com
Galleria	http://galleria.io
AD Gallery	http://coffeescripter.com/code/ad-gallery
Plugins for text layout	
UI Layout	http://layout.jquery-dev.net
Masonry	http://masonry.desandro.com
Columnizer	http://welcome.totheinter.net/columnizer-jquery-plugin
jsColumns	http://code.google.com/p/js-columns
jLayout	http://www.bramstein.com/projects/jlayout/jquery-plugin.html
Plugins for forms	
Malsup jQuery Form	http://jquery.malsup.com/form
Ideal Forms	http://code.google.com/p/idealforms
Bassistance Validation	http://bassistance.de/jquery-plugins/jquery-plugin-validation
jqTransform	http://www.dfc-e.com/metiers/multimedia/opensource/jqtransform
Niceforms	http://www.emblematiq.com/lab/niceforms
Plugins for interface design	
jQuery UI	http://plugins.jquery.com
Wijmo	http://wijmo.com
Plugins for mobile development	
jQuery Mobile	http://www.jquerymobile.com
jQTouch	http://www.jqtouch.com

Description

- The table above lists some of the most useful plugins. But if you need a plugin for other purposes, just search for it. You'll probably find it.

- In section 3 of this book, you'll learn how to use jQuery UI, and in section 5, you'll learn how to use jQuery Mobile.

Figure 11-2   Some of the most useful plugins

How to use any plugin

Figure 11-3 shows how to use any plugin after you find the one you want. First, if you haven't already done so, you study the documentation for the plugin so you know what HTML and CSS it requires and what methods and options it provides. Usually, you'll do this as you evaluate the plugin to see if it does what you want and if its documentation tells you everything you need to know.

Second, you usually download the files for the plugin and save them on your web server. This download is often in the form of a zip file, and it will always include at least one JavaScript file. In addition, it may include CSS or image files that are used by the plugin.

The download may also include two versions of the main JavaScript file. If you want to review the code for the file, you can open the full version in your text editor. But the one you should use for your applications is the compressed version, which usually has a name that ends with min.js.

For some plugins, the files are also available from a Content Delivery Network (CDN). If you want to access the files that way, you can record the URLs for the files. Then, you can use those URLs in the link and script elements for the files.

Third, if a plugin requires one or more CSS files, you code the link elements for them in the head element of the HTML. Then, you code the script elements for the JavaScript files for the plugin. Usually, only one JavaScript file is required, but some plugins require more than one. At this point, you're ready to use the plugin.

So fourth, you code the HTML and CSS for the page so it is appropriate for the plugin. And fifth, you code the JavaScript for using the plugin. This can be in an external file or it can be within the head element of the HTML.

This procedure is illustrated by the example in this figure, which uses the bxSlider plugin. Here, the script elements show that the element for the plugin must come after the element for the jQuery library. That's because all jQuery plugins use the jQuery library. As the first caution in this figure points out, not coding these script elements in this sequence is a common error.

The HTML that follows shows the elements that the plugin requires. In particular, the id attribute for the unordered list is set to "slider" so the jQuery can select that element when it calls the bxSlider method of the plugin.

This is followed by the jQuery code for using this plugin. Here, the bxSlider method is called as the first statement within the function for the ready method for the document. This method name is followed by a set of braces that contains the code for setting two options for the method: displaySlideQty and moveSlideQty. This is the way you pass options to any plugin method, and you should already be familiar with this syntax.

Before you continue, note the second caution in this figure. That is that some plugins require a specific version of jQuery, which may not be the latest version. As you'll see in chapter 17, jQuery Mobile is an example of this.

General steps for using a plugin within your web pages

1. Study the documentation for the plugin so you know what HTML and CSS it requires as well as what methods and options it provides.

2. If the plugin file or files are available via a Content Delivery Network (CDN) and you want to access them that way, get the URLs for them. Otherwise, download the file or files for the plugin, and save them in one of the folders of your web site.

3. In the head element of the HTML for a page that will use the plugin, code the link elements for any CSS files that are required. Also, code the script elements for the JavaScript files that are required. These script elements must be after the one for the core jQuery library because all jQuery plugins use the core library.

4. Code the HTML and CSS for the page so it is appropriate for the plugin.

5. Write the jQuery code that uses the methods and options of the plugin.

The script elements for the jQuery library and the bxSlider plugin

```
<!-- the script element for the core jQuery library -->
<script src="http://code.jquery.com/jquery-1.8.3.min.js"></script>
<!-- the script element for the plugin when it has been downloaded -->
<script src="js/jquery.bxSlider.min.js"></script>
```

The HTML used by the bxSlider plugin

```
<ul id="slider">
    <li><img src="images/building_01_thumb.jpg"></li>
    <!-- more li elements -->
    <li><img src="images/building_05_thumb.jpg"></li>
</ul>
```

The jQuery for using the bxSlider plugin

```
$(document).ready(function(){
    $("#slider").bxSlider(
        {
            displaySlideQty: 2,        // a plugin option
            moveSlideQty: 2            // another plugin option
        }
    );
});
```

Two cautions

- Make sure that you include a script element for jQuery and make sure that the script element for the plugin comes after it. Not doing one or the other is a common error.

- Some plugins won't work with the latest version of jQuery. So if you have any problems with a plugin, check its documentation to see which version of jQuery it requires.

Description

- Some plugins can be accessed via a CDN, but most must be downloaded and stored on your server.

- Most plugins require the use of methods and most offer options. A few, however, only require that you code the HTML in a specific way.

Figure 11-3   How to use any plugin

How to use four of the most useful plugins

Now, you'll get a close-up view of four of the most useful plugins. This will introduce you to the power of plugins. It will also show you how the procedure in the last figure works with specific plugins.

How to use the Lightbox plugin for images

Figure 11-4 presents the Lightbox plugin. This is a popular plugin that displays a larger version of a thumbnail image when the user clicks on the thumbnail image. This image is displayed in a modal dialog box, which means that it must be closed before the user can continue. The image in this box has a thick white border, and it may have a caption below it. The part of the web page that's outside of the dialog box is darkened. To close the dialog box, the user clicks on the "X" in the bottom right corner.

If images are grouped in sets, this plugin not only displays the dialog box for the thumbnail, it also displays the image number and total number of images below the image, as in "Image 3 of 5". This is illustrated by the example in this figure. Also, when the mouse hovers over the left or right side of an image, previous and next buttons are displayed. Then, if the user clicks on a button (or the right or left side of an image), the display is moved to the previous or next image.

As the link and script elements in this example show, this plugin requires both CSS and JavaScript files. These elements use the names of the downloaded files. Remember, though, that the script element for the plugin must come after the script element for the jQuery library.

Next, this figure shows the HTML for using this plugin. The key points are that the img elements identify the thumbnail images; these elements must have rel attributes with the value "lightbox"; and these img elements must be within <a> elements that use the href attributes to identify the larger images. To provide for a set of images, you code a group name within brackets at the ends of the rel attributes for the img elements.

Once all of that's done, you're done, because the Lightbox plugin is one of the few plugins that you don't have to initiate by calling one of its methods. In other words, no JavaScript code is required. It just works!

A web page that uses the Lightbox plugin

The URL for this plugin

http://lokeshdhakar.com/projects/lightbox2/

The link and script elements for the Lightbox plugin

```
<!-- the link element for the CSS file -->
<link href="lightbox.css" rel="stylesheet">
<!-- the script element for the plugin -->
<script src="js/lightbox.js"></script>
```

The HTML for the Lightbox plugin

```
<a href="images/building_01.jpg" rel="lightbox[vecta]"
    title="Front of building">
    <img src="images/building_01_thumb.jpg"></a>
<a href="images/building_02.jpg" rel="lightbox[vecta]"
    title="Left side of building">
    <img src="images/building_02_thumb.jpg"></a>
<!-- more img elements within <a> elements -->
```

Description

- The Lightbox plugin can be used to open a larger version of a thumbnail image. This plugin works for a single image or a set of images.

- When the user clicks on an image in a set of images, the larger version is displayed with the rest of the page darkened and a caption and a counter below the image. Also, when the mouse pointer moves over the larger image, next or previous buttons appear.

- The Lightbox download includes a CSS file, a plugin file, an image that's displayed when the slides are loading, and images for the close, next, and previous buttons. However, this plugin doesn't require any jQuery coding.

- The HTML for a Lightbox consists of img elements within <a> elements as shown above. The src attributes of the image elements identify the thumbnail images. The href attributes of the <a> elements identify the larger images. The title attribute of each <a> element can be used to provide a caption that is shown below the image.

- The rel attributes of the <a> elements must be "lightbox". If you want to define a set of elements, you specify a unique name in brackets after the word *lightbox*.

Figure 11-4   How to use the Lightbox plugin for images

How to use the bxSlider plugin for carousels

Figure 11-5 presents the bxSlider plugin for creating carousels. In the example, this plugin displays two images at a time, and the user can move to the next or previous images by clicking on the buttons to the right and left of the images. However, you can change many aspects of how this plugin works by setting its options. You can also use the Lightbox plugin with the bxSlider plugin so a larger image is displayed if the user clicks on an image in the carousel.

If you download the JavaScript file for this plugin, the script element can refer to it as shown in this figure. As part of the download, you'll also get a set of images that can be used with this plugin. Another way to access the JavaScript file is to get it from the bxSlider.com site with a script element like this:

```
<script src="http://bxslider.com/sites/default/files/
            jquery.bxSlider.min.js">
</script>
```

One way to set up the HTML for use with this plugin is shown in this figure. Here, img elements are coded within the li elements of an unordered list, and the src attributes of the img elements identify the images that are displayed. However, you can code whatever elements you want within the li elements. Another way to set this up is to code div elements within a top-level div element.

To run the carousel using its default options, you code this jQuery statement within the ready function of a jQuery application:

```
$("#slider").bxSlider();
```

To set some of its options, you code a set of braces that contains name/value pairs as shown in the example in this figure. Here, the number of slides that are displayed at one time is set to 2, and the number of slides that are moved when the next or previous button is clicked is also set to 2.

By default, the bxSlider plugin will display next and prev links in the bottom left corner of the carousel. But you can change the text links to buttons by setting the nextImage and previousImage options so they point to the images you want to use. Beyond that, this plugin provides many other options that affect the way the carousel works. To get a better understanding of that, you can review the examples on this plugin's web site. Then, you can review the documentation for the options to see what's available.

To change the placement of the next and previous links or images, you also need to code some CSS that uses the bx.next and bx.prev classes. You won't find these classes in the HTML, though, because they're added to the DOM by the plugin. You can also use these classes to change the default links to images, which is the way the application in this example works. To see the CSS that's used, you can review the CSS file for the downloaded application.

Although it isn't necessary and it isn't done in this example, it's a good practice to code the width and height attributes for the img elements and set them to the exact size of the images. That way, the browser can reserve the space for the images and continue rendering the page while the images are being loaded.

A web page that uses the bxSlider plugin for a carousel

The URL for this plugin

http://bxslider.com

The script element for the bxSlider plugin

```
<script src="js/jquery.bxSlider.min.js"></script>
```

The HTML for the bxSlider plugin

```
<ul id="slider">
    <li><img src="images/building_01_thumb.jpg"></li>
    <li><img src="images/building_02_thumb.jpg"></li>
    <li><img src="images/building_03_thumb.jpg"></li>
    <li><img src="images/building_04_thumb.jpg"></li>
    <li><img src="images/building_05_thumb.jpg"></li>
</ul>
```

The jQuery for using the plugin

```
$(document).ready(function(){
    $("#slider").bxSlider(
        { displaySlideQty:2,
          moveSlideQty:2 }
    );
});
```

Description

- The bxSlider plugin makes it easy to develop a carousel like the one above.

- The HTML for the images can be an unordered list that contains one list item for each slide as shown above. Or, it can be a top-level div element that contains one div element for each slide.

- The bxSlider plugin provides many options. Two of the most useful are: displaySlideQty and moveSlideQty. The first one determines how many slides are displayed at one time; the second one determines how many slides are moved at one time.

- By default, "next" and "prev" links that move to the next or previous slide appear below the slides. To change the location of the links and to change the links to buttons, you can use CSS to apply styles to the bx.next and bx.prev classes that are added to the DOM by the plugin. You can see how this works in the downloaded application.

- It's a good practice to code the width and height attributes for img elements to the exact sizes of the images. Then, the browser can reserve the right amount of space for the images and continue rendering the page while the images are being loaded.

Figure 11-5   How to use the bxSlider plugin for carousels

How to use the Cycle plugin for slide shows

Figure 11-6 presents the Cycle plugin, which makes it easy to develop a slide show. There are two versions of this plugin, a full version and a lite version. These options are similar, but the lite version offers fewer options and requires less storage. For instance, the lite version only offers the fade effect as the transition between slides. In contrast, the full version provides 27 different effects that can be used for the transitions.

The HTML for this plugin works with the children of a selected div element. These children are usually either img elements or div elements. When you use div elements, you can code whatever you want within them, including headings, text, lists, and images.

The jQuery for using this plugin calls the cycle method and provides a list of options. In the example in this figure, the fx option sets the effect that will be used for the transitions; the speed option sets the speed of the transition; the timeout option sets the time between transitions; and the pause option is set to 1 (which is equivalent to "true") so the slide show pauses when the user hovers the mouse over a slide.

If you go to the web site for this plugin, the home page has demonstrations of some of the effects that can be used for transitions. Next, you can click on the link for the Effects Browser page to see a listing of all of the available effects, and if you click on the name of one of these effects, you'll see a demonstration of it. Then, you can return to the home page and click on the link for the Options Reference page to see a listing of all the options that are available.

Incidentally, this example illustrates the proper use of the width and height attributes for img elements. These attributes are set to the exact sizes of the images. As a result, the browser can reserve the space for these images and continue rendering the page while the images are being loaded.

A web page that uses the Cycle plugin for slide shows

On June 6th, 2012, Vecta Corp. moved into its new 4 story, 35,000 square foot facilty. Below are a few pictures of the new facility.

The URL for this plugin

http://jquery.malsup.com/cycle/

The script element for the Cycle plugin

```
<script src="js/jquery.cycle.all.js"></script>
```

The HTML for the Cycle plugin

```
<div id="slideshow">
    <img src="images/building_01.jpg" width="420" height="315">
    <img src="images/building_02.jpg" width="420" height="315">
    <img src="images/building_03.jpg" width="420" height="315">
</div>
```

The jQuery for using the plugin

```
$(document).ready(function(){
    $("#slideshow").cycle({
        fx: "scrollHorz",        // sets the transition effect
        speed: 500,              // sets speed of transition
        timeout: 2000,           // sets time between slides
        pause: 1                 // pauses slide during mouseover
    });
});
```

Description

- The Cycle plugin makes it easy to develop a slide show. It treats the children of a div element as the slides. Those children are usually img elements or div elements.

- This plugin comes in two versions: a full version and a lite version. The lite version is like the full version but it provides for fewer options.

- The full version of this plugin provides many different options including 27 different effects that can be used for the transition between images.

- If you study some of the demonstrations for this plugin, you'll get a better idea of how you can use its many options.

Figure 11-6   How to use the Cycle plugin for slide shows

How to use the jLayout plugin for two-column layouts

Figure 11-7 shows you how to use the jLayout plugin for creating a two-column layout without using CSS. This is a simple use of this relatively complicated plugin which has many other options for page layout. In fact, this plugin can be used to lay out complete pages, including headers and footers. Even for this simple two-column use of it, though, script elements are required for three of the six JavaScript files that the download includes.

The HTML for creating a two-column layout with this plugin consists of a top-level div element that contains two other div elements, one for each column. The class attributes for these columns must be "column1" and "column2".

Then, the jQuery code for this plugin selects the top-level div element and calls the layout method. It also passes the layout options to this plugin. In this example, the type option is set to "grid", the hgap option sets the gap between columns to 27 pixels, and the items option sets the widths of the two columns. In this case, the column widths are the same, but they don't have to be.

Of course, you can get the same result by using CSS. But using this plugin simplifies the CSS, which is especially helpful for developers who aren't that good with CSS.

If you study the examples and documentation for this plugin, you'll see that you can use it for many different types of layouts. However, it isn't easy to figure out how to use it for other layouts. At some point, then, it's easier to use CSS to do the formatting than it is to use this plugin for it. This is the type of tradeoff that you often have to consider when you're evaluating the use of plugins.

A web page that uses the the jLayout plugin to create two columns

The URL for this plugin

http://www.bramstein.com/projects/jlayout/jquery-plugin.html

The script elements for the jLayout plugin

```
<script src="js/jquery.sizes.js"></script>
<script src="js/jlayout.grid.js"></script>
<script src="js/jquery.jlayout.js"></script>
```

The HTML for the jLayout plugin

```
<div id="layout">
    <div class="column1">
        <!-- the content for the first column goes here -->
    </div>
    <div class="column2">
        <!-- the content for the second column goes here -->
    </div>
</div>
```

The jQuery for using the plugin

```
$(function() {
    $("#layout").layout({
        type: "grid",
        hgap: 27,
        items: [$(".column1").width(210), $(".column2").width(210)]
    });
});
```

Description

- The jLayout plugin makes it easy to develop a two-column layout as shown above without using CSS. This plugin also provides for many other layouts.

- The HTML for a two-column layout consists of a top-level div element that contains two other div elements: one for each column. The div elements for the columns must have class attributes with the values "column1" and "column2".

- For a two-column layout, the type option determines the type of layout, the hgap option specifies the number of pixels between the columns, and the items option specifies the widths of the columns.

Figure 11-7   How to use the jLayout plugin for two-column layouts

How to create your own plugins

One of the features of jQuery is that it provides an *API* (*Application Programming Interface*) that lets you create your own plugins. Since it sometimes makes sense to do that, this topic shows you how. Keep in mind, though, that it takes time to develop your own plugins. So before you start the development of a plugin, you should ask yourself a few questions.

First, have you done a thorough search for a plugin that does what you want to do so you don't have to create your own? Second, is the plugin that you plan to create one that you will use for many web pages? Third, are you sure your plugin will improve the effectiveness and usability of your web pages? If you can answer "yes" to questions like these, it probably does make sense to create the plugin.

The structure of a plugin

The first two examples in figure 11-8 show two ways to structure a plugin. In both examples, the plugin function is wrapped within an *Immediately Invoked Function Expression* (*IIFE*):

```
(function($) {
    // the plugin goes here
})(jQuery);
```

Here, the IIFE receives the jQuery library as a parameter. That way, the scope of the library is limited to the plugin, and you can continue to use the $ sign in the other jQuery code for an application just as you've learned in previous chapters. If a plugin isn't coded this way, it can cause conflicts with other libraries and plugins that use the $ sign.

Within the IIFE, the only code that changes from one plugin to another is the method name and the code that implements the plugin. In the function for the plugin, the each method is called for the object that the plugin is applied to, which is referred to by the this keyword. Then, if the object consists of more than one element, the plugin function is applied to each element.

At the end of the plugin function in the first example, the return statement returns the object, again by using the this keyword. This means that the plugin method can be chained with other methods. In second example, the return statement precedes the this.each method. This gets the same result as the first example, and this is the way professionals usually code this structure.

The example after the two structures presents a simple plugin. Here, the each method contains one alert method that uses the text method to display the text of the this object. If this object consists of only one element, this method displays one alert dialog box. If this object consists of more than one element, this method displays one alert dialog box for each element.

Because this plugin is stored in a file named jquery.selection.js, the script element for using this plugin uses that name in its src attribute. Then, the jQuery for using this plugin makes a selection and calls the displaySelection method of the plugin to operate upon the selection. In this example, the selection is all of the h2 elements in an element with "faqs" as its id attribute. As a result, one alert dialog box will be displayed for each h2 element.

The structure of a plugin

One way to code this structure

```
(function($){
    $.fn.methodName = function() {
        this.each(function() {
            // the code for the plugin
        });
        return this;
    }
})(jQuery);
```

The way most professionals code this structure

```
(function($){
    $.fn.methodName = function() {
        return this.each(function() {
            // the code for the plugin
        });
    }
})(jQuery);
```

A simple Selection plugin that uses this structure

The jQuery for a plugin in a file named jquery.selection.js

```
(function($){
    $.fn.displaySelection = function() {
        return this.each(function() {
            alert("The text for the selection is '" + $(this).text() + "'");
        });
    }
})(jQuery);
```

The script element for this plugin

```
<script src="jquery.selection.js"></script>
```

The jQuery for using this plugin

```
$(document).ready(function(){
    $("#faqs h2").displaySelection();
});
```

Naming conventions for plugin files

```
jquery.pluginName.js
```

The API standards for plugins

- The plugin should support implicit iteration.
- The plugin should preserve chaining by returning the selected object.
- The plugin definitions should end with a semicolon.
- The plugin options should provide reasonable defaults.
- The plugin should be well-documented.

Description

- For many plugins, most of the code will be in the function of the each() method.
- When the plugin finishes, the this object should be returned to the calling application.

Figure 11-8   The structure of a plugin

Figure 11-8 also shows the naming conventions for plugin files as well as the API standards for plugins. To support "implicit iteration", you use the each method within the plugin function. To preserve chaining, you return the this object. Beyond that, you should be sure to end all method definitions with a semicolon, and you should provide reasonable defaults if your plugin offers options. Above all, your plugin should be well documented if it's going to be used by others.

How to code a plugin that highlights menu items

Now that you know the structure of a plugin, figure 11-9 shows how to create a plugin that sets CSS styles for the items in a menu that consists of <a> elements within the li elements of an unordered list. This plugin also highlights an item when the mouse enters the item, and it returns the item to its original styles when the mouse leaves the item.

The code for this plugin uses the second structure in the previous figure. Within its each method, the first statement selects the <a> elements within the li elements of the element that the plugin is applied to. It stores these elements in a variable named items.

Then, the plugin uses the jQuery css method to apply six styles to the items in the items variable, which are the <a> elements in the menu. Note here that the css methods are chained to the items object. That's possible because each css method returns the object that it was applied to.

Next, the plugin provides functions for the mouseover and mouseout events of the <a> elements in the items variable. The function for the mouseover event changes the background color and color for the item. The function for the mouse-out event returns the background color and color for the item to the original colors.

Because the plugin is stored in a file named jquery.highlight.js, the script element for the plugin reflects this. Then, the jQuery to activate the plugin selects the unordered list by its id and calls the highlightMenu method of the plugin.

A menu that is highlighted by the highlightMenu plugin

The HTML for a menu that can be highlighted by the plugin

```
<ul id="vecta_menu">
    <li><a href="index.html">Home</a></li>
    <li><a href="aboutus.html">About Us</a></li>
    <!-- the rest of the links for the menu -->
</ul>
```

The highlightMenu plugin in a file named jquery.highlight.js

```
(function($){
    $.fn.highlightMenu = function() {
        return this.each(function() {
            var items = $("li a");
            items.css("font-family", "arial, helvetica, sans-serif")
                 .css("font-weight", "bold")
                 .css("text-decoration", "none")
                 .css("background-color", "#dfe3e6")
                 .css("color", "#cc1c0d")
                 .css("width", "125px");
            items.mouseover(function() {
                $(this).css("background-color", "#000")
                       .css("color", "#fff");
            });
            items.mouseout(function() {
                $(this).css("background-color", "#dfe3e6")
                       .css("color", "#cc1c0d");
            });
        });
    }
})(jQuery);
```

The script element for the plugin

```
<script src="jquery.highlight.js"></script>
```

jQuery that uses the highlightMenu plugin

```
$(document).ready(function() {
    $("#vecta_menu").highlightMenu();
});
```

Description

- The code in the highlightMenu plugin sets CSS styles for the links within the selected lists. It also changes two of those styles for the mouseover and mouseout events.

Figure 11-9   A plugin that highlights the items in a menu

How to add options to a plugin

To make a plugin more useful, you usually provide some options for it. To do that, you can use the coding technique that is illustrated in figure 11-10.

To start, you code an options parameter in the function for the plugin method. This is highlighted in the figure. This parameter will receive all of the options that are set by the user in name/value pairs within an object.

As the API standards for plugins in figure 11-8 point out, a plugin should always provide defaults for the options so the users don't have to set the options if they don't want to. To do that, you can use the $.extend method to set up the defaults as shown in this example. Here, a variable named defaults is set to the object that's created by the $.extend method.

The first parameter of the $.extend method consists of name/value pairs that provide the properties for the object that's created, and the second parameter is set to the options that are passed to the plugin, which are also treated as object properties. Then, when this method is executed, the user options are merged with the default options and the user options replace any default options with the same name. The result is that the default variable contains one property for each option that is either the default property or the property that the user set to override the default property.

Within the each method for this plugin, a variable named *o* is created and set to the object for the options. Then, you can refer to these options within the plugin function by using object notation. For instance,

`o.hoverBgColor`

refers to the option named hoverBgColor and returns the value of that option. When this is assigned to an <a> element, it sets the background color either to the default or the option that the user set.

This figure also shows the code for using the plugin and setting its options. In this case, the user overrode just two of the options. This, of course, is where the plugin documentation should make it easy to find out what the names of the options are and how they should be coded. Without documentation, the users of this plugin will have to study the plugin code to figure out how to set the options, and untrained users may not be able to do that.

Incidentally, you still need to provide some CSS rule sets for a menu that is highlighted by this plugin. For instance, you need to set the display property for the <a> elements in the menu to block. You need to set the padding and margins for the list items. And you need to set the list-style property of the list items to "none".

The highlightMenu plugin with options

```
(function($){
    $.fn.highlightMenu = function(options) {
        var defaults = $.extend({
                "bgColor"       : "#000000",
                "color"         : "#ffffff",
                "hoverBgColor"  : "#cccccc",
                "hoverColor"    : "#000000",
                "linkWidth"     : "125px",
        }, options);

        return this.each(function() {
            var items = $("li a");
            var o = defaults;

            items.css("font-family", "arial, helvetica, sans-serif")
                .css("font-weight", "bold")
                .css("text-decoration", "none")
                .css("background-color", o.bgColor)
                .css("color", o.color)
                .css("width", o.linkWidth);

            items.mouseover(function() {
                $(this).css("background-color", o.hoverBgColor)
                        .css("color", o.hoverColor);
            });

            items.mouseout(function() {
                $(this).css("background-color", o.bgColor)
                        .css("color", o.color);
            });
        });
    }
})(jQuery);
```

jQuery that uses the highlightMenu plugin and sets just two of its options

```
$(document).ready(function() {
    $("#vecta_menu").highlightMenu({
        bgColor: "#dfe3e6",
        color: "#cc1c0d"
    });
});
```

Description

- To provide options for a plugin, you code a parameter for the plugin that will receive the options that the user sets. In the example above, this parameter is named "options".

- To set the default options, you use the $.extend method, which creates an object from the name/value pairs in its first parameter. Then, it merges those pairs with the name/value pairs in its second parameter, which are the options set by the user. This replaces the pairs in the first parameter that have the same names, so the user options override the defaults.

- To refer to the options in the object that's created, you use object, dot, property notation.

Figure 11-10   The highlightMenu plugin with options

A web page that uses two plugins

This chapter ends by showing the code for a page that uses two plugins. This illustrates how two or more plugins can be used for a single page.

The user interface

Figure 11-11 presents the user interface for this web page. Here, a slide show is displayed beneath the heading for the page. It uses the Cycle plugin to cycle through the images for three products. However, this slide show pauses if the user hovers the mouse over an image.

Then, in the left column of the page, the highlightMenu plugin is used to highlight the items in the menu. This is the custom plugin that's shown in the previous figure.

The script elements

This figure also shows the script elements that this application requires. The first one is for the core jQuery library. The second one is for the Cycle plugin. And the third one is for the highlight plugin.

In this case, the script elements for both of the plugins must come after the script element for the jQuery library. However, it doesn't matter what sequence the script elements for the plugins are in.

The page layout

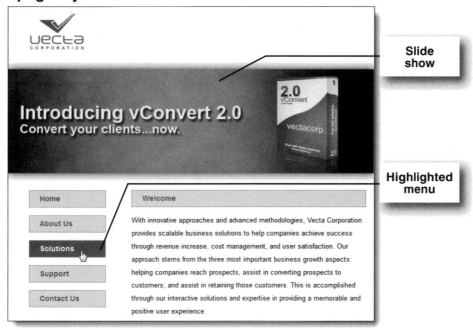

The script elements in the head section of the HTML

```
<!-- script element for the jQuery library -->
<script src="http://code.jquery.com/jquery-1.8.3.min.js"></script>

<!-- script element for the Cycle plugin -->
<script src="js/jquery.cycle.all.js"></script>

<!--  script element for the custom highlightMenu plugin -->
<script src="js/jquery.highlight.js"></script>
```

Description

- This web page uses two plugins.
- The Cycle plugin cycles through the images for three Vecta Corp products.
- The highlightMenu plugin in figure 11-10 is used to format the menu and highlight any menu item that has the mouse over it.
- The script elements for the plugins must come after the script element for the core jQuery library, but it doesn't matter which one comes first.

Figure 11-11   The user interface and script elements for the Vecta Corp page

The HTML for the elements used by the plugins

Figure 11-12 presents the HTML for the portions of the web page that use the plugins. This starts with the div element that contains the three images for the slide show. It is followed by the unordered list for the menu that will be highlighted by the highlight plugin.

The jQuery for using the plugins

This figure also shows the jQuery for using the plugins. Notice that both plugins are called from the event handler for the ready event. As a result, they start as soon as the page is ready.

Since you already know how to use these plugins, you shouldn't have any trouble understanding the code for calling them. The only difference from what you've already seen is that some of the options are set differently.

The HTML for the Cycle and highlightMenu plugins

```html
<section>
    <!-- the slides used by the Cycle plugin -->
    <div id="slideshow">
        <img src="images/rotator01.jpg" width="697" height="240"
            alt="vProspect 2.0">
        <img src="images/rotator02.jpg" width="697" height="240"
            alt="vConcert 2.0">
        <img src="images/rotator03.jpg" width="697" height="240"
            alt="vRetain 1.0">
    </div>

    <!-- the menu used by the custom highlightMenu plugin -->
    <nav>
        <ul id="vecta_menu">
            <li><a href="index.html">Home</a></li>
            <li><a href="aboutus.html">About Us</a></li>
            <li><a href="solutions.html">Solutions</a></li>
            <li><a href="support.html">Support</a></li>
            <li><a href="contactus.html">Contact Us</a></li>
        </ul>
    </nav>

    <!-- the rest of the html -->
</section>
```

The jQuery that uses the Cycle and highlightMenu plugins

```javascript
$(document).ready(function() {
    // set up the Cycle plugin
    $("#slideshow").cycle({
        fx: "fade",
        speed: 1000,
        pause: 1
    });

    // set up the highlightMenu plugin
    $("#vecta_menu").highlightMenu({
        bgColor: "#dfe3e6",
        color: "#cc1c0d",
        hoverBgColor: "#cc1c0d",
        hoverColor: "#fff",
        linkWidth: "125px"
    });
});
```

Figure 11-12   The HTML and jQuery for the plugins used by the Vecta Corp page

Perspective

Now that you've finished this chapter, you should be able to find and use plugins for common web development functions. This by itself can improve your productivity as you develop web pages, and often the plugin functions will work better than the ones you could write by yourself.

If you need to create a plugin of your own, you should be able to do that too. However, you should only develop your own plugin if the plugin function is clearly needed, isn't already available, and will be reused often.

Terms

plugin
API (Application Programming Interface)
IIFE (Immediately Invoked Function Expression)

Summary

- If you need a common function for a web page, chances are that a *plugin* is already available for it. By using a plugin, you can often save hours of work and do the job even better than you would have done it on your own.

- Perhaps the best way to find a plugin is to do a Google search. However, you can also go to code repositories like Google Code, GitHub, and Sourceforge.

- Some plugins can be accessed from a Content Delivery Network (CDN), but others need to be downloaded and saved on your server. The downloads for some plugins consist of only a single JavaScript file, but some include files like CSS and image files.

- To access a plugin, you code a script element for it in the head element of the HTML document. This script element must come after the script element for the jQuery library, because all jQuery plugins use that library.

- To use a plugin, you call its method within the ready event handler for a page. If the plugin requires options, you code the options as part of the method call.

- Four of the most useful plugins are Lightbox for displaying images, bxSlider for carousels, Cycle for slide shows, and jLayout for two-column page layouts.

- When you create a plugin, you use jQuery's *Application Programming Interface (API)* for plugins. This API describes the way the plugins should be coded.

- To adhere to the plugin API, you code each plugin within an *Immediately Invoked Function Expression (IIFE)* to prevent any conflicts over the use of the $ sign. In most cases, you also use the jQuery each function to operate on each of the selected elements. And when the plugin function is finished, you always return the object for the selected elements so the plugin method can be chained.

Exercise 11-1   Experiment with the Cycle plugin

In this exercise, you'll experiment with the Cycle plugin and the slide show that's in figure 11-6. You'll also review the documentation for this plugin. This will give you a better of idea of how you can use plugins.

Review the application

1. Use your text editor to open the HTML file in this folder:

   `c:\jquery\exercises\ch11\cycle\`

2. Note that the jQuery for using the Cycle plugin is in a script element. Then, run the application to see how it works.

Experiment with the effects

3. Go to the web site for the Cycle plugin, which is at this URL:

   `http://jquery.malsup.com/cycle/`

   Review the effect demos on the Home page. Then, try the shuffle and curtainX effects with your slide show.

4. Go back to the web site for the Cycle plugin, and click on the Effects Browser link. Then, click on any of the effects that are listed to see how that effect works. If you're interested, try one or more of these effects in your slide show.

Experiment with the options

5. Go back to the Home page of the web site for the Cycle plugin, and click on the Intermediate Demos (Part 2) link to get a better idea of how you can use options. Then, click on the Back button and click on the Options Reference link to learn more about the options.

6. If you're interested, try using one or more of these options.

Check out the download

7. Go back to the Home page of the web site for the Cycle plugin, and click on the Download the Cycle Plugin link in the upper left corner of the page. This goes to a page that offers links for Cycle Plugin and Cycle Lite Plugin.

8. Click on the Cycle Lite Plugin link, and note that the JavaScript for this plugin is opened in a new tab or window of your browser. Although this isn't the way most downloads work, this is relatively common with plugins.

9. Download the Cycle Lite code to your system. To do that, create a new Javascript file in the js folder for the Cycle application that is named jquery.cyclelite.js. Then, select all of the Cycle Lite code in the browser, copy it to the clipboard, and paste it into the new file.

10. Open the Cycle Lite file in your text editor, and note that this plugin has the standard plugin structure that's shown in figure 11-9.

Exercise 11-2   Experiment with the Selection plugin

This exercise has you experiment with the Selection plugin in figure 11-9 and to demonstrate that the standard plugin structure facilitates chaining.

1. Use your text editor to open the HTML file and the two JavaScript files in this folder:

    `c:\jquery\exercises\ch11\selection\`

2. The Selection plugin is in the file named jquery.selection.js, and the jQuery for using that plugin is the first statement within the ready event handler in the file named faqs.js. Note that this statement selects all h2 elements in the "faqs" element before calling the plugin method. If you look at the HTML for this application, you can see that it includes three h2 elements.

3. Run the application to see that the text for the three h2 elements are displayed in alert dialog boxes. Then, change the selection to all h1 elements and run the application again to see that the text for the one h1 element is displayed.

4. To prove that the standard plugin structure facilitates chaining, chain the css method that follows to the call to the plugin method in the faqs.js file:

    `css("color", "red")`

    Then, test this change. It should change the color of the h1 element to red after the alert dialog box is displayed.

Exercise 11-3   Create a Reveal plugin

In this exercise, you'll create a relatively simple plugin named Reveal. This plugin will set up click event handlers for the selected elements. Alternate clicks of a selected element will first show and then hide the next sibling element.

1. Use your text editor to open the files in this folder:

    `c:\jquery\exercises\ch11\reveal\`

2. In the jquery.reveal.js file, you can see the standard plugin structure with the method name set to reveal. In the faqs.js file, you can see the jQuery for the FAQs application. But the Reveal plugin should do what this code does. So copy the code for the toggle method into the each method of the reveal file.

3. Modify the code in the reveal file so it will show and hide the next siblings for whatever elements are selected by this method. Then, in the HTML file, add a statement to the last script element that calls the reveal method for the h2 elements of the "faqs" section. Since this HTML file already contains a script element for the Reveal plugin, you can now test this application. It should show and hide the answers of the FAQs application.

4. Note, however, that this plugin can be used for any application that works like this. The user just has to change the selection that's used. Now, to make this plugin more useful, add a statement at the start of the loop for the each method that hides the next siblings of the selected elements. Then, delete the rule set in the CSS file that hides the div elements, and test this change.

Section 3

jQuery UI essentials

jQuery UI (User Interface) is a free, open-source, JavaScript library that extends the jQuery library by providing themes, widgets, interactions, and effects. In chapter 12 of this section, you'll get off to a fast start with jQuery UI by learning how to use widgets like accordions, tabs, and sliders to enhance your web pages. Then, in chapter 13, you'll learn how to use jQuery UI's interactions and effects.

The information presented in this section is based on version 1.8.23 of jQuery UI. As this book went to press, though, version 1.9.0 of jQuery UI was released. This new version includes three new widgets, as well as changes to some of the existing components of jQuery UI. Although the new widgets aren't presented here, you shouldn't have any trouble learning how to use them after reading chapter 12. And, although the applications shown in this section were written for version 1.8.23 of jQuery UI, they will continue to work with version 1.9.0.

The jQuery UI web site has also been modified for version 1.9.0, and we show how to use the updated web site in chapter 12. That way, you'll be able to build a jQuery UI download and use the jQuery UI documentation without any trouble. Keep in mind, though, that jQuery UI and the jQuery UI web site are updated frequently. So don't be surprised if what you see on the web site doesn't match what's shown here.

12

Get off to a fast start with jQuery UI themes and widgets

In this chapter, you'll get off to a fast start with jQuery UI by learning how to use its themes and widgets. As you will see, widgets can add useful features to your web pages with a minimum of development time. That's why they're used by many web sites. In fact, widgets may be the only jQuery UI components that you will want to use in your web pages.

Introduction to jQuery UI...**344**
What jQuery UI is and where to get it.. 344
The jQuery UI components 346

How to build and use a jQuery UI download **348**
How to build a download..348
How to use ThemeRoller to build a custom theme 350
How to use the downloaded folders and files............................352

How to use jQuery UI widgets.......................................**354**
How to use any widget...354
How to use the Accordion widget..356
How to use the Tabs widget 358
How to use the Button and Dialog widgets 360
How to use the Autocomplete widget..362
How to use the Datepicker widget 364
How to use the Slider widget...366
How to use the Progressbar widget 368

A web page that uses jQuery UI **370**
The user interface 370
The link and script elements...370
The HTML for the widgets..372
The jQuery for the widgets..374

Perspective **376**

Introduction to jQuery UI

To get you started with jQuery UI, you'll first learn what it is, where to get it, and what components it contains.

What jQuery UI is and where to get it

jQuery UI (User Interface) is a free, open-source, JavaScript library that extends the use of the jQuery library by providing higher-level features that you can use with a minimum of code. To provide those features, the jQuery UI library uses the jQuery library. In fact, you can think of jQuery UI as the official plugin library for jQuery.

Figure 12-1 shows the home page and the URL for the jQuery UI web site. But you can also get to this site by clicking on the UI link at the top of the jQuery home page. And you can get back to the jQuery home page by clicking on the jQuery tab to the left of the jQuery UI tab.

This figure also summarizes the four types of features that jQuery UI provides. *Themes* provide the formatting for widgets, and they are implemented by a CSS style sheet that's part of the jQuery UI download. When you build this download as described later in this chapter, you can select one of the 24 predefined themes that come with jQuery UI. You can also create a custom theme if none of these 24 are right for you.

Widgets are features like accordions, tabs, and date pickers. In this chapter, you'll learn how to use many of the widgets that are currently provided by jQuery UI. In the next chapter, you'll learn how to use interactions and effects.

The jQuery UI web site

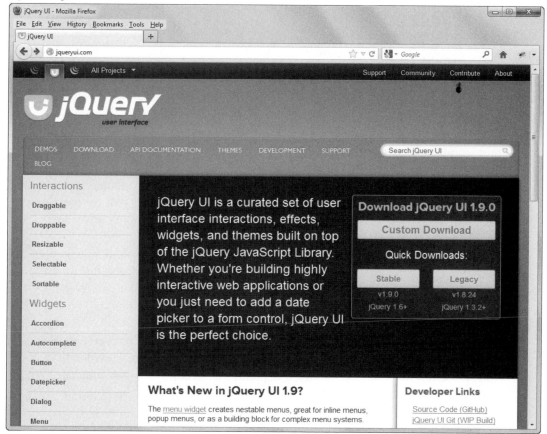

The URL for jQuery UI

http://jqueryui.com/

The four types of features provided by jQuery UI

Name	Description
Themes	24 predefined themes as well as a ThemeRoller application that lets you create a custom theme. A theme is implemented by a CSS style sheet.
Widgets	Accordions, tabs, date pickers, and more.
Interactions	Draggable, droppable, resizable, and more.
Effects	Color animations, class transitions, and more.

Description

- *jQuery UI* is a free, open-source, JavaScript library that extends the jQuery library by providing higher-level features. jQuery UI uses jQuery and can be thought of as the official plugin library for jQuery.

- The jQuery UI web site can be accessed by the URL above or by clicking on the UI link at the top of the home page for the jQuery web site.

Figure 12-1   What jQuery UI is and where to get it

The jQuery UI components

Figure 12-2 summarizes most of the components that are supported by jQuery UI. When you build a jQuery UI download, you decide which of these components you want to use in your web pages. Naturally, the fewer you choose, the smaller the jQuery UI file that has to be loaded into a user's browser.

The core jQuery UI components in the first group in this figure are divided into core, widget, mouse, and position. Core is always required when you use jQuery UI. Widget is required if you use widgets. Mouse is required if you use interactions. And position is required if you use elements that require positioning relative to other elements on a web page.

The next three groups list many of the widgets, interactions, and effects that jQuery UI currently provides. Of these, the widgets are the ones that get the most use. However, if you aren't going to use some of these widgets, you can exclude them from your download.

Note that this table doesn't include the three new widgets included in version 1.9.0 of jQuery UI. These are the menu, spinner, and tooltip widgets. Because you use the same basic techniques to work with these widgets that you do to work with the other widgets that you'll see in this chapter, you shouldn't have any trouble using them if you ever need to.

In contrast to widgets, many web sites don't use any of the interactions. If that's the case for your web site, you can exclude them from your download. Note, however, that the Dialog widget depends on both the Draggable and Resizable interactions, so you have to include these interactions if you're going to include the Dialog widget.

The power of the jQuery UI interactions is that they can be applied to any HTML element. For instance, you can make the items in an unordered list sortable, or you can make a row within a table selectable. For uses like those, you need to include the interactions in your download. In chapter 13, you'll learn how to use the interactions.

The jQuery UI effects can be used with interactions and widgets. For instance, an effect can be used to control how a new tab is displayed in a Tabs widget. In addition, jQuery UI effects can be used with HTML elements that aren't a part of jQuery UI. In chapter 13, you'll also learn how to use the effects.

UI core components

Name	Description
Core	Provides the core functionality. It is required for all interactions and widgets.
Widget	Provides the base functionality for all widgets.
Mouse	Provides the base functionality for all interactions that require the mouse.
Position	Required for all interactions that require the positioning of elements.

Widgets

Name	Description
Accordion	An accordion.
Autocomplete	A text box that displays a list of suggested items based on the user entries.
Button	A customizable button.
Dialog	A modal dialog box that is resizable and draggable.
Slider	A slider that can display a range of values.
Tabs	A set of tabs that reveals a tab's contents when the tab is clicked.
Datepicker	A calendar that can be toggled from a textbox or displayed inline.
Progressbar	A status indicator that can be used to display progress or percentage values.

Interactions

Name	Description
Draggable	Makes an element on a web page draggable.
Droppable	Defines targets that draggable objects can be dropped within.
Resizable	Makes an element on a web page resizable.
Selectable	Makes an element selectable with a mouse.
Sortable	Makes a list of items sortable.

Effects

Name	Description
Effects core	Required for all of the effects.
Blind	Creates a blind effect similar to vertical blinds on a window.
Bounce	Bounces an element up and down or side to side.
Clip	Clips the element on and off.
Drop	Moves an element in one direction and hides it at the same time.
Explode	Explodes an element in all directions. Also supports imploding.
Fade	Fades the element in or out.
Fold	Folds an element horizontally and then vertically.
Highlight	Highlights an element's background with a color for a specified length of time.
Pulsate	Pulsates an element for a certain amount of time by changing the opacity.
Scale	Grows or shrinks an element and its content.
Shake	Shakes an element up and down or side to side for a specified amount of time.
Slide	Slides an element in and out of the screen.
Transfer	Transfers an element from one element to another.

Figure 12-2   The jQuery UI components

How to build and use a jQuery UI download

In contrast to a jQuery download, you have to build a jQuery UI download before you download it. That lets you select the components for the download, which lets you keep the download to the minimum size that you need for your web pages.

How to build a download

Figure 12-3 shows the Download Builder page that you get to by clicking on the button or link in the jQuery UI home page. This is the page that lets you select the components that you want in the download. This page includes a components list, a drop-down Theme list, and a Download button.

The Components list includes all of the components in the four groups that are summarized in the previous figure: UI core, Interactions, Widgets, and Effects. To start, all of the components are selected. This results in a JavaScript library that is roughly 200KB in size. Then, to reduce this size, you can deselect (uncheck) the components that you aren't going to use. However, if you try to uncheck a component that is required by another component, a message will be displayed indicating that both components will be removed. For instance, this happens if you try to uncheck the Draggable component without first unchecking the Droppable and Dialog components because these components depend on the Draggable component. Then, you can continue by removing all the dependent components or by canceling the operation.

For many web sites, you can uncheck all or most of the interactions and effects. If, for example, you're going to use only a few of the widgets and you're not going to use the Dialog widget, you can uncheck all of the other widgets, the interactions, and the effects.

After you select the components you want, you can select a theme from the 24 that are in the drop-down Theme list or choose No Theme. Or, if you want to create a custom theme, you can click on the "design a custom theme" link, which will direct you to the ThemeRoller page in the next figure.

You can also set the name of the folder that your theme will be saved in. Otherwise, the folder for the theme will be given a default name. In addition, you can set the scope for the theme. You do this when you want to apply different themes to different areas of a page.

When you're confident that you have everything the way you want it, you can click the Download button, which will download a zipped folder to your computer. Then, you can unzip the folder to use the files it contains in your applications. You'll learn more about this download and how to use it in figure 12-5.

The Download Builder page

Download Builder

Version
1.9.0

Components
☑ Toggle All

UI Core
☑ Toggle All

A required dependency,
contains basic functions and
initializers.

☑ Core	The core of jQuery UI, required for all interactions and widgets.
☑ Widget	Provides a factory for creating stateful widgets with a common API.
☑ Mouse	Abstracts mouse-based interactions to assist in creating certain widgets.
☑ Position	Positions elements relative to other elements.

Interactions
☑ Toggle All

These add basic behaviors
to any element and are used
by many components below.

☑ Draggable	Enables dragging functionality for any element.
☑ Droppable	Enables drop targets for draggable elements.
☑ Resizable	Enables resize functionality for any element.
☑ Selectable	Allows groups of elements to be selected with the mouse.
☑ Sortable	Enables items in a list to be sorted using the mouse.

Widgets
☑ Toggle All

Full-featured UI Controls -
each has a range of options
and is fully themeable.

☑ Accordion	Displays collapsible content panels for presenting information in a limited amount of space.
☑ Autocomplete	Lists suggested words as the user is typing.
☑ Button	Enhances a form with themable buttons.

How to build your custom jQuery UI library and download your files

1. From the home page, click the Download link in the navigation bar or the Custom Download button. That will take you to the Download Builder page.

2. Select or deselect the interactions, widgets, and effects until the checked boxes identify the components that you want in your download. The fewer you select, the smaller your download will be.

3. If you want to select a theme for the download, use the drop-down list at the bottom of the page. Or, if you want to build a custom theme, click on the link above the drop-down list. That will take you to the ThemeRoller page in the next figure.

4. After you select a theme or design a custom theme and return to the page above, click the Download button to download a zipped folder that contains the jQuery UI files.

Figure 12-3   How to build a download

How to use ThemeRoller to build a custom theme

If you prefer to "roll your own" theme, maybe to match the color scheme used by your web site, you can use jQuery UI's ThemeRoller application to do that. The use of this application is summarized in figure 12-4.

Interestingly, the left sidebar on the ThemeRoller page is a Tabs widget that has Roll Your Own, Gallery, and Help tabs. Also, within the Roll Your Own tab, an Accordion widget is used for the eleven categories that you can change. As this accordion shows, you can customize a variety of CSS properties. The best way to find out what's available is to review this page yourself, and you'll get a chance to do that in the exercises at the end of this chapter.

In this example, the Font Settings panel has been opened, and the font weight has been changed to bold. As soon as a setting is changed, the change is reflected in the widgets to the right of the sidebar. In this case, for example, the headings in the accordion have been changed from normal to bold.

If you click on the Gallery tab of the ThemeRoller sidebar, you'll see that the left sidebar shows how the 24 predefined themes look in a Datepicker widget. Next, if you click on the Datepicker widget for a theme, you'll see how that theme is applied to the other widgets that are to the right of the sidebar. Then, if you like a predefined theme, you can click on the Download button that's below that theme to go back to the Download Builder page with that theme selected in the drop-down Theme list.

Another alternative is to click the Edit button that's below a theme. That will send you back to the Roll Your Own tab with all of the properties within each category set to the base properties for that theme. Then, you can make any changes to those settings, and click the Download Theme button to go back to the Download Builder page with Custom Theme selected in the drop-down Theme list.

The ThemeRoller page

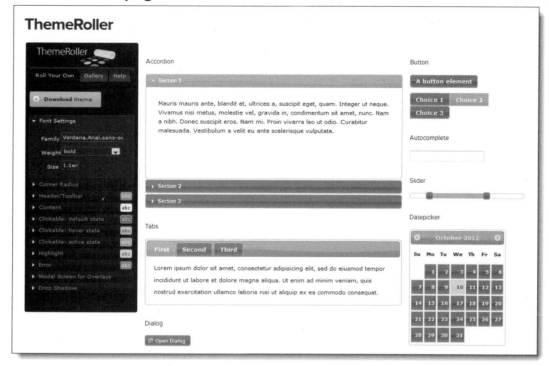

How to use ThemeRoller to create a custom theme

- Use the accordion in the left sidebar to customize the properties for any of the items in the list. After you change a setting, you can see its effect in the widgets to the right of the sidebar.

- When you're satisfied with your theme, click the Download Theme button. That will return you to the Download Builder page with Custom Theme selected in the drop-down Theme list.

Description

- jQuery UI has 24 predefined themes that you can select from the Themes list in the Download Builder page. Beyond that, jQuery UI's ThemeRoller lets you create your own custom theme.

- If you want to start a custom theme from one of the predefined themes, click the Gallery tab in the sidebar of the ThemeRoller page. That will show you what that theme will look like when applied to the widgets. Then, you can select one of those themes by clicking its Download button or you can return to the Roll Your Own tab by clicking its Edit button.

- The accordion in the left sidebar for ThemeRoller lists the customizable properties for a theme. The widgets to the right of the sidebar show how the custom properties will look.

- If you prefer to use your own CSS style sheet instead of a jQuery UI style sheet, you don't have to select a theme from the Download Builder page or use ThemeRoller to build your own theme.

Figure 12-4   How to use ThemeRoller to build a custom theme

How to use the downloaded folders and files

The first bitmap in figure 12-5 shows the files and folders that are included in the zip file for a jQuery UI download. As you can see, the download is organized into three main folders (css, development-bundle, and js), plus an index.html file. This index file displays a page that showcases some of the jQuery UI components.

The css folder in the download includes the CSS style sheet for your theme, as well as the images required by the widgets including arrows, icons, backgrounds, and more. This style sheet and the images folder are in a folder with a name that reflects your theme. In this case, I chose the "smoothness" theme so the style sheet and images are in that folder.

The development-bundle folder contains demos, documentation, style sheets, JavaScript files, and more. Although the index.html file requires some of these files, you won't need any of these for your web pages. So, if you don't intend to use any of these files, you can delete the entire development-bundle folder and the index.html file.

The js folder in the download contains the files for the latest jQuery and jQuery UI libraries. However, if you want to get the latest jQuery file from the jQuery CDN, you will only need the jQuery UI file for your web pages.

After you download these files, you'll want to use your text editor or IDE to open the CSS file. Then, you can review the rule sets in this well-documented file to get an idea of how many classes are supported. These are the styles that are applied to widgets, but you can also use these styles to format your own HTML elements.

To use the required files and the image folder in your applications, you can use a folder structure like the one in the second bitmap in this figure. Here, the accordion application has a css folder that contains the same folders (smoothness and images) and files as the css folder in the download. It also has a js (JavaScript) folder that contains the jQuery UI file for the download.

Then, to include the jQuery UI CSS and JavaScript files in a web page, you use the link and script elements that are shown next in this figure. Here, the link element points to the jQuery UI CSS file in the css/smoothness folder. The first script element points to the CDN address for the latest jQuery library. And the second script element points to the jQuery UI JavaScript file in the js folder. Please note that the script element for the jQuery UI file must follow the script element for the jQuery file because jQuery UI uses jQuery.

The last script element either points to the developer's external JavaScript file or it contains the JavaScript code. If the code that's needed is short, it is often embedded within the script element in the HTML document. Otherwise, an external JavaScript file can be used.

The components of a jQuery UI download

A typical folder structure for a jQuery UI application

How to include the downloaded files in your application

```
<!-- the link element for the jQuery UI stylesheet -->
<link rel="stylesheet"
    href="css/smoothness/jquery-ui-1.8.23.custom.css">
</link>

<!-- the script elements for the jQuery and jQuery UI libraries -->
<script src="http://code.jquery.com/jquery-1.8.3.min.js"></script>
<script src="js/jquery-ui-1.8.23.custom.min.js"></script>

<!-- the script element for your external JavaScript file or your code -->
<script></script>
```

Description

- A jQuery UI download consists of a zip file that contains the CSS file and images for the theme that has been selected, the jQuery and jQuery UI files that are required, and a development bundle that consists of demonstrations, documentation, and more.

- The index.html file in the download can be used to start the demonstrations and documentation.

- If the jQuery UI download is based on a predefined theme, the CSS library and associated images will be stored in a folder with that theme name.

- The only downloaded folders and files that you need to include in your applications are the CSS file, the images folder and files, and the jQuery UI file. You can also use the jQuery file, but an alternative is to use a CDN to get the latest jQuery file.

Figure 12-5   How to use the downloaded folders and files

How to use jQuery UI widgets

The best way to get off to a fast start with jQuery UI is to begin using its widgets. That will show you how you can quickly add features like accordions and tabs to your web pages with a minimum of code. In the topics that follow, you'll learn how to use eight of the widgets that are currently supported by jQuery UI.

How to use any widget

The next seven figures show how to use the eight widgets in their basic forms. That may be all the information that you need for using these widgets in your own web pages. All of these widgets, however, provide options, events, and methods that go beyond what these figures present. So, if you want to see how else these widgets can be used, you can review the jQuery UI documentation for the widgets, which is excellent.

For instance, figure 12-6 shows how to use the documentation for the Accordion widget. A good way to start is to click on the names of the examples in the right side bar to see how the widget can be used. Then, you can click on the View Source link to see the source code that makes the example work. After that, you can review the options, methods, and events for the widget by clicking on the API Documentation link.

After you're comfortable with the way a widget works, you're ready to implement it on a web page, which you do in three stages. First, you code the link and script elements for jQuery UI in the head element of the HTML as shown in the previous figure. Second, you code the required HTML for the widget. Third, you code the jQuery for running the widget. If you've read the plugins chapter, you'll see that this is how any plugin works.

In the jQuery example in this figure, you can see the general structure for the jQuery code that's required for a widget. First, the code for using the widget is within the ready event handler. Second, a jQuery selector is used to select the HTML element that's used for the widget. Third, the method for running the widget is called. Fourth, any options for the widget are coded within braces in the parameter for the method. This too is how any plugin works.

The accordion documentation on the jQuery UI web site

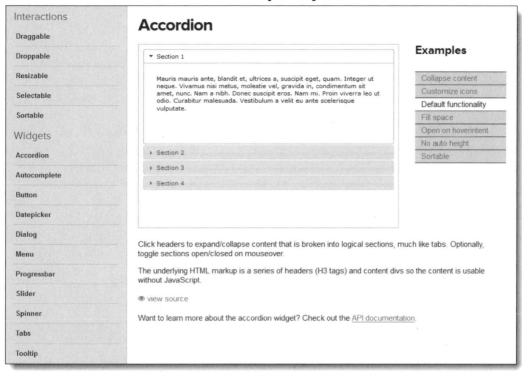

How to use the jQuery UI documentation

- In the left sidebar, click on a widget name to display an overview.
- In the right sidebar, click on an example name to see a working example, then click on the View Source link to see the code for the example.
- Click the API Documentation link to display information about the widget's options, methods, and events.

The jQuery for using a widget

```
$(document).ready(function(){
    $("selector").widgetMethod({
        // option settings
    });
});
```

Description

- To use a jQuery UI widget, you code the HTML and jQuery for the widget.
- In the jQuery, you code a selector, the method to be used, and the options.

Figure 12-6   How to use any widget

How to use the Accordion widget

Figure 12-7 shows how to use an Accordion widget, which consists of two or more headings and the contents for those headings. By default, an accordion starts with the panel for the first heading displayed, and only one panel can be open at a time. Then, when the user clicks on one of the other headings, the contents for that heading are displayed and the contents for the first heading are hidden.

As the HTML in this figure shows, an Accordion widget consists of a top-level div element that contains one h3 element and one div element for each item in the accordion. Within each h3 element, you code an <a> element that has an href attribute equal to the hash code (#). The exception is if you're using version 1.9.0 or later of jQuery UI. In that case, the <a> element isn't required.

In the jQuery for an accordion, you select the top-level div element of the accordion and call the accordion method with or without options. Often, you'll use this method without options because its defaults work the way you want them to.

In the example in this figure, though, two options are coded. The event option changes the event that causes the contents of a heading to be displayed from the "click" to the "mouseover" event, but you could also use other events to activate the accordion. Then, the collapsible option is set to true, which means that all of the panels can be closed at the same time. To close the open panel, you click on its heading or move the mouse over its heading.

Another option that you may want to use is the animated option. This option lets you specify the effect that's used when a panel is opened or closed. Normally, though, using an effect doesn't enhance the usability of the Accordion widget.

Although the basic formatting for an accordion is done by the CSS style sheet for jQuery UI, you can use your own style sheet to format the contents of a panel. In fact, you usually need to do that when the panel consists of several different types of HTML elements.

An Accordion widget

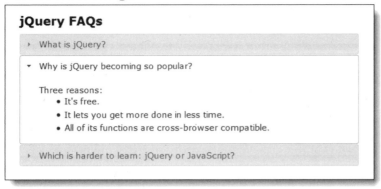

The HTML for the accordion

```
<div id="accordion">
    <h3><a href="#">What is jQuery?</a></h3>
    <div>
        <!-- the content for the panel -->
    </div>
    <h3><a href="#"> Why is jQuery becoming so popular?</a></h3>
    <div>
        <!-- the content for the panel -->
    </div>
    <h3><a href="#">Which is harder to learn: jQuery or JavaScript?</a></h3>
    <div>
        <!-- the content for the panel -->
    </div>
</div>
```

The jQuery for the accordion

```
$(document).ready(function(){
    $("#accordion").accordion({
        event: "mouseover",
        collapsible: true
    });
});
```

Description

- The HTML consists of <a> elements within h3 elements that provide the headers for the panels, followed by div elements that contain the contents for the panels. These elements should be within an outer div element that represents the accordion.

- The href attributes of the <a> elements should be set to the # symbol.

- In the jQuery, the accordion method is used to implement the accordion widget for the div element that represents the accordion.

- By default, a panel is opened when its header is clicked, one panel always has to be open, and effects aren't used for opening and closing the panels. To change the defaults, you can use the event, collapsible, and animated options.

- The basic formatting of the accordion is done by the CSS for jQuery UI, but you can use CSS to format the contents within the panels.

Figure 12-7   How to use the Accordion widget

How to use the Tabs widget

Figure 12-8 shows how to use the Tabs widget. This widget has the same general function as an Accordion widget, but it displays the contents of a panel when the related tab is clicked.

As this figure shows, the HTML for a Tabs widget consists of a top-level div element that represents the widget. Then, this element contains an unordered list that contains the headings for the tabs, followed by one div element for each tab that contains the content of the tab. To relate the tab headings to their respective div elements, the href attributes of the <a> elements within the li elements are set to the ids of the div elements.

To activate a Tabs widget with jQuery, you just select the top-level div element and call the tabs method. Usually, you don't need to set any options because the defaults work the way you want them to. However, you can use the event option to change the event for opening a tab from the click event to some other event. You can also use the fx option to add animation to the way the tabs are opened and closed.

Here again, the basic formatting for a Tabs widget is done by the CSS style sheet for jQuery UI. However, you can use your own style sheet to format the contents of a panel. In fact, you usually need to do that when the panel consists of several different types of HTML elements.

A Tabs widget

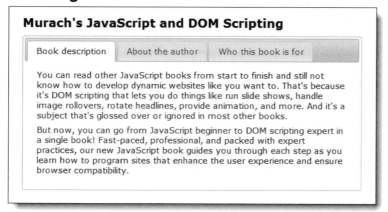

The HTML for the tabs

```
<div id="tabs">
    <ul>
        <li><a href="#tabs-1">Book description</a></li>
        <li><a href="#tabs-2">About the author</a></li>
        <li><a href="#tabs-3">Who this book is for</a></li>
    </ul>
    <div id="tabs-1"><!-- the content --></div>
    <div id="tabs-2"><!-- the content --></div>
    <div id="tabs-3"><!-- the content --></div>
</div>
```

The jQuery for the tabs

```
$(document).ready(function(){
    $("#tabs").tabs();
});
```

Description

- The HTML should consist of a div element that contains an unordered list that represents the tabs, followed by div elements that contain the contents for the tabs.

- The heading for each tab should be in an <a> element within an li element of the list. The href attribute for each tab should point to the id of the div element that contains the contents for the tab.

- In the jQuery, the tabs method is used to implement the Tabs widget for the div element that represents the tabs.

- By default, a tab is switched to when its header is clicked, but you can change that by using the event option. You can also use the fx option to add animation to the way tabs are opened and closed.

- After you learn how to use Ajax in chapter 14, you can use the ajaxOptions option to get the contents for a tab from a web server via Ajax.

- The basic formatting of the tabs is done by the CSS for jQuery UI, but you can use CSS to format the contents within the panels.

Figure 12-8   How to use the Tabs widget

How to use the Button and Dialog widgets

Figure 12-9 shows how the Button and Dialog widgets work. The HTML for a Button widget is often an input element of the "button" type, but this widget also works with the "submit", "reset", "radio", and "checkbox" types, and with <a> elements too.

When a Button widget is activated by the jQuery button method, the HTML is converted into a button that uses the jQuery UI theme. Other than that, the button works its normal way. In the example in this figure, the Button widget is coded as an <a> element that contains an img element for a book, and jQuery UI changes its appearance. When the user clicks on it, the dialog box is opened.

In contrast, the HTML for a Dialog widget consists of a div element that contains the contents for the dialog box. The title attribute of this element can be used to specify the heading for the dialog box. And the contents of this element can contain any HTML elements.

When the dialog box is displayed, it is both draggable and resizable. This means that you can drag the box by its title bar, and you can resize the box by dragging the resize handle in the lower right corner. You can also close the box by clicking on the "X" icon in the upper right corner.

To display a Dialog widget with jQuery, you use the dialog method. If, for example, you want to display a dialog box right after a page is ready, you select the div element for the dialog box and call the dialog method. If you want the user to have to close the dialog box before continuing, you can also set the *modal* option to "true".

Usually, you want to open a dialog box when some event occurs, like clicking on a Button widget. Then, you use the jQuery code that's shown in this figure. First, the button method is called to convert the HTML for the button to a Button widget. Then, an event handler for the click event of the button is set up. Within that event handler, the dialog method of the dialog box is called to display the box. Here, the modal option is set to true so the user has to close the dialog box before proceeding. That's why the page behind the dialog box in this figure is dimmed.

You may also need to use some of the other options for a Dialog widget. If, for example, you want to change the height or width of the dialog box, you can set the height or width option. If you don't want the dialog box to be draggable and resizable, you can set those options to false. You can also use the title option to set the title for a dialog box if you don't want to use the title attribute for that purpose.

If you want to add one or more buttons, like an OK button, to a dialog box, you can use the buttons option to do that. If you look at the documentation for this option, you'll see that this is easy to do. The documentation also shows how to code the function for closing the dialog box when a button is clicked.

Incidentally, the Dialog widget is generally considered to be a nice improvement over the JavaScript technique for opening another window and using it as a dialog box. That's especially true because most browsers have built-in features for blocking popup windows.

A Button widget that activates a Dialog widget

The HTML for the Button and Dialog widgets

```
<a id="book"><img src="images/javascriptbook.jpg" alt="JavaScript book"
    width="159" height="192" /></a>
<div id="dialog" title="JavaScript and DOM Scripting" style="display:none;">
    <!-- the content for the dialog box -->
</div>
```

The jQuery for the Button and Dialog widgets

```
$(document).ready(function(){
    $("#book").button();
    $("#book").click(function() {
        $("#dialog").dialog({ modal: true });
    });
});
```

Description

- The HTML for a Button widget can be an input element with any of these type attributes: button, submit, reset, radio, or checkbox. It can also be an <a> element. When activated, jQuery UI styles a Button widget so it looks like a button.

- The HTML for a Dialog widget consists of a div element that contains the contents for the dialog box. The title attribute for this element can provide the heading for the dialog box, but that can also be done by using the title option of the jQuery UI dialog method.

- To prevent the Dialog widget from appearing when the page loads, set its display property to "none". You can do that in a style attribute or in the CSS for the widget.

- In the jQuery, use the button method to activate the Button widget. Then, in the click event handler for the button, use the dialog method to display the Dialog widget.

- jQuery UI provides many options for Dialog widgets. For instance, if the *modal* option is set to true, the box must be closed before the user can proceed. The width option can be used to change the width of the box from its default of 300 pixels. And the buttons option can be used to add buttons to the box that can be used to close the box.

- By default, a dialog box is resizable and draggable, but you can change those options by setting them to false.

Figure 12-9   How to use the Button and Dialog widgets

How to use the Autocomplete widget

Figure 12-10 shows how to use an Autocomplete widget. As the user types one or more characters into the text box for this widget, a list drops down that shows the items that contain those characters. Then, the user can select one of those items by clicking on it or by pressing the down-arrow key to go to an item and the Enter key to select that item. That item then replaces what's typed in the text box.

Note that the items that are displayed in the list don't have to start with the letters you type. In the list shown here, for example, both HTML and XHTML contain the characters "ht", but only HTML starts with those letters.

The HTML for this widget consists of a div element that contains an input element. The class attribute of the div element should be set to ui-widget, which is a jQuery UI class that styles the input element and auto-completion list. Note, however, that the input element doesn't contain a type attribute. Instead, jQuery UI will make sure that this element works as a text or search box.

To implement an Autocomplete widget with jQuery, you first define a variable that contains an array of all of the items that can be in the auto-completion list. Then, you select the input element for the widget and call the autocomplete method. The one option for this method that must be set is the "source" option that points to the variable that contains the items array.

This figure also mentions some other options that you might want to use for an Autocomplete widget. If the list for this widget is so long that you want to get it from the server, you can use Ajax and JSON to get the list without making an HTTP request for another web page. You'll learn how to use Ajax and JSON in chapter 14. After that, you can study the documentation for this widget to see how it can work with these technologies.

An Autocomplete widget

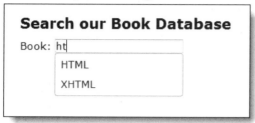

The HTML for the Autocomplete widget

```
<div class="ui-widget">
    <label for="books">Book: </label>
    <input id="books">
</div>
```

The jQuery for the Autocomplete widget

```
$(document).ready(function(){
    var murachBooks =
        ["ADO.NET", "ASP.NET", "C#", "C++", "CICS", "CSS", "COBOL",
         "DB2", "HTML", "IMS", "Java", "JavaScript", "LINQ", "MySQL",
         "Oracle SQL", "OS/390", "PHP", "VB", "Web Development",
         "Web Programming", "XHTML", "z/OS JCL"];
    $("#books").autocomplete({
        source: murachBooks
    });
});
```

Description

- The HTML for an Autocomplete widget consists of a div element with its class attribute set to "ui-widget". This div element should contain an input element with no type attribute.

- The "ui-widget" class is a jQuery UI class that's used to style the input element and the auto-completion list.

- In the jQuery, define a variable that contains an array of the items for the list in the Autocomplete widget. You can code as many items as you want in this array.

- To activate the Autocomplete widget in the jQuery, use the autocomplete method for the widget and set the source option to the name of the variable that you used for the array.

- You can use the delay option to set the number of milliseconds after a character is entered before the Autocomplete widget is activated; the default is 300 milliseconds. You can also use the minLength option to specifiy the minimum number of characters that must be entered before this widget is activated; the default is 1.

- After you learn how to use Ajax and JSON in chapter 14, you can use the documentation for this widget to learn how to get the items that are displayed by the widget from a web server. If you do that, you usually change the minLength option to 3 or more so the Ajax call isn't done too soon.

Figure 12-10   How to use the Autocomplete widget

How to use the Datepicker widget

Figure 12-11 shows how to use a Datepicker widget that is associated with a text box. Then, when the user clicks in the text box, a calendar is displayed. After the user selects a date, the calendar is hidden and the selected date appears in the text box.

To implement a Datepicker widget, you code a text box in the HTML. Then, you select that text box in the jQuery and call the datepicker method. By default, the calendar looks like the one in this figure with the current date displayed in mm/dd/yyyy format. But many options are available for customizing the date format, language, selectable date ranges, and more.

In the second jQuery example in this figure, three options are set. The first option sets the minimum date to the current date, which is done by assigning a new Date object to the option. The second option sets the maximum date that the widget will accept to 45 days after the current date. And the third option displays a panel beneath the calendar that contains Today and Done buttons. If the user clicks the Today button after moving to another month, the calendar returns to the month that contains the current date. If the user clicks the Done button, the calendar is closed.

A Datepicker widget with no options set

The HTML for the Datepicker widget

```
<label>Arrival date:</label>
<label><input type="text" id="datepicker"></label>
```

The jQuery for the Datepicker widget with no options

```
$(document).ready(function(){
    $("#datepicker").datepicker();
});
```

The jQuery for the Datepicker widget with three options

```
$(document).ready(function(){
    $("#datepicker").datepicker({
        minDate: new Date(),
        maxDate: +45,
        showButtonPanel: true
    });
});
```

Description

- The HTML for a Datepicker widget is a text box.
- The jQuery for a Datepicker widget is a call to the datepicker method.
- By default, the Datepicker widget is displayed when the user moves the focus into the text box, and the current date is highlighted.
- jQuery UI provides many options for the Datepicker widget. For instance, minDate sets the minimum date that the user can select; maxDate sets the maximum date that the user can select; changeMonth and changeYear when set to true provide controls that let the user select the month and year that should be displayed; numberOfMonths sets the number of months that should be displayed; and showButtonPanel displays a bar at the bottom of the widget with Today and Done buttons.

Figure 12-11   How to use the Datepicker widget

How to use the Slider widget

Figure 12-12 shows how to use the Slider widget. This widget lets the user drag the slider to the position that represents a specific value. You can use this widget to limit the values that the user can select to valid values so the entry doesn't have to be validated.

The example in this figure shows how to use a slider in conjunction with a text box that shows the value set by the slider. In this case, the HTML for the Slider widget is preceded by the HTML for the text box.

The HTML for a Slider widget consists of just a div element. Then, the jQuery selects that element and calls the slider method, usually with one or more options. For instance, the example in this figure sets the starting value to 50, the minimum value to 1, and the maximum value to 100. As a result, the user must select a value from 1 to 100 by sliding the slider.

This example also sets the slide option to a function that is called each time the slider is moved by the mouse. This function has two parameters: the first one is for the event object of the slide event, and the second one is for the object that contains the value that has been set by the slider. Within this function, the text box with "employees" as its id is selected, and the val method is used to set its value to the value set by the slider (ui.value). That way, the value in the text box will always be the same as the one selected by the slider.

After the code for the slider method, the ready event handler contains one more statement. That statement selects the text box and sets its value to 50, which is the same as the starting value for the slider. As a result, the text box value and the slider value will be the same from the start.

A Slider widget

The HTML for the Slider widget

```
<div id="size">
    <label>Company size: </label>
    <input type="text" id="employees" style="border:0;">
</div>
<div id="slider" style="width:100px;"></div>
```

The jQuery for the Slider widget

```
$(document).ready(function(){
    $("#slider").slider({
        value: 50,
        min: 1,
        max: 100,
        slide: function(event, ui) {
            $("#employees").val(ui.value);
        }
    });
    $("#employees").val(50);
});
```

Description

- The HTML for a slider consists of a div element. To set the size of the slider, you can set the CSS width and height properties. In the HTML above, this is done with a style attribute, but you can also do this in the CSS style sheet.

- In this example, the HTML for the slider is preceded by the HTML for a text box that is used to display the value that's set by the slider.

- In the jQuery for the slider, use the slider method to activate the slider, and use the value, min, and max options to set the starting, minimum, and maximum values for the slider.

- You can also use the slide option to provide a function for the slide event. In the example above, this function sets the value in the text box to the value set by the slider as the slider is moved by the mouse.

- The last line of code in the example above sets the initial value of the text box to 50 so it is the same as the initial value that's set for the slider.

- Other options for the Slider widget let you change the way the slider works. For instance, you can set the orientation option to "vertical" so the slider goes up and down instead of left and right. You can set the range option to true to provide a range of values that are specified in the values option. And you can set the step option to a numerical value that determines the size of the interval or step that each slider move makes.

Figure 12-12   How to use the Slider widget

How to use the Progressbar widget

Figure 12-13 shows how to use a Progressbar widget. This widget is designed to show the progress for a process, ranging from 0 to 100 percent. As a result, the value of this widget must be updated as the process progresses.

The HTML for a Progressbar widget consists of one div element. By default, this element will be as wide and high as its parent container, but you can resize it by using CSS so it looks like a progress bar. Then, to activate this widget with jQuery, you select the div element and call the progressbar method, usually with a value option that sets the starting percentage of progress. In this example, that value is set to 10 percent.

To change the value of the progress bar as the process progresses, you can use the method in the second jQuery example in this figure. Here, you pass two parameters to the progressbar method. The first is "value", and the second one is the updated value for the widget.

Of course, to use this method, you need to get periodic updates that tell you what percent of the process has been completed. Then, you can update the value of the Progessbar widget after each update. How you get these updates depends upon the process that you're monitoring, but if you can get the updates, using the Progressbar widget is an easy way to show the progress.

A Progressbar widget

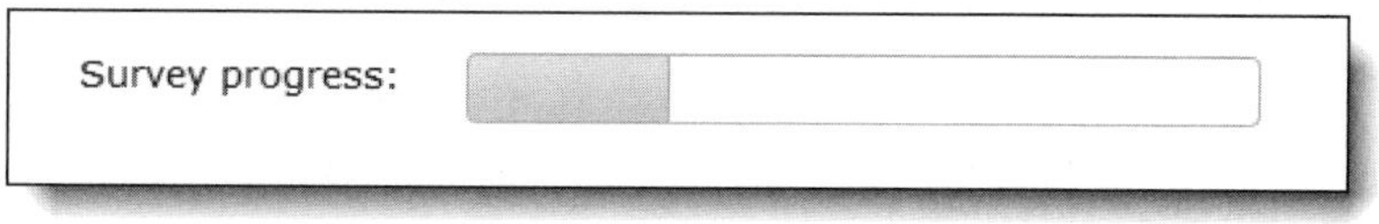

The HTML for the Progressbar widget

```
<div id="progressbar" style="width:300px; height:25px;"></div>
```

The jQuery for activating the Progressbar widget

```
$(document).ready(function(){
    $("#progressbar").progressbar({value: 10});
});
```

The jQuery for changing the value of the ProgressBar widget

```
$("#progressbar").progressbar("value", 25);
```

Description

- The HTML for a Progressbar widget consists of a div element.
- The default height and width for a Progressbar widget is 100% of its container element, but you can change that by setting the height and width properties of its div element. In the HTML above, the height and width properties are set by the style attribute, but you can also do this in the CSS style sheet.
- In the jQuery, use the progressbar method to activate the widget. By default, the Progressbar's starting value is zero, but you can use the value option to change that.
- To change the value of the Progressbar widget while an action is in progress, you can use the progessbar method with the first parameter set to "value" and the second parameter set to the updated value.
- To use this widget effectively, you need to get periodic data that indicates the progress of the process that is being monitored. Then, you can update the value of the widget.

Figure 12-13   How to use the Progressbar widget

A web page that uses jQuery UI

This chapter ends by showing the code for a web page that uses five of the jQuery UI widgets. This shows how two or more widgets can be used for a single page.

The user interface

Figure 12-14 presents the user interface for this web page. Here, a Dialog widget is used to give information about the web site's support documentation, a Tab widget is used within a form to get data entered by the user, and a Button widget is used for the Submit Form button.

Beyond that, a Slider widget is used in the Company tab to get the range for the number of employees in the company. Also, a Datepicker widget is used to get a date in the Additional tab. If you run this application on your own computer, you'll get a better feel for how these widgets work.

The link and script elements

This figure also shows the link and script elements that this application requires. The first link element is for the jQuery UI CSS style sheet. The second one is for the developer's CSS style sheet.

Similarly, the first script element is for the jQuery library. The second one is for the jQuery UI library. And the third is for the developer's external jQuery file. This of course is the required sequence for these libraries because the developer's jQuery uses both the jQuery and the jQuery UI library, and the jQuery UI library uses the jQuery library.

The page layout

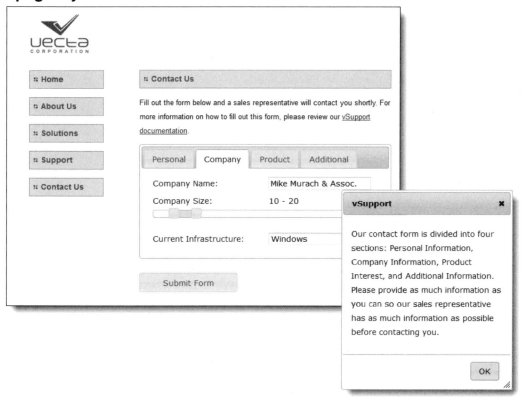

The link and script elements for the web page

```
<!-- jQuery UI style sheet reference. Smoothness is the theme used. -->
<link href="css/smoothness/jquery-ui-1.8.23.custom.css" rel="stylesheet">

<!-- Normal style sheet used for layout and general formatting. -->
<link href="styles.css" rel="stylesheet">

<!-- jQuery reference to the library on jQuery's CDN. -->
<script src="http://code.jquery.com/jquery-1.8.3.min.js"></script>

<!-- jQuery UI library reference. -->
<script src="js/jquery-ui-1.8.23.custom.min.js"></script>

<!-- The developer's external JavaScript file -->
<script src="vecta_corp.js"></script>
```

Description

- This web page uses three of the jQuery widgets within a form element: a Tabs widget to get data from the user; a Dialog widget to display a help dialog box when the user clicks on the vSupport Documentation link; and a Button widget for the Submit Form button.

- Within the Tabs widget, a Slider is used in the Company tab to get the company size range, and a Datepicker widget is used in the Additional tab to get a contact date.

Figure 12-14   The user interface, link, and script elements for the Vecta Corp page

The HTML for the widgets

Figure 12-15 presents the HTML for the portions of the web page that use the widgets. Since you've already seen these widgets in action, you should have no problem understanding this HTML. Note, however, that all five widgets are coded within a form element.

The HTML for the widgets

```
<form id="contactusForm">
    <p>Fill out the form below and a sales representative will contact
        you shortly. For more information on how to fill out this form,
        please review our <a href="#" id="help">vSupport documentation</a>.
    </p>
    <!-- DIALOG WIDGET -->
    <div id="helpdialog" title="vSupport" style="display:none;">
        <p>Our contact form is divided into four sections: ... </p>
    </div>
    <!-- TABS WIDGET -->
    <div id="tabs">
        <ul>
            <li><a href="#tabs-1">Personal</a></li>
            <li><a href="#tabs-2">Company</a></li>
            <li><a href="#tabs-3">Product</a></li>
            <li><a href="#tabs-4">Additional</a></li>
        </ul>
        <div id="tabs-1">
            .
            .
            .
        </div>
        <div id="tabs-2">
            .
            .
            .
            <label>Company Size:</label>
            <input type="text" id="employees" style="border:0;">
            <!-- SLIDER WIDGET -->
            <div id="slider"></div><br>
            .
            .
            .
        </div>
        <div id="tabs-3">
            .
            .
            .
        </div>
        <div id="tabs-4">
            .
            .
            .
            <!-- DATEPICKER WIDGET -->
            <input type="text" id="datepicker"><br>
        </div>
    </div>
    <!-- BUTTON WIDGET -->
    <input type="submit" id="submitbutton" value="Submit Form">
</form>
```

Figure 12-15   The HTML for the widgets of the Vecta Corp page

The jQuery for the widgets

Figure 12-16 shows the jQuery for the widgets. Notice that the methods for all five widgets are called from the event handler for the ready event. Here again, since you already know how to use these widgets, you shouldn't have any trouble understanding the code for using them.

Note, however, that the jQuery code for the dialog box uses the buttons option to add an OK button to the box. Then, the function for this button indicates that the dialog box should be closed when the OK button is clicked.

Also note that the jQuery code for the slider includes range and values options. Because the range option is set to true, the values option can include two values that identify the starting range as 11-20. Then, the user can change that range by dragging the ends of the slider.

The jQuery for the widgets

```
$(document).ready(function(){
    // DIALOG WIDGET
    $("#help").click(function() {
        $("#helpdialog").dialog({
            buttons: { OK: function() { $(this).dialog("close"); }
            }
        });
    });

    // TABS WIDGET
    $("#tabs").tabs();

    //SLIDER WIDGET
    $("#slider").slider({
        min: 1,
        max: 100,
        range: true,
        values: [11, 50],
        slide: function(event, ui) {
            $("#employees").val(ui.values[0] + " - " + ui.values[1]);
        }
    });
    $("#employees").val(11 + " - " + 50);

    //DATEPICKER WIDGET
    $("#datepicker").datepicker();

    // BUTTON WIDGET
    $("#submitbutton").button();
});
```

Figure 12-16   The jQuery for the widgets of the Vecta Corp page

Perspective

Now that you've completed this chapter, you should be able to build a download for jQuery UI that includes a predefined theme or a custom theme. In addition, you should be able to use all of the jQuery UI widgets presented in this chapter. That gets you off to a fast start with jQuery UI because the widgets are the most widely-used jQuery UI components.

Terms

jQuery UI (User Interface)
theme
widget
modal

Summary

- *jQuery UI (User Interface)* is a JavaScript library that extends the jQuery library. Since the jQuery UI library uses the jQuery library, the script element for jQuery UI must come after the script element for jQuery.

- Before you download the jQuery UI library, you can build a custom download that can include a predefined or custom *theme* that is used to style the jQuery UI components that you use. This theme is implemented by a CSS style sheet that is part of the download.

- As you build a jQuery UI download, you can also select the components for the features that you're going to use, including interactions, widgets, and effects. As you would expect, the fewer components you select, the smaller the jQuery UI file that has to be loaded into the user's browser.

- The most widely-used jQuery UI components are the *widgets* that include the Accordion, Tabs, Button, Dialog, Autocomplete, Datepicker, Slider, and Progressbar widgets.

- To use a widget, you code the prescribed HTML for it. Then, in the jQuery, you select the widget and run its primary method, often with one or more options.

Exercise 12-1   Experiment with the Accordion widget

In this exercise, you'll review the jQuery UI demos and documentation for the Accordion widget. Then, you'll make some minor modifications to the application that uses this widget.

Review the demos and documentation for the widget

1. Go to the jQuery UI web site at this URL:
    `http://jqueryui.com/`
    Then, click on the link for the Accordion widget in the left sidebar.

2. Use the accordion at the top of the page to see how it works. Then, click the View Source link below the accordion to display the code that implements it, and review this code. In particular, notice that the accordion method doesn't use any options.

3. Select one or more of the examples to the right of the accordion to see how they change the way the accordion works, and review the jQuery code to see what options are used.

4. Click the API Documentation link and review the options on the page that's displayed.

Review the application

5. Open the HTML file for the accordion application in this folder:
    `c:\jquery\exercises\ch12\accordion\`
    Then, run the application to see how it works.

6. Modify the jQuery code for the accordion so the panels are displayed when the user double-clicks on them rather than when the mouse moves over them. Test this change.

7. Modify the jQuery code so all of the panels are closed when the application starts. To do that, use the active option. Then, test this change.

Exercise 12-2   Experiment with the Datepicker widget

In this exercise, you'll review the jQuery UI demos and documentation for the Datepicker widget. Then, you'll make some modifications to an application that uses this widget.

1. Go to the jQuery UI web site. Then, click on the link for the Datepicker widget in the left sidebar.

2. Try some of the demos for this widget, view the source code to get a better idea of how this widget works, and review the API documentation.

3. Open the HTML file for the datepicker application in this folder:
    `c:\jquery\exercises\ch12\datepicker\`
    Then, run the application to see how it works.

4. Modify the jQuery code so the user can't enter a date before the current date or more than 6 months from the current date. To refer to the current date, you can use a Date object. To refer to 6 months from the current date, you can use the string "+6m". Then, test the application.

5. Modify the jQuery code so the Datepicker widget is displayed when the user clicks the calendar.jpg image that's in the images folder. To learn how to do that, you'll need to review the documentation for the showOn, buttonImage, and buttonImageOnly options. Then, test the application.

Exercise 12-3   Review the pages for building a download

1. Go to the jQuery UI web site at this URL:

    `http://jqueryui.com/`

    Then, click the Custom Download button near the upper right corner to display the Download Builder page.

2. Review the components that are available. Then, drop down the list of themes at the bottom of the page to see what's available.

3. Click the "design a custom theme" link above the drop-down list of themes to display the ThemeRoller page. Then, display the Gallery tab in the left sidebar to see that it lists the available themes and shows how each theme looks when applied to a Datepicker widget.

4. Click on the Datepicker widget for one or more of the themes to see what they look like when applied to the other widgets shown in the main part of the page.

5. Click on the Edit button below one of the themes. You will be returned to the Roll Your Own tab, and the properties of the theme you selected will be listed in the Accordion widget.

6. Make any changes you'd like to the properties of the theme to see how they look when applied to the widgets shown on the page. When you're done, click the Download Theme button at the top of the sidebar to return to the Download Builder page.

7. If you want to create a download that uses the custom theme, remove the checkmark from any components that you don't want to include in the download.

8. When you have just the components you want selected, click the Download button and respond to the dialog boxes that are displayed. Then, unzip the download folder and review the files it contains.

13

How to use jQuery UI interactions and effects

In addition to the widgets that you learned about in the previous chapter, a jQuery UI download can include interactions and effects. Although interactions and effects aren't used as widely as widgets, they provide the basis for some interesting jQuery applications. In this chapter, you'll learn how to use them.

How to use interactions..**380**
Introduction to interactions 380
How to use the draggable and droppable interactions.............................382
How to use the resizable interaction...384
How to use the selectable interaction 386
How to use the sortable interaction 388

How to use effects..**390**
Introduction to effects..390
How to use individual effects 392
How to use color transitions 394
How to use class transitions..396
How to use visibility transitions 398

Perspective **400**

How to use interactions

The jQuery UI *interactions* provide behaviors that you can apply to HTML elements. As a result, they provide the basis for some interesting jQuery applications.

Introduction to interactions

Figure 13-1 starts by presenting an example of an interaction. Here, the resizable interaction is applied to a div element that is formatted to look similar to a dialog. Notice in the HTML that a class is assigned to both the div element and the h3 element it contains. These classes are included in the jQuery UI CSS file that's part of a jQuery UI download. As you'll see in the examples of interactions in the figures that follow, classes like these are used frequently with interactions.

To use an interaction, you code jQuery UI methods with or without options just like you do when you use widgets. In this figure, for example, the resizable method is used to make the element with an id of "dialog" resizable. Then, the four options specify the minimum and maximum height and width for the resizable element.

This figure also lists the jQuery UI interactions that you were introduced to in the previous chapter. As you learn about these interactions in the pages that follow, keep in mind that the jQuery UI web site provides excellent documentation and demos for them. So, use this chapter to get started with interactions, and use the documentation and demos when you need to expand upon what you've learned.

An element that uses the resizable interaction

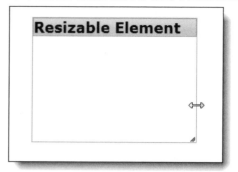

The HTML for the element

```
<div id="dialog" class="ui-widget-content">
    <h3 class="ui-widget-header">Resizable Element</h3>
</div>
```

The jQuery for the interaction

```
$(document).ready(function() {
    $("#dialog").resizable({
        maxHeight: 250,
        maxWidth: 350,
        minHeight: 150,
        minWidth: 200
    });
});
```

The five jQuery UI interactions

- Draggable
- Droppable
- Resizable
- Selectable
- Sortable

Description

- jQuery UI *interactions* can be used to provide interactivity that would be difficult to code with JavaScript.
- Like widgets, interactions have options that control how they work.
- Interactions rely on classes within the CSS for the jQuery UI more so than widgets do.
- The documentation and demos for interactions on the jQuery UI web site is excellent.

Figure 13-1   Introduction to the jQuery UI interactions

How to use the draggable and droppable interactions

Figure 13-2 shows how to use the draggable and droppable interactions. Here, the user can drag any of the three products at the top of the page and drop it onto the shopping cart at the bottom of the page.

As the HTML in this figure shows, draggables and droppables are defined as div elements. In this case, the three div elements that define draggable objects contain images. In contrast, the div element that defines the droppable area contains a <p> element that identifies the area as a cart.

The jQuery that implements the draggable and droppable interactions starts by selecting the first three div elements and calling the draggable method. This method includes the cursor option, which identifies the cursor that should be displayed as an element is dragged. You can see this cursor over the element that's being dragged in the web page.

Next, the jQuery selects the fourth div element and calls the droppable method. This method includes a drop event with a callback function that indicates what happens when an element enters the drop area. In this case, the addClass method is used to assign the ui-state-highlight class to the element. This class will set the background color of the drop area to a light yellow and set the text color to a dark gray. Then, it uses the find method to get the <p> element that's a descendant of the div element, and it uses the html method to change the text in the <p> element to indicate that an item has been added to the cart.

In most cases, you'll use the draggable and droppable interactions together as shown here. Although you can use the draggable interaction without the droppable interaction, it usually doesn't make sense to let a user drag an element without providing a place to drop it.

A draggable element as it's being dragged onto a droppable element

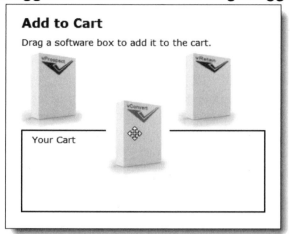

The HTML for the elements

```
<div id="vprospect"><img src="images/vprospect.png"></div>
<div id="vconvert"><img src="images/vconvert.png"></div>
<div id="vretain"><img src="images/vretain.png"></div>
<div id="cart"><p>Your Cart</p></div>
```

The jQuery for the interactions

```
$(document).ready(function() {
    $("#vprospect, #vconvert, #vretain").draggable({ cursor: "move" });
    $("#cart").droppable({
        drop: function() {
            $(this).addClass(
                "ui-state-highlight").find("p").html("vSolution added!");
        }
    });
});
```

Description

- The HTML for a draggable element consists of a div element that contains the draggable element.

- The HTML for a droppable element consists of a div element that defines the area where a draggable element can be dropped.

- In the jQuery, the draggable method is used to make a div element draggable, and the droppable method is used to make a div element the target of a draggable element.

- jQuery UI provides a variety of options for the draggable method, many of which control how and where an element can be dragged.

- jQuery UI also provides options for the droppable method. For example, the accept option identifies the elements that a droppable will accept, and the tolerance option indicates when a draggable object is considered to be over a droppable.

- To control what happens when a draggable object is dropped, you can code a callback function for the drop event of the droppable.

Figure 13-2   How to use the draggable and droppable interactions

How to use the resizable interaction

Figure 13-3 shows how to use the resizable interaction. Here, the interaction is applied to a text area so it can be enlarged to make room for the user to enter more text. However, the resizable interaction can be used with any HTML element.

The HTML for the text area consists of just an opening tag with an id and a closing tag. Then, the jQuery selects the text area by its id and calls the resizable method. In this example, the handles option is included on this method to indicate which directions the area can be enlarged. Here, "se" stands for southeast, which refers to the bottom right corner.

When you provide for resizing an element by dragging a corner, stripes appear near that corner. Often, though, those stripes aren't inside the corner as shown here. To fix that, you can override the properties of the class that's assigned to the element based on the value of the handles option. In the CSS in this figure, for example, the bottom and right properties of the ui-resizable-se class are specified.

Before I go on, you should realize that some browsers automatically provide for resizing a text area by dragging its bottom right corner. Other browsers, however, especially older ones, don't provide for this feature. Because of that, it's best to use the resizable interaction whenever you want the user to be able to enlarge a text area by dragging it. Keep in mind, though, that a vertical scroll bar is added to a text area if more text is entered than can be displayed at one time. In most cases, that's sufficient.

A text area that can be resized

Questions / Comments:

```
We are a small publishing company that has been in
business for 40 years. We are looking for new ways
to grow our customer base, particularly in the
college market.
```

The HTML for the text area

```html
<p>Questions / Comments:</p>
<textarea id="questions"></textarea>
```

The jQuery for the interaction

```javascript
$(document).ready(function() {
    $("#questions").resizable({
        handles: "se"
    });
});
```

The CSS for the interaction

```css
.ui-resizable-se {
    bottom: 13px;
    right: 2px;
}
```

Description

- The resizable interaction can be used with any HTML element. To enable the resizable interaction, you use the jQuery resizable method.

- By default, you can drag the bottom right corner or the right or bottom side of an element to resize it. To change this default, you use the handles option. The values you code for this option refer to directions. For example, "se" stands for southeast, which refers to the bottom right corner.

- If an element can be resized by dragging a corner, stripes appear near the corner of the element. If the stripes don't appear where you want them, you can move them by overriding properties of the appropriate jQuery UI CSS class.

- To restrict the size of an element, you can use the minWidth, minHeight, maxWidth, and maxHeight options. You can also use the containment option to restrict the bounds of the element.

Figure 13-3 How to use the resizable interaction

How to use the selectable interaction

Figure 13-4 shows how to use the selectable interaction, which is often used to provide a more visual means of selecting one or more options. In this case, the selectable interaction is used to select one or more of three products represented by images.

In the HTML in this figure, you can see that the selectable elements are coded as items within a list. Note, however, that any HTML element or group of elements can be selectable. For example, div elements are often used with the selectable interaction.

The jQuery for this example starts by selecting the list element that contains the selectable elements and calling the selectable method. Within this method, a callback function is coded for the stop method, which occurs when the interaction ends. In this case, the selectable interaction ends each time a product is selected. That's because the only way to select multiple images is to hold down the Ctrl key and then click on them. In contrast, if you're working with elements that contain text, you can select multiple elements by dragging around them. Then, the sortable interaction ends when you release the mouse button.

The callback function for the stop method selects all elements that have been assigned to the ui-selected class. Because this class is automatically assigned to an element when it's selected, this includes all selected elements. Then, the each method is called on each selected element. The callback function for this method starts by selecting the span element that is coded within the label that follows the selectable list. Then, the html method is used to add text to the span element. Notice here that this text includes the id of the selected element, which is referred to by using the this keyword.

Because no properties are defined by default for the ui-selected class, a selected element doesn't appear any differently than elements that aren't selected. To change that, you can include CSS for this class. In this example, this class adds a border around the selected elements.

A selected element in a list of selectable elements

The HTML for the list of selectable elements

```
Select the product that you're interested in:<br>
<ol id="solutions">
    <li id="vProspect"><img src="images/logo_vprospect.gif"></li>
    <li id="vConvert"><img src="images/logo_vconvert.gif"></li>
    <li id="vRetain"><img src="images/logo_vretain.gif"></li>
</ol>
<label><span id="selected"></span></label>
```

The jQuery for the interaction

```
$(document).ready(function() {
    $("#solutions").selectable({
        stop: function() {
            $(".ui-selected").each(function() {
                $("#selected").html("Product selected: " + this.id);
            });
        }
    });
});
```

The CSS for the interaction

```
.ui-selected {
    border: 1px solid #000;
}
```

Description

- The selectable interaction can be used to make any HTML element or group of elements selectable. To enable the selectable interaction, you use the selectable method. Then, you can select one or more elements using standard techniques.

- Although it's common to define selectable elements as list items, you can also use other elements such as div elements.

- By default, all of the elements within a selectable object are selectable. To change that, you can use the filter option to identify the selectable elements.

- When an element is selected, the ui-selected class is automatically assigned to it. To control how an element is displayed when it's selected, you can override the properties of this class.

- To perform an operation when a selectable interaction ends, you can code a callback function for the stop event of the element. Within this function, you can refer to each selected element using the .ui-selected class.

Figure 13-4   How to use the selectable interaction

How to use the sortable interaction

Figure 13-5 shows how to use the sortable interaction to provide for sorting a group of HTML elements. When an element is sortable, the user can drag it from one location to another. As you can see in this figure, when an element is positioned between two other sortable elements, a placeholder appears. Then, the user can drop the element onto that placeholder to change the sort sequence.

In most cases, you'll use the sortable interaction with an unordered list as shown in this figure. However, you can also use this interaction with any group of HTML elements.

Notice in the HTML shown here that the ui-state-default class is assigned to each line item in the sortable list. This class provides the default appearance shown in this figure. Of course, you can override this class to change the appearance.

In the jQuery for the sortable interaction, you select the element that contains the sortable items. Then, you call the sortable method on this element. In this example, the placeholder option is included on this method. This option assigns the ui-state-highlight class to the placeholder that appears as a sortable element is dragged.

By default, the ui-state-highlight class changes the border around the place-holder to a light yellow and the background color of the placeholder to an even lighter yellow. In this figure, though, you can see that the height property has been added to this class. The value of this property will cause the placeholder to be about the same height as the sortable elements.

A sortable list as one of the items is dragged downward

The HTML for the sortable list

```
<ul id="vsupport">
    <li class="ui-state-default">Blog / How-To Articles</li>
    <li class="ui-state-default">Discussion Forum</li>
    <li class="ui-state-default">Knowledge Base</li>
    <li class="ui-state-default">Phone Support</li>
    <li class="ui-state-default">Wiki Support</li>
</ul>
```

The jQuery for the interaction

```
$(document).ready(function() {
    $("#vsupport").sortable({
        placeholder: "ui-state-highlight"
    });
});
```

The CSS for the interaction

```
.ui-state-highlight {
    height: 1.5em;
}
```

Description

- The sortable interaction can be used to make a group of HTML elements sortable. To enable the sortable interaction, you use the sortable method.

- Although it's common to define sortable elements as list items, you can also use other elements such as div elements.

- To move an element, just drag it to a new location within the list. When the element is positioned between two other sortable elements, a placeholder appears and you can drop the element on that placeholder.

- To stylize the elements in a sortable list, you can assign the ui-state-default class to the sortable elements. To stylize the placeholder for a list, you can assign the ui-state-highlight class to the placeholder option of the sortable method.

Figure 13-5   How to use the sortable interaction

How to use effects

In the topics that follow, you'll learn the basic skills for using the many effects that jQuery UI provides.

Introduction to effects

Figure 13-6 presents the jQuery UI *effects*. The table at the top of this figure lists the effects that are included in the effects core component. These effects extend the effects provided by jQuery. For example, jQuery UI extends the animate method to provide for animating color transitions.

This figure also lists the 15 individual effects that jQuery UI provides. You can apply these effects to widgets and interactions as well as other HTML components.

To use these effects, you must include the jQuery UI core effects component in your download. In addition, you must include the specific component for an effect. To use the blind effect, for example, you must include the "Effects Blind" component. The two exceptions are the puff and size effects, which don't have separate components of their own. Instead, they require the "Effects Scale" component.

Here again, the jQuery UI web site provides excellent documentation and demos. So, use this chapter to get started with effects, and use the documentation and demos when you need to expand upon what you've learned.

As you learned in chapter 8, when you use one of the basic jQuery effects, you can apply a jQuery UI *easing* to it. If you would like to see a full list and demonstrations of these easings, you can go to the URL in this figure.

jQuery UI core effects

Effect	Description
Color transitions	Provides for animating background color, border colors, text color, and outline color.
Class transitions	Provides for animations while a class is being added, deleted, or changed.
Easing	Provides easing effects to animated elements.
Visibility transitions	Provides for applying an individual effect to an element while showing, hiding, or toggling the element.

jQuery UI individual effects

Blind	Fade	Scale
Bounce	Fold	Shake
Clip	Highlight	Size
Drop	Puff	Slide
Explode	Pulsate	Transfer

The URL for demonstrations of the easings on the jQuery UI web site

`http://jqueryui.com/effect/#easing`

Description

- The jQuery UI core effects component extends jQuery functionality by providing color transitions, class transitions, easing, and visibility transitions.

- The jQuery UI library includes 15 individual effects that you can apply to widgets, interactions, and even your own non-jQuery UI HTML elements. Each of these effects requires the core effects component as well as an individual effect component.

- The documentation and demos for effects on the jQuery UI web site are excellent.

- In figure 8-9 of chapter 8, you learned how to use *easings* with effects and animations. For a full list and demonstrations of all the jQuery UI easings, you can go to the URL shown above.

Figure 13-6   Introduction to the jQuery UI effects

How to use individual effects

To use the individual effects, you call the effect method shown in figure 13-7. In the syntax for this method, you can see that the only required parameter is the name of the effect. In addition to this parameter, though, you can code one or more options, a duration, and a callback function.

In the example in this figure, the highlight and pulsate effects are applied to the sortable list you saw in figure 13-5. If you refer back to that figure, you'll see that the HTML for the list in this figure is identical. However, two events have been added to the sortable method in the jQuery.

The first event, start, is triggered when the sorting interaction starts. That happens when the user starts to drag a sortable element. Then, the callback function for this event calls the effect method of the element that's being dragged and causes it to pulsate once per second. That's why this element appears to be dimmed in the web page in this figure.

One option is also coded for this effect. This option, times, controls the number of times that the element pulsates. The default is five, but the option in this example changes it to three.

Notice here that the callback function for the start method accepts two parameters: event and ui. Although the event parameter isn't used in this example, the item property of the ui parameter is used to identify the element that's currently being dragged. You'll use this parameter often to refer to the current item in a group of items.

The second event, update, is triggered when the user stops dragging a sortable element and its position changes in the list. The callback function for this event accepts event and ui parameters just like the callback function for the start event. Then, the item property of the ui parameter is used to select the element that was dragged to a new position, and the effect method is called to apply the highlight effect to that element using the specified color for two seconds.

The syntax for the effect method

```
effect(effect[, {options}][, duration][, callback])
```

A sortable list that uses highlight and pulsate effects

The HTML for the sortable list

```
<ul id="vsupport">
    <li class="ui-state-default">Blog / How-To Articles</li>
    <li class="ui-state-default">Discussion Forum</li>
    <li class="ui-state-default">Knowledge Base</li>
    <li class="ui-state-default">Phone Support</li>
    <li class="ui-state-default">Wiki Support</li>
</ul>
```

The jQuery for the effects

```
$(document).ready(function() {
    $("#vsupport").sortable({
        placeholder: "ui-state-highlight",
        start: function(event, ui) {
            $(ui.item).effect("pulsate", { times: 3 }, 1000);
        }
        update: function(event, ui) {
            $(ui.item).effect("highlight", { color: "#7fffd4" }, 2000);
        }
    });
});
```

Description

- You can use the jQuery UI effect method to apply an individual effect to one or more elements. The only argument that's required by this method is the name of the effect.

- If you code a callback function as a parameter of the effect method, the function is called after the effect is executed.

- If you code the effect method within a callback function, the function should accept event and ui parameters. The event parameter contains information about the original browser event, and the ui parameter contains information about the selected item.

- You can also use some of the individual effects with the show, hide, and toggle methods. For more information, see figure 13-10.

Figure 13-7 How to use individual effects

How to use color transitions

Figure 13-8 shows how to use *color transitions* to animate a change from one color to another. To do that, you use the animate method that you learned about in chapter 8. Then, you include the new color properties in the properties map, and you include a duration that indicates how long it takes the colors to change. This makes for a smoother transition from one color to another.

The example in this figure uses a text area to illustrate how color transitions work. Here, the user can click on a link to increase the size of the text area. When that happens, the background color and text color of the text area also change.

The jQuery for this example contains an event handler for the click event of the link. Within this event handler, the animate method is called on the text area. Then, the properties map for this method includes the four properties that change the width, height, background color, and text color. Finally, the duration parameter is coded so the transition takes place over a period of one second.

Note that when you specify a color for a color transition, you must use a color name, an RGB (red-green-blue) value, or a hex value. That means you can't use the CSS3 color specifications.

A text area that grows and changes color when a link is clicked

The HTML for the text area and link

```
<textarea id="comments" style="width:350px;height:125px;"></textarea><br>
<a href="#" id="grow_textarea">Increase text area</a>
```

The jQuery for the transition

```
$(document).ready(function() {
    $("#grow_textarea").click(function() {
        $("#comments").animate({
            width: 500,
            height: 200,
            backgroundColor: "#ededed",
            color: "green"
        }, 1000 );
    });
});
```

Color properties that can be animated

color	borderRightColor
backgroundColor	borderTopColor
borderBottomColor	outlineColor
borderLeftColor	

Description

- The animate method has been extended by jQuery UI to support *color transitions.*
- To use color transitions, you include the color properties in the properties map for the animate method.
- You can use a color name, an RGB value, or a hex value to specify a color.
- Please refer to chapter 8 for more information on coding the animate method.

Figure 13-8   How to use color transitions

How to use class transitions

Figure 13-9 shows how to use *class transitions*. Class transitions provide for changing the class that's assigned to one or more elements over a specified period of time so the change is gradual. You can use class transitions with the jQuery addClass, removeClass, and toggleClass methods that you learned about in chapter 7. You can also use them with the switchClass method, which is part of the jQuery UI core effects component.

The example in this figure shows how you can use a class transition to change the font size for a paragraph of text. To change the font size, the user can click the Medium, Large, or X-Large button on the page. Then, the event handler for the click event of the button that's clicked is executed.

You can see these event handlers in the jQuery code in this figure. For each handler, a function named setSize is called with a value that indicates the name of the class that should be assigned to the paragraph. These classes are defined in the CSS as shown here.

The setSize function starts by calling the removeClass method to remove any classes that are currently assigned to the paragraph. Then, this function calls the addClass method to add the class with the name that was passed to the function. This change takes place over a period of one second.

The syntax of the methods for class transitions

```
addClass(className[, duration])
removeClass([className][, duration])
toggleClass(className[, duration])
switchClass(removeName, addName[, duration])
```

Text before and after its size is changed

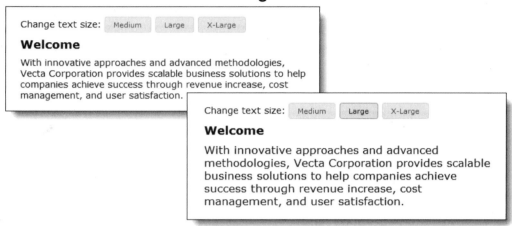

The HTML for the class transition

```
Change text size:
<input type="button" id="button1" value="Medium">
<input type="button" id="button2" value="Large">
<input type="button" id="button3" value="X-Large">
<h2>Welcome</h2>
<p id="p1">... INSERT CONTENT HERE ...</p>
```

The jQuery for the class transitions

```
$(document).ready(function() {
    $("#button1").click(function() { setSize("medium"); });
    $("#button2").click(function() { setSize("large"); });
    $("#button3").click(function() { setSize("x_large"); });

    function setSize(size) {
        $("#p1").removeClass();
        $("#p1").addClass(size, 1000);
    }
});
```

The CSS for the classes

```
.medium {font-size: 100%;}
.large {font-size: 120%;}
.x_large {font-size: 150%;}
```

Description

- jQuery UI provides for animating the transition between two classes over a specified duration. The animation can be applied to any properties that contain numeric values.

- *Class transitions* can be applied using the addClass, removeClass, toggleClass, and switchClass methods.

Figure 13-9   How to use class transitions

How to use visibility transitions

Figure 13-10 shows how to use *visibility transitions* to apply individual effects to an element as it's displayed or hidden. To do that, you use the show, hide, and toggle methods that you learned about in chapter 8. You can see the syntax of these methods at the top of this figure. Except for the method name, this syntax is the same as the syntax of the effect method you saw in figure 13-7.

To illustrate how visibility transitions work, the example in this figure presents a menu that has a submenu that can be displayed or hidden. Here, the main menu is implemented as an unordered list, and each list item contains an <a> element. Then, the third list item is followed by a div element that contains a submenu that consists of three <a> elements.

The jQuery for this example contains an event handler for the click event of the menu item that contains the submenu. Within this event handler, the div element that contains the submenu is selected, and the toggle method is called for it. If the submenu is hidden when this method is called, it causes the submenu to be displayed. If the submenu is displayed, it causes it to be hidden.

Two parameters are coded on the toggle method. The first one is for the effect that will be used to display and hide the submenu. In this case, the blind effect is used, which causes the submenu to be lowered and raised like vertical blinds. The second parameter is for the duration of the effect, which in this case is half a second.

The syntax of the methods for visibility transitions

```
{show|hide|toggle}(effect[, {options}][, duration][, callback])
```

A visibility transition that's used to show and hide a submenu

The HTML for a menu with an item that contains a submenu

```
<ul>
    <li><a href="index.html">Home</a></li>
    <li><a href="aboutus.html">About Us</a></li>
    <li><a href="#" id="solutions">Solutions</a></li>
    <div id="solutions_menu">
        <a href="solutions.html#vprospect">vProspect 2.0</a>
        <a href="solutions.html#vconvert">vConvert 2.0</a>
        <a href="solutions.html#vretain">vRetain 1.0</a>
    </div>
    <li><a href="support.html">Support</a></li>
    <li><a href="contactus.html">Contact Us</a></li>
</ul>
```

The jQuery for the visibility transition

```
$(document).ready(function() {
    $("#solutions").click(function() {
        $("#solutions_menu").toggle("blind", 500);
    });
});
```

Description

- jQuery UI provides for applying individual effects to elements using the show, hide, and toggle methods.

- All of the individual effects shown in figure 13-6 except for bounce, highlight, pulsate, shake, size, and transfer can be applied with these methods.

Figure 13-10   How to use visibility transitions

Perspective

With the information in this chapter, you should now be able to use any of the jQuery UI components. That includes the widgets you learned about in the last chapter, as well as the interactions and effects you learned about in this chapter. Keep in mind, though, that the interactions and effects have many more options and events than what's presented here. So you may need to do some additional research to get them to work exactly the way you want them to.

Terms

interaction	color transition
effect	class transition
easing	visibility transition

Summary

- The jQuery UI *interactions* provide for enhancing the usability of HTML elements. The five interactions include draggable, droppable, resizable, selectable, and sortable.

- To use an interaction, you select the element you want to apply it to and then call its method, often with one or more options and events.

- In many cases, you use classes in the jQuery UI download to format an element during different stages of an interaction.

- *Effects* can be divided into two categories: the effects that are included in the jQuery UI core effects component, and the individual effects that are implemented as separate components.

- To use the individual effects, you call the effect method on the element you want to apply the effect to. This method names the effect and can also include options, a duration, and a callback function that's called after the effect is executed.

- The jQuery UI core effects include color transitions, class transitions, visibility transitions, and easing.

- To implement a *color transition*, you include color properties in the properties map for the animate method, along with a duration parameter.

- To implement a *class transition*, you use the jQuery addClass, removeClass, and toggleClass methods or the jQuery UI switchClass method. With all four methods, you can provide a duration parameter.

- To implement a *visibility transition*, you use the show, hide, or toggle method, and you specify the effect for the transition in the first parameter.

Exercise 13-1   Use the sortable interaction

In this exercise, you'll experiment with a sortable list like the one in figure 13-5. Then, you'll add some options and events to the sortable method for this list. As you do this exercise, you may need to or want to refer to the documentation and demos on the jQuery UI web site.

Review the application

1. Use your text editor to open the HTML file in this folder:
   `c:\jquery\exercises\ch13\sortable\`

2. Run the application. Then, try to drag one of the items outside the list including below the last item to see what happens.

Add three more options to the sortable method

3. Add the containment option to the sortable method with either "parent" or the id of the element that contains the list items ("#vsupport") as its value. Then, run the application and notice that you can't drag an item to the right or left of the list, below the last item in the list, or above the first item in the list.

4. Comment out the containment option. Then, add the items option to indicate that all of the items in the list are sortable except for the last item. To do that, add a class named "sortable" to all of the list items in the HTML except the last one, and use this class (.sortable) as the value of the items option. Run the application to see that you can no longer drag the last item.

5. Add the revert option to the sortable method, and set its value to true. Then, run the application, drag an item to a new location, and notice that the item glides into its new location instead of snapping there.

Add two events to the sortable method

6. Add a start event to the sortable method with a callback function that accepts the event and ui parameters like the start option in figure 13-7. Within this function, use the removeClass method to remove the ui-state-default class from the item that's currently being dragged. To refer to this item, use the item property of the ui parameter. Then, use the addClass method to add the ui-state-active class to the item.

7. Run the application and drag an item to a new location. Notice that as you start dragging, the appearance of the item changes. However, the appearance doesn't change back when you drop it in its new location.

8. To fix that, add a stop event to the sortable method. The callback function for this event should work like the function for the start event, except it should remove the ui-state-active class and add the ui-state-default class. Run the application one more time to see that an item returns to its original appearance when it's dropped in a new location.

Exercise 13-2   Use transitions

In this exercise, you'll enhance an application that uses jQuery effects and animations by adding jQuery UI color and visibility transitions.

Review the application

1. Use your text editor to open the HTML file in this folder:

   `c:\jquery\exercises\ch13\animation\`

2. Run the application, and notice the jQuery animation that's done for the "jQuery FAQs" heading. Then, click on one of the subheadings to display the answer for the question, and click on the heading again to hide it.

Enhance the animation for the heading

3. Using figure 13-8 as a guide, add color animations to the heading. In the first animation, change the background color from its starting value of white to blue and the text color from its starting value of blue to red. In the second animation, reverse those color changes.

Enhance the effects for the subheadings

4. Using figure 13-10 as a guide, change the slideUp and slideDown methods in the toggle method for the h2 headings to hide and show methods with visibility transitions. For the show method, use the jQuery UI bounce effect over 500 milliseconds. For the hide method, use the jQuery UI puff effect over 1500 seconds.

5. Go to this URL to review the effects that jQuery UI provides:

   `http://jqueryui.com/effect/`

   Then, try two of the other effects in this application.

Section 4

Ajax, JSON, and API essentials

The three chapters in this section show you how to use Ajax, how to use JSON data, and how to use Ajax with the APIs (Application Programming Interfaces) for some of the most popular web sites. These are important skills for developing modern web sites.

In chapter 14, you'll learn how to use Ajax to load HTML, XML, and JSON data from a web server without loading a new web page. This chapter also shows you how to use Ajax with the API for Google Blogger to load blogs. This is a typical use of Ajax.

Then, in chapter 15, you'll learn how to use Ajax with the APIs for three other popular web sites: YouTube, Twitter, and Flickr. And in chapter 16, you'll learn how to use the API for Google Maps. When you complete these chapters, you'll be able to apply what you have learned as you explore the APIs for other web sites.

14

How to use Ajax, JSON, and Blogger

This chapter shows you how to use Ajax to update a web page with HTML, XML, or JSON data without loading a new web page into the browser. Since Ajax is commonly used to get data from popular web sites, this chapter also shows how to use Ajax with the API for Google's Blogger.

Introduction to Ajax **406**
How Ajax works 406
Common data formats for Ajax............................... 408
The members of the XMLHttpRequest object......................................410
How to use the XMLHttpRequest object 412

How to use the jQuery shorthand methods for Ajax **414**
The jQuery shorthand methods for working with Ajax 414
How to use the load method to load HTML data......................................416
How to use the $.get or $.post method to load XML data 418
How to use the $.getJSON method to load JSON data 420
How to send data with an Ajax request 422

How to use the $.ajax method for working with Ajax **424**
The syntax of the $.ajax method 424
How to use the $.ajax method to load data....................................426

How to use Ajax with the API for Google's Blogger **428**
Introduction to Google's Blogger 428
How to use the API for Blogger...430
How to use an online JSON editor to review the feed from a web site.......432
How to use Ajax and JSON to display Blogger posts.................................434

Perspective **436**

Introduction to Ajax

The four topics that follow introduce you to Ajax, the types of data that are commonly used with Ajax, and the XMLHttpRequest object that is the basis for Ajax.

How Ajax works

Ajax is the acronym for *Asynchronous JavaScript and XML*. As shown in figure 14-1, Google's Auto Suggest feature is a typical Ajax application. As you type the start of a search entry, Google uses Ajax to get the terms and links of items that match the characters that you have typed so far. Ajax does this without refreshing the page so the user doesn't experience any delays. This is sometimes called a "partial page refresh."

To make this work, all modern browsers provide an *XMLHttpRequest object* (or *XHR object*) that is used to send an Ajax request to the web server and to receive the returned data from the server. In addition, JavaScript is used in the browser to issue the request, parse the returned data, and modify the DOM so the page reflects the returned data. In many cases, a request will include data that tells the server what data to return.

On the web server, an application program or script is commonly used to return the data that is requested. Often, these programs or scripts are written before the JavaScript developers use them so they know how their requests must be coded. Otherwise, the JavaScript developers and the server-side developers need to coordinate so the Ajax requests can be processed by the server scripts.

The two diagrams in this figure show how a normal HTTP request is made and processed as well as how an Ajax request is made and processed. The main difference is that the server returns an entire page for a normal HTTP request so the page has to be loaded into the browser. In contrast, an Ajax request sends an XMLHttpRequest object to get data and the server returns only the data. In addition, JavaScript is used to send the request, process the returned data, and script the DOM with the new data. As a result, the web page doesn't have to be reloaded.

Because this Ajax technology is so powerful, it is commonly used by web sites like Facebook and Google Maps. When you post a comment to a friend's Facebook page, for example, the comment just appears. And when you move the cursor off of a Google Map, the map is automatically adjusted. In neither case is the page reloaded.

Beyond that, web sites like YouTube and Twitter provide *Application Programming Interfaces* (*APIs*) that show how to use Ajax to get data from their sites. This means that you can get data from these sites to enhance your own web pages. Since this is a skill that every modern web develop should have, this chapter shows you how to use the API for Google's Blogger, which is a typical API. Then, in the next two chapters, you'll learn how to use the APIs for four other web sites: YouTube, Twitter, Flickr, and Google Maps.

Google's Auto Suggest is an Ajax application

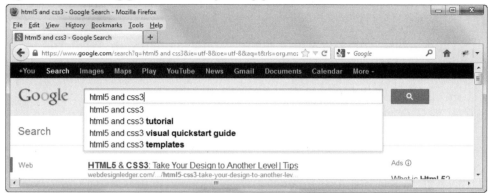

How a normal HTTP request is processed

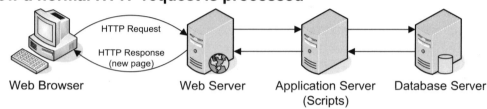

How an Ajax XMLHttpRequest is processed

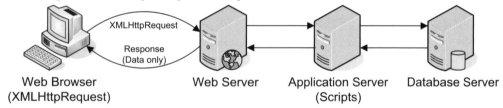

Description

- *Ajax* stands for *Asynchronous JavaScript and XML.* Unlike normal HTTP requests, Ajax lets you receive data from a web server without reloading the page. This is sometimes known as a "partial page refresh."

- As the Ajax name implies, JavaScript is essential to the use of Ajax because JavaScript not only sends the requests but also processes the responses and updates the DOM with the new data.

- To send an Ajax request, JavaScript uses a browser object known as an *XMLHttpRequest (XHR) object.* This object can include data that tells the application server what data is being requested.

- An XHR object is often processed by a program or script on the application server that's written in a language like PHP or ASP.NET. Then, the JavaScript programmer has to coordinate the Ajax requests with the application scripts.

- Today, web sites like Google's Blogger, YouTube, Twitter, and Flickr provide *APIs* (*Application Programming Interfaces*) that let you use Ajax to get data from their sites.

Figure 14-1   How Ajax works

Common data formats for Ajax

Figure 14-2 presents the three common data formats for Ajax applications. The easiest one to use is HTML, which you're already familiar with. When you use Ajax to load HTML data into a web page, you don't have to parse the data because it already includes the HTML tags for the data. In contrast, you do have to parse the data when you work with XML or JSON data.

Today, *XML (eXtensible Markup Language)* is the most popular format when working with Ajax, so much so that XML is part of the Ajax name. XML is an open-standard, device-independent format for exchanging data across the Internet, and its syntax and document tree mimic that of HTML. The downside to XML is that it's relatively difficult to use JavaScript and jQuery to parse the data in XML files.

JSON, pronounced "Jason", stands for *JavaScript Object Notation*, and its popularity for working with Ajax is growing quickly. This format is easy to understand, and most server-side languages already provide functions for JSON encoding. PHP, for example, has the json_encode() function, and ASP.NET has the DataContractJsonSerializer class.

JSON is based on a subset of the JavaScript programming language, and it uses conventions that are familiar to programmers of C-style languages like C, C++, Java, and JavaScript. Since its structure is a hierarchy of name/value pairs that are returned as an object, it is relatively easy to parse the JSON data with JavaScript and jQuery.

Although HTML, XML, and JSON are the three most popular data formats for working with Ajax, they aren't the only ones that are supported. In fact, you can also use plain text, YAML, and CSV files with Ajax.

The common data formats for Ajax

Format	Description	File extension
HTML	Hypertext Markup Language	html
XML	eXtensible Markup Language	xml
JSON	JavaScript Object Notation	json is often used

XML data

```
<?xml version="1.0" encoding="utf-8"?>
<management>
    <teammember>
        <name>Agnes</name>
        <title>Vice President of Accounting</title>
        <bio>With over 14 years of public accounting ... </bio>
    </teammember>
    <teammember>
        <name>Wilbur</name>
        <title>Founder and CEO</title>
        <bio>While Wilbur is the founder and CEO ... </bio>
    </teammember>
</management>
```

JSON data

```
{"teammembers":[
    {
        "name":"Agnes",
        "title":"Vice President of Accounting",
        "bio":"With over 14 years of public accounting... "
    },
    {
        "name":"Wilbur",
        "title":"Founder and CEO",
        "bio":"While Wilbur is the founder and CEO ... "
    }
]}
```

Description

- The common data formats for working with Ajax are HTML, XML, and JSON.

- *XML (eXtensible Markup Language)* is an open-standard, device-independent format that must be parsed by JavaScript or jQuery in the browser.

- *JSON (JavaScript Object Notation)* is fast becoming the most popular format for Ajax applications. In general, JSON files are smaller and faster than XML files. They are also easier to parse since JSON data is returned as JavaScript objects.

- Most server-side languages have methods that can be used to encode JSON data on the server. PHP 5, for instance, has the json_encode() method, and ASP.NET 4 has the DataContractJsonSerializer class.

- For more information on JSON APIs that are built into your favorite programming language, you can visit www.json.org.

Figure 14-2   Common data formats for Ajax

The members of the XMLHttpRequest object

Figure 14-3 presents all of the *members* (methods, properties, and events) of the XMLHttpRequest object. This object is behind every Ajax request, no matter what type of data is being requested. You'll see how the members of this object are used in the application in the next figure.

The two methods that are used with every request are the open and send methods. The open method is used to open a connection for a request. As you can see in the parameters for the open method, this method specifies whether the request is a GET or POST request and it provides the URL for the request.

After the open method is issued, the send method is used to send the request. If necessary, this method can include a data parameter that tells the server what data to return.

As you can see in the list of properties, the readyState property indicates the state of the request, the status and statusText properties provide the status code and status message that's returned by the server, and the responseText and responseXML properties provide the returned data in plain or XML format.

The last member in this figure is the onreadystatechange event that can be used for an event handler that processes the returned data. You'll see how this works in the next figure.

Incidentally, the GET and POST methods are the same ones that are used for an HTML form. When you use the GET method, the data is sent to the web server as part of the URL, but the total amount of data that can be sent is limited. When you use the POST method, the data that is sent is hidden and unlimited.

Members of the XMLHttpRequest object

Method	Description
abort()	Cancels the current request.
getAllResponseHeaders()	Returns a string that contains the names and values of all response headers.
getResponseHeader(*name*)	Returns the value of a specific response header.
open(*method,url*[,*async*] [,*user*][,*pass*])	Opens a connection for a request. The parameters let you set the method to GET or POST, set the URL for the request, set asynchronous mode to true or false, and supply a username and password if authentication is required. When asynchronous is used, the application continues while the request is being processed.
send([*data*])	Starts the request. This method can include data that gets sent with the request. This method must be called after a request connection has been opened.
setRequestHeader(*name,value*)	Specifies a name and value for a request header.

Property	Description
readyState	A numeric value that indicates the state of the current request: 0 is UNSENT, 1 is OPENED, 2 is HEADERS_RECEIVED, 3 is LOADING, and 4 is DONE.
responseText	The content that's returned from the server in plain text format.
responseXml	The content that's returned from the server in XML format.
status	The status code returned from the server in numeric format. Common values include 200 for success and 404 for not found.
statusText	The status message returned from the server in text format.

Event	Description
onreadystatechange	An event that occurs when the state of the request changes.

Description

- The table above shows the *members* (methods, properties, and events) that can be used with the XMLHttpRequest object.

Figure 14-3   The members of the XMLHttpRequest object

How to use the XMLHttpRequest object

Figure 14-4 shows how you can use the XMLHttpRequest object to get XML data from the web server without refreshing the web page. Here, the first example shows a portion of the XML file, but you can assume that this file includes all of the team members with full data in the bio fields. Then, the second example shows the div element that will receive the data returned by the XHR object.

The third example shows the JavaScript code for using an XHR object to send an Ajax request and receive the returned data. This is coded within the event handler for the ready event. The first statement in this JavaScript code uses the *new* keyword to create a new XHR object. This is followed by an event handler for the onreadystatechange event. The first statement in this handler is an if statement that tests whether the readyState property is 4 and the status property is 200, which means that the request has finished and was successful. If that's true, the if statement parses the returned data. Otherwise, it does nothing.

To parse the data, the first statement in the handler saves the responseXML property of the XHR object in a variable named xmlDoc. Then, the next statement uses the JavaScript getElementsByTagName method to store the data for each team member in an array variable named team. Next, it sets a variable named html to an empty string. This is the variable that the for loop that follows will fill with the formatted data for the team members.

In the for loop, one statement is executed for each team member in the team array. This statement uses the getElementsByTagName method to get the name, title, and bio data for each team member in the array. It also concatenates this data to the html variable along with br elements that provide the spacing between the data items. When the for loop finishes, the first statement after it saves the data in the html variable in the div element with "team" as its id. That will display the data as shown in the web page at the top of this figure.

At this point, though, the Ajax request hasn't been sent. The code has just set up the event handler for after it has been sent. To send the request, the open method that follows the event handler opens the connection for the request. It sets the method for the request to GET, provides the URL for the XML data, and sets asynchronous to true. In this case, the URL parameter is a relative URL that shows that the team.xml file is in the same folder as the file that contains the JavaScript.

Then, the send method sends the request. Once that's done, the onreadystatechange event will occur, and the event handler will parse the returned data if the request was successful.

With the exception of the ready event method, this example uses JavaScript instead of jQuery. This should give you some idea of how the XHR object has been traditionally used. Please note, however, that jQuery could be used for this application. In fact, with the advent of jQuery, Ajax programming has become much easier. Just keep in mind that the XHR object is used with every Ajax request, whether or not jQuery is used to issue the request.

A web page that uses the XHR object and JavaScript to load XML data

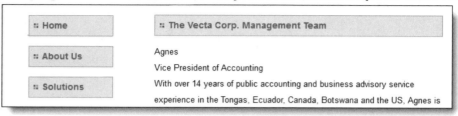

The XML file (team.xml)

```
<?xml version="1.0" encoding="utf-8"?>
<management>
    <teammember>
        <name>Agnes</name>
        <title>Vice President of Accounting</title>
        <bio>With over 14 years of public accounting ... </bio>
    </teammember>
    ...
</management>
```

The HTML div element that receives the data

```
<div id="team"></div>
```

The JavaScript for getting and parsing the data

```
$(document).ready(function() {
    xhr = new XMLHttpRequest();
    xhr.onreadystatechange = function() {
        if (xhr.readyState == 4 && xhr.status == 200) {
            xmlDoc = xhr.responseXML;
            var team = xmlDoc.getElementsByTagName("teammember");
            var html = "";
            for (i = 0; i < team.length; i++) {
                html +=
                    xmlDoc.getElementsByTagName("name")[i]
                        .childNodes[0].nodeValue + "<br>" +
                    xmlDoc.getElementsByTagName("title")[i]
                        .childNodes[0].nodeValue + "<br>" +
                    xmlDoc.getElementsByTagName("bio")[i]
                        .childNodes[0].nodeValue + "<br><br>";
            }
            document.getElementById("team").innerHTML = html;
        }
    }
    xhr.open("GET", "team.xml", true);
    xhr.send();
});
```

Description

- This application uses the XHR object to load all of the team members in the file named team.xml on the web server and display them in the div element with "team" as its id.

- The event handler for the onreadystatechange event parses the data returned by the method if the readyState property is 4 and the status property is 200.

Figure 14-4   How to use the XMLHttpRequest object

How to use the jQuery shorthand methods for Ajax

In this topic, you'll learn how to use the shorthand methods for working with Ajax that are provided by jQuery.

The jQuery shorthand methods for working with Ajax

Figure 14-5 summarizes the jQuery methods for working with Ajax. Here, the load method is used to get HTML data. The $.get and $.post methods are commonly used to get XML data, which is the default data type for these methods. And the $.getJSON method is used to get JSON data.

The examples show how these methods work. The first example uses the load method to load the HTML from a file named solutions.html. The second example uses the $.get method to load XML data. And the third example uses the getJSON method to load JSON data.

In the second example, the $.get method is coded with three parameters. The first parameter is the URL for a PHP script that will process the Ajax request. The second parameter passes data to the request in the form of a string. This data will be used by the PHP script to determine what data is returned. The third parameter names the function that will be called if the request is successful.

In the third example, the URL parameter for the $.getJSON method is for a JSON file. This method doesn't have a data parameter, and its success parameter consists of an embedded function that will be called if the request is successful.

The $.each method is also included in this figure. This method is commonly used for processing the data that's returned by an Ajax request. You'll see how this works in figure 14-8.

The shorthand methods for working with Ajax

Method	Description
`load(url[,data][,success])`	Load HTML data.
`$.get(url[,data][,success[,dataType])`	Load data with a GET request.
`$.post(url[,data][,success[,dataType])`	Load data with a POST request.
`$.getJSON(url[,data][,success])`	Load JSON data with a GET request.

The parameters for the shorthand methods

Parameter	Description
`url`	The string for the URL to which the request is sent.
`data`	A map or string that is sent to the server with the request, usually to filter the data that is returned.
`success`	A function that is executed if the request is successful.
`dataType`	A string that specifies the type of data (html, xml, json, script, or text). The default is XML.

The $.each method for processing the data that's returned

Method	Description
`$.each(collection, callback)`	The collection parameter is an object or array. The callback parameter is a function that's done for each item in the collection.

A load method

```
$("#solution").load("solutions.html");
```

A $.get method that includes data and calls a success function

```
$.get("getmanager.php", "name=agnes", showManager);
```

A $.getJSON method with an embedded function

```
$.getJSON("team.json", function(data){
    // the statements for the success function
}
```

Description

- jQuery includes several shorthand methods that let you request and receive HTML, XML, or JSON data.

- All of the shorthand methods let you include data that will let the web server filter the results of the request so only the right results are returned. You can send this data as a query string (as in the second example above) or as a map (see figure 14-9).

- The only difference between the $.get and $.post methods is the method that is used for the request (GET or POST). These are the same methods that you specify when you set up an HTML form.

- The $.each method is an expanded form of the each method that can be used to process the items in the returned data (see figure 14-8).

Figure 14-5   The jQuery shorthand methods for working with Ajax

How to use the load method to load HTML data

Figure 14-6 shows how to use the load method to load HTML data with an Ajax request. For this example, three div elements are coded within a file named solutions.html. The ids for these elements are "vprospect", "vconvert", and "vretain", which refer to three products. Then, one of these div elements is loaded when the user clicks on the link for the product.

You can see how this works in the jQuery for this application. It consists of the event handlers for the click events of the three links. In the load methods for these links, the URL not only consists of the name of the HTML file but also a reference to the div element for that link. For instance, #vconvert in the code that follows

```
$("#solution").load("solutions.html #vconvert");
```

gets the HTML for the div element with vconvert as its id.

The one benefit of using HTML data with Ajax requests is that the data is already within HTML elements that can be formatted by the CSS for the page. In other words, you don't have to parse the data that is returned by the request. In contrast, you do need to parse the XML or JSON data that is returned, as you will see in the next two figures.

By the way, you should know that if you test the load method with the Firefox, IE, or Safari browsers, it should work even if the HTML files are on your file server. If you're using Chrome or Opera, though, the HTML files need to be on a web server.

A web page that loads HTML elements when one of the links is clicked

The HTML for the user Interface

```
<p>Which Vecta Corp. solution are you interested in learning about?</p>
<a id="vprospect" href="#">vProspect 2.0</a> |
<a id="vconvert" href="#">vConvert 2.0</a> |
<a id="vretain" href="#">vRetain 1.0</a><br>
<div id="solution"></div>
```

The start of the second div element in the solutions.html file

```
<div id="vconvert">
    <p><strong>vConvert 2.0</strong></p>
    <p><img src="images/logo_vconvert.gif" width="63" height="36" >
        Create a highly user-friendly and easy-to-navigate information ...
    </p>
    <ul>
        <li>Build a visual and functional user front end that ... </li>
        <li>Cause the desired emotional response in a user to ...</li>
        ...
    </ul>
</div>
```

The jQuery that loads the data when a link is clicked

```
$(document).ready(function() {
    $("#vprospect").click(function() {
        $("#solution").load("solutions.html #vprospect");
    });
    $("#vconvert").click(function() {
        $("#solution").load("solutions.html #vconvert");
    });
    $("#vretain").click(function() {
        $("#solution").load("solutions.html #vretain");
    });
});
```

Description

- The load function can only load content from files on the same server as the page making the call.

- During testing, you'll be able to load files from the file system in Firefox, IE, and Safari, but Chrome and Opera require all of the files to be on an actual web server.

Figure 14-6 How to use the load method to load HTML data

How to use the $.get or $.post method to load XML data

The example in figure 14-7 shows how to use the $.get method to load XML data from a web server. Remember, though, that the $.post method works the same way, except the POST method is used to send the request.

The first parameter in the $.get method in this example gives the URL for the XML file that will be loaded by the request. Here again, this URL is relative to the file that contains the jQuery code. Then, the second parameter is the function that will be used to process the returned data. The parameter for this function is the data that's returned by the request.

Within this function, the first statement sets the value of the HTML div element that will receive the processed data to an empty string. Then, to process the returned data, it issues the find method for the data that's returned to find the children of the XML item named "management". Those children are the items named "teammember", and the each method is chained to the children so it can be used to process each of the team members.

The first statement in the each method sets a new variable named xmlDoc to the value of the this keyword, which is the team member that's being processed. Then, the next statement appends the data for that team member to the div element that will receive the processed data. Within the parameter for the append method, three find methods get the data for the "name", "title", and "bio" items in the returned data, and the text method gets the text for those items.

To keep this application simple, the formatting for the data that's returned is limited. Specifically, the name field is parsed into an h3 element, and br elements are added after the title and bio fields to add spacing after these fields.

To test the use of the $.get and $.post methods, the files named in the URL have to be on a web server, not a file server. Specifically, the XML file must be in the same domain as the web page that's making the request. This is required because of the *cross-domain security policy* that is used by most browsers.

A web page that loads XML data

The XML file (team.xml)

```
<management>
    <teammember>
        <name>Agnes</name>
        <title>Vice President of Accounting</title>
        <bio>With over 14 years of public accounting ... </bio>
    </teammember>
    ...
</management>
```

The HTML div element that receives the data

```
<div id="team"></div>
```

The jQuery

```
$(document).ready(function(){
    $.get("team.xml", function(data){
        $("#team").html("");
        $(data).find("management").children().each(function() {
            var xmlDoc = $(this);
            $("#team").append("<h3>" +
                xmlDoc.find("name").text() + "</h3>" +
                xmlDoc.find("title").text() + "<br>" +
                xmlDoc.find("bio").text() + "<br>");
        });
    });
});
```

Description

- The $.get and $.post methods work the same except for the method that's used to send the data in the XHR request.

- You can use the jQuery find method to get the data in an XML file. Here, the first find method starts a chain that gets the children (team members) of the management data that's returned, and the other three find methods get the name, title, and bio fields for each team member.

Figure 14-7   How to use the $.get or $.post method to load XML data

How to use the $.getJSON method to load JSON data

Figure 14-8 shows how to use the $.getJSON and $.each methods to load JSON data. In the $.getJSON method, the first parameter provides the URL for the JSON file with json as its extension. Then, the second parameter is the function that processes the JSON data if the request is successful. Note that the parameter in this function, data, is an object that will receive the data for the request.

Within the success function, the first $.each method processes each collection of items in the returned object. In this case, the object contains a single collection of team members. The first parameter for this function is the object returned by the request. Then, the second parameter is a function that processes each item in the collection using another $.each method. Here, each item is a team member.

The first parameter of the second $.each method is the this keyword, which refers to the current team member. Then, because the data for each team member consists of key/value pairs, the function for the second parameter accepts a key and a value. Within this function, the name, title, and bio items are appended to the div element with "team" as its id.

To refer to the value of each data item in the inner loop, this example uses object notation like this:

```
value.name
```

This refers to the name item in the object for the current item in the inner loop. If, for example, this inner loop is being executed for the second team member, the data for value.name is Damon, and the data for value.title is Director of Development. This shows how much easier it is to parse JSON data than XML data.

In general, to test the use of the $.getJSON method, the file named in the URL has to be on a web server, not a file server. It must also be in the same domain as the web page that's making the request. However, a simple application like this one where the URL points to a JSON file instead of a file for processing the request and returning JSON can be tested on your file server or computer.

A web page that loads JSON data

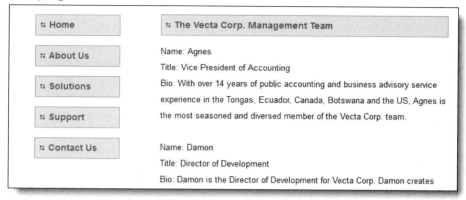

The JSON file (team.json)

```
{"teammembers":[
    {
        "name":"Agnes",
        "title":"Vice President of Accounting",
        "bio":"With over 14 years of public accounting... "
    },
    {
        "name":"Damon",
        "title":"Director of Development",
        "bio":"Damon is the Director of Development for ... "
    }
]}
```

The HTML div element that receives the data

```
<div id="team"></div>
```

The jQuery

```
$(document).ready(function(){
    $.getJSON("team.json", function(data){
        $.each(data, function() {
            $.each(this, function(key, value) {
                $("#team").append(
                    "Name: " + value.name + "<br>" +
                    "Title: " + value.title + "<br>" +
                    "Bio: " + value.bio + "<br><br>"
                );
            });
        });
    });
});
```

Description

- To process the returned JSON data, you can use nested $.each methods. The function in the first method will process each collection in the returned data (in this case, a single collection of team members).

- The function in the second $.each method will process each item (team member) in the collection. It will have two parameters that represent the key and value of each item. Then, you can use object notation to get the fields in the returned data.

Figure 14-8   How to use the $.getJSON method to load JSON data

How to send data with an Ajax request

Figure 14-9 shows how to send data with an Ajax request. To do that, you use the data parameter of a shortcut method to supply either a string or a map that contains the data. In this figure, the first example uses a string to send one name/value pair that asks for a "name" data item that has a value of "wilbur". The second example uses a map (or object literal) that's coded within braces to send the same name/value pair.

The $.get methods in both of these examples also include a third parameter that names the function that is called if the request is successful. Then, you code this function after the $.get method. This function has one parameter that receives the data returned by the Ajax request. Of course, you can also embed the function within the parameter the way it's done in the other examples in this chapter.

In some Ajax applications, forms are used to get the data that should be sent with a request. In that case, you can use the helper methods in this figure to package the data that's sent with the request. The serialize method collects the entries for a form as a string. The serializeArray method collects the entries for a form as an array of name/value pairs.

The next example in this figure shows how the serialize method works with a request for data. Here, the first statement in the ready event handler uses the serialize method to encode the form entries as a string and save that string in a variable named "formData". This is followed by a $.get method that uses the formData variable as its data parameter.

Whenever you send data with an Ajax request, you have to coordinate the data that you send with your request with the way the script on the server is written. For instance, you can tell from the first two examples that the PHP script in the file named getmanager.php accepts a data item named name, but what other data items can you send with a request?

Two ways to send data with an Ajax request

A $.get method that uses a string for the data parameter

```
$(document).ready(function() {
    $.get("getmanager.php", "name=wilbur", showManager);
    function showManager(data) {
        // process data
    }
});
```

A $.get method that uses a map for the data parameter

```
$(document).ready(function() {
    $.get("getmanager.php", {name:wilbur}, showManager);
    function showManager(data) {
        // process data
    }
});
```

The helper methods for working with Ajax

Function	Description
serialize()	Encode a set of form elements as a string that can be used for the data parameter of an Ajax request.
serializeArray()	Encode a set of form elements as an array of name/value pairs that can be used for the data parameter of an Ajax request.

The HTML for a form

```
<form id="contactForm">
    <!-- the controls for the form -->
</form>
```

jQuery that uses the serialize method

```
$(document).ready(function() {
    var formData = $("#contactForm").serialize();
    $.get("processcontact.php", formData, processReturnedData);
    function processReturnedData(data) {
        // the statements for the success function
    }
});
```

Description

- When you send data with an Ajax request, the URL is for a server-side script such as a PHP file. Then, the script is responsible for returning the data in XML or JSON format.

- The data parameter in a jQuery shortcut method is a name/value pair that can be set either as a query string or a map (object literal).

- The jQuery helper functions for Ajax make it easy to package form data before sending it to the server.

Figure 14-9   How to send data with an Ajax request

How to use the $.ajax method for working with Ajax

Although you can use the shortcut methods for many Ajax applications, the $.ajax method provides more options for making Ajax requests. You'll learn about this method next.

The syntax of the $.ajax method

Figure 14-10 presents the syntax of the $.ajax method, including some but not all of the options for this method. Besides a function that is executed when the request is successful, this method has options for functions that are done before the request is sent, whenever the request finishes, after the data is returned but before it is passed to the success function, and when an error occurs. These functions give you more control over the way the method works.

Note in this summary that all four of these functions can have parameters. One of these parameters is jqXHR, which refers to the jQuery XHR object (or *jqXHR object*). This object is a superset of the standard XHR object that includes the properties of the XMLHttpRequest object. This means that you can use the properties in figure 14-3 with this object.

In the beforeSend function, you can use the settings parameter to set properties in the jqXHR object before it is sent with the request. In the complete, error, and success functions, the jqXHR object is passed to the function. The status parameter in these functions returns a string that represents the status of the request. And the error parameter in an error function returns the text portion of the HTTP status.

The jsonp option is used to provide the name of a JSONP parameter that gets passed to the server. *JSONP*, or "JSON with padding", lets you request data from a server in a different domain, which is typically prohibited by web browsers due to their cross-domain security policies. JSONP does this by using a callback function that puts a script element in the DOM that tricks the browser into thinking that the file is actually on the client. JSONP is often used by the APIs for web sites, and you'll see how that works in the next chapter.

Other options for the $.ajax method let you provide a password and username if they are needed for authentication. They also let you determine whether the returned data can be cached by the browser and how long a request can last before it times out as a failed request.

The syntax of the $.ajax method

```
$.ajax({ options })
```

Some of the options for the $.ajax method

Options	Description
url	The string for the URL to which the request is sent.
beforeSend(*jqXHR, settings*)	A function that is executed before the request is sent. It can pass two parameters: the jqXHR object and a map of the settings for this object.
cache	A Boolean value that determines if the browser can cache the response.
complete(*jqXHR, status*)	A function that is executed when the request finishes. It can receive two parameters: the jqXHR object and a string that represents the status of the request.
data	A map or string that is sent to the server with the request, usually to filter the data that is returned.
dataType	A string that specifies the type of data (html, xml, json, script, or text).
error(*jqXHR, status, error*)	A function that is executed if the request fails. It can receive three parameters: the jqXHR object, a string that represents the type of error, and an exception object that receives the text portion of the HTTP status.
jsonp	A string containing the name of the JSONP parameter to be passed to the server. Defaults to "callback".
password	A string that contains a password that will be used to respond to an HTTP authentication challenge.
success(*data, status, jqXHR*)	A function that is executed if the request is successful. It can receive three parameters: the data that is returned, a string that describes the status, and the jqXHR object.
timeout	The number of milliseconds after which the request will time out in failure.
type	A string the specifies the GET or POST method.
username	A string that contains a user name that will be used to respond to an HTTP authentication challenge.

Description

- The $.ajax method provides options that give you more control over the way the Ajax request works, such as providing a function for handling errors.
- The *jqXHR object* is jQuery's superset of the standard XMLHttp Request object that provides the properties of that object.
- *JSONP*, or "JSON with padding", is a complement to JSON data that lets you request data from a server in a different domain, which is typically prohibited by web browsers due to their cross-domain security policies. You'll see this used in the next chapter.

Figure 14-10   The syntax of the $.ajax method

How to use the $.ajax method to load data

When successful, the application in figure 14-11 is like the one in figure 14-7. However, the $.ajax method sets the timeout option to 10000 milliseconds so it will time out with an error after 10 seconds. In addition, it provides two functions besides the function for successful completion.

In the beforeSend option, you can see the function that is executed before the Ajax request is sent. It just displays "Loading ..." in the div element that will receive the requested data, as shown in this figure. Of course, you could make this more interesting by displaying an animated gif like a progress indicator or a spinning wheel.

In the error option, you can see the function that is executed if an error occurs. This function is coded with three parameters: "xhr" for the jqXHR object, "status" for the string that describes the type of error that occurred, and "error" for the text portion of the HTTP status. Within the function, an alert method is used to display the status of the request (xhr.status), a hyphen, and then the text portion of the HTTP status (error). If, for example, a 404 error occurs, an alert dialog box like the one in this figure will be displayed. This, of course, is a common error when the URL that's specified can't be found.

In the success option, you can see the function for processing the data that's returned. This function has a parameter named "response" that will receive the data returned by the request. The first statement in this function uses the html method to set the data in the div element with "team" as its id to an empty string. This replaces the "Loading..." message that was displayed while the request was being processed.

This statement is followed by a jQuery statement that uses the find method to find the "management" data in the XML file, uses the children method to get the children (team members) within the management data, and uses the each method to process the data for each child. In the function for the each method, a variable named xmlDoc is set to the this keyword, which is the team member that's being processed by the each loop.

Then, the next statement uses the append method to append the data for the current team member to the div element with "team" as its id. To do that, it uses the find method to get the data for the name, title, and bio fields and the text method to get the text for these fields. This method also encloses the name value in an <h3> element, and it adds br elements after the title and bio fields to provide spacing after these fields.

A web page with a loading message and an alert dialog box for errors

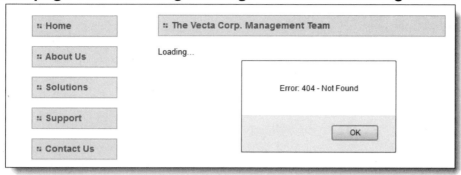

The XML file

```
<management>
    <teammember>
        <name>Agnes</name>
        <title>Vice President of Accounting</title>
        <bio>With over 14 years of public accounting ... </bio>
    </teammember>
    ...
</management>
```

The HTML div element that receives the data

```
<div id="team"></div>
```

The jQuery

```
$(document).ready(function() {
    $.ajax({
        type: "get",
        url: "team.xml",
        beforeSend: function() {$("#team").html("Loading...");},
        timeout: 10000,
        error: function(xhr, status, error) {
            alert("Error: " + xhr.status + " - " + error);
        },
        dataType: "xml",
        success: function(data) {
            $("#team").html("");
            $(data).find("management").children().each(function() {
                var xmlDoc = $(this);
                $("#team").append("<h3>" +
                    xmlDoc.find("name").text() + "</h3>" +
                    xmlDoc.find("title").text() + "<br>" +
                    xmlDoc.find("bio").text() + "<br>");
            });
        }
    });
});
```

Description

- When successful, this application works like the one in figure 14-7. However, it also provides a timeout value and two functions besides the one for successful completion of the request.

Figure 14-11   How to use the $.ajax method to load data

How to use Ajax with the API for Google's Blogger

Once you know how to use Ajax, you have the skills that you need for getting data from popular web sites like YouTube, Twitter, and Flickr. In fact, you can get data from any web site that provides an API for that.

To give you an idea of how this works, this chapter will now show you how to use Ajax with the API for Google's Blogger. The goal here is not so much to show you how to use Blogger, but rather how to use the API for any web site. Then, the next two chapters show you how to use the APIs for other popular web sites.

Introduction to Google's Blogger

Figure 14-12 introduces Google's Blogger. Blogger is a free, Google application that makes it easy to create your own blog on the Google site. For instance, the browser window at the top of this figure shows a fictitious blog for Vecta Corp. The URL for this blog is vectacorp.blogspot.com, and you can choose any available name for your blog.

To get started with Blogger, you need to get a key for its API. To do that, you can use the procedure in this figure. All that's required is a Google account. After you complete the Quota Request form and click the Submit button, you have to wait for an email that gives further instructions. Once you receive that email along with your API key, you're ready to create your own blog.

A fictitious blog on Google's Blogger at http://vectacorp.blogspot.com

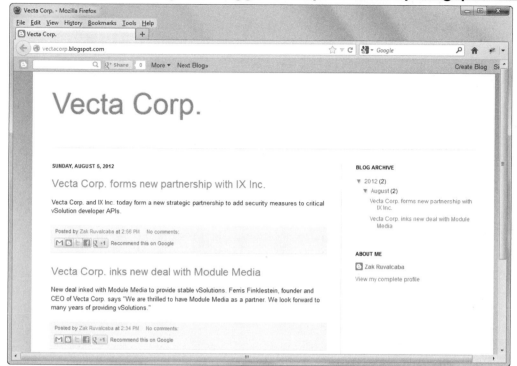

The URL for Google's Blogger
www.blogger.com

The URL for Google APIs
https://code.google.com/apis/console/

How to get a key for the Blogger API

1. Go to the URL for Google APIs that's shown above, and log in.

2. If this is the first time you've used the Google APIs, you'll be redirected to a welcome screen where you can click a "Create project" button. Then, click that button to go to the Console page.

3. Scroll down and click the "Request access" link for the Blogger API.

4. Fill out the Quota Request form, and click Submit when finished.

5. Wait for an email that confirms your request and provides the final steps that you need to follow for approval.

Description

- Blogger is a free, Google application that lets you create your own blog. To do that, you just need to open a Google account and get an API key as shown above.

- With Blogger, you can use with any available name for your blog followed by blogspot.com. For instance, the URL for the fictitious Vecta Corp blog shown above is: http://vectacorp.blogspot.com.

Figure 14-12   Introduction to Google's Blogger

How to use the API for Blogger

Figure 14-13 shows how to use the API for Blogger. The documentation for this API shows how to use Ajax and JSON to access the data in a blog. To start, you should click the Getting Started link and learn how Blogger works. There, you'll learn that a blog consists of posts, comments, pages, and users.

Then, you can click on the Using the API link to get the details on how to work with posts, comments, pages, and users. The start of that documentation is shown in the browser window at the top of this figure. If, for example, you click on the "Retrieving posts for a blog" link, you'll learn that you need to use a URL like the one in this figure. Within this URL, you code the blog id for your blog, assuming that's the blog that you want to retrieve. At the end of this URL, you code your API key in a key/value pair.

The documentation also shows the data items that are available for a post. To give you an idea of what they are, some of them are summarized in the table in this figure. For instance, "published" provides the date that a post was first published, and "author.image" provides the URL for the author's image file. This same type of documentation is available for comments, pages, and users, and you can review that documentation on your own.

The API documentation for Blogger

The URL for the start of the API documentation

https://developers.google.com/blogger/docs/3.0/getting started

The format of a URL for getting posts

https://www.googleapis.com/blogger/v3/blogs/BLOG-ID/posts?key=API-KEY

Some of the data items for working with posts

Item	Description
`published`	The date when the post was first published.
`updated`	The date when the post was last updated.
`url`	The URL for the post.
`title`	The title for the post.
`content`	The main content for the post.
`author.id`	The author's id.
`author.displayName`	The author's name.
`author.url`	The URL for the author's profile.
`author.image`	The URL for the author's image file.
`replies.totalItems`	The total number of replies to the post.

Description

* All blogs are assigned a blog id that you must use along with your API key to get the JSON feed for your blog.

* A blog consists of posts, comments, pages, and users, and the API documentation shows how to work with all of them including the data items that are available.

Figure 14-13   How to use the API for Blogger

How to use an online JSON editor
to review the feed from a web site

For many web sites, the API documentation is difficult to understand. Then, to save time, you may want to review the JSON feed that you want to use. That way, you can see what data it actually contains, and that may save you a few hours of studying the documentation.

To review the JSON feed for a web site, you can use the online JSON editor that's illustrated in figure 14-14. To start, you type or paste the URL for the JSON feed in the address bar of your browser and press the Enter key. That will display the JSON in the browser window. Unfortunately, that data is likely to be unformatted and difficult to read. In fact, it may be displayed in a single line. That's where the online JSON editor comes in.

To use this editor, select all of the JSON in your browser window (press Ctrl+A on a Windows system), copy it to the clipboard, switch to the URL for the editor that's shown in this figure, and paste the JSON into the left pane of the editor. Then, click the Format button to see formatted JSON, like the JSON shown in this example.

Next, click on the right arrow button between the two panes of the editor. That will display the JSON data in the right pane in structured format. Last, click on the Expand All button above this pane to see all of the JSON data in this format.

Now, if you look in the right pane, it's easy to tell what data items the feed contains. For instance, this example shows the kind, id, blog.id, published, updated, url, selfLink, and title items. Note that all of these are contained within an items item. You'll see how this works in the next figure.

This illustrates the potential that an online JSON editor has for saving you time. To use one, you just need to use the API documentation to figure out what the URLs are for the feeds you want to use. Then, you can use the JSON editor to decide what data items you want to use.

The Blogger feed for Vecta Corp's blog in an online JSON editor

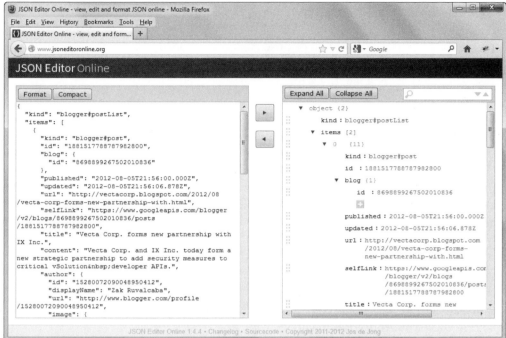

The URL for the online JSON editor

www.jsoneditoronline.org

The URL for the Vecta Corp blog (this should all be on one line)

**www.googleapis.com/blogger/v2/blogs/8698899267502010836/posts?
key=AIzaSyByJiL407voPRmQyNAYZKWxBC5FuI1BIdQ**

The procedure for reviewing a feed in the online JSON editor

1. Type or paste the URL for the feed into the address bar of your browser. Then, press the Enter key to see the contents of the JSON feed in the browser window.

2. Copy all of the JSON, go to the URL for the online JSON editor (above), and paste the JSON into the left pane of the editor.

3. Click the Format button at the top of the left pane to see the formatted JSON data.

4. Click the right arrow button between the panes to see a structured version of the data. Then, click on the Expand All button at the top of the right pane to see all of the data in the feed.

Description

- When the documentation for an API is difficult to understand, you can often save time by reviewing the data in the JSON feed for an application. That way, you can tell exactly what data your application is going to get.

- In the example above, the JSON feed for the Vecta Corp blog is displayed in an online JSON editor. This makes it easy to tell what data items the feed contains.

Figure 14-14   How to use an online JSON editor to review the feed from a web site

How to use Ajax and JSON to display Blogger posts

Figure 14-15 shows how you can use Ajax and JSON to display the posts for your own blog. To start, you can code a global variable that stores the value of your API key. This is a lengthy string of characters that you can paste into your code. Then, you can use this at the end of the URL option in the $.ajax method.

Next, you can code another global variable that will be used for the HTML that the Blogger data will be parsed into. After that, you should code this statement:

```
$.support.cors = true;
```

This allows for cross-domain JSON requests, even in browsers like IE that don't fully support them. Although you can sometimes use JSONP instead, that doesn't always work. In those cases, you can include the statement above, which enables Cross-Origin Resource Sharing (CORS).

Finally, you can code a ready event handler with the $.ajax method for getting the Blogger posts. In the URL option for this method, you code the URL for getting the Blogger data in a single line (not the two lines that this URL had to be broken into for this figure). Within this URL, you code the blog id for your blog. At the end of this URL, you code your API key.

In the success option for this method, you can use the $.each method to process the data for each post. The first parameter for this method can be data.items, which represents the data for all of the posts, and the second parameter is the function that is executed for each post.

Within this second function, the first parameter is the index of each post, which you don't need to use, and the second parameter is the object that contains the values of the data items for each post. Then, you can use the value object to get the data items for the post. For instance, value.url is the URL for the post, and value.author.displayName is the name for the author.

Remember that the primary goal here is to show you how to use the API for a web site and then use Ajax and JSON to get data from that web site. Of course, there's a lot more that you can do with Blogger, but this should get you started.

A web page that displays Blogger posts

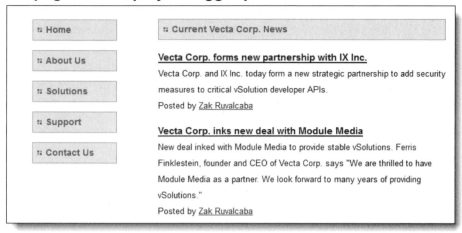

The HTML div element that receives the blog posts

```
<div id="posts"></div>
```

The jQuery for using Blogger

```
var apikey = "";    // your key goes between the quotation marks
var html = "";
$.support.cors = true;
$(document).ready(function() {
    $.ajax({
        // the url option that follows must be coded in a single line
        // the number in the url is the id for the blog
        url:"https://www.googleapis.com/blogger/v2/blogs/
            8698899267502010836/posts?key=" + apikey,
        dataType: "json",
        success: function(data) {
            $.each(data.items, function(index, value) {
                html += "<h3><a href='" + value.url + "'>" + value.title
                    + "</a></h3>"
                    + value.content
                    + "<br>Posted by <a href='" + value.author.url + "'>"
                    + value.author.displayName + "</a>";
            });    // end each method
            $("#posts").html(html);
        }    // end ajax options
    });    // end ajax method
});    // end ready
```

Description

- The data for the posts that are returned from Blogger consists of one set of items for each post. Then, the $.each method can be used to process the items within each set.

- In the function for the $.each method, the first parameter receives the index for each post. The second parameter receives a value object for the post. Then, object notation can be used to access the data items within the value object.

Figure 14-15   How to use Ajax and JSON to display Blogger posts

Perspective

Now that you've completed this chapter, you should be able to use jQuery to make Ajax requests that return HTML, XML, and JSON data from your server. You should also be able to use Ajax to get data from Google's Blogger. Because this is a typical use of Ajax and JSON, the next chapter shows you how to use Ajax with the APIs for YouTube, Twitter, and Flickr.

Terms

Ajax (Asynchronous JavaScript and XML)	member
XMLHttpRequest (XHR) object	cross-domain security policy
API (Application Programming Interface)	jqXHR object
XML (eXtensible Markup Language)	JSONP
JSON (JavaScript Object Notation)	

Summary

- *Ajax*, which standards for *Asynchronous JavaScript and XML*, lets you get data from a web server without refreshing the page. This means that a page can display new information based on the user's actions without the normal delays.

- To make an Ajax request possible, modern browsers provide an *XMLHttp-Request (XHR) object*. This object is used to make the request as well as receive the returned the data. An enhanced version of this object called the *jqXHR object* is used with Ajax requests that are done with jQuery.

- When you use Ajax, you use JavaScript (or jQuery) to make the request, process the returned data, and update the DOM so the data is displayed on the web page.

- The three common data formats for Ajax are HTML, XML (*eXtensible Markup Language*), and *JSON (JavaScript Object Notation)*. Because JSON makes it easier to parse the returned data, its popularity is growing rapidly.

- To make Ajax programming easier, jQuery provides shortcut methods like the $.get and $.getJSON methods, the $.ajax method, the $.each method, and two serialize methods for packaging form data so it can be used with an Ajax request.

- Many Ajax requests are processed on the web server by programs or scripts in languages like PHP or ASP.NET. Then, the web developers have to coordinate their Ajax requests with the programs or scripts that process the requests.

- JSONP, or "Jason with Padding", lets you get JSON data from a server in a different domain. This gets around the *cross-domain security policy* that most browsers have.

- Many popular web sites such as Blogger, YouTube, Twitter, and Flickr provide *APIs (Application Programming Interfaces)* that let you use Ajax to get data from their sites. Two ways to prepare for using a web site are studying the API documentation and using an online JSON editor to review the feed for a site.

Exercise 14-1   Modify the Blogger application

This exercise works with the Blogger application that gets JSON data from the Blogger web site. That way, you won't have to deploy this application on a web server in order to run the application and test your modifications to it.

Review the Blogger application, web site, and documentation

1. Use your text editor to open the HTML file in this folder:

    `c:\jquery\exercises\ch14\blogger\`

    After you review the JavaScript code in the last script element, run this application to see how it works.

2. Go to the Blogger home page in your browser by using this URL:

    `www.blogger.com`

    If you're interested, take a tour of this site.

3. Go the start of the Blogger API document in your browser by using this URL:

    `https://developers.google.com/blogger/docs/3.0/getting started`

    Then, scroll through that page to see what it offers.

4. Click on the "Using the API" link in the left sidebar to go to the API documentation. Then, click on the "Retrieving posts for a blog" link and scroll through that documentation. It shows the format for the URL for retrieving posts as well as the data items that you can get for a post.

Use an online JSON editor to review the Vecta Corp feed for posts

5. Carefully enter the URL that follows into the address bar of your browser, or copy the parts of this URL from the application to the address bar (this should all be on one line):

    `https://www.googleapis.com/blogger/v2/blogs/8698899267502010836/`
    `posts?key=AIzaSyByJiL407voPRmQyNAYZKWxBC5FuIlBIdQ`

    Then, press the Enter key. This should display the feed for the Vecta Corp blog in the browser window, although that data won't be formatted. Then, select all of this feed and copy it to the clipboard.

6. Switch to the online JSON editor at this address:

    `www.jsoneditoronline.org`

    Then, paste the JSON feed from the clipboard into the left pane.

7. Click the Format button at the top of the left pane to format the JSON. Click the right arrow button between the panes to structure the data for the feed in the right pane. And click the Expand All button at the top of the right pane to show all of the data in the feed. Is this data easier to understand than the API documentation for posts?

Add an error function to the $.ajax method

8. In your text editor for this application, add an error option to the $.ajax method. This method should be like the one in figure 14-11 that displays an error message in an alert dialog box when an error occurs.

9. Delete one digit from the blog id in the URL for the $.ajax method. Then, save the file and test this application. It should display an error message.

10. After you get this to work, undo the error that you introduced and test again to make sure it works correctly.

Use the $.getJSON method and display two more items

11. Comment out the entire $.ajax method. Then, below this method, code a $.getJSON method that gets the same result, but without the error function. Then, test this change.

12. Modify the $.getJSON method so it displays two more data items for each post: the publication date and the number of replies. These items should be displayed right after the other items for each post. To get the names of these items, you can refer back to the data in the online JSON editor. Then, test this change.

Do more experimentation?

13. If you want to try other aspects of Ajax, JSON, and Blogger coding, experiment on your own. That's a great way to learn.

15

How to use the APIs for YouTube, Twitter, and Flickr

In the last chapter, you learned how to use Ajax and JSON. You also learned how to use the API for Blogger, because working with another web site is a common use for Ajax and JSON. Now, in this chapter, you'll learn how to use Ajax and JSON with the APIs for three more web sites: YouTube, Twitter, and Flickr.

How to use Ajax with YouTube..**440**

How to use the API for YouTube 440

The query parameters and data items that you'll use the most 442

How to list videos by channel.. 444

How to list videos by search term 446

How to play videos in a video player on your site.................................... 448

How to use Ajax with Twitter...**450**

How to use the API for Twitter..450

How to display the tweets for a user..452

How to convert the URLs within tweets to links 454

How to display a timestamp for each tweet..456

How to use Ajax with Flickr..**458**

How to use the API for Flickr 458

The query parameters and data items that you'll use the most 460

How to display titles and descriptions for a Flickr photo feed...................462

How to display a gallery of Flickr photos 464

Perspective **466**

How to use Ajax with YouTube

YouTube, of course, is the most popular web site for viewing videos. However, YouTube also provides an API that lets other web sites access its videos and even play them on their own sites.

How to use the API for YouTube

Figure 15-1 shows the starting page for the YouTube API and the URL for getting to that page. Unlike many other APIs, the YouTube API lets you access public videos without any authentication. It also lets you play them on your web site.

Because this API provides so many capabilities, it is relatively complicated. A good place to start, though, is the Data API because it's the one that lets you retrieve different types of video feeds. The most common type of feed is videos that are selected by a search term. Another type of feed is one that selects videos based on a user's channel. In this chapter, you'll learn how to use both of these types of feeds.

Of course, YouTube provides for many other types of feeds. For instance, you can select videos from a user's playlist, subscriptions, favorites, and contacts. But you've got to start somewhere, and selecting videos by search terms and channels is a good place to start.

The web page for the start of the YouTube API

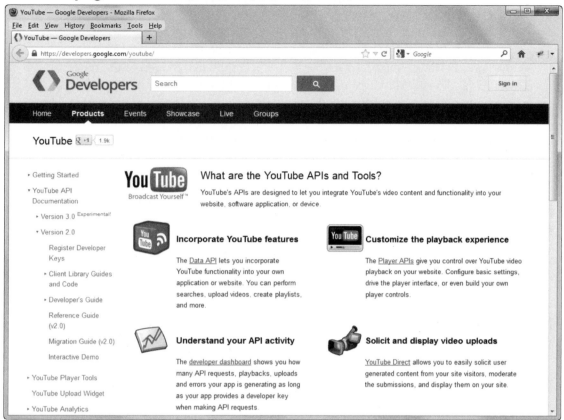

The URL for the YouTube API

https://developers.google.com/youtube/

Description

- YouTube provides a powerful API that lets you search for and play videos within your own web pages.

- Unlike many other APIs, the YouTube API allows for unauthenticated access to public videos, but on a read-only basis.

- The API lets you access videos by id, user channel, playlist, search term, and more. It also lets you construct a video player on your web page that plays YouTube videos.

- YouTube's Data API is the one that lets you retrieve videos, so clicking on the Data API link on the home page is a good way to get started with this API. From there, you can go on to the Developer's Guide and Reference Guide.

- Because the YouTube API offers so many capabilities, it is also a relatively difficult API. However, the examples that follow will help you get started with it.

Figure 15-1   How to use the API for YouTube

The query parameters and data items that you'll use the most

Figure 15-2 starts by showing you how to build the URLs for some common feeds. For all URLs, you start with the base URL shown at the top of the page. Then, you add one of the three extensions shown in the first table in this figure, followed by one or more of the query parameters shown in the second table.

For instance, this URL, which must be coded in a single line,

```
http://gdata.youtube.com/feeds/api/users/microsoft/uploads?
max-results=5&alt=json
```

will get a feed that returns the data for five videos for a user channel named "microsoft". Here, users/microsoft/uploads has been added to the base URL, and that is followed by two query parameters. The first one says that the data for 5 videos should be returned, and the second one says that JSON should be used for the feed, which will be true for all of the examples in this chapter.

Similarly, the URL after the second table in this figure adds /videos to the base URL and follows that with three parameters. Here, the first parameter is vq, which says that "apple" should be used for the search term.

In addition to the vq, max-results, and alt parameters, you can use the orderby parameter to determine the order in which the videos are returned. By default, the videos are returned in order of relevance, but other options such as the date published are common. You'll see how to use this option in the example in figure 15-4.

The third table in this figure summarizes some of the common data items that you'll use in your applications. For instance, published.$t gets the date and time that the video was published, and title.$t gets the title for the video. Also, gd$rating.average gets the average rating for a video, and yt$statistics.viewCount gets the total number of views that a video has had. In the applications in the next three figures, you'll see how some of these data items are used.

To get a better idea of what a feed contains, remember that you can use the procedure in figure 14-14 of the last chapter to display the JSON data in an online JSON editor that makes it easier to see the structure of the data. There, you'll see that $t is actually a data item that is subordinate to the id, published, updated, title, content, and name data items. That's why these data items have to be followed by .$t as shown in the table.

Incidentally, the default format for a YouTube feed is the Atom Syndication Format, which is an XML language and a W3 standard. Another common format that YouTube supports is RSS. In this chapter, though, JSON is used for all of the web feeds.

The base URL for YouTube videos

```
http://gdata.youtube.com/feeds/api
```

The URL extensions for retrieving different types of videos

URL Addition	Description
/standardfeeds/most_popular	Retrieve most popular videos.
/users/*user*/uploads	Retrieve videos by user channel.
/videos?vq=*search_term*	Retrieve videos by search term.

Common query parameters

Parameter	Description
vq	Search term.
max-results	Number of videos to retrieve.
orderby	Method used to order entries. Options are relevance, published, rating, and viewcount. Relevance is the default.
alt	The format for the feed. The default is atom, but json is a popular alternative.

A URL that gets videos by search term with three query parameters

```
http://gdata.youtube.com/feeds/api/videos?vq=apple&maxresults=5&alt=json
```

Common data items

Data item	Description
entry	The collection of returned items.
id.$t	The unique identifier for the video.
published.$t	The date and time that the video was published.
updated.$t	The date and time that the video was last updated.
category	A collection of categories that the video is associated with, such as scheme and term.
title.$t	The title for the video.
content.$t	Descriptive text for the video.
link[*index*]	An array of the links for a video. For example, link[0].href is the URL for the video on YouTube.
author[*index*].name.$t	A collection of the authors of the video. For example, author[0].name.$t is the name of the first author.
media$group.media$content[*index*].url	A collection of the URLs for video players.
media$group.media$thumbnail[*index*].url	A collection of the URLs for thumbnail images.
gd$rating	A collection that includes the average rating (average) and the number of raters (numRaters) for a video.
yt$statistics	A collection that includes the number of views the video has had (viewCount) as well as the number of users that have made the video a favorite (favoriteCount).

Figure 15-2   The query parameters and data items that you'll use the most

How to list videos by channel

Figure 15-3 shows an application that lists the data for five videos for a user channel (although only three are shown in this figure). In this case, that channel is "microsoft". Then, it uses four of the data items for each video: the link to the video on YouTube's web site, the title of the video, the date the video was published, and the name of the video's author.

In the $.getJSON method for this application, you can see that a $.each method is used to process the data for each video, and that data is referred to as

```
data.feed.entry
```

Then, the first four statements in the $.each method create variables for the four data items that are taken from the feed. Because YouTube provides multiple links for a video, the url variable is set equal to

```
item.link[0].href
```

This sets the variable equal to the href attribute of the first link (index 0) that's returned, because that's the URL that points to the video on YouTube's web site. Similarly, the fourth statement sets the author variable equal to the first author name in the collection because YouTube provides for more than one author.

The third statement is also interesting. It sets the variable equal to the published item in the feed. However, it also chains the substring method to this data item, which extracts the first 10 characters from the item. That's done because the published item not only includes the date, but also the time, and the first ten characters are just the date in this format: yyyy/mm/dd.

Once these variables are set up, the next statement creates a variable named text that puts the url variable within an <a> element so it will link to the You-Tube video. It also puts the title variable in the content for this <a> element so that's what will show in the link. Last, this statement puts the datepublished and author variables within text and follows that with two br elements for spacing. Then, the last statement in the $.each function appends the text variable to the div element that's used to display the content in the browser window.

Like the application in the last chapter that displays Blogger posts, the jQuery for this application starts by enabling CORS. That way, this application will work in browsers like Internet Explorer that don't fully support cross-domain requests. As you'll see in the applications in this chapter that get data from Twitter and Flickr, though, this isn't always necessary.

A web page that lists the videos for Microsoft's channel by relevance

Microsoft unveils a new look
Published: 2012-08-23 by Microsoft

Iñigo Sancho Te Enseña El Asus Zen Book
Published: 2012-07-05 by Microsoft

Cloud Computing's Role in Job Creation
Published: 2012-03-21 by Microsoft

The URL for this application (always in a single line)

```
http://gdata.youtube.com/feeds/api/users/microsoft/uploads?
max-results=5&alt=json
```

The div element that will receive the YouTube data

```
<div id="youtube"></div>
```

The jQuery

```
$.support.cors = true;
$(document).ready(function(){
    var url = "http://gdata.youtube.com/feeds/api/users/microsoft/uploads?
            max-results=5&alt=json";

    $.getJSON(url, function(data) {
        $.each(data.feed.entry, function(i,item) {

            // create four variables for each video
            var url = item.link[0].href;
            var title = item.title.$t;
            var datepublished = item.published.$t.substring(0, 10);
            var author = item.author[0].name.$t;

            // format the data with <a> and <br> tags
            var text =
                "<a href='" + url + "'>" + title + "</a><br>" +
                "Published: " + datepublished + " by " + author +
                "<br><br>";

            // append the data to the div element in the HTML
            $("#youtube").append(text);
        });
    });
});
```

Description

- This application uses four of the data items in the previous figure.
- The function for the $.each method is performed once for each of the five entries in the feed (data.feed.entry).
- The substring method for the published field extracts the first 10 characters from the field, which is the date portion of the field.

Figure 15-3   How to list YouTube videos by channel

How to list videos by search term

Figure 15-4 shows an application that lists the data for the five latest videos for the search term: buster posey (although only three are shown in this figure). Here, the data items that are used are the same as the ones in the previous figure. So what's different is the way the URL for the feed is constructed. In particular, the vq parameter for the URL must provide the search term.

The jQuery for this application consists primarily of an event handler for the click event of the Search button in the HTML. The first statement in this handler sets the contents of the div element that will receive the data from the feed to an empty string. This replaces the contents from the previous search.

This is followed by a statement that sets a variable named searchTerm to an empty string and an if statement that puts the search term that the user entered into this variable, unless the entry is an empty string. In that case, the else clause displays an error message.

The statement after that builds the URL by adding the user entry to the vq parameter in the base string and also adding the max-results, orderby, and alt parameters. Here, the orderby parameter is set to "published", which causes the videos to be returned in the order they were published with the most recent videos first. Then, the $.getJSON method uses that URL to get the feed for the search term. The function for this method, which processes the data in the feed, is the same as the one in the previous figure.

A web page that lists the latest videos for a search term

The URL for retrieving a video by search term

```
http://gdata.youtube.com/feeds/api/videos?vq=search_term
```

The HTML for the search field and button

```
Search by keyword: <input type="text" size="30" id="search">
<input type="button" value="Search" id="btnSearch">
```

The div element that will receive the YouTube data

```
<div id="youtube"></div>
```

The jQuery

```
$.support.cors = true;
$(document).ready(function(){
    $("#btnSearch").click(function() {
        // clear the data from the previous feed
        $("#youtube").html("");

        // make sure user has entered a search term
        var searchTerm = "";
        if (!$("#search").val() == "") {
            searchTerm = $("#search").val();
        } else {
            alert("You must enter a search term!");
        }

        // build the URL for the next feed
        var url = "http://gdata.youtube.com/feeds/api/videos?vq=" +
                  searchTerm + "&max-results=5&orderby=published&alt=json";

        // process the feed
        $.getJSON(url, function(data) {
        // same as in the previous figure
        });
    });
});
```

Description

- This is like the application in the previous figure except that it creates the URL for the $.getJSON method based on the user's entry in the search box.

Figure 15-4   How to list YouTube videos by search term

How to play videos in a video player on your site

Figure 15-5 presents an application that is similar to the last application except that it gets the data for videos based on a search for a user channel. Beyond that, it plays the videos in an onsite video player!

In the jQuery, the start of the click event handler for the Search button is similar to the one in the previous figure. It sets the HTML for the div element that will receive the data from the feed to an empty string. It gets the channel name that's entered by the user. And it builds the URL for getting the feed for that channel. It also sets the HTML for the div element that will display the video player to an empty string. Although this div element isn't shown here, it works just like the first div element.

Within the $.each method in the $.getJSON method, the first four statements are similar to those in the previous two examples. Note, however, that setting up the url variable requires the use of different data items:

```
var url = item.media$group.media$content[0].url
```

That's because this url is going to return a video player for each video. Here, the media$content entry is a collection of entries for the Flash and 3GPP formats (used in 3G capable phones). Then, to access the link for the Flash format, you set the index to zero. That returns a URL that can be used to build a Flash-based, video player.

The next statement creates the text that will be displayed for each video. This statement is also similar to the one in the previous two examples. The main difference is that the URL for the video is assigned to the title attribute of the <a> tag. That way, the URL can be retrieved and the video can be displayed on the page when the link is clicked.

The next event handler is for the click event of an <a> element. After this event handler clears any existing HTML from the div element for the video player, it gets the URL that was stored in the title attribute. Then, a string that contains object, param, and embed elements is created. Here, the object element sets the size for the player. Then, the value attribute for the param element that follows is set to the value of the url variable. To provide for browser compatibility, the two param elements are followed by an embed element with its src attribute set to the value of the url variable. That way, the videos will play in browsers like Firefox and Safari, as well as in Internet Explorer.

Of course, this doesn't explain exactly what's going on with the object, param, and embed elements, but this is the way you need to set this code up. To keep it simple, you can just paste the code for this application into your own pages whenever you need to include a video player.

A web page that plays the videos for a channel search in a video player

The jQuery

```
$.support.cors = true;
$(document).ready(function() {
    $("#btnSearch").click(function() {
        $("#youtube").html("");
        $("#video").html("");

        var channel = $("#channel").val();
        var channelUrl = "http://gdata.youtube.com/feeds/api/users/" +
                          channel + "/uploads?max-results=5&alt=json";

        $.getJSON(channelUrl, function(data) {
            $.each(data.feed.entry, function(i,item) {
                var url = item.media$group.media$content[0].url;
                var title = item.title.$t;
                var datepublished = item.published.$t.substring(0, 10);
                var author = item.author[0].name.$t;
                var text = "<h3><a href='#' title='" + url + "'>" + title +
                           "</a></h3>" +
                           "<p>Published: " + datepublished + " by " +
                           author + "</p><br>";
                $("#youtube").append(text);
            });

            $("a").click(function() {
                $("#video").html("");
                var url = $(this).attr("title");
                var text =
                  "<object width='425' height='344'>" +
                  "<param name='movie' value='" + url + "'></param>" +
                  "<param name='allowFullScreen' value='true'></param>" +
                  "<embed src='" + url +
                  "' type='application/x-shockwave-flash'
                      allowfullscreen='true' width='425'
                      height='344'></embed>" +
                  "</object>";
                $("#video").append(text);
            });
        });
    });
});
```

Figure 15-5   How to play YouTube videos in a video player on your site

How to use Ajax with Twitter

Twitter, of course, is the popular web site for posting tweets. The good news is that the API for Twitter lets you retrieve any user's tweets without authorization. This means you can display them on your own web site.

Be aware, however, that the Twitter JSON feed currently limits you to 150 views per hour. Once you exceed that limit, it won't display the feed until the hour has passed. For the purposes of this book, though, that shouldn't be a problem.

How to use the API for Twitter

Figure 15-6 shows how to use the API for Twitter. This API provides basic functions like connecting to a user's timeline and parsing tweets, as well as advanced functions like connecting to Twitter using Web Services, mobile applications, and more.

Since this is a relatively simple API, you can get started with it quite easily. To get you going, this chapter shows you how to parse a user's timeline, which can be used to display your own tweets on your own web page so your visitors can see what you've been tweeting.

As this figure shows, the base URL for Twitter feeds let you return the data in JSON format. In this chapter, though, the three examples use a form of JSON called JSONP.

JSONP was briefly mentioned in the last chapter, but here's that information again. *JSONP*, or "JSON with padding" is a complement to JSON data. It provides a way to request data from a server in a different domain, which is typically prohibited by web browsers due to their *cross-domain security policies*. JSONP does this by using a callback function that puts a script element in the DOM that tricks the browser into thinking that the file is actually on the client.

The fourth query parameter in the first table in this figure is the one that provides for the JSONP callback function. To do that, this parameter is set to a question mark (?). That's all it takes to use JSONP with Twitter. If this parameter is omitted, the JSON feed won't be parsed correctly by the JavaScript.

The other parameters are screen_name, count, and include_rts. The screen_name parameter specifies the user for the timeline that should be returned. The count parameter specifies the maximum number of entries to return. Note that retweets are included in the count, although they're not returned by default. If you want to include retweets, you can set the include_rts parameter to 1 (true).

The first two data items in the second table in this figure are the ones you commonly use with tweets. The other ones are for the user that posted the tweets. You'll see how the first two are used in the three applications that follow.

The web page for the Twitter API

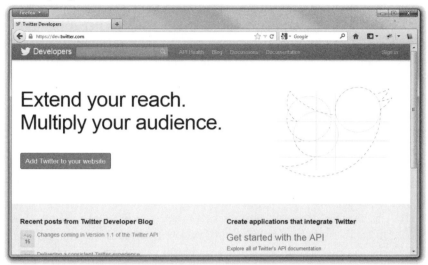

The URL for the Twitter API

`https://dev.twitter.com`

The base URL for a user's Twitter timeline that returns JSON

`http://api.twitter.com/1/statuses/user_timeline.json`

Common query parameters

Parameter	Description
`screen_name`	The user's timeline to return.
`count`	The maximum number of entries to return. Retweets are included in the count even if they're not returned. The default is 20.
`include_rts`	If set to 1 (true), retweets are included. The default is 0 (false).
`callback`	Optional unless the return format is JSONP, which it is in the examples in this chapter. Then, this parameter must be coded as callback=?.

A URL that gets tweets by user with four query parameters (on one line)

```
"http://api.twitter.com/1/statuses/user_timeline.json?
screen_name=microsoft&count=5&include_rts=1&callback=?"
```

Common data items

Data item	Description
`text`	A tweet in a user's timeline. It may contain URLs that the tweeter embedded in the tweet.
`created_at`	The date and time that the tweet was made.
`user.location`	The location of the user.
`user.url`	The URL for the user's web site.
`user.followers_count`	The number of followers of the user.
`user.friends_count`	The number of friends of the user.

Figure 15-6   How to use the API for Twitter

How to display the tweets for a user

Figure 15-7 shows how to display the tweets for a user using JSONP data. Here, the URL that's declared for this application is for JSON data, and the four parameters specify microsoft as the user, 5 as the number of tweets to return, true for including retweets, and ? as the callback function for JSONP.

In the function for the $.getJSON method for this application, only the text data item is used. It includes all of the information shown in the example at the top of this figure for each tweet. To add spacing between the tweets, two br elements are coded after each tweet. Then, when the $.each method finishes, the append method is used to append the tweets to the div element in the HTML after an h3 element that provides a heading for the tweets.

Of course, you could enhance this application by providing a search box that lets the users enter the name of the user whose tweets they would like to review. Then, the users could easily switch from one set of tweets to another. You could also format the tweets and provide the tweet date as you'll see in the next two applications.

A web page that displays tweets from Microsoft

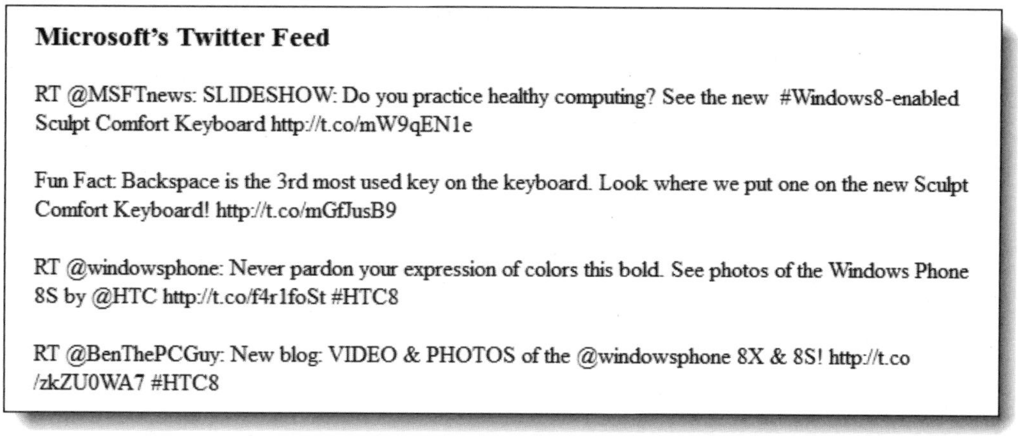

Microsoft's Twitter Feed

RT @MSFTnews: SLIDESHOW: Do you practice healthy computing? See the new #Windows8-enabled Sculpt Comfort Keyboard http://t.co/mW9qEN1e

Fun Fact: Backspace is the 3rd most used key on the keyboard. Look where we put one on the new Sculpt Comfort Keyboard! http://t.co/mGfJusB9

RT @windowsphone: Never pardon your expression of colors this bold. See photos of the Windows Phone 8S by @HTC http://t.co/f4r1foSt #HTC8

RT @BenThePCGuy: New blog: VIDEO & PHOTOS of the @windowsphone 8X & 8S! http://t.co/zkZU0WA7 #HTC8

The HMTL element that will receive the data from the feed

```
<div id="twitter"></div>
```

The jQuery

```
$(document).ready(function(){
    var url = "http://api.twitter.com/1/statuses/user_timeline.json?
               screen_name=microsoft&count=5&include_rts=1&callback=?";
    var tweet = "";

    $.getJSON(url, function(data) {
        $.each(data, function(i,item) {
            tweet += item.text + "<br><br>";
        });
    $("#twitter").html(
        "<h3>Microsoft&rsquo;s Twitter Feed</h3>").append(tweet);
    });
});
```

Description

- The URL for connecting to a user's Twitter feed must include the user's screen name.
- Because this application retrieves JSONP data, the callback query parameter must be coded as shown above.

Figure 15-7   How to display the tweets for a user

How to convert the URLs within tweets to links

Figure 15-8 shows you how to enhance the formatting of the tweets so any URLs in the tweets are converted to clickable links. Then, the user can click on a link to go to the page that's represented by the URL. Otherwise, this application is the same as the one in the previous figure, so it only uses the text data item.

The difference in the jQuery for this application is that a function named convertUrlToLink is used to find the URLs in the tweets and convert them to links. This function uses plain JavaScript, not jQuery, and you don't have to understand what it does, especially since this book doesn't present the JavaScript features that it uses. If you want to use it, you can just copy the function into your code and call it as shown in this figure.

If you are interested in the JavaScript code for this function, here's a brief description. The first line of code sets up a regular expression that will find a URL and saves this expression in a variable named exp. The /i at the end of this regular expression means that case-sensitivity should be ignored when performing the search for a URL.

Then, the second line of code calls the replace method of a string (the text for the tweet). The first parameter for this method is the regular expression in the exp variable. The second parameter is a string that contains "$1" twice. Here, the $1 represents the URL that the regular expression found. As a result, this URL is plugged into the string in two places, and that string replaces the value of the text data item that came from the tweet. The result is that the URL is the value of the href attribute in an <a> element as well as the text in that element.

You can see this in the example at the top of this figure. This means the user can click on the URL link to go to the page it refers to.

A web page that displays tweets with clickable URL links

Microsoft's Twitter Feed

RT @MSFTnews: SLIDESHOW: Do you practice healthy computing? See the new #Windows8-enabled Sculpt Comfort Keyboard
http://t.co/mW9qEN1e

Fun Fact: Backspace is the 3rd most used key on the keyboard. Look where we put one on the new Sculpt Comfort Keyboard!
http://t.co/mGfJusB9

RT @windowsphone: Never pardon your expression of colors this bold. See photos of the Windows Phone 8S by @HTC
http://t.co/f4r1foSt #HTC8

RT @BenThePCGuy: New blog: VIDEO & PHOTOS of the @windowsphone 8X & 8S!
http://t.co/zkZU0WA7 #HTC8

The modified $.getJSON method that calls a convertUrlToLink function

```
$.getJSON(url, function(data) {
    $.each(data, function(i,item) {
        tweet += convertUrlToLink(item.text) + "<br><br>";
    });
    $("#twitter").html(
        "<h3>Microsoft&rsquo;s Twitter Feed</h3>").append(tweet);
});
```

The convertUrlToLink function

```
function convertUrlToLink(text) {
    // a regular expression that can be used to find a URL in a tweet
    var exp =
        /(\b(https?):\/\/[-A-Z0-9+&@#\/%?=~_|!:,.;]*[-A-Z0-9+&@#\/%=~_|])/i;

    // a statement that uses the search method with the regular expression
    // to find any URL and then enclose it with an <a> element
    return text.replace(exp,"<br><a href='$1'>$1</a>");
}
```

Description

- This application just shows how to find a URL within a tweet and enclose it in an <a> element so it will be a clickable link in the browser.

- The convertUrlToLink function uses a JavaScript regular expression with the replace method, and neither is presented in this book. However, you can use this function by copying it into your code, even if you don't understand how it works.

- In brief, the regular expression in this example is a standard expression that will find a URL within a block of text. The replace method uses that expression to find a URL and then replaces the URL with an <a> element that has the URL ($1) as its href attribute as well as its contents.

Figure 15-8 How to convert the URLs within tweets to links

How to display a timestamp for each tweet

Figure 15-9 shows how you can enhance a tweet by adding a timestamp to it. To do that, the jQuery uses the created_at data item for the tweet. But rather than just display that date, this application calls a function named formatTime to format the date and time in a way that's more interesting for the user. For instance, the timestamp for the first tweet in this example is "about 2 hours ago". Other than that, this application is the same as the one in the previous figure.

Here again, the function that's used is written in JavaScript and some of the date and time methods it uses aren't presented in this book. However, you can use this function just by copying it into your code and then calling it whenever you want to convert a tweet date and time to the format that's shown.

In case you're interested, the first statement in this function creates a string that represents a valid date. This is necessary because the value in the created_at data item is in a format that Internet Explorer doesn't recognize as a date. So, this statement creates a date string that Internet Explorer does recognize.

The next two statements in this function convert the tweet date and time into the number of milliseconds since January 1, 1970. The fourth statement gets the current date and time in milliseconds. And the fifth statement subtracts the tweet value in milliseconds from the current date value in milliseconds, divides that by 1000 so the result is in seconds, and stores the result in the variable named timeago.

The rest of this function uses if, else if, and else clauses to determine if the value of the variable timeago is less than a minute, less than two minutes, less than 45 minutes, less than 90 minutes, less than a day, less than two days, or two days or more. If the condition for one of these clauses is true, an appropriate message is returned. If, for example, timeago is 42, "less than a minute ago" is returned. Or, if timeago is 2400 (40 x 60), "40 minutes ago" is returned.

This example and the previous one show that you sometimes need to use JavaScript skills that aren't presented in this book. That's especially true when you want to do something that jQuery doesn't provide methods for. So eventually, you'll probably want to learn more about JavaScript. To do that, we of course recommend *Murach's JavaScript and DOM Scripting*.

A web page that displays a timestamp for each tweet

Microsoft's Twitter Feed

RT @MSFTnews: SLIDESHOW: Do you practice healthy computing? See the new #Windows8-enabled
Sculpt Comfort Keyboard
http://t.co/mW9qEN1e
about 2 hours ago

Fun Fact: Backspace is the 3rd most used key on the keyboard. Look where we put one on the new Sculpt
Comfort Keyboard!
http://t.co/mGfJusB9
about 3 hours ago

RT @windowsphone: Never pardon your expression of colors this bold. See photos of the Windows Phone
8S by @HTC
http://t.co/f4r1foSt #HTC8
about 5 hours ago

The modified $.getJSON function that calls the formatTime function

```
$.getJSON(url, function(data) {
    $.each(data, function(i,item) {
        tweet += urlToLink(item.text) + "<br>" +
                    formatTime(item.created_at) + "<br><br>";
    });
    $("#twitter").html(
        "<h3>Microsoft&rsquo;s Twitter Feed</h3>").append(tweet);
});
```

The formatTime function

```
function formatTime(tweetDateTime) {
    var dateTimeString = tweetDateTime.substr(4, 7) +
                            tweetDateTime.substr(26) +
                            tweetDateTime.substr(10, 15);
    var tweetDate = new Date(dateTimeString);
    var tweetTime = tweetDate.getTime();
    var currentTime = new Date().getTime()
    var timeago = parseInt((currentTime - tweetTime) / 1000);

    if      (timeago < (1*60)) return "less than a minute ago";
    else if(timeago < (2*60)) return "about a minute ago";
    else if(timeago < (45*60)) return
        (parseInt(timeago / 60)).toString() + " minutes ago";
    else if(timeago < (90*60)) return "about an hour ago";
    else if(timeago < (24*60*60)) return
        "about " + (parseInt(timeago / 3600)).toString() + " hours ago";
    else if(timeago < (48*60*60)) return "1 day ago";
    else return (parseInt(timeago / 86400)).toString() + " days ago";
}
```

Description

- This application shows how to convert the date for a tweet to a user-friendly
  representation of the time that takes the user's time zone into consideration.

Figure 15-9   How to display a timestamp for each tweet

How to use Ajax with Flickr

Flickr is a web site that lets you store photos on it for free. This means that you can access your photos anywhere you are as long as you can connect to this web site. Since you can also store a description for each photo that includes a thumbnail image and text within HTML tags, this site can also be used as a simple Content Management System (CMS).

How to use the API for Flickr

Figure 15-10 shows the URL for Flickr and the URL for the API for Flickr. In the web page for the API, you can see that Flickr refers to its API as "The App Garden."

The App Garden encourages developers to write new applications that use the Flickr API. The Garden also has a link (http://www.flickr.com/services/) that showcases some of the custom applications that people have developed. To get you started with this API, though, this chapter presents two relatively simple applications.

The Flickr feed that's used the most is the "public photos & videos" feed. This feed allows unauthenticated, public access to any Flickr photos. Other available feeds include those that are summarized in the table in this figure.

The web page for the Flickr API

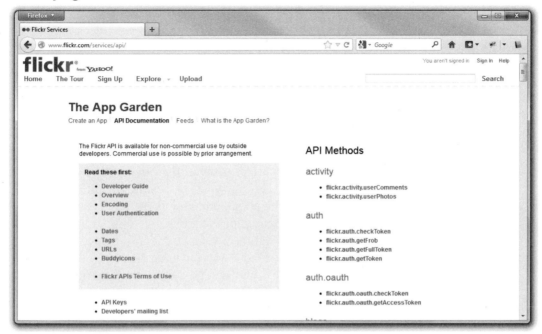

The URL for Flickr
http://www.flickr.com

The URL for the Flickr API
http://www.flickr.com/services/api/

Flickr feeds

Feed	Description
Public photos & video	Returns public content matching specified criteria.
Friends photostream	Returns public content for the contacts, friends, and family of a specified user.
Public favorites for a user	Returns public favorites for a user.
Group discussions	Returns recent discussions for a specified group.
Group pools	Returns items recently added to a specified group.
Forum discussions	Returns recent topics from the Flickr forum.
Recent activity	Returns recent activity for a specified user.
Recent comments	Returns recent comments by a specified person.

Description
- Flickr is a web site that lets you store your photos on it for free. That means you can access your photos wherever you are.
- Flickr provides an API called "The App Garden" that lets you retrieve public photos without authorization, although you do need to know the user ids for a photo feed.

Figure 15-10   How to use the API for Flickr

The query parameters and data items that you'll use the most

Figure 15-11 presents the base URL for retrieving a public photo feed, and the first table presents the common parameters that are used with that URL. Then, the example after the table shows how those parameters can be used. There, the id parameter specifies the id of a Flickr user. The format parameter specifies that the data is JSON. The jsoncallback parameter specifies that JSONP will be used. And the tags parameter specifies that only the photos with the "vectacorp" tag should be returned.

The second table in this figure summarizes some of the Flickr data items that are commonly used for a photo feed. For instance, title is the title of a photo, link is the URL for the Flickr page for the photo, media.m is the URL for the photo itself, and description is the description for the photo.

Note, however, that the description item includes a thumbnail image of the photo in an <a> link that has the URL for the Flickr page for the photo. It also includes <p> tags for the text. This means that you can display the description in a web page without applying your own HTML tags to it. In effect, this works like a simple Content Management System (CMS).

But also note that the description starts with a <p> element that contains an <a> link that accesses the Flickr page for whoever posted the photo. As you will see in the application in the next figure, you may want to remove these <p> elements from the descriptions for some applications.

The base URL for retrieving a public photo stream
http://api.flickr.com/services/feeds/photos_public.gne

Common query parameters

Parameter	Description
id	A user id.
ids	A comma-delimited list of user ids.
tags	A comma-delimited list of tags.
tagmode	Controls whether the returned items must match all of the tags specified (tagmode=all) or any of the tags specified (tagmode=any).
format	The format of the returned feed. Atom 1.0 is the default.
lang	The display language of the feed. The default is English.
jsoncallback	Optional unless the return format is JSONP, which it is in the examples in this chapter. Then, this parameter must be coded as jsoncallback=?.

A URL that gets a JSON feed for a specific user's id (in one line)
http://api.flickr.com/services/feeds/photos_public.gne?
id=82407828@N07&format=json&jsoncallback=?&tags=vectacorp

Common data items

Data item	Description
items	The collection of returned items.
title	The title of the photo.
link	The URL for the Flickr page for the photo or video.
media.m	The URL for the photo.
date_taken	The date the photo was taken.
description	Descriptive text for a photo, plus a thumbnail image in an <a> element that links to the full photo on the Flickr site. This data is formatted with HTML tags so it's ready for display.
published	The date and time the image or video was uploaded to Flickr.
author	The author's username and email.
tags	The filtering tags for an an image or video.

The description for the first item in the JSON feed for the URL above
```
"description":
    "<p><a href=\"http://www.flickr.com/people/82407828@N07/\">
        zakruvalcaba<\/a> posted a photo:<\/p>
    <p><a href=\"http://www.flickr.com/photos/82407828@N07/7550727644/\"
        title=\"Wilbur\">
        <img src=\"http://...\" alt=\"Wilbur\" /><\/a><\/p>
    <p>While Wilbur is the founder and CEO of Vecta Corp, ....<\/p>"
```

Description

- The description member of the feed for a photo or video includes a thumbnail image and descriptive text that are formatted by HTML tags. This means that you can display the description in a web page without applying any HTML tags to it.

Figure 15-11   The query parameters and data items that you'll use the most

How to display titles and descriptions for a Flickr photo feed

Figure 15-12 shows how to display the title and descriptions for the photos in a Flickr feed. In the example at the top of this figure, you can see the title and description for the first photo in the feed. Here, the title of the photo is "Wilbur" and the description starts with a thumbnail photo of the full photo. If you click on this thumbnail, the Flickr page for this photo will be displayed.

In the jQuery code for this application, you can see the parameters that are used for the URL and the $.getJSON method that's used to load the Flickr data. Then, the $.each method is used to process the returned data in the usual way.

The only aspect of this code that's new is the last statement in the each method. After the title and description data have been concatenated to the variable named html, the replace method is used to replace the first <p> element in the data for each photo with an empty string. This is the element that contains the <a> link to the Flickr page for the person who posted the photo.

To get this replacement to work right, the first parameter in the replace method must exactly match the data in the description. To make sure you get this right, you can paste the URL for the feed into the address bar of your browser and open the feed. Then, you can copy and paste the data that you want to replace.

Incidentally, this application and the next one get the photos for a Flickr user that represents a fictitious company, Vecta Corp. This user has uploaded photos that have either the vectacorp tag, as in this figure, or the vectacorpbuilding tag, as in the next figure. For each tag, there are just five photos, but that's enough to show you how the Flickr API works.

A web page that displays titles and descriptions for a photo feed

The HMTL element that will receive the data from the feed

```
<div id="team"></div>
```

The jQuery

```
$(document).ready(function(){
    var url = "http://api.flickr.com/services/feeds/photos_public.gne?
            id=82407828@N07&format=json&jsoncallback=?&tags=vectacorp";

    $.getJSON(url, function(data) {
        var html = "";

        $.each(data.items, function(i, item){
            html += "<h3>" + item.title + "</h3>";
            html += item.description;

            // this statement replaces the code at the start of the
            // description with an empty string
            html = html.replace(
                "<p><a href=\"http://www.flickr.com/people/82407828@N07/\">\
                zakruvalcaba<\/a> posted a photo:<\/p>", "");
        });

        $("#team").html(html);
    });
});
```

Description

- This application displays just two items from the Flickr feed: title and description. However, the description item includes the thumbnail image for the photo as well as descriptive information that includes HTML tags (see the feed in the previous figure).

- This application also removes the unwanted <p> element at the start of the description item by replacing it with an empty string.

- Because the thumbnail image is within an <a> element, clicking on it goes to the full image on the Flickr site.

- When used like this, Flickr becomes a simple Content Management System (CMS).

Figure 15-12   How to display titles and descriptions for a Flickr photo feed

How to display a gallery of Flickr photos

Figure 15-13 shows how Flickr photos can be used in a gallery of images. Here, thumbnail images are displayed in the gallery. Then, when the user clicks on one of those thumbnails, the full image is displayed with Lightbox, the plugin that you learned how to use in chapter 11.

In the URL for this application, the tags parameter specifies the vectacorp-building tag instead of the vectacorp tag. As a result, this application gets the feed for a different set of photos than the previous application used.

This time, the jQuery uses the title and media.m data items in the feed. The first statement in the $.each method starts an <a> element with media.m (the URL for the photo) as the href attribute and title as the title attribute. This means that clicking on this link will cause the photo to be displayed. This statement also sets the rel attribute to "lightbox[vecta]", which will automatically activate the Lighthouse plugin when a link is clicked and use the title attribute as the caption of the photo.

The second statement in the $.each method puts an img element within the <a> link. Since its src attribute is set to media.m, the img element will display the photo. Note, however, that the width and height attributes set this image to 120 x 100 pixels, so they will be displayed in thumbnail size.

Then, the third statement in the $.each method ends the <a> element, and the last statement in the $.getJSON method sets the HTML for the div element that will receive the data to the HTML that has just been built. The overall result is that thumbnail images are displayed in the image gallery, and clicking on one of these images will display the full image in Lightbox.

A web page that displays a gallery of Flickr photos

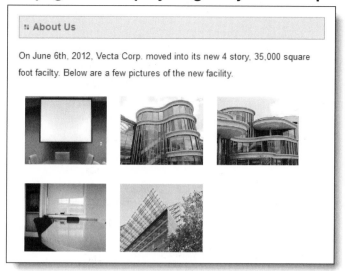

The HMTL element that will receive the data from the feed

```
<div id="newbuilding"></div>
```

The jQuery

```
$(document).ready(function(){
    var url = "http://api.flickr.com/services/feeds/photos_public.gne?
        id=82407828@N07&format=json&jsoncallback=?&tags=vectacorpbuilding";

    $.getJSON(url, function(data){
        var html = "";

        $.each(data.items, function(i, item){
            html += "<a href=" + item.media.m + " title=" + item.title +
                " rel=lightbox[vecta]>";
            html += "<img src=" + item.media.m +
                " width=120 height=100>";
            html += "</a>";
        });

        $("#newbuilding").html(html);
    });
});
```

Description

- This application gets the URLs for Flickr photos and puts them within img elements within <a> elements. To limit the size of these images when they're displayed, the width and height attributes for the img elements are set to 120 and 100 pixels.

- This application also uses the Lightbox plugin to display the full photos when an image in the gallery is clicked. To make that work, the rel attributes of the <a> elements are set to lightbox[vecta].

Figure 15-13   How to display a gallery of Flickr photos

Perspective

Now that you've completed this chapter, you should know how to use the APIs for three more web sites. You should also realize that the APIs for some sites (like Twitter) are quite simple, but the APIs for others (like YouTube) are complicated. Our goal in this chapter was to give you enough information to get you started with YouTube, Twitter, and Flickr so you can take it from there.

In the next chapter, you'll learn how to use the API for Google Maps, which is another complicated API. After that, our hope is that you'll have the confidence to dig into the API for any web site and figure out how to use it to do what you want.

Terms

JSONP
cross-domain security policy

Summary

- One of the common uses of Ajax and JSON is to get feeds from popular web sites like YouTube, Twitter, and Flickr.

- The APIs for YouTube, Twitter, and Flickr show you how to build the URLs for feeds, including the use of query parameters. They also summarize the data items that are provided by the feeds.

- If you have trouble understanding the API documentation for some web sites, you can display one of its feeds in your browser or in an online JSON editor. That usually makes the data structure easier to understand.

- *JSONP* is often used for web site feeds because it provides a way to request data from a server in a different domain, which is typically prohibited by the *cross-domain security policies* of web browsers. To use JSONP with a typical API, you set a query parameter like callback or jsoncallback to a question mark (?).

Exercise 15-1 Modify the YouTube application

This exercise has you review the YouTube application in figure 15-4 and then modify it so it displays a thumbnail image for each video in the list.

Review the YouTube application, web site, and API

1. Use your text editor to open the HTML file in this folder:

   `c:\jquery\exercises\ch15\youtube_search\`

   Then, run this application to see how it works.

2. Go to the start of the YouTube API by using this URL:

   `https://developers.google.com/youtube/`

   Then, scroll through that page to see what it offers.

3. Click on the Data API link to go to that documentation. Then, review that page and click on any of the links to get more information. If you take 5 or 10 minutes to experiment with this documentation, you'll probably agree that it's relatively difficult to use.

Use an online JSON editor to review the YouTube feed for a search

4. Carefully enter the URL that follows into your browser's address bar and press Enter:

   `http://gdata.youtube.com/feeds/api/videos?vq=oprah&max-results=5&alt=json`

   This should display the feed for Oprah in the browser window, but the data won't be formatted. Then, select all of this feed and copy it to the clipboard.

5. Switch to the online JSON editor at this address:

   `www.jsoneditoronline.org`

   Then, paste the JSON feed from the clipboard into the left pane.

6. Click the Format button at the top of the left pane to format the JSON. Click the right arrow button between the panes to structure the data in the right pane. And click the Expand All button to show all of the data in the feed. Then, scroll through this data to find the data items in figure 15-2 as well as many more.

Add a thumbnail image to the listing for each video

7. Use your text editor to create a new variable named thumbnail in the $.each method for this application. This variable should receive the URL for the first thumbnail image for each video by using this data item:

   `item.media$group.media$thumbnail[0].url`

8. Add an img element to the end of the text variable for this application that uses the thumbnail variable as the value of the src attribute for the element. This will display the thumbnail image after the other items for each video. Then, test this enhancement.

16

How to use the API for Google Maps

In the last chapter, you learned how to use the APIs for three of the most popular web sites to get content from those sites for your own web pages. Now, you'll learn how to use the API for Google Maps so you can add a map to your web site and provide driving directions between two points on the map.

Introduction to Google Maps **470**
Introduction to the Google Maps API 470
The classes for adding a Google map to a web page 472
The script element for the Google Maps API.................................474
How to add a Google map to a web page 474

How to display markers on a map **476**
The classes and methods for geocoding and markers.................476
How to create an address list that displays markers....................478

How to display messages on a map...............................**480**
The classes and methods for messages and markers.................. 480
How to add messages to markers..482
How to add custom messages to markers 484
How to add Flickr images to messages 486

How to display driving directions..................................**488**
The classes and methods for directions and listeners 488
How to display driving directions on your own site....................490

Perspective **492**

Introduction to Google Maps

You've probably used more than one Google map by now, either on the Google Maps web site or on another web site. If so, you know how easy one is to use. You may have also used Google Maps to get directions from one point to another.

The good news is that you can add Google maps to your own web site, either for free or for a small fee. At this writing, for example, Google Maps allows 25,000 free map requests per day, before it starts charging a small fee. That means that you can use your web site to show your customers your location on a Google map and even provide driving directions from your customers' locations to yours.

Introduction to the Google Maps API

In figure 16-1, you can learn how to get started with the Google Maps API. To start, you can use the documentation to learn about the API. When you display this documentation, you'll see that it is extensive. That of course is because this API provides so many capabilities, but that also makes this API difficult to comprehend and use.

For instance, the screen in this figure shows the start of the Table of Contents for the API Reference. But that Table of Contents scrolls down for many pages, and it's hard to figure out how to get started with it. Then, if you click on one of the items in the Table of Contents, you go to another level of complexity.

In this chapter, though, you'll learn how to use this API to develop some of the most useful map applications. If you refer to the API as you read this chapter, you'll realize that this chapter has done its best to simplify what you need to know. You'll also realize that this chapter presents just a small fraction of the classes and methods that this API provides. Later, if you want to use Google Maps for other applications, you'll have to dig into this documentation on your own.

If you're going to use the Google Maps API for your own web site or a web site that you're developing (not for a school project), you should get an API key by using the procedure in this figure. Then, you'll be able to monitor your application's usage of this API. This also provides a way for Google to contact you if your application exceeds the maximum number of free requests that Google allows.

The URL for the Google APIs Services Console

`code.google.com/apis/console/`

The base URL for the documentation for the Google Maps API

`developers.google.com/maps/documentation/javascript/reference`

The web page for the start of the API reference

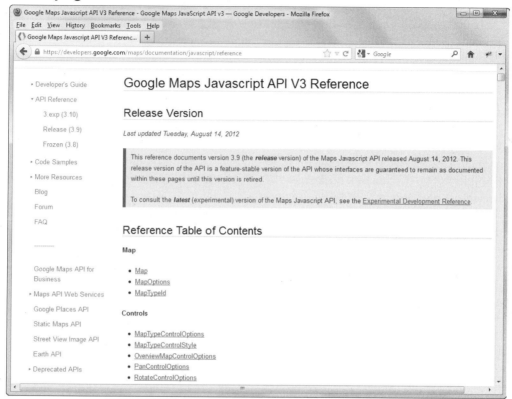

How to get a key for the Google Maps API

1. Go to the URL for the APIs services console that's shown above, and log in.

2. If this is the first time you've used the Google APIs, you'll be redirected to a welcome screen where you can click a "Create project" button. Then, click that button to go to the Console page.

3. Click on the Services link in the left sidebar.

4. Scroll down and enable the API v3 by changing its switch from "off" to "on".

Description

- You should use an API key with the Google Maps API so you can monitor your application's usage of the API.

- Google Maps allows up to 25,000 free requests per day before charging a small fee.

- The documentation for the Google Maps API is extensive, which makes it difficult to use. However, the examples in this chapter will get you started with it.

Figure 16-1   Introduction to the Google Maps API

The classes for adding a Google map to a web page

Unlike some of the other APIs that you've seen, the Google Maps API consists of classes that provide the methods and properties that you need for adding Google maps to your web pages. For instance, the first table in figure 16-2 summarizes three of the classes that you use for adding a map to a web page.

Because the documentation is so extensive for the Google Maps classes, it's sometimes useful to use a URL to go to the documentation for a class. For instance, you can go to the documentation for the LatLng class by adding #LatLng to the base URL at the top of this figure. This is true for any of the classes that are presented in this chapter. Just add the pound sign and the class name to the base URL in the address bar.

You may remember from earlier chapters that the *constructor* for a *class* creates an *object* from that class. That constructor may require one or more parameters. For instance, the constructor for the Map class in the first table requires two parameters. The first one identifies the HTML element that will receive the map. The second one provides one or more options for the map. When this constructor is executed, it creates a Map object, and the map for that object is displayed in the HTML element of the page.

Similarly, the constructor for the LatLng class requires two parameters. The first one is for the latitude of a point in a map, and the second one is for the longitude of that point. When this constructor is executed, it creates a LatLng object that can be used to mark the center of a map.

The MapTypeId class in the first table is a different type of class that isn't used to create objects. Instead, it provides the names for *constants* that can be used with other classes. These constants identify the type of map that should be displayed.

The second table in this figure summarizes the three required options for the second parameter of the constructor for a Map object. Then, the example after that table shows how the three options and classes are used to add a map to a web page. First, a variable named mapOptions is created that contains three options. The zoom option is set to 8, which is a good starting value for most maps. The center option is set to a LatLng object that's created by the LatLng constructor. And the mapTypeId option is set to the ROADMAP constant in the MapTypeId class. After this variable is created, it is used as the second parameter in the constructor for the Map class.

The first parameter in this constructor is set to the HTML element that has its id attribute set to "map". Note, however, that this is followed by a get(0) method. This is a jQuery method that gets the DOM object for that element, which is required by the Map constructor. Note too that the Map constructor is preceded by the new keyword just as the LatLng constructor is preceded by that keyword. This keyword is required whenever you use a constructor to create a new object.

When the Map constructor is executed, it uses the Google Maps API to create the specified map and display it in the HTML element that's specified by the first parameter. In this example, the map is also stored in a variable named "map", but that isn't necessary unless you need to refer to it later.

The base URL for the Google Maps API reference

developers.google.com/maps/documentation/javascript/reference

The placeholders for specific classes

```
#Map
#MapTypeId
#LatLng
```

The classes for adding a map to a web page

Class	Description
Map(*element, options*)	This constructor creates a Map object. The first parameter specifies the HTML element that receives the map. The second parameter provides options for the map.
LatLng(*latitude, longitude*)	This constructor creates a LatLng object based on its latitude and longitude parameters.
MapTypeId	This class provides constants for the four map types: ROADMAP, HYBRID, SATELLITE, and TERRAIN.

The required options for the Map constructor

Option	Setting
zoom	A number that provides the initial zoom level.
center	A new LatLng object that identifies the center of the map.
mapTypeId	A MapTypeId constant that specifies the map type.

How to use the three classes to create a map object

```
var mapOptions = {
    zoom: 8,
    center: new google.maps.LatLng(33.4936111, -117.1475),
    mapTypeId: google.maps.MapTypeId.ROADMAP
};
var map = new google.maps.Map($("#map").get(0), mapOptions);
```

Description

- A *constructor* for a *class* creates a new *object* from that class. For instance, the constructor for the Map class creates a Map object. Then, the methods of the class can be called from the Map object. The new keyword must be used with any constructor.

- The constructor for a Map object can include many options in its second parameter, but only the three in the table above are required.

- For the zoom option, you can experiment with the values until you get the map the way you want it, but 8 is a good value to start your experimentation with.

- To provide the value for the center option, the new keyword is used with the LatLng constructor.

- To provide the value for the mapTypeId option, one of the constants in the MapTypeId class is used.

- To create a Map object, you use a jQuery selector to identify the HTML element that will receive the map. Then, you use the get(0) method to get the DOM object for that element.

Figure 16-2   The classes for adding a Google map to a web page

The script element for the Google Maps API

Figure 16-3 shows how to use the classes of the previous figure to add a map to a web page. But note first that a script element is required that refers to the Google Maps API. This is required for every application for this chapter, although it isn't shown in the other figures, and it can be coded before or after the one for jQuery because the Google Maps API doesn't use jQuery.

Note that the URL for this API includes a key parameter that you can use to specify your API key. Although this parameter isn't required, Google recommends that you include it. To get an API key, you can follow the procedure in figure 16-1.

How to add a Google map to a web page

Figure 16-3 also shows the HTML for the div element that will receive the map in this example, and the jQuery for displaying the map in that element. Here, the jQuery code is the same as in the previous figure. First, a variable with the three required map options is created. Then, the Map constructor is used to create the map with those options and display it in the div element. Here again, you don't need to store the Map object in a variable unless you're going to need to refer to that map later on in your code.

In this example, the LatLng constructor for the center option is coded with actual latitude and longitude values, which represent Temecula, California. You can do that if you happen to know the values that you want to use. However, you can also use geocoding to get those values as shown in the next two figures.

Once you add a Google map to a web page, it works just like a map on the Google Maps web site. As a result, the user can use the controls to zoom in or out of the map or to move the map up, down, right, or left. The user can also drag the map up, down, right, or left. To reveal different portions of the map based on the user's actions, Google Maps uses Ajax.

A web page that displays a Google map

The script element for the Google Maps API (on one line)

```
<script src="https://maps.googleapis.com/maps/api/js?key=your_api_key
&sensor=false"></script>
```

The HTML for the div element that will receive the map

```
<div id="map"></div>
```

The jQuery

```
$(document).ready(function(){
    var mapOptions = {
        zoom: 8,
        center: new google.maps.LatLng(33.4936111, -117.1475),
        mapTypeId: google.maps.MapTypeId.ROADMAP
    };
    var map = new google.maps.Map($("#map").get(0), mapOptions);
});
```

Description

- To use the Google Maps API for a web page, you must always include a script element like the one above. Although the API key is optional, Google recommends you include it.

- When you use the Map constructor to create a Google map, the map is displayed in the HTML element that is identified by the first parameter of the constructor. To get the DOM object for this element, you use the jQuery get method with a parameter of zero.

- In this example, the LatLng method is used with actual values for the latitude and longitude parameters. Often, though, you'll use geocoding to get those parameter values, as shown in the next two figures.

- When you add a Google map to a web page on your site, the users can use the controls on the map and drag the map horizontally and vertically just as they would with a map at the maps.google.com web site.

Figure 16-3   How to add a Google map to a web page

How to display markers on a map

In the topics that follow, you'll learn how to add markers to a map. As part of that, you'll learn how to use geocoding to get the latitude and longitude for an address.

The classes and methods for geocoding and markers

Figure 16-4 presents the classes and methods that you need for geocoding and for adding a marker to a map. *Geocoding* refers to the conversion of an address into a location that consists of the latitude and longitude for the location, and vice versa. That's what the Geocoder class and its geocode method do.

As the second table in this figure shows, the geocode method has two parameters. The first one is for the request, or GeocoderRequest object, which can have several properties including the two properties in the third table in this figure. If the conversion is from an address to a location, the address property should be used. If the conversion is from a location to an address, the location property should be used.

The second parameter of the geocode method is a callback function that receives the results of the request in the form of a GeocoderResult object. This object contains several properties including those in the fourth table in this figure.

This method is illustrated by the first example in this figure. Here, the first parameter is a request object that consists of an address (4340 N Knoll, Fresno, CA) so the conversion will be to a LatLng object for the location of that address. Then, the second parameter is a callback method that receives the result object as its parameter. In this case, that parameter is referred to as results.

The alert statement in the callback method shows how to get the location from the result object. To get the formatted_address property of the object, this code is used:

```
results[0].formatted_address
```

Here, the index refers to the first item in the object, which can be an array. Then, to get the location property of the object, this code is used:

```
results[0].geometry.location
```

Note, that both properties are available in the result object, even though the address was part of the request. Note too that the lat method is used to get the latitude of the location, and that the lng method could be used to get its longitude.

The next example in this figure shows how to use the constructor for the Marker method. Although this method can be coded with many options, only the position and map options are required. Here, the position option is coded as a new LatLng object, and the map option is coded with the name of the variable that the map is stored in. When this constructor is executed, the marker is added to the map.

The classes for geocoding and creating markers

Class	Description
`Geocoder`	This constructor creates a Geocoder object that provides methods that communicate with Google servers and return geocodes.
`Marker(options)`	This constructor creates a Marker object that marks a position on a map. Two of the commonly-used options are position, which gives the location of the marker as a LatLng object, and map, which identifies the map for the marker.

One of the methods of the Geocoder class

Method	Description
`geocode(request, callback)`	Sends a GeocoderRequest object to Google servers that contains an address or a location and returns a GeocoderResult object that contains the results in an array.

Two of the properties of the GeocoderRequest object

Property	Description
`address`	The address of the request as a string.
`location`	The location of the request as a LatLng object.

Three of the properties of the GeocoderResult object

Property	Description
`address_components`	The components of the address. From this property, you can use long_name and short_name to get those properties.
`formatted_address`	The formatted address as a string.
`geometry.location`	The location of the request as a LatLng object. From this property, you can use the lat() and lng() methods to get the latitude and longitude of the location.

How to use the geocode method

```
geocoder = new google.maps.Geocoder();
geocoder.geocode({address: "4340 N Knoll, Fresno, CA"}, function(results) {
    alert("Latitude for " + results[0].formatted_address + " is " +
        results[0].geometry.location.lat());
});
```

How to create a Marker object

```
var marker = new google.maps.Marker({
    position: new google.maps.LatLng(36.799793, -119.858135),
    map: map});        // assuming the Map object is in a variable named map
```

Description

- *Geocoding* refers to the conversion of addresses into locations, and vice versa. This conversion is done by the geocode method of the Geocoder class.

- To add a marker to a map, you create a Marker object.

Figure 16-4   The classes and methods for geocoding and markers

How to create an address list that displays markers

Figure 16-5 shows how to use the constructors and methods that you just learned about to add a marker to a web page. Here, a marker is added when a user clicks on one of the city links in the right sidebar. In fact, this application will add a marker for each link that's clicked, which is how three markers are shown on the map.

The HTML for this map consists of a div element for the map and a ul element for the city links. A style sheet is used to float both these elements so they appear as shown.

In the jQuery for this application, you can see that the first statement in the ready event handler creates a Geocoder object named geocoder. This is followed by the statements that create the map. These are the same statements that you saw in figure 16-3.

Then, the Geocoder object is used by the click event method that creates event handlers for each of the links. Within the function for this method, the first statement uses the this keyword and the text method to get the address from a link and stores it in a variable named "address". This is typical jQuery code that you learned in section 2.

Next, the geocode method of the Geocoder object is used to get the location of the address for each link and return the results in its callback function. Then, within that callback function, a Marker object is created using the location that's returned by the geocode method for the position option and the map that has been created for the map option. Later, when the user clicks on a city link and the Marker object is created, it is added to the map.

A marker is added to the map when the user clicks on an address link

The HTML for the map and links

```
<div id="map"></div>
<ul id="links">
    <li><a href="#">Los Angeles, CA</a></li>
    <li><a href="#">Temecula, CA</a></li>
    <!-- the li elements for other cities -->
</ul>
```

The jQuery

```
$(document).ready(function(){
    var geocoder = new google.maps.Geocoder();
    var myLatLng = new google.maps.LatLng(33.4936111, -117.1475);
    var mapOptions = {zoom: 8, center: myLatLng,
                    mapTypeId: google.maps.MapTypeId.ROADMAP};
    var map = new google.maps.Map($("#map").get(0), mapOptions);

    $("#links a").click(function() {
        var address = $(this).text();   // gets address from <a> element
        geocoder.geocode({address: address}, function(results) {
            new google.maps.Marker({
                position: results[0].geometry.location,
                map: map
            });
        });
    });
});
```

Description

- In the click event handler for the address links, the geocode method converts the address to a location object and passes that object to its callback function.

- Within the callback function, the Marker constructor uses the results object to get the position for the marker. When the Marker object is created, it is added to the map.

Figure 16-5   How to create an address list that displays markers on a map

How to display messages on a map

Now, you'll learn how to display messages for the markers on a map. To do that, you're going to learn how to use three more classes and several new methods.

The classes and methods for messages and markers

Figure 16-6 presents three more classes, several methods for those classes, and two methods of the Marker class. In brief, the InfoWindow class provides methods that let you add a message to a marker. The OverlayView class provides three methods that let you add an overlay to a map in the form of a custom message. And the MapCanvasProjection class provides a method that lets you position a custom message.

You might note here that the MapCanvasProjection class doesn't have a constructor. Instead, a MapCanvasProjection object is created by the getProjection method of the OverlayView map class. This is another way that objects can be created from a class.

The last table in this figure presents two of the methods of the Marker class that was introduced in the last two figures. The getPosition method gets the latitude and longitude coordinates of a marker that's on a map, which can be used to position a message. The setMap method puts a marker on a map, or, if its parameter is set to null, it removes the marker from the map.

You'll see all of these classes and methods illustrated in the three figures that follow. As you study the applications for these figures, you can refer back to the tables in this figure.

The classes for adding messages to markers

Class	Description
`InfoWindow(options)`	This constructor creates an object that works as a message balloon for a marker. Its content option provides the content for the balloon, and the content can be coded with plain text or HTML.
`OverlayView()`	This constructor creates an object that can be used to overlay objects on the map.
`MapCanvasProjection`	An object is created from this class when the getProjection method of an OverlayView object is called.

One method of the InfoWindow class

Method	Description
`open(map, marker)`	Opens the message balloon for the map and marker.

Three methods of the OverlayView class

Method	Description
`draw()`	Draws or updates the overlay.
`setMap(map)`	Adds the overlay to the map.
`getProjection()`	Returns a MapCanvasProjection object for the overlay.

One method of the MapCanvasProjection class

Method	Description
`fromLatLngToContainerPixel(` `    markerPosition)`	Returns the pixel coordinates for a marker's position.

Two methods of the Marker class

Method	Description
`getPosition()`	Gets the latitude and longitude coordinates of the marker.
`setMap(map)`	Renders the marker on the specified map. If the parameter is null, it removes the marker from the map.

Description

- You'll see these classes and methods in action in the three figures that follow.

Figure 16-6   The classes and methods for messages and markers

How to add messages to markers

Figure 16-7 shows how to add a message to a marker by using the InfoWindow class. Here again, a marker is added to the map when the user clicks on a city link. But this time, a message is also added. Also, when one marker is added to the map, the previous one is removed.

In the jQuery code for this application, the first statement in the ready event handler declares a variable named marker. That way, it will be available when the click event method is executed. Then, the next four statements create the Geocoder object and the map, just as in figure 16-5.

In the click event handler, the first statement is the same as before, but the second statement tests to see whether the variable named marker contains a value. If it does, the setMap method for the marker is set to null, which removes the marker from the map. The first time the if statement is executed, of course, the marker will be null, so the setMap method won't be executed.

Next, in the callback function for the geocode method, the marker is created just as in figure 16-5. This is followed by a statement that creates an InfoWindow object that specifies the content for this object. Note here that this content can include HTML elements. The last statement in this function uses the open method of the InfoWindow object to specify that the window (or message balloon) should be opened for the map and marker that's specified by the parameters.

A marker and message are added when the user clicks on a link

The jQuery

```
$(document).ready(function(){
    var marker;
    var geocoder = new google.maps.Geocoder();
    var myLatlng = new google.maps.LatLng(33.4936111, -117.1475);
    var mapOptions = {zoom: 8, center: myLatlng,
        mapTypeId: google.maps.MapTypeId.ROADMAP};
    var map = new google.maps.Map($("#map").get(0), mapOptions);

    $("#links a").click(function() {
        var address = $(this).text();  // gets address from <a> element
        if (marker) { marker.setMap(null); } // deletes current marker
        geocoder.geocode({address: address}, function(results) {
            marker = new google.maps.Marker({
                position: results[0].geometry.location,
                map: map
            });
            // adds message balloon
            var infoWindow = new google.maps.InfoWindow({
                content: "This is: <h3>" + address + "</h3>"}
            );
            infoWindow.open(map, marker);
        });
    });
});
```

Description

- As in figure 16-5, this application adds a marker to the map when the user clicks on an address link. This time, though, an InfoWindow object is used to add a message at the location of the marker, and only one marker can be displayed at one time.

- The HTML for this application is the same as in figure 16-5.

Figure 16-7   How to add messages to markers

How to add custom messages to markers

Figure 16-8 shows how to add custom messages to markers by using the OverlayView and MapCanvasProjection classes and another of the Marker methods. Here, the message balloon is actually an HTML div element with its id attribute set to "message". This div element is styled by a separate style sheet.

In the jQuery code, the first five statements are the same as in the previous figure. The start of the click event handler for the address links is also the same as in the previous figure. But after the marker is set in the function for the geocode method, the code changes.

Still in the function for the geocode method, an OverlayView object is created. Then, its draw method is executed, and the function for this method starts by creating a point variable that is going to contain the location of the marker for the link in pixels. This variable will be used later on to position the custom message.

To get the location of this point, the getProjection method of the overlay object creates a MapCanvasProjection object for the overlay. Then, the fromLatLngToContainerPixel method of the MapCanvasProjection object is used to get the location of the marker in pixels. The parameter for this method is the position for the marker, which is returned by the getPosition method of the marker for the link. (You may be wondering who dreams this stuff up, but that's the way you get the location value that you want.)

Once that value is calculated, the rest is easy. Still in the function for the draw method of the overlay object, the html method is used to add the contents of the message to the HTML div element with the "message" id. Then, the show method is used to show this div element, and the css method that's chained to the show method places the message near the marker by setting its top and left properties relative to the value in the point variable, which represents the y and x coordinates in pixels.

At this point, though, the message hasn't been displayed in the web page. To do that, the last statement in the function for the geocode method issues the setMap method for the overlay object. Then, the message is displayed over the map that's specified by the parameter.

In this example, the content for the message balloon contains some HTML, including an <a> element that links to the Google Maps web site. This URL includes a daddr parameter for the address of the marker. This is simply intended to show that you can get creative with the content for a message balloon.

A web page that displays a custom message for a marker

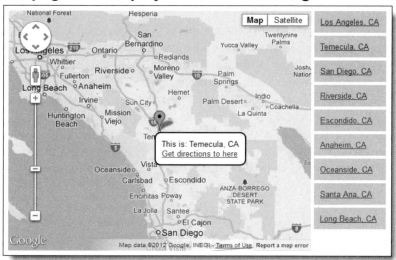

The HTML for the message balloon

```
<div id="message" style="display:none;"></div>
```

The jQuery

```
$(document).ready(function(){
    // same first five statements as in the previous figure
    $("#links a").click(function() {
        var address = $(this).text();
        if (marker) { marker.setMap(null); }
        geocoder.geocode({address: address}, function(results) {
            marker = new google.maps.Marker({
                position: results[0].geometry.location,
                map: map
            });
            var overlay = new google.maps.OverlayView();
            overlay.draw = function() {
                var point =
                    overlay.getProjection().fromLatLngToContainerPixel(
                        marker.getPosition());
                $("#message").html(
                    "This is: " + address +
                    "<br><a href=http://maps.google.com/maps?daddr=" +
                    address + ">Get directions to here</a>");
                $("#message").show().css({
                    top: point.y + 10,
                    left: point.x
                });
            };
            overlay.setMap(map);
        });
    });
});
```

Description

*   After OverlayView and Marker methods get the position of the marker in pixels, the html and css methods create and position the HTML, which is styled by a style sheet.

Figure 16-8   How to add custom messages to markers

How to add Flickr images to messages

Figure 16-9 shows how a message balloon for a marker can be enhanced by an image that's retrieved from the Flickr web site. This combines skills that you learned in the last two chapters with the skills you're learning now. The application in this figure is like the one in the last figure except that it displays a Flickr image in the message balloon for a city.

The jQuery code for this application is just like the code for the previous figure until you get to the comment in the middle of the click event handler. After that, the first statement creates a URL for Flickr that uses the address of a link to get a related photo. Then, the second statement uses the $.getJSON method and the $.each method to get the image for the address and store it in the HTML div element for the marker.

This is followed by the chained show and css methods that are like the ones in the previous figure. Here again, the function for the geocode method ends by issuing the setMap method of the overlay object, so the message is displayed.

A web page that displays a Flickr image for the location

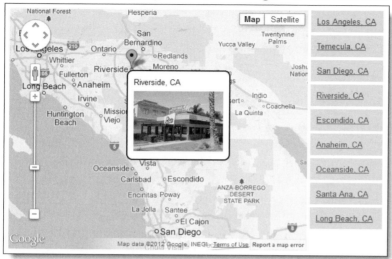

The code for setting up the click event handlers for the links

```
$("#links a").click(function() {
    var address = $(this).text();
    if (marker) { marker.setMap(null); }
    geocoder.geocode({address: address}, function(results) {
        marker = new google.maps.Marker({
            position: results[0].geometry.location,
            map: map
        });
        var overlay = new google.maps.OverlayView();
        overlay.draw = function() {
            var point =
                overlay.getProjection().fromLatLngToContainerPixel(
                    marker.getPosition());
            // the changed code for this application follows
            var url =
                // the url that follows has to be coded in a single line
                "http://api.flickr.com/services/feeds/photos_public.gne?
                format=json&jsoncallback=?&tags=" + address;
            $.getJSON(url, function(data) {
                $.each(data.items, function(i, item){
                    $("#message").html(address + "<br><img src=" +
                        item.media.m + " width=150 height=100>");
                });
            });
            $("#message").show().css({
                top: point.y + 10,
                left: point.x
            });
        };
        overlay.setMap(map);
    });
});
```

Description

- This is like the application in the previous figure except that it gets an image from Flickr using Ajax and JSON and then puts the image in the HTML for the message.

Figure 16-9   How to add Flickr images to messages

How to display driving directions

If you use a Google Map to show your users the location of your company, you may also want to provide driving directions to that location. In the next two figures, you'll learn how to do that.

The classes and methods for directions and listeners

The first three tables in figure 16-10 summarize the classes and methods that you need for providing driving directions. In brief, you use the DirectionsService class and one of its methods to get the directions. Then, you use the DirectionsRenderer class and three of its methods to display the directions.

The first example in this figure shows how to use these classes and methods. This assumes that the DirectionsService and DirectionsRenderer objects have already been created. Then, a variable is set up for the three required properties of a request. Here, the origin property is set to the position of a marker, the destination property is set to the position of another marker, and the travelMode property is set to the DRIVING constant of the TravelMode class.

This is followed by a statement that uses the route method of a DirectionsService object to get the directions. In the callback function for this method, the setDirections method of the DirectionsRenderer object is used to display the results. The parameter for this method is the result object returned by the request.

The last table in this figure summarizes three methods of the event namespace that you can use to provide event handlers for events. In the terminology of the Google Maps API and many programming languages, a *listener* listens for an event and directs it to the event handler for that event. When you use the listener methods, you don't have to first create an object because the event namespace is always available to a Google Maps application.

To add a listener to an application, you use the addListener method, which has three parameters: the object for the event, the event, and the event handler. This is illustrated by the example after this table. Here, the addListener method is used to listen for the click event of a marker. When that event occurs, an event object is passed to the event handler, which is then executed. One of the properties of this event object, the latLng property, can be used to get the location of the click on the map.

Once you create a listener, you can use the trigger method to trigger its event. Also, if you save the listener for an event handler in a variable, you can use the removeListener method to remove it later on. You'll see this illustrated in the application in the next figure.

The classes for retrieving and displaying driving directions

Class	Description
`DirectionsService()`	This constructor creates an object that can be used to retrieve driving directions from the Google server.
`DirectionsRenderer()`	This constructor creates an object that can be used to render driving directions.
`TravelMode`	This class provides contants for four travel modes: DRIVING, BICYCLING, TRANSIT, and WALKING.

One method of the DirectionsService class

Member	Description
`route(request, callback)`	Issues a directions request. Its first parameter is a DirectionsRequest object that has three required properties: origin (starting location), destination, and travel mode. This method returns a DirectionsResult object and a DirectionsStatus object.

Three members of the DirectionsRenderer class

Member	Description
`setMap(map)`	Specifies the map for which directions will be rendered.
`setPanel(panel)`	Specifies the HTML div element that will receive the directions.
`setDirections(result)`	Renders the result of a directions request in a div element.

A typical directions request

```
var request = {
    origin: marker1.getPosition(),
    destination: marker2.getPosition(),
    travelMode: google.maps.TravelMode.DRIVING
};
directionsService.route(request, function(result, status) {
    directionsRenderer.setDirections(result);
});
```

Three methods of the event namespace for using event handlers

Method	Description
`addListener(object, event, handler)`	Registers an event handler for an object and event. It returns an event object that has properties related to the event.
`removeListener(listener)`	Removes the specified listener.
`trigger(object, event)`	Fires the specified event for the specified object.

How to use the addListener method to register an event handler

```
google.maps.event.addListener(marker, "click", function(event) {
    // code for the event handler
});
```

Figure 16-10   The classes and methods for directions and listeners

How to display driving directions on your own site

Figure 16-11 presents an application that provides driving directions on its own site. Here, the directions are displayed to the right of the map after the user clicks on two points in the map, and the positioning of the map and the directions is done by a style sheet.

To start, the ready event for this application creates a new DirectionsService object and stores it in a variable named directionsService. Then, because this application works with two different markers, it declares an array named markers that will be used to store the markers. Finally, after the map is added to the web page, a listener is created for the click event of the map.

To create the listener, the first parameter of the addListener method is set to the variable named "map", which contains the Map object. The second parameter is set to "click", which is the event that will be listened for. Then, in the function (event handler) for this listener, a new marker is created when the user clicks on the map. This function uses the latLng property of the event object that's passed to the event handler to set the position for the marker. After that, the push method of the markers array is used to add the marker to the array.

The next statement in the event handler is an if statement that tests whether the number of markers in the array is greater than one. If it is, the user has already clicked on two points in the map so two markers have been created. Then, the statements for this clause are executed. Otherwise, nothing else is done by the event handler.

If the statements in the if clause are executed, the first statement removes the listener. That way, the user can't add a third marker to the map. Next, the event handler sets up variables for the two markers by copying them from the array with the indexes set to 0 and 1.

This is followed by a statement that creates a new DirectionsRenderer object and stores it in a variable named directionsRenderer. Then, the setMap method of this object sets its map to the map that has been created, and the setPanel method sets its display panel to the div element with "directions" as its id attribute. Note here that the get(0) method has to be chained to the selector so the setPanel method receives the DOM object for the div element.

The next statement creates a variable named "request" that will be used as the request object in the statement that follows. Its origin property is set to the position of the first marker. Its destination property is set to the position of the second marker. And its travelMode property is set to the DRIVING constant of the TravelMode class. To get the positions for the two markers, the getPosition method of the Marker objects are used.

At this point, both the DirectionsService and DirectionsRenderer objects are ready to get the directions and display them. Then, the last statement in the if clause of the listener issues the route method of the DirectionsService object with the request variable as its first parameter. This method also returns the result and status and passes them to its callback function.

Within the callback function, the if statement checks the status object to see if the request was successful. This uses yet another class named DirectionsStatus with the OK constant. If it is successful, the setDirections method of the DirectionsRenderer object displays the result in the "directions" div element.

A web page that displays the driving directions between two points

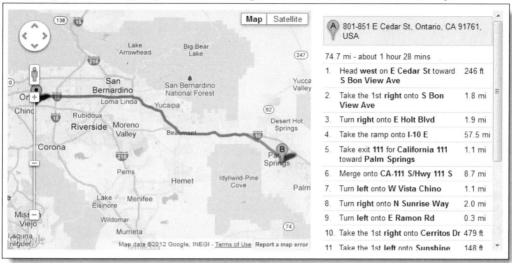

The HTML for the map and directions panel

```html
<div id="map"></div>
<div id="directions"></div>
```

The jQuery

```javascript
$(document).ready(function(){
    var directionsService = new google.maps.DirectionsService();
    var markers = [];
    var myLatlng = new google.maps.LatLng(33.4936111, -117.1475);
    var mapOptions = {zoom: 8, center: myLatlng, mapTypeId:
        google.maps.MapTypeId.ROADMAP};
    var map = new google.maps.Map($("#map").get(0), mapOptions);

    var listener =
            google.maps.event.addListener(map, "click", function(event) {
        var marker =
            new google.maps.Marker({position: event.latLng, map: map});
        markers.push(marker);
        if (markers.length > 1) {
            google.maps.event.removeListener(listener);
            var marker1 = markers[0];
            var marker2 = markers[1];
            var directionsRenderer = new google.maps.DirectionsRenderer();
            directionsRenderer.setMap(map);
            directionsRenderer.setPanel($("#directions").get(0));
            var request = { origin: marker1.getPosition(),
                destination: marker2.getPosition(),
                travelMode: google.maps.TravelMode.DRIVING };
            directionsService.route(request, function(result, status) {
                if (status == google.maps.DirectionsStatus.OK) {
                    directionsRenderer.setDirections(result); }
            });
        }
    });
});
```

Figure 16-11   How to display driving directions on your own site

Perspective

If you've been referring to the documentation for the Google Maps API as you've read this chapter, you know that the documentation is both extensive and complicated. That's why the goal of this chapter has been to get you started with some of the basic classes and methods and some of the common map applications.

With this start, we hope you'll be able to develop variations of the chapter applications on your own. We also hope you'll be able to explore the Maps documentation and figure out how to develop other types of map applications.

Terms

constructor	constant
class	geocoding
object	listener

Summary

- The Google Maps API consists primarily of *classes* that provide *constructors* that are used to create *objects* from the classes. Then, the objects can be used to call the methods for developing map applications.

- Some of the classes in the GoogleMaps API aren't used to create objects. Instead, they provide *constants* that can be used to provide values.

- When you use the constructor for a Map object, you must provide zoom, center, and mapTypeId options. You must also provide the DOM object that represents the div element that the map should be displayed in. When the Map object is created, it is automatically displayed in the div element.

- *Geocoding* refers to the process of converting an address to a location, or vice versa. To do that, you use a Geocoder object and its geocode method.

- When you use the constructor of the Marker class to create a marker object, you must provide the position of the marker and the name of the map. Then, when the Marker object is created, a marker is automatically added to the map.

- To provide message balloons for the markers on a map, you can use the objects and methods of the InfoWindow, OverlayView, MapCanvasProjection, and Marker classes.

- A *listener* is used to listen for a specific event on a specific object and run an event handler when that event occurs.

- To display the directions between two points in a map, you can use the objects and methods of the DirectionsService and DirectionsRenderer classes.

Exercise 16-1   Enhance a map application

In this exercise, you'll review some of the Google Maps documentation, and you'll enhance a map application so it shows your home town with a marker and a custom message, and then provides directions from your home town to any spot that's clicked on the map.

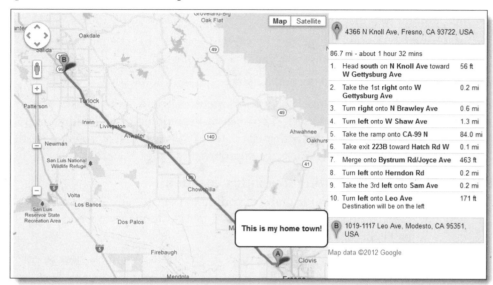

Review the Google Map application and the Google Maps API

1. Use your text editor to open the HTML file in this folder:

    `c:\jquery\exercises\ch16\map\`

    Then, run this application to see that all it does is display a map.

2. Go to the start of the documentation for the Google Maps API by using this URL:

    developers.google.com/maps/documentation/javascript

    Then, click on the API Reference link in the left sidebar. This presents a list of the many classes that you can click on to review the documentation for a class.

3. Try drilling down into the links for the Map class. To start, click the Map link in the Table of Contents. Note in the constructor for this class that the second parameter has a link to MapOptions. Next, click on that link to see the properties for that parameter, including the required zoom, center, and mapTypeId properties. Then, click on the LatLng link for the center property to see the methods that you can use with a LatLng object. This should give you some idea of how difficult it can be to work with this API.

4. If you're going to use Google Maps for your own web site (not for a course), you should get an API key for using it. To do that, go to the Google APIs Services Console by using this URL:

    code.google.com/apis/console/

    Then, use the procedure in figure 16-1 to get the API key.

Enhance the map

5. At the start of the ready method for the map application, use geocoding to get the location of your home town. Then, make the enhancements that follow by placing the code within the callback function for the geocode method.

6. To start, store the location that's returned by the request in a variable named myLatLng. Then, move the code that displays the map so it's executed within the callback function for the geocode method, and change the center option of the map to the myLatLng variable. When you test this change, your home town should be the center of the map that's displayed.

7. Using figure 16-5 as a guide, add a marker for your home town to the map.

8. Using figure 16-8 as a guide, add a custom message above the marker that says: "This is my home town!" This message should be placed within an h3 element. When the message is displayed, the style sheet that's provided for this application will format the message appropriately.

Provide directions for getting to another location

9. Using figure 16-11 as a guide and still coding in the callback function for the geocode method, code a listener that adds a marker to the map when the user clicks on it. Then, remove the listener.

10. Again using figure 16-11 as a guide, display directions that show how to get from your home town to the point where the user clicked. The style sheet that's provided for this application will display the directions to the right of the map.

If you have the time, do more experimentation. That's the best way to learn.

Section 5

jQuery Mobile essentials

jQuery Mobile is a JavaScript library that extends the jQuery library. jQuery Mobile makes it easier than ever to build web sites with native interfaces for mobile devices.

In chapter 17 of this section, you'll get off to a fast start with jQuery Mobile by learning the basic jQuery Mobile skills. Then, chapter 18 presents the rest of the skills that you need for getting the most from jQuery Mobile. When you complete this section, you'll be ready to develop mobile web sites at a professional level.

17

Get off to a fast start with jQuery Mobile

In this chapter, you'll learn how to build web sites with native interfaces for mobile devices like cell phones and PDAs. To do that, you'll use a jQuery library called jQuery Mobile.

How to work with mobile devices 498
How to provide pages for mobile devices...498
How to use a JavaScript plugin to redirect mobile browsers
to a mobile web site 500
How to set the viewport properties..502
Guidelines for designing mobile web pages...504
Guidelines for testing mobile web pages..504

How to get started with jQuery Mobile............................506
What jQuery Mobile is and where to get it 506
How to include jQuery Mobile in your web pages......................................508
How to create one web page with jQuery Mobile.......................................510
How to code multiple web pages in a single HTML file.............................512
How to use dialogs and transitions 514
How to create buttons 516
How to create a navigation bar 518

How to style web pages with jQuery Mobile 520
How to work with the default styles 520
How to apply theme swatches to HTML elements......................................522
How to use ThemeRoller to roll your own theme 524

A mobile web site for Vecta Corp 526
The layout of the web site..526
The HTML for the mobile web site..528
The style sheet for the mobile web site...528

Perspective 532

How to work with mobile devices

Many different types of mobile devices are in use today, and these devices are frequently used to access web sites. Because the screens on these devices are much smaller than standard computer screens, a web site that's designed to be used on the desktop can be difficult to work with on a mobile device. To accommodate mobile users, then, web developers typically provide web pages that are designed for mobile devices.

How to provide pages for mobile devices

Today, the biggest companies provide full versions of their web sites as well as mobile versions. This is illustrated in the Home pages in figure 17-1. One is for the full version of a site; the other is for the mobile version.

To detect mobile devices and redirect them to the mobile versions of the sites, the full versions of the sites use either client-side or server-side code. For instance, JavaScript or jQuery can be used to do that in the browser, and a scripting language like PHP can be used to do that on the web server. You'll learn more about this in the next figure.

When you use this technique, one common convention for the mobile site name is to precede the domain name for the main site with m. For instance, the name for the mobile version of vectacorp.com will be m.vectacorp.com. A second convention is to store the mobile site in a subdirectory of the main site as in vectacorp.com/mobile.

If you don't have the resources to create a mobile version of your web site, another alternative is shown in this figure. That is to use a CSS feature called *media queries* to provide different style sheets for computers and mobile devices, even though the HTML is the same for both. That way, you can hide or resize some of the components of the web pages when they're displayed on mobile devices. The trouble with this is that media queries aren't supported by all browsers.

The good news is that jQuery Mobile makes it easier than ever to create a mobile version of a web site. That means that smaller companies should now be able to afford mobile versions of their sites. In that case, media queries won't be necessary.

The Home pages for a full web site and the mobile version of the site

Two ways to redirect a user to the mobile version of the site

- Use JavaScript or JQuery to detect mobile devices and redirect them to the mobile version of the site.

- Use a server-side scripting language such as PHP to detect mobile devices and redirect them to the mobile version of the site.

How to provide a different style sheet for a mobile device

- CSS3 provides a feature called *media queries* that lets you provide a different style sheet for mobile devices. For instance, this link element could be used to provide a style sheet for devices that have a width of less than 480 pixels:

```
<link rel="stylesheet" href="styles/mobile.css"
      media="only screen and (max-device-width: 480px)">
```

Then, another link element could be used to provide a style sheet for devices that have a width of more than 480 pixels. For more information, go to:

http://www.w3.org/TR/css3-mediaqueries/

- The downside is that older browsers don't support this feature, so this technique isn't backward compatible.

Description

- At present, the best way to provide for mobile devices is to redirect the user to a mobile version of the main web site.

- If you don't have a mobile version of your web site, one alternative for mobile devices is to use *media queries* to provide a style sheet for mobile devices that makes the full version of the site more usable on those devices.

Figure 17-1   How to provide pages for mobile devices

How to use a JavaScript plugin to redirect mobile browsers to a mobile web site

Because there are so many different types of mobile devices and mobile browsers, it would be difficult to code and maintain a JavaScript application that redirects mobile browsers to the mobile version of a web site. So when you need to do that, a good way to get started is to look for a plugin that does what you want.

One web site that provides scripts for detecting browsers is the Detect Mobile Browsers site shown in figure 17-2. It provides scripts for clients and servers that detect mobile browsers and redirect them to the mobile versions of the sites. As you can see, it provides these scripts in many different languages, including ASP.NET, JSP, PHP, and Python for servers as well as JavaScript and jQuery for browsers.

The procedure in this figure shows how to use the JavaScript version of the application. In brief, you download the JavaScript file, which has a txt extension. Next, you use your editor to modify the URL at the end of the file so it points to a page in your mobile web site, rename the file so it has a js instead of a txt extension, and deploy the file to your web server. Then, you code a script element that includes this file in any web page that you want redirected to the mobile site when a mobile browser is detected.

The home page for Detect Mobile Browsers

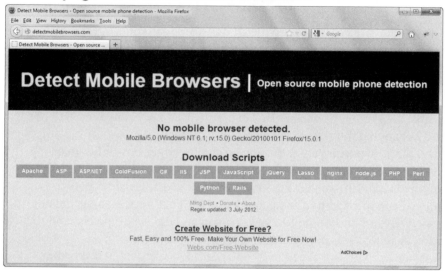

The URL for Detect Mobile Browsers

http://www.detectmobilebrowser.com

The end of the code in the downloaded file (detectmobilebrowser.js.txt)

...||window.opera,'http://detectmobilebrowser.com/mobile');

The end of the code after the URL has been edited

...||window.opera,'http://www.vectacorp.com/mobile');

The script element for any page that wants to redirect to a mobile site

```
<script src="detectmobilebrowser.js"></script>
```

How to use the JavaScript plugin for mobile browser detection

1. Go to the URL above. Then, click on the JavaScript button under the Download Scripts heading to download a file named detectmobilebrowser.js.txt.

2. Open the file in your text editor, and move the cursor to the end of the JavaScript code, which will include a URL like the one above. Then, change this URL to the path of the mobile site that you want the user redirected to.

3. Save your work, close the file, and rename the file so the .txt extension is removed. Then, deploy the file to your web server.

4. In any web page that you want to redirect to the mobile web site, code a script element that refers to the file that you've just deployed.

Description

*   The Detect Mobile Browsers web site offers many server-side and client-side scripts that will redirect a mobile device from the full version of a site to the mobile version.

*   After you modify the URL in the JavaScript plugin so it points to the correct mobile page, you need to provide a script element for it on every page that you want redirected.

Figure 17-2   How to use a JavaScript plugin to redirect users to a mobile web site

How to set the viewport properties

When you develop a web site for mobile devices, you can use a special meta element that lets you configure a device's *viewport*. This meta element is presented in figure 17-3.

To start, you should know that the viewport on a mobile device works differently from the viewport on a computer screen. On a computer screen, the viewport is the visible area of the web page. However, the user can change the size of the viewport by changing the size of the browser window.

In contrast, the viewport on a mobile device can be larger or smaller than the visible area and determines how the page content appears in that area. In this figure, for example, you can see that the first web page is displayed without a meta element so the entire width of the page is visible. That's because the default width of the viewport for an iPhone like the one shown here is 980 pixels, and the width of the page that's displayed is 697 pixels.

In contrast, the second web page has a viewport meta element that sets the viewport to the width of the device and the scale to .5. This makes the pages of the full web site easier to work with on a mobile device.

To configure the viewport, you use a meta element with the name attribute set to "viewport". Then, for the content attribute, you can specify any of the properties that are summarized in this figure to set the dimensions and scaling of the web page within the mobile device.

In practice, if the pages you're designing are for mobile devices, you can use a viewport meta element like the first example in this figure. You'll see that illustrated in the application at the end of this chapter.

However, if you're trying to set the viewport for a full web site, that may take some experimentation. For example, the second viewport meta element in this figure sets the width of the viewport to the width of the device and the scale to .5. That's illustrated by the page on the right at the top of this figure.

Beyond that, you can experiment with the content properties until you get something that works for your full web site. But a better solution is to develop a mobile version of your web site, and jQuery Mobile makes that easier than ever.

A web page on an iPhone before and after scaling

No viewport meta element

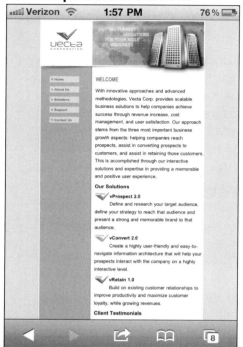

width=device-width, initial-scale=.5

Basic settings for a mobile web site

```
<meta name="viewport" content="width=device-width, initial-scale=1">
```

Typical settings for the pages of a full web site

```
<meta name="viewport" content="width=device-width, initial-scale=.5">
```

Content properties for viewport metadata

Property	Description
width	The width of the viewport in pixels. You can also use the device-width keyword to indicate that the viewport should be as wide as the screen.
height	The height of the viewport specified in pixels. You can also use the device-height keyword to indicate that the viewport should be as tall as the screen.
initial-scale	A number that indicates the initial zoom factor that's used to display the page.
minimum-scale	A number that indicates the minimum zoom factor for the page.
maximum-scale	A number that indicates the maximum zoom factor for the page.
user-scalable	Indicates whether the user can zoom in and out of the viewport. Possible values are yes and no.

Description

- The *viewport* on a mobile device determines the content that's displayed on the page. It can be larger or smaller than the visible area of the screen.

Figure 17-3   How to set the viewport properties

Guidelines for designing mobile web pages

If you create web pages specifically for mobile devices, you should follow some general guidelines so it's easy for users to work with those pages. Figure 17-4 presents these guidelines.

In general, you want to simplify the layout and content of your pages. This is illustrated by the two pages in this figure. The first shows the home page for the mobile version of a large web site. This page consists primarily of links to the major types of products that the site offers. The second page shows a product list after the user has drilled down into the site. If you review the full version of this site, you'll get a better idea of just how much the full version has been simplified.

Guidelines for testing mobile web pages

Figure 17-4 also presents some guidelines for testing mobile web pages. Because there are so many different mobile devices, it's important to test a mobile web page on as many devices and in as many browsers as possible. Although the best way to test a mobile web page is to deploy the page on a web server and then display it on a variety of devices, that isn't always possible. In that case, you may want to use the device emulators and browser simulators that are available for many of the mobile devices and browsers.

In most cases, you need to download the required emulator or simulator from the manufacturer's web site so you can run it on your desktop. In a few cases, though, you can run the emulator or simulator online. To do that, though, you sometimes need to deploy the web page so it can be accessed online. Also, when you use an emulator or a simulator, it may not always provide accurate results, although it should approximate what a page will look like.

To capture the screens for this chapter, I used my iPhone. To do that, I first deployed the pages to my web server. Then, I used the Safari browser on my iPhone to display the pages. To capture each page image, I held down the Home button and pressed the Power button. After I captured all of the page images, I copied the images from my iPhone to my computer.

If you don't have a web server where you can deploy the mobile pages, one easy option is to size your browser window so it's about the size of a mobile device. That will give you a good idea of what the pages will look like on a mobile device. I recommend downloading and using Safari if you do not have access to an iPhone. This will give you the most the accurate representation of how an element will look and function within an iPhone using jQuery Mobile.

Another option is to use a mobile device simulator like the one that's built into the latest release of Dreamweaver. Or, you can try to find one on the web, like the iPhone simulator that's available at:

`www.testiphone.com`

With this simulator, though, your web pages have to be on a web server and the simulation is something less than perfect. What you want of course is a site that provides simulators for multiple devices that work in a realistic way.

Two pages from the mobile web site for <u>www.orvis.com</u>

The Home page

A product list

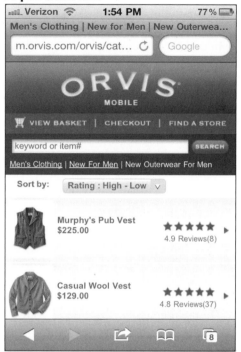

Guidelines for designing mobile web pages

* Keep your layout simple so the focus is on the content. One-column layouts typically work best.
* Include only essential content.
* Keep images small and to a minimum.
* Avoid using Flash. Most mobile devices, including the iPhone, don't support it.
* Include only the essential navigation in the header of the page. The other navigation should be part of the content for the page.
* Make links and other elements large enough that the user can easily manipulate them.
* Use relative measurements so the page looks good regardless of the scale.

Guidelines for testing mobile web pages

* Test all pages on as many different mobile devices and in as many different mobile browsers as possible.
* The best way to test mobile web pages is to deploy them to your web server and test them on the devices themselves.
* When you can't test your pages on the devices themselves, you can use device emulators and browser simulators.

Figure 17-4   Guidelines for designing and testing mobile web pages

How to get started with jQuery Mobile

Throughout this book, you have learned how to use jQuery and jQuery UI to enhance your web pages. Now, in this chapter, you'll learn how to use the jQuery Mobile library to develop mobile web sites. Although there are other ways to develop mobile web sites, we think jQuery Mobile sets a standard that other development methods are going to have a hard time beating.

What jQuery Mobile is and where to get it

As figure 17-5 summarizes, *jQuery Mobile* is a free, open-source, cross-platform, JavaScript library that you can use for developing mobile web sites. This library lets you create pages that look and feel like the pages of a native mobile application.

Although jQuery Mobile is fairly new, the current version provides all of the features that you need for developing an excellent mobile web site. Also, since jQuery Mobile's popularity is increasing rapidly, newer versions are in the works. At this writing, the current stable version is 1.1.1, but the beta version of 1.2.0 has already been released.

To include jQuery Mobile in your pages, you can download the required JavaScript and CSS libraries from the jQuery Mobile web site, deploy them to your web server, and then include them in your mobile web pages. Or, you can use a Content Delivery Network as we've done with the latest version of jQuery throughout the book.

The jQuery Mobile web site (www.jquerymobile.com)

The two jQuery libraries that you need
- jQuery (the core library)
- jQuery Mobile

Description
- jQuery Mobile is a free, open-source, JavaScript library that makes it easier to develop web sites for mobile devices. It is used in combination with the core jQuery library.

- jQuery Mobile lets you store multiple pages in a single HTML file; create dialog boxes, buttons, and navigation bars; format your pages without coding your own CSS; lay out pages with two columns, collapsible content blocks, and accordions; and much more.

- jQuery Mobile is supported by most devices including iPhone iOS, Android, Black-Berry, Windows Phone, Palm WebOS, and Symbian.

- The jQuery Mobile web site features all of the documentation, sample code, and downloads that you need for beginning your work with mobile devices.

- To download jQuery Mobile, go to its web site (www.jquerymobile.com). However, you won't need to do that if you include it from a CDN (see figure 17-6).

Figure 17-5   What jQuery Mobile is and where to get it

How to include jQuery Mobile in your web pages

To use jQuery Mobile, you need to include the three files listed at the top of figure 17-6 in your web pages: the jQuery file, the jQuery Mobile file, and the jQuery Mobile CSS style sheet. As this figure shows, there are two ways to do that.

The first way to include the three files is illustrated by the first example in this figure. Here, the link element for the CSS file and the script elements for the jQuery and jQuery Mobile files use a Content Delivery Network. At this writing, Microsoft and jQuery are the only CDNs that you can use for getting the jQuery Mobile library, and this example uses the jQuery CDN.

The benefit to using a CDN is that you don't have to manage the jQuery and jQuery Mobile versions on your server as new ones become available. Instead, you just have to change the version numbers in the link and script elements for these files.

The second way is to download the three files and deploy them on your system or web server. To do that, you download the compressed zip files, extract the files from the zip files, and copy the files to your web server.

Then, for each web page that uses jQuery Mobile, you code one link element that includes the CSS file and two script elements that include the jQuery and jQuery Mobile files. This is illustrated by the second example in this figure. Here, the names for the current versions of the files are retained. Although you can change those names once they're on your server, keeping the downloaded names makes it easy to tell which versions of the files you're using.

No matter which method you use, you must code the script element for jQuery Mobile after the one for jQuery. That's because jQuery Mobile uses the jQuery library.

The three files that you need to include for jQuery Mobile applications

- The jQuery JavaScript file
- The jQuery Mobile JavaScript file
- The jQuery Mobile CSS style sheet

Two ways to include the jQuery files

- Include the files from a Content Delivery Network (CDN) like Microsoft or jQuery.
- Download and deploy the files on your web server. Then, include them from the server.

How to include the jQuery Mobile files from a Content Delivery Network

```
<!-- include the jQuery Mobile stylesheet -->
<link rel="stylesheet"
    href="http://code.jquery.com/mobile/1.1.1/jquery.mobile-1.1.1.min.css">

<!-- include the jQuery and jQuery Mobile JavaScript files -->
<script src="http://code.jquery.com/jquery-1.8.3.min.js"></script>
<script
    src="http://code.jquery.com/mobile/1.1.1/jquery.mobile-1.1.1.min.js">
</script>
```

How to include the jQuery Mobile files when they're on your web server

```
<!-- include the jQuery Mobile stylesheet -->
<link rel="stylesheet" href="jquery.mobile-1.1.1.min.css">

<!-- include the jQuery and jQuery Mobile JavaScript files -->
<script src="http://code.jquery.com/jquery-1.8.3.min.js"></script>
<script src="jquery.mobile-1.1.1.min.css"></script>
```

Description

- To use jQuery, you need to include the three files shown above. The first two are the JavaScript files for jQuery and jQuery Mobile. The third is the CSS file for the jQuery Mobile style sheet.
- jQuery Mobile is continually being improved and enhanced, so check the web site often for the latest version.
- At this writing, only Microsoft and jQuery provide *Content Delivery Networks* (*CDNs*) that can be used to access the jQuery Mobile files.
- The jQuery and jQuery Mobile filenames always include the version number. At this writing, the latest stable version of jQuery Mobile is 1.1.1.
- If you download and deploy the jQuery files to your system, you can change the filenames so they're simpler. But that way, you can lose track of what versions you're using and when you need to upgrade to newer versions.

Figure 17-6   How to include jQuery Mobile in your web pages

How to create one web page with jQuery Mobile

To give you an idea of how jQuery Mobile works, figure 17-7 shows how to create one web page with it. In the HTML for a page, you use data-role attributes to identify the components of the page: page, header, content, and footer. You also use an h1 element for the content of the header, and an h4 element for the content of the footer.

In the page that's displayed, you can see how jQuery Mobile automatically formats these components. Here the text for both the header and footer is centered in white type against a black background, while the text for the content is black against a gray background. This is the default styling that's done by jQuery Mobile, and it's similar to the styling for a native iPhone application.

Within the header, footer, and content components, you can code the HTML for whatever content you need. You'll see this illustrated in the examples that follow. However, this simple example should give you some idea of how easy it is to code and format a single web page.

A web page that uses jQuery Mobile

The HTML for the mobile web page

```
<div data-role="page">
    <header data-role="header">
        <h1>Header</h1>
    </header>

    <section data-role="content">
        <p>The page content</p>
    </section>

    <footer data-role="footer">
        <h4>Footer</h4>
    </footer>
</div>
```

Description

- The HTML for a typical web page that uses jQuery Mobile will contain div, header, section, and footer elements.

- The data-role attribute is used to identify the different parts of a mobile web page. To identify the four major parts of a mobile web page, set the values of this attribute to "page", "header", "content", and "footer".

- In the header, the content should be coded within an h1 element. In the footer, the content should be coded within an h4 element.

- In the section with "content" as its data-role attribute, you can code whatever elements you need.

- The style sheet for jQuery Mobile formats the web page based on the values in the data-role attributes.

Figure 17-7   How to create one web page with jQuery Mobile

How to code multiple web pages in a single HTML file

In contrast to the way you develop the web pages for a web site that will be displayed on a computer screen, jQuery Mobile lets you create multiple pages in a single HTML file. This is illustrated by figure 17-8. Here, you can see two pages of a site along with the HTML for these pages. What's surprising is that both pages are coded within a single HTML file.

For each page, you code one div element with a unique id for each. Then, within each of those div elements, you code the HTML5 header, content, and footer elements. Later, when the HTML file is loaded, the first page in the body of the file is displayed.

To link between the pages in an HTML file, you use standard HTML place-holders. For instance, the <a> element within the second li element for the first page goes to the page with the div element that has "solutions" as its id attribute. Similarly, the <a> element in the first li element for the second page goes to the page with the div element that has "home" as its id. In this example, the <a> elements are displayed as buttons in a navigation bar, which you'll learn more about in figure 17-11. However, the principle is the same no matter how the links are displayed.

Although this example shows only two pages, you can code many pages within a single HTML file. Remember, though, that all of the pages along with their images are loaded with the single HTML file. As a result, the load time will become excessive if you store too many pages in a single file. When that happens, you can divide your pages into more than one HTML file.

Keep in mind too that because all the pages of a multi-page file are loaded at once, the ids used throughout all the pages must be unique. Even if pages are coded in separate files, though, the ids must be unique across the pages. That's because when the user displays another page, jQuery Mobile adds that page to the DOM instead of replacing it.

Two web pages that use jQuery Mobile

The HTML for the two pages in the body of one HTML file

```
<div data-role="page" id="home">
    <header data-role="header">
        <h1>Vecta Corp</h1>
        <div data-role="navbar">
            <ul>
                <li><a href="#home">Home</a></li>
                <li><a href="#solutions">Solutions</a></li>
                <li><a href="#contactus">Contact Us</a></li>
            </ul>
        </div>
    </header>
    <section data-role="content">
        <!-- the contents of the section -->
    </section
    <footer data-role="footer"><h4>&copy; 2012</h4></footer>
</div>
<div data-role="page" id="solutions">
    <header data-role="header">
        <h1>Vecta Corp</h1>
        <div data-role="navbar">
            <ul>
                <li><a href="#home">Home</a></li>
                <li><a href="#solutions">Solutions</a></li>
                <li><a href="#contactus">Contact Us</a></li>
            </ul>
        </div>
    </header>
    <section data-role="content">
        <!-- the rest of the section and the footer -->
```

Description

- To code more than one page in a file, set the id attribute for each page to a place-holder value that can be referred to by the <a> elements of other pages.

Figure 17-8   How to code multiple web pages in a single HTML file

How to use dialogs and transitions

Figure 17-9 shows how to create a *dialog* that opens when a link is tapped. To do that, you code the dialog just as you would any page. But in the <a> element that goes to that page, you code a data-rel attribute with "dialog" as its value.

As the examples in this figure show, the jQuery Mobile CSS file formats a dialog differently than a normal web page. By default, a dialog will have a dark background with white foreground text, and the header and footer won't span the width of the page. A dialog box will also have an "X" in the header that the user must tap to return to the previous page.

When you code an <a> element that goes to another page or dialog, you can also use the data-transition attribute to specify one of the six *transitions* that are summarized in the table in this figure. Each of these transitions is meant to mimic an effect that a mobile device like an iPhone uses. In general, these transitions won't work in desktop browsers, but they will work in the Safari browser. That makes it easy to test them on your computer.

Incidentally, the transitions work even if the pages are stored in separate files. That's because jQuery Mobile automatically creates an Ajax request for a page that's in a different file than the one for the current page. Then, the next page is added to the DOM, and the transition works as if both pages were in the same file. This is sometimes referred to as "Hijax." If you want to stop this default behavior, you can set the <a> element's data-ajax attribute to "false". Then, the transition will work the way it does for a standard web page.

A page and a dialog that have the same HTML

The web page

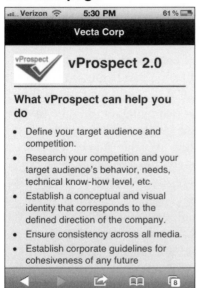

The dialog

The transitions that can be used

Transition	Description
slide	The next page slides in from right to left.
slideup	The next page slides in from bottom to top.
slidedown	The next page slides in from top to bottom.
pop	The next page fades in from the middle of the screen.
fade	The next page fades into view.
flip	The next page flips from back to front similar to a playing card being flipped over. This transition isn't supported on some devices.

HTML that opens the web page with the "fade" transition

```
<a href="#vprospect" data-transition="fade">
```

HTML that opens the page as a dialog with the "pop" transition

```
<a href="#vconvert" data-rel="dialog" data-transition="pop">
```

Description

- The HTML for a *dialog* is coded the way any page is coded. However, the <a> element that links to the page includes the data-rel attribute with "dialog" as its value. To close the dialog, the user taps the X in its header.

- To specify the way a page or a dialog is opened, you can use the data-transition attribute with one of the values in the table above. If a device doesn't support the transition that you specify, the attribute is ignored.

- The styling for the way a dialog is displayed is done by the jQuery Mobile CSS file. The contents of a dialog may need to be formatted by the developer's style sheet.

Figure 17-9   How to use dialogs and transitions

How to create buttons

Figure 17-10 shows how to use buttons to navigate from one page to another. To do that, you just set the data-role attribute for an <a> element to "button", and jQuery Mobile does the rest.

However, you can also set some other attributes for buttons. If, for example, you want two or more buttons to appear side by side, like the first two buttons in this figure, you can set the data-inline attribute to "true".

If you want to add one of the 18 icons that are provided by jQuery Mobile to a button, you also code the data-icon attribute. For instance, the third button in this example uses the "delete" icon, and the fourth button uses the "home" icon. All of these icons look like the icons that you might see within a native mobile application. Incidentally, these icons are not separate files that the page must access. Instead, they are provided by the jQuery Mobile library.

If you want to group two or more buttons horizontally, like the Yes, No, and Maybe buttons in this figure, you can code the <a> elements for the buttons within a div element that has "controlgroup" as its data-role attribute and "horizontal" as its data-type attribute. Or, to group the buttons vertically, you can change the data-type attribute to "vertical".

If you set the data-rel attribute for a button to "back" and the href attribute to the pound symbol (#), the button will return to the page that called it. In other words, the button works like a Back button. This is illustrated by the last button in the content for the page.

The last two buttons show how buttons appear in the footer for a page. Here, the icons and text are white against a black background. In this case, the class attribute for the footer is set to "ui-bar", which tells jQuery Mobile that it should put a little more space around the contents of the footer.

A mobile web page that displays buttons

The icons that are provided by jQuery Mobile

delete	arrow-l	arrow-r	arrow-u	arrow-d	search
plus	minus	check	gear	refresh	forward
back	grid	star	alert	info	home

The HTML for the buttons in the section

```html
<!-- For inline buttons, set the data-inline attribute to true -->
<a href="#" data-role="button" data-inline="true">Cancel</a>
<a href="#" data-role="button" data-inline="true">OK</a>
<!-- To add an icon to a button, use the data-icon attribute -->
<a href="#" data-role="button" data-icon="delete">Delete</a>
<a href="#" data-role="button" data-icon="home">Home</a>
<!-- To group buttons, use a div element with the attributes that follow -->
<div data-role="controlgroup" data-type="horizontal">
    <a href="#" data-role="button">Yes</a>
    <a href="#" data-role="button">No</a>
    <a href="#" data-role="button">Maybe</a>
</div>
<!-- To code a Back button, set the data-rel attribute to back -->
<a href="#" data-role="button" data-rel="back" data-icon="back">
    Back to previous page</a>
```

The HTML for the buttons in the footer

```html
<footer data-role="footer" class="ui-bar">
    <a href="http://www.facebook.com" data-role="button"
        data-icon="plus">Add to Facebook</a>
    <a href="http://www.twitter.com" data-role="button"
        data-icon="plus">Tweet this Page</a>
</footer>
```

Description

- To add a button to a web page, you code an <a> element with its data-role attribute set to "button".

Figure 17-10   How to create buttons

How to create a navigation bar

Figure 17-11 shows how you can add a navigation bar to a web page. To do that, you code a div element with its data-role attribute set to "navbar". Within this element, you code a ul element that contains li elements that contain the <a> elements for the items in the navigation bar. Note, however, that you don't code the data-role attribute for the <a> elements.

To change the color for the items in the navigation bar, the code in this example includes the data-theme attribute with a value of "b" for each item. As a result, jQuery Mobile changes the background color of each item from black, which is the default, to an attractive blue. In addition, this code sets the class attribute for the active button to "ui-btn-active" so jQuery Mobile changes the color for the active button to a lighter blue. This shows how you can change the formatting that's done by jQuery Mobile, and you'll learn more about that next.

A mobile web page with a navigation bar

The HTML for the navigation bar

```
<header data-role="header">
    <h1>Vecta Corp</h1>
    <div data-role="navbar">
        <ul>
            <li><a href="#home"
                    data-icon="home" data-theme="b">Home</a></li>
            <li><a href="#solutions" class="ui-btn-active"
                    data-icon="star" data-theme="b">Solutions</a></li>
            <li><a href="#contactus"
                    data-icon="grid" data-theme="b">Contact Us</a></li>
        </ul>
    </div>
</header>
```

How to code the HTML for a navigation bar

- Code a div element within the header element. Then, set the data-role attribute for the div element to "navbar".
- Within the div element, code a ul element that contains one li element for each item.
- Within each li element, code an <a> element with an href attribute that uses a placeholder for the page that the link should go to. Then, set the data-icon attribute to the icon of your choosing.
- For the active item in the navigation bar, set the class attribute to "ui-btn-active". Then, the color of this item will be lighter than the other items in the navigation bar.
- You should also use the data-theme attribute to apply a jQuery Mobile theme to each item in the navigation bar. Otherwise, the buttons in the bar will be the same color as the rest of the header. To learn more about applying themes, see figure 17-13.

Description

- A navigation bar is a type of jQuery UI toolbar. The other types of toolbars are the header bar and footer bar that you learned about in figure 17-7.
- Navigation bars are commonly coded within the header for a web page as shown above.

Figure 17-11   How to create a navigation bar

How to style web pages with jQuery Mobile

As you've already seen, jQuery Mobile automatically formats the components of a web page based on its own style sheet. Now, you'll learn more about that, as well as how to adjust the default styling that jQuery Mobile uses.

How to work with the default styles

Figure 17-12 shows the default styles that jQuery Mobile uses for common HTML elements. For all of its styles, jQuery Mobile relies on the browser's rendering engine so its own styling is minimal. This keeps load times fast and minimizes the overhead that excessive CSS would impose on a page.

In general, jQuery Mobile's styling works the way you want it to. For instance, the black type on the gray background is consistent with the formatting for native mobile applications.

To fine tune that styling, though, you often need to provide your own CSS style sheet. For instance, the spacing before and after HTML elements may not be the way you want it. Or, you may want to add top or bottom borders to elements. Then, you can use the border, margin, and padding properties in your own style sheet to get this formatting the way you want it.

The default styles for common HTML elements

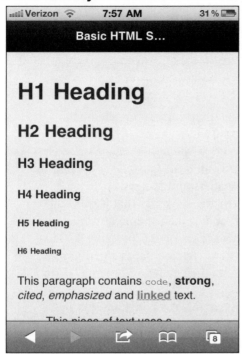
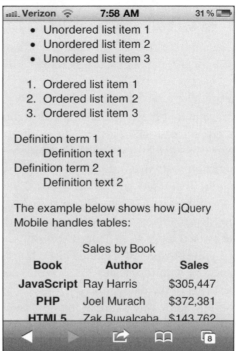

Description

- By default, jQuery Mobile automatically applies styles to the HTML elements for a page. These styles are not only attractive, but also mimic a browser's native styles.

- By default, jQuery Mobile applies a small amount of padding to the left, right, top, and bottom of each mobile page.

- By default, links are slightly larger than normal text. This makes it easier for the user to tap the links.

- By default, links are underlined with blue as the font color.

- To get the formatting for a page the way you want it, especially for borders and spacing before and after an element, you often need to use your own style sheet.

Figure 17-12   The default styles that jQuery Mobile uses

How to apply theme swatches to HTML elements

The styles that jQuery Mobile uses are provided by its default *theme*, which is meant to mimic the appearance of a native mobile application. This theme includes some global settings, such as the font family, as well as five *swatches* that control the color schemes that are used by various elements. Figure 17-13 summarizes these five swatches.

Note that these swatches are designed to visually prioritize the elements on a page, and the swatches in this figure are listed in the order of priority. For example, swatch "a" is used for headers and footers by default because these elements typically have visual priority. In contrast, swatch "c" is used for content by default to provide maximum contrast with the headers and footers.

In some cases, you will want to change the theme swatches that jQuery Mobile uses by default. One way to do that is to code a data-theme attribute with the swatch letter as its value. You saw this in the navigation bar in figure 17-11, and you can see this in the HTML for the second navigation bar in this figure. Here, the data-theme attribute applies theme "e" to the header and theme "d" to the items in the navigation bar.

The other way to apply theme swatches is to set the class attribute for an element to a class name that indicates a swatch. This is illustrated by the first example after the table. Here, the class attribute is used to apply both the "ui-bar" and "ui-bar-b" classes to the div element. As a result, jQuery Mobile first applies its default styling for a bar to the element and then applies the "b" swatch to that styling.

Please note that the table in this figure says to use swatch e sparingly. That's because it uses an orange color that works okay for accenting an item, but isn't attractive in large doses. This is illustrated by the second header and navigation bar in this figure, which tends to be jarring when you see it in color.

In general, it's best to stay with the default styles and the first three themes, which usually work well together. Then, you can experiment with themes d and e when you think you need something more.

Two headers and navigation bars that illustrate the use of theme swatches

Header "a", bar "b"   **Header "e", bar "d"**

The HTML for the second header and navigation bar

```
<header data-role="header" data-theme="e">
    <h1>Solutions</h1>
    <div data-role="navbar">
        <ul>
            <li><a href="#home" data-icon="home"
                    data-theme="d">Home</a></li>
            <li><a href="#solutions" data-icon="star"
                    data-theme="d" class="ui-btn-active">Solutions</a></li>
            <li><a href="#contactus" data-icon="grid"
                    data-theme="d">Contact Us</a></li>
        </ul>
    </div>
</header>
```

The five swatches in the jQuery Mobile default theme

Swatch	Description
a	Black background with white foreground. This is the default.
b	Blue background with white foreground.
c	Light gray background with a black foreground. Text will appear in bold.
d	Dark gray background with black foreground. Text will not appear in bold.
e	Orange background with black foreground. Use for accents, and use sparingly.

Two ways to apply a swatch

By using a data-theme attribute

```
<li><a href="#home" class="ui-btn-active"
        data-icon="home" data-theme="b">Home</a></li>
```

By using a class attribute that indicates the swatch

```
<div class="ui-bar ui-bar-b">Bar</div>
```

Description

- jQuery Mobile includes a default *theme* that consists of global settings, including the font and the corner radius of buttons and boxes, and swatches.

- The *swatches* define different color combinations for various elements and are designed to give a visual priority to the elements on a page, where swatch "a" has the highest priority and swatch "e" has the lowest priority.

- Although you can apply swatches to change the appearance of elements, you often need to use your own style sheet to get other types of formatting, like borders, margins, and padding, the way you want it.

Figure 17-13   How to apply theme swatches to HTML elements

How to use ThemeRoller to roll your own theme

In addition to changing the theme swatches that are applied, you can "roll your own" theme. To do that, you can use jQuery Mobile's ThemeRoller application, which is summarized in figure 17-14. This application lets you set custom properties for the jQuery Mobile elements as a whole as well as set the properties for swatches a, b, and c.

To change the color for a component of a swatch, you just drag it from the color palette at the top of the page to the component. If, for example, you want to change the swatch A color for a link to a darker blue, you drag the color to the link that's shown for that swatch. You can also use the collapsible panels for a tab in the left sidebar to adjust other properties. When you've made all of the changes that you want to make, you download the CSS file for the theme that you've created as described in this figure and deploy it to your web server.

To use your own theme for the pages in an HTML file, you add a link element to the file that refers to the downloaded CSS file. Note, however, that this link element must come after the one for the jQuery Mobile CSS file. Once that's done, the custom styles that you've created will override the default styles.

As a practical matter, you may decide that you don't need to roll your own theme for your web site. That's because the default styles do a good job of simulating native user interfaces. If you want to improve on that, though, the ThemeRoller is there for you.

Roll your own theme with ThemeRoller

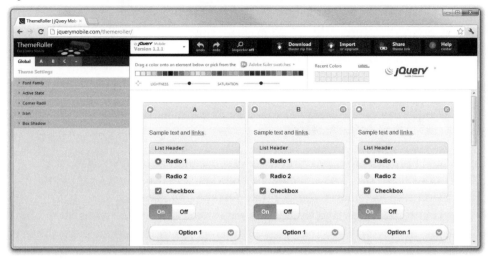

The URL for ThemeRoller
jquerymobile.com/themeroller/

How to roll your own theme

1. Adjust the global properties or the properties for a swatch by using the collapsible panels for a tab and by dragging colors from the color palette to specific elements.

2. When you're satisfied with your theme, click the "Download theme zip file" button in the navigation bar at the top of the page.

3. In the Download Theme dialog box, enter a name for your theme. Then, click the Download Zip button to download a zip file that contains the CSS file for the theme.

4. Extract and deploy the CSS file on your web server.

How to use your own theme

- Add a link element that refers to the CSS file to each HTML file that uses the theme. This link element must come after the one for the jQuery Mobile CSS file.

Description

- ThemeRoller lets you create your own custom themes based on the default jQuery Mobile theme.

- You can choose the colors for a swatch from ThemeRoller's color library or from Adobe's Kuler swatches.

- The collapsible panels in the Global tab of the sidebar let you adjust the font, the active state of an element, the corner radius of a box, the icons used, and box shadows.

- The collapsible panels in tabs A, B, and C let you customize the colors of the header and footer bar, the content body, and the normal, hover, and pressed states of buttons.

- If you click on the last tab (the one with the plus sign), another swatch is added.

Figure 17-14   How to use ThemeRoller to roll your own theme

A mobile web site for Vecta Corp

To show how the features you've just learned work together in a complete web site, this chapter ends by presenting four pages of a mobile site that uses jQuery Mobile. This should give you a better idea of how you can use jQuery Mobile to build your own sites.

The layout of the web site

Figure 17-15 presents four pages of the mobile version of the Vecta Corp web site. That includes the Home, Solutions, and Contact Us pages, as well as the dialog for the vProspect solution that is offered by the company.

On the Home, Solutions, and Contact Us pages, you can see the navigation bar that lets the user switch from one page to another. On the Solutions page, the user can tap one of the three "Read more" links to open the dialog for that solution.

On the Contact Us page, you can see a phone number, a mailing address, and an email address. If the user taps on the phone number, the user's device will try to call that number. If the user taps on the email address, the user's device will try to start an email to that address.

The page layouts for a simple mobile web site that uses jQuery Mobile

The Home page

The Solutions page

The vProspect dialog

The Contact Us page

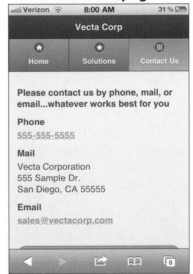

Description

- When the user taps a button or a link for another page, the page is opened.
- When the user taps the phone number on the Contact Us page, the device's phone feature will try to call the number.
- When the user taps the email address on the Contact Us page, the device's email feature will try to start an email for that address.
- When the user taps the button at the bottom of the Contact Us page, the previous page is reopened.

Figure 17-15   A mobile web site for Vecta Corp

The HTML for the mobile web site

Figure 17-16 presents the HTML for this web site in three parts. Since this HTML uses the features that you've just learned, you should understand it without any help. In case you're interested, though, here are a few highlights.

In the head section in part 1, the viewport metadata specifies a width equal to the device width and an initial scale and maximum scale of 1. This should work for all mobile devices, including iPhones and Android devices.

This is followed by the link elements for the jQuery Mobile CSS file and the developer's CSS file. This second file is used to add the top borders to the h3 headings in the pages and to set the spacing before and after some of the elements. These link elements are followed by the script elements for jQuery and jQuery Mobile, both of which point to the files in a Content Delivery Network.

In the body section in part 1, you can see the HTML for the Home page of the site. Since this page is first in the file, it is the one that will be displayed when the HTML file is loaded. Other than the data-role attributes and the navigation bar attributes, this page uses normal HTML code.

In part 2 of this figure, you can see the code for the Solutions page. To go from this page to the dialogs for the three products, each product description ends with a "Read more" link. To add a little fun, three different transitions are used to go to and from the dialogs: slideup, slidedown, and flip. If you run this application in the Safari browser on your computer, you'll be able to see the differences in these transitions.

If you look at the way the Solutions page is displayed in figure 17-15, you can tell that the styles in the developer's style sheet have been used to provide top borders to the h3 elements. They have also been used to set the margins and padding for the elements. Otherwise, this formatting wouldn't be satisfactory.

In part 3 of this figure, you can see the code for the vProspect dialog. It will open as a dialog because the link in the Solutions page is coded with the data-rel attribute set to "dialog".

You can also see the code for the Contact Us page. Here, <a> elements are used for the phone number and email address. That's why the device will try to call the phone number when the phone number is tapped and will try to start an email message when the email address is tapped.

This page ends with the code for a button that has its data-rel attribute set to "back". As a result, this button will return to the previous page. If, for example, the user clicked the Contact Us button in the Home page to get to the Contact Us page, this button will return the user to the Home page. If the user clicked it from the Solutions page, it will return the user to the Solutions page.

The style sheet for the mobile web site

The developer's style sheet for this application uses simple CSS to apply top borders, margins, and padding to some of the elements in the HTML. If you want to review this style sheet, you can review the file in the downloaded application.

The HTML for the head section and the Home page

```
<head>
    <meta charset="utf-8">
    <meta name="viewport" content="width=device-width,
        initial-scale=1, maximum-scale=1">
    <title>Vecta Corp. Mobile</title>
    <!-- style sheets -->
    <link rel="stylesheet"
        href="http://code.jquery.com/mobile/1.1.1/jquery.mobile-1.1.1.min.css">
    <link rel="stylesheet" href="styles.css">
    <!-- JavaScript files -->
    <script src="http://code.jquery.com/jquery-1.8.3.min.js"></script>
    <script
        src="http://code.jquery.com/mobile/1.1.1/jquery.mobile-1.1.1.min.js">
    </script>
</head>

<body>
<div data-role="page" id="home">
    <header data-role="header">
        <h1>Vecta Corp</h1>
        <div data-role="navbar">
            <ul>
                <li><a href="#home" data-icon="home"
                        class="ui-btn-active" data-theme="b">Home</a></li>
                <li><a href="#solutions" data-icon="star"
                        data-theme="b">Solutions</a></li>
                <li><a href="#contactus" data-icon="grid"
                        data-theme="b">Contact Us</a></li>
            </ul>
        </div>
    </header>
    <section data-role="content">
        <h2>Why people choose Vecta</h2>
        <p>Vecta Corp provides software packages that help companies increase
            sales in three ways:</p>
        <ul>
            <li>Finding prosects</li>
            <li>Converting prospects to customers</li>
            <li>Retaining customers</li>
        </ul>
        <p>To find out more, go to <a href="#solutions">Solutions</a>.</p>

        <h3>What our clients say</h3>
        <q>Throughout the years we have worked with Vecta Corp, we have always
            been amazed at their level of dedication and professionalism.</q>
        <cite>Zak Ruvalcaba, CEO<br>Module Media, Inc.</cite>
        <q>Incredible results from an incredible effort by the Vecta Corp.
            team! We are very pleased with the business benefits we have
            received by working with them.</q>
        <cite>Robin Banks, CEO<br>Profits Financial, Inc.</cite>
    </section>
    <footer data-role="footer"><h4>&copy; 2012</h4></footer>
</div>
```

Figure 17-16   The HTML for the Vecta Corp mobile site (part 1 of 3)

The HTML for the Solutions page

```
<div data-role="page" id="solutions">
    <header data-role="header">
        <h1>Vecta Corp</h1>
        <div data-role="navbar">
        <ul>
            <li><a href="#home" data-icon="home"
                    data-theme="b">Home</a></li>
            <li><a href="#solutions" data-icon="star" class="ui-btn-active"
                    data-theme="b">Solutions</a></li>
            <li><a href="#contactus" data-icon="grid"
                    data-theme="b">Contact Us</a></li>
        </ul>
    </div>
    </header>

    <section data-role="content">
        <p>Vecta Corp provides scalable business solutions to help companies
            achieve success through revenue increase, cost management, and user
            satisfaction.</p>

        <h3>vProspect 2.0</h3>
        <img src="images/logo_vprospect.gif" width="84" height="48">
        <p>Define and research your target audience, define your strategy to
            reach that audience and present a strong and memorable brand to
            that audience.
            <a href="#vprospect" data-rel="dialog" data-transition="slideup">
                Read more...</a></p>

        <h3>vConvert 2.0</h3>
        <img src="images/logo_vconvert.gif" width="84" height="48">
        <p>Create a highly user-friendly and easy-to-navigate information
            architecture that will help your prospects interact with the
            company on a highly interactive level.
            <a href="#vconvert" data-rel="dialog" data-transition="slidedown">
                Read more...</a></p>

        <h3>vRetain 1.0</h3>
        <img src="images/logo_vretain.gif" width="84" height="48">
        <p>Build on existing customer relationships to improve productivity
            and maximize customer loyalty, while growing revenues.
            <a href="#vretain" data-rel="dialog" data-transition="flip">
                Read more...</a></p>
    </section>
    <footer data-role="footer">
        <h4>&copy; 2012</h4>
    </footer>
</div>
```

Figure 17-16   The HTML for the Vecta Corp mobile site (part 2 of 3)

The HTML for the vProspect and the contactus pages

```
<div data-role="page" id="vprospect">
    <header data-role="header">
        <h1>Vecta Corp</h1>
    </header>
    <section data-role="content">
        <img src="images/logo_vprospect.gif" width="84" height="48">
        <h2>vProspect 2.0</h2>
        <h3>What vProspect can help you do</h3>
        <ul>
            <li>Define your target audience and competition.</li>
            <li>Research your competition and your target audience&rsquo;s
                behavior, needs, technical know-how level, etc.</li>
            <li>Establish a conceptual and visual identity that corresponds to
                the defined direction of the company.</li>
            <li>Ensure consistency across all media.</li>
            <li>Establish corporate guidelines for cohesiveness of any future
                developments.</li>
            <li>Define and/or re-define your service and/or product
                offerings.</li>
            <li>Define expansion plans and strategies.</li>
            <li>Implement Search Engine Optimization of all Online
                materials.</li>
        </ul>
    </section>
</div>

<div data-role="page" id="contactus">
    <header data-role="header">
        <h1>Vecta Corp</h1>
        <div data-role="navbar">
        <ul>
            <li><a href="#home" data-icon="home" data-theme="b">Home</a></li>
            <li><a href="#solutions" data-icon="star" data-theme="b">
                Solutions</a></li>
            <li><a href="#contactus" data-icon="grid" class="ui-btn-active"
                data-theme="b">Contact Us</a></li>
        </ul>
        </div>
    </header>
    <section data-role="content">
        <h4>Please contact us by phone, mail, or email...whatever works best
            for you</h4>
        <h4>Phone</h4><p><a href="tel:555-555-5555">555-555-5555</a></p>
        <h4>Mail</h4>
        <p>Vecta Corporation<br>555 Sample Dr.<br>San Diego, CA 55555</p>
        <h4>Email</h4>
            <p><a href="mailto:sales@vectacorp.com">sales@vectacorp.com</a>
            </p><br>
        <a href"#" data-role="button" data-rel="back" data-icon="back"
            data-theme="b">Back to previous page</a>
    </section>
    <footer data-role="footer"><h4>&copy; 2012</h4></footer>
</div>
</body>
```

Figure 17-16   The HTML for the Vecta Corp mobile site (part 3 of 3)

Perspective

Now that you have completed this chapter, you should be able to build simple web sites with jQuery Mobile. You should also realize that jQuery Mobile has made the task of building a mobile web site much easier. In the next chapter, you'll learn how to use many of the other features that jQuery Mobile offers.

Terms

media query	dialog
viewport	transition
scale	theme
jQuery Mobile	swatch

Summary

- The best way to provide web pages for mobile devices is to build a separate web site for those devices. Then, you can use client-side or server-side code to detect mobile devices and redirect them from your full web site to your mobile web site.

- The *viewport* on a mobile device determines the content that's displayed. To control how that works, you can code a viewport meta element in the head section of a page.

- *jQuery Mobile* is a JavaScript library that's designed for developing mobile web sites. jQuery Mobile uses the core jQuery library along with its own CSS file.

- To include the jQuery Mobile and jQuery libraries in a web page, you code script elements in the head section. Because jQuery Mobile uses jQuery, the script element for jQuery Mobile must be coded after the one for jQuery.

- jQuery Mobile lets you code the HTML for many mobile pages in a single HTML file. jQuery Mobile also supports the use of dialogs, transitions, buttons, navigation bars, and more.

- By default, jQuery Mobile uses a *theme* that provides formatting that relies on a browser's native rendering engine. jQuery Mobile also provides five *swatches* that you can use to adjust the default formatting without using CSS style sheets of your own.

- If you want to roll your own theme, jQuery Mobile's ThemeRoller application lets you do that.

Exercise 17-1   Experiment with the mobile web site

In this exercise, you'll first test the mobile version of the Vecta Corp web site that's presented in this chapter. Then, you'll make some simple modifications to it.

Open and test the mobile web site for Vecta Corp

1. Use your text editor to open the HTML page in this folder:
    `c:\jquery\exercises\ch17\vectacorp\`

2. Test this page and the navigation from one page to another within the site. The easiest way to do that is to run the page in your web browser and then reduce the size of the browser window so it's about the size of a mobile window. As you go from page to page, remember that all of the pages come from one HTML file.

3. If you have Safari on your system, open it and start the Vecta Corp web site. That way, you'll be able to see the transitions that are used when you open a dialog. Then, on the Solutions page, click on all three "Read more" links to see the differences in the slideup, slidedown, and flip transitions.

4. From the Home page, click on the Contact Us button in the navigation bar. Then, click on the bottom button in the Contact Us page, and note that you return to the Home page. Next, do that same starting from the Solutions page, and note that you are returned to the Solutions page.

Modify the way the pages work and test these changes

5. Modify the code for the button at the bottom of the Contact Us page so it always returns to the Solutions page, no matter how the user got there.

6. Change the first link on the Solutions page so the first product page is opened as a page, not as a dialog. Next, add a button at the bottom of this page that goes to the Contact Us page. When you test this, compare the product page with one of the product dialogs to see the differences in the formatting.

7. Create a new page that has "aboutus" as its id. This page should have the same navigation bar as the other pages, but its contents should contain just one heading that says: "About Us". Then, in the Home page, change the paragraph and link that goes to the Solutions page so it goes to the About Us page and reads like this:

    To find out more about us, go to About Us.

8. Temporarily delete or comment out the link for the developer's style sheet. Then, run the web site to see the default formatting. This demonstrates the need for a developer's style sheet. Now, restore the link to the style sheet, and run the application again.

9. Add a data-theme attribute to the header of the Home page that changes the default theme to "e", and change the theme for the buttons in the navigation bar on the Home page from "b" to "d". Test the change to see what you think of the results. Then, change the themes back the way they were.

18

How to enhance a jQuery Mobile web site

In the last chapter, you were introduced to jQuery Mobile. Now, you'll learn how to enhance your mobile pages with content formatting, list views, and form controls.

How to use the jQuery Mobile documentation...............**536**
The components of jQuery Mobile..536
The data attributes of jQuery Mobile.......................................536
The events and methods of jQuery Mobile 536

How to use jQuery Mobile for content formatting **538**
How to lay out content in grids..538
How to use collapsible content blocks......................................540
How to use collapsible sets 542

How to use jQuery Mobile for list views..........................**544**
How to use basic lists..544
How to use split button lists and inset lists 546
How to use list dividers and count bubbles 548
How to use search filter bars...550

How to use jQuery Mobile for forms...............................**552**
How to use text fields and text areas 552
How to use sliders and switches 554
How to use radio buttons and check boxes...............................556
How to use select menus..558
How to submit a form 560

An enhanced mobile web site for Vecta Corp.................**562**
The layout of the web site 562
The HTML...564
The style sheet 564

Perspective **568**

How to use
the jQuery Mobile documentation

This chapter and the last chapter are designed to get you started fast with jQuery Mobile by showing you the common ways that its components are used. Keep in mind, however, that these chapters don't present everything there is to know about jQuery Mobile. For that, there's the jQuery Mobile web site, and the three topics that follow present a few highlights.

The components of jQuery Mobile

In figure 18-1, you can see the index page for the demos and documentation for the latest stable release of jQuery Mobile. This page is divided into three sections: Overview, Components, and API. All three parts are excellent and can be used to enhance the quick start treatment of this book.

In the Components section, the first three entries are Pages & Dialogs, Toolbars, and Buttons, which you learned about in chapter 17. The next three entries are Content Formatting, Form Elements, and List Views, which you'll learn about in this chapter. If you need more information about any of these components, you'll find it here.

The data attributes of jQuery Mobile

As you use the components of jQuery Mobile, it's often hard to keep track of what data attributes are available. That's when the Data Attribute Reference in the API section of the documentation can be useful. In this figure, for example, the portion of the reference that applies to buttons is shown. It neatly summarizes the attributes that can be used with buttons.

In figure 17-10 of the last chapter, you can see examples of the most useful data attributes for buttons, but this shows that there are a few more. For instance, the data-iconpos attribute lets you specify the position of an icon, and the data-mini attribute when set to true produces a smaller version of the button. In the same way, this reference can be useful when you're working with other components.

The events and methods of jQuery Mobile

When you use jQuery Mobile, you can use its events, methods, and utilities whenever they are needed. However, one of the strengths of jQuery Mobile is that it uses these events, methods, and utilities automatically, so you don't need to code them yourself. For that reason, the two chapters in this book don't show you how to use them. If you're interested, though, the second and third items in the API section of the documentation are there for you.

The URL for the demos and documentation of jQuery Mobile 1.1.1

`http://jquerymobile.com/demos/1.1.1/index.html`

The start of the jQuery Mobile documentation

The data attribute reference for buttons

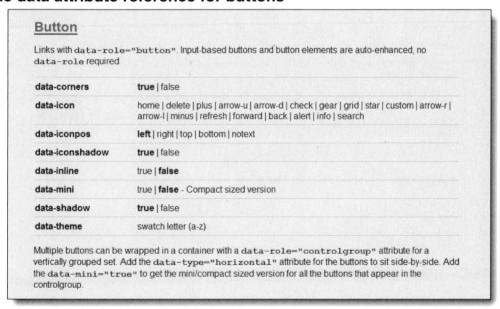

Button

Links with `data-role="button"`. Input-based buttons and button elements are auto-enhanced, no `data-role` required

data-corners	**true** | false
data-icon	home | delete | plus | arrow-u | arrow-d | check | gear | grid | star | custom | arrow-r | arrow-l | minus | refresh | forward | back | alert | info | search
data-iconpos	**left** | right | top | bottom | notext
data-iconshadow	**true** | false
data-inline	true | **false**
data-mini	true | **false** - Compact sized version
data-shadow	**true** | false
data-theme	swatch letter (a-z)

Multiple buttons can be wrapped in a container with a `data-role="controlgroup"` attribute for a vertically grouped set. Add the `data-type="horizontal"` attribute for the buttons to sit side-by-side. Add the `data-mini="true"` to get the mini/compact sized version for all the buttons that appear in the controlgroup.

Description

- This chapter and the last chapter are designed to get you started fast with jQuery Mobile by showing you the common ways that its components are used.

- The jQuery Mobile documentation, which is excellent, presents all the ways that its components can be used, including the use of its data attributes.

Figure 18-1   How to use the jQuery Mobile documentation

How to use jQuery Mobile for content formatting

Content formatting in jQuery Mobile provides for grids, collapsible content blocks, and collapsible sets. You'll learn how to use these components in the three topics that follow.

How to lay out content in grids

Figure 18-2 shows how to lay out content in grids that consist of rows and columns. In this example, the grid consists of just two columns, but jQuery Mobile provides for up to five columns. In most cases, though, you'll limit the columns to what you can see on a page at one time.

To create columns and rows, you use jQuery Mobile classes that indicate the number of columns and identify the content for each column. In this figure, for example, you can see that all the columns are coded within a section element with the ui-grid-a class. This class is used to format the content into two columns. Then, the content of the first column is coded within a div element with the ui-block-a class, and the content of the second column is coded within a div element with the ui-block-b class.

If you need to extend this code to create additional columns, you can do that by using additional classes. For a three-column grid, for example, you set the class for the section to ui-grid-b. For a four-column grid, you set this class to ui-grid-c. And for a five-column grid, you set this class to ui-grid-d.

After that, you just add the div elements for the additional columns. Then, the third column uses the ui-block-c class, the fourth column uses the ui-block-d class, and the fifth column uses the ui-block-e class.

A mobile web page with a grid that has two columns

The HTML for the two columns

```
<section class="ui-grid-a">
    <div class="ui-block-a">
        <img src="images/agnes.gif" alt="Agnes">
        <h4><a href="#agnes">Agnes Agnew</a></h4>
        <p>VP of Accounting</p>
        <!-- the code for the other speakers in the first column -->
    </div>
    <div class="ui-block-b">
        <img src="images/mike.gif" alt="Mike">
        <h4><a href="#mike">Mike Masters</a></h4>
        <p>VP of Marketing</p>
        <!-- the code for the other speakers in the second column -->
    </div>
</section>
```

How to code the HTML for two columns

- Code a section (or div) element for the two-column area, and set its class to "ui-grid-a".

- Within this section, code one div element for each column, and set the class for these elements to "ui-block-a" and "ui-block-b".

- In the div elements for the columns, code the content for the columns.

Description

- jQuery Mobile lets you lay out content in grids that consist of columns and rows.

- The ui-block-a and ui-block-b classes are formatted by jQuery Mobile so they float left. As a result, the div elements in the example above are displayed in two columns.

- To lay out a page with three columns, set the class for the top-level section or div element to "ui-grid-b" and set the class for the third column to "ui-block-c". This can continue for up to five columns.

Figure 18-2   How to lay out content in grids

How to use collapsible content blocks

Figure 18-3 shows how to use content blocks that collapse so just a heading is displayed. This is similar to how the jQuery UI accordion works, except that more than one content block can be displayed at the same time.

To create *collapsible content blocks*, you code a div element for each block and set its data-role attribute to "collapsible". Then, by default, all of the blocks will be collapsed when the page is first displayed as shown in the first web page in this figure. If that's not what you want, you can set the data-collapsed attribute for one or more blocks to "false". In the code in this figure, this attribute has been added to the second content block. The result is shown in the second web page.

Note that the text that's displayed in the button for a content block is the content of the header element that's coded at the beginning of the block. In this figure, an h3 element is used for the header, but you can use any header element from h1 through h6. The element you use doesn't affect how the text is displayed.

A mobile web page with collapsible content blocks

With all blocks collapsed

With the second block expanded

The HTML for the collapsible content blocks

```
<div data-role="collapsible">
    <h3>Agnes Agnew</h3>
    <img src="images/agnes.gif" alt="Agnes">
    <h4>Agnes Agnew<br>VP of Accounting</h4>
    <p>With over 14 years of public accounting and business...</p>
</div>
<div data-role="collapsible" data-collapsed="false">
    <h3>Mike Masters</h3>
    <img src="images/mike.gif" alt="Mike">
    <h4>Mike Masters<br>VP of Marketing</h4>
    <p>Mike serves as the Vice President of Sales and Marketing...</p>
</div>
<!-- the div elements for the other content blocks -->
```

How to code the HTML for collapsible content blocks

- Code a div element for each content block with the data-role attribute set to "collapsible".

- By default, each content block will be collapsed when the page is first displayed. To expand a content block, add the data-collapsed attribute with its value set to "false".

- Within each div element, code a header element (h1 through h6) with the text that will be displayed when a block is collapsed, followed by the HTML for the content.

Description

- More than one *collapsible content block* can be expanded at the same time.

- jQuery Mobile automatically adds the plus and minus icons for the content blocks.

Figure 18-3   How to use collapsible content blocks

How to use collapsible sets

Figure 18-4 shows how to use collapsible sets. *Collapsible sets* are similar to collapsible content blocks, except that the content of only one block can be displayed at one time. In other words, a collapsible set works like a jQuery UI accordion.

To create a collapsible set, you code a section or div element with its data-role attribute set to "collapsible-set". Then, within this element, you code collapsible content blocks like the ones you saw in the last figure. The only difference is that you can only set the data-collapsed attribute to "false" for one of the blocks.

A mobile web page with a collapsible set

With all blocks collapsed

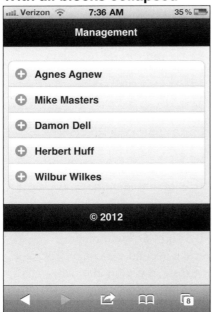

With the first block expanded

The HTML for the collapsible set

```
<section data-role="collapsible-set">
    <div data-role="collapsible" data-collapsed="false">
        <h3>Agnes Agnew</h3>
        <img src="images/agnes.gif" alt="Agnes">
        <h4>Agnes Agnew<br>VP of Accounting</h4>
        <p>With over 14 years of public accounting and...</p>
        <a href="mailto:agnes@vectacorp.com" data-role="button"
            class="ui-bar">Email Agnes</a>
    </div>
    <!-- the div elements for the other content blocks -->
</section>
```

How to code the HTML for a collapsible set

- Code a section (or div) element for the collapsible set, and set its data-role attribute to "collapsible-set".

- Code the content blocks within the set the same way you code collapsible content blocks (see figure 18-3).

Description

- In contrast to collapsible content blocks, only one block in a *collapsible set* can be expanded at the same time. This works just like a jQuery UI accordion.

- jQuery Mobile automatically adds the plus and minus icons for the content blocks.

Figure 18-4   How to use collapsible sets

How to use jQuery Mobile for list views

In jQuery Mobile, a *list view* consists of a list of items that link to other pages. In the topics that follow, you'll learn how to create and format list views so they work the way you want them to.

How to use basic lists

Figure 18-5 shows you how to create a basic list. To do that, you code a ul element and set its data-role attribute to "listview". Then, within each li element for the list, you code an <a> element with an href attribute that identifies the page to be displayed when the list item is tapped.

The first web page in this figure shows the default appearance for a list. Here, the content of each link is displayed along with a right-arrow indicator. You can also number the items in the list as shown in the second web page. To do that, you code the li elements within an ol element instead of a ul element.

Note that because each element in a list displays another page, you can use any of the six transitions you learned about in the last chapter to display that page. To do that, you just code the data-transition attribute on the <a> element. If you want the page to slide into view, for example, you can set this attribute to "slide".

Mobile web pages with a list view

A basic list

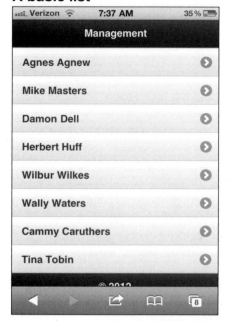

A numbered list

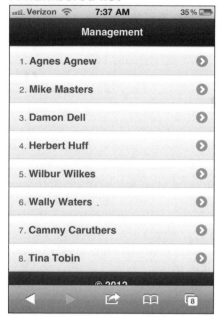

The HTML for the first list view

```html
<ul data-role="listview">
    <li><a href="#agnes">Agnes Agnew</a></li>
    <li><a href="#mike">Mike Masters</a></li>
    <li><a href="#damon">Damon Dell</a></li>
    <li><a href="#herbert">Herbert Huff</a></li>
    <li><a href="#wilbur">Wilbur Wilkes</a></li>
    <li><a href="#wally">Wally Waters</a></li>
    <li><a href="#cammy">Cammy Caruthers</a></li>
    <li><a href="#tina">Tina Tobin</a></li>
</ul>
```

How to code the HTML for a basic list

- Code a ul element with its data-role attribute set to "listview".

- Within the ul element, code one li element for each item in your list.

- Within each li element, code an <a> element that links to another page. This element can contain any content you want.

- To create a numbered list, change the ul element to an ol element.

Description

- *List views* are used to display lists of items that link to other pages when tapped.

- jQuery Mobile automatically adds a right-arrow indicator to the right side of each list item.

Figure 18-5   How to use basic lists

How to use split button lists and inset lists

In most cases, you'll want the items in a list to display the same page no matter where the user taps on them. Occasionally, though, you may want to provide list items that can link to two different pages. To do that, you can use *split button lists* as shown in figure 18-6.

In the web pages at the top of this figure, you can see that the list items have two distinct areas: the main portion of the list item and the indicator at the right side of the list item. To create a list like this, you code a second <a> element within each list item. The href attribute of this element should indicate the page that's displayed when the indicator is tapped.

When you use a split button list, you can also change the indicator that's displayed for each list item. To do that, you code the data-split-icon attribute with one of the icon values you learned about in the last chapter. In the second list shown in this figure, for example, the indicator has been changed to a gear.

This example also illustrates an *inset list*. This type of list is typically used when a page contains content other than the list. As you can see, an inset list is formatted with rounded corners, and it is inset from the left and right sides of the screen. To create an inset list, you simply set the data-inset attribute of the ul element to "true".

In the examples in this figure, it's clear that more information about a manager will be displayed when the user taps the main portion of a list item. But how does the user know what will happen when the indicator is tapped? The answer is that the user won't know unless the indicator makes it clear. To indicate that an email will be started, for example, the indicator should be an envelope. Fortunately, you can create custom icons like this for use in your applications. To learn how to do that, you can refer to the documentation for button icons. Then, you can apply this technique to the items in a list.

Mobile web pages with a split button list

With the defaults

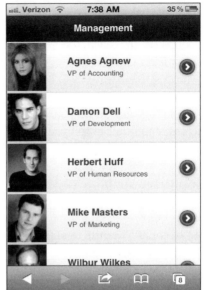

With an inset list and special icon

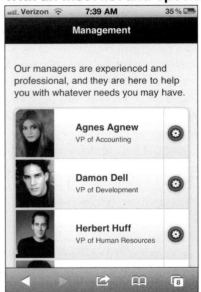

The HTML for the first list

```
<ul data-role="listview">
    <li>
        <a href="#agnes">
            <img src="images/agnes.gif" alt="Agnes">
            <h3>Agnes Agnew</h3>
            <p>VP of Accounting</p>
        </a>
        <a href="mailto:agnes@vectacorp.com" title="Send Email">
            Send Email</a>
    </li>
    <!-- the li elements for the other items -->
</ul>
```

The ul element for the second list

```
<ul data-role="listview" data-split-icon="gear" data-inset="true">
```

How to code the HTML for a split button list

- Code the list just as you would a basic list (see figure 18-5).
- Add a second <a> element for each list item that links to a page other than the page that the first <a> element for the item links to. This element should include a title attribute that can be used for accessibility.
- To change the indicator, add the data-split-icon attribute to the ul element with its value set to the name of the icon you want to use. See figure 17-10 for a list of the icons.
- To create an inset list, add the data-inset attribute with a value of "true".

Description

- *Split button lists* let you divide each list item into two tappable areas.
- *Inset lists* are typically used when a page has content other than the list.

Figure 18-6   How to use split button lists and inset lists

How to use list dividers and count bubbles

Figure 18-7 shows how to add two additional elements to list views: list dividers and count bubbles. As you can see in the first web page in this figure, *list dividers* provide a way of dividing list items into groups. In this case, the employees for a company are grouped into executives, managers, and other employees.

In contrast, the second web page shows that *count bubbles* provide a way of displaying the number of items in a list item that represents a group. In this case, the list items represent the groups of executives, managers, and other employees, and the count bubbles indicate the number of employees in each group.

To create a list divider, you simply add an li element wherever you want the divider to appear in the list. Then, you set the data-role attribute for this element to "list-divider", and you set the content to what you want displayed in the divider.

To add a count bubble to a list item, you add a span element after the content for the <a> element. Then, you set the class for this element to ui-li-count, and you code the number you want displayed for the content of this element.

Mobile web pages with list dividers and count bubbles

With list dividers

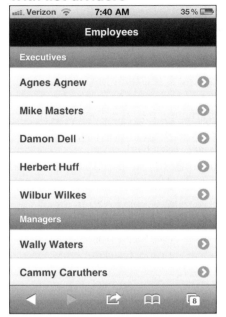

With count bubbles

The HTML for the first list

```html
<ul data-role="listview">
    <li data-role="list-divider">Executives</li>
    <li><a href="#agnes">Agnes Agnew</a></li>
    <li><a href="#mike">Mike Masters</a></li>
    <li><a href="#damon">Damon Dell</a></li>
    <li><a href="#herbert">Herbert Huff</a></li>
    <li><a href="#wilbur">Wilbur Wilkes</a></li>
    <li data-role="list-divider">Managers</li>
    <li><a href="#wally">Wally Waters</a></li>
    <li><a href="#cammy">Cammy Caruthers</a></li>
    <li><a href="#tina">Tina Tobin</a></li>
    <!-- the li elements for the other items -->
</ul>
```

The HTML for the second list

```html
<ul data-role="listview">
    <li><a href="#emps">Executives<span class="ui-li-count">368</span>
    </a></li>
    <li><a href="#mgrs">Managers<span class="ui-li-count">25</span>
    </a></li>
    <li><a href="#execs">Other Employees<span class="ui-li-count">5</span>
    </a></li>
</ul>
```

How to code the HTML for a list divider

- Add an li element with its data-role attribute set to list-divider.

How to code the HTML for a count bubble

- Code a numeric value within a span element and set the class attribute of the span element to ui-li-count.

Figure 18-7   How to use list dividers and count bubbles

How to use search filter bars

If a list contains many items, you can make individual items easier to locate by adding a search feature to the list. To do that, you use a *search filter bar* as shown in figure 18-8.

To add a search filter bar to a list, you set the data-filter attribute of the ul element to "true". Then, when the page is first displayed, the filter bar will appear above the list as shown in the first web page in this figure. At that point, the user can filter the list by entering one or more characters into the filter box. In the second web page in this figure, for example, the list items have been filtered so that only the items that contain the character "w" are displayed.

Notice that when a list is filtered, an X icon appears at the right end of the filter bar. Then, the user can tap this icon to remove the filter.

A mobile web page that uses a search filter bar

Before filtering

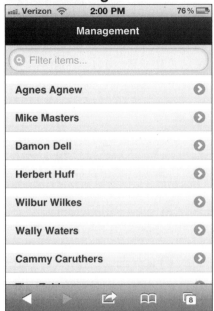

After filtering

The HTML for the filter bar and list

```
<ul data-role="listview" data-filter="true">
    <li><a href="#agnes">Agnes Agnew</a></li>
    <li><a href="#mike">Mike Masters</a></li>
    <li><a href="#damon">Damon Dell</a></li>
    <li><a href="#herbert">Herbert Huff</a></li>
    <li><a href="#wilbur">Wilbur Wilkes</a></li>
    <li><a href="#wally">Wally Waters</a></li>
    <li><a href="#cammy">Cammy Caruthers</a></li>
    <li><a href="#tina">Tina Tobin</a></li>
    <li><a href="#johnny">Johnny Jimenez</a></li>
    <li><a href="#larry">Larry Lowe</a></li>
    <li><a href="#ginny">Ginny Gerard</a></li>
    <li><a href="#stephen">Stephen Smith</a></li>
</ul>
```

How to code the HTML for a search filter bar

- Add the data-filter attribute to the ul element and set its value to "true".

How to use a search filter bar

- Type one or more characters into the filter box. The items in the list are filtered so that only the items that contain the characters you entered are displayed.

- When a list is filtered, an X icon appears at the right end of the search box. The user can tap this icon to remove the filtering.

Figure 18-8   How to use search filter bars

How to use jQuery Mobile for forms

In addition to the jQuery Mobile components you've already learned about, you can use jQuery Mobile to create forms with controls like the ones you saw in chapter 10. In fact, all of the jQuery Mobile form controls are enhanced versions of the standard HTML form controls. So if you know how to code these controls, you won't have any trouble coding the jQuery Mobile controls.

How to use text fields and text areas

Figure 18-9 shows you how to use the text field and text area controls. These controls are similar except that a text area control can accept multiple lines of text.

To create a text field, you code an input element with its type attribute set to any valid HTML5 value. In this figure, for example, the type attribute of the first two fields is set to "text", the type attribute of the third field is set to "tel", and the type attribute of the fourth field is set to "email". jQuery Mobile can use these values to determine if there's a special keypad that can make data entry more efficient. When the user taps on the text field that has the type "tel", for example, the numeric keypad is displayed as shown in the second web page in this figure.

In addition to the type attribute, you should include id and name attributes on the input element. Then, you can precede this element with a label element that identifies the text field. This element should include a for attribute that has the same value as the text field's id attribute.

To create a text area, you code a textarea element with id and name attributes. In addition, you code a label element with a for attribute just like you do for a text field.

By default, the labels for text fields and text areas are displayed above the controls as shown in the web pages in this figure. In most cases, that's what you want. If you want to display the labels to the left of the controls, though, you can do that by wrapping the labels and controls in a div element that has its data-role attribute set to "fieldcontain".

A mobile web page with text fields and a text area

With text fields and a text area

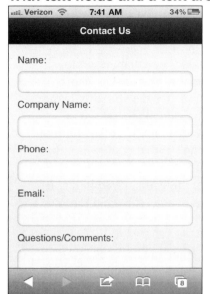

With a keypad for numeric input

The HTML for the text fields and text area

```
<label for="name">Name:</label>
<input type="text" name="name" id="name">
<label for="companyname">Company Name:</label>
<input type="text" name="companyname" id="companyname">
<label for="phone">Phone:</label>
<input type="tel" name="phone" id="phone">
<label for="email">Email:</label>
<input type="email" name="email" id="email">
<label for="questions">Questions/Comments:</label>
<textarea name="questions" id="questions"></textarea>
```

How to code the HTML for a text field or text area

- For a text field, code an input element, set the type to a valid HTML5 value, and include id and name attributes.
- For a text area, code a textarea element with id and name attributes.
- Code a label element before the text field or text area to identify the control. Include a for attribute with its value set to the value of the control's id attribute.

Description

- By default, a label is displayed above its associated control. To display it to the left of the control, wrap the label and control in a div element with its data-role attribute set to "fieldcontain".
- You can set the type attribute of a text field to any HTML5 value, including text, password, tel, email, number, and url.
- When the user taps on a field with certain input types, a special keypad is displayed that makes data entry more efficient for that type.

Figure 18-9   How to use text fields and text areas

How to use sliders and switches

Figure 18-10 shows how to use sliders and switches. A slider provides for selecting a value from a range of values. In contrast, a switch provides for selecting a binary on/off or true/false value.

To create a slider, you code an input element with its type attribute set to "range". Then, you set minimum and maximum values for the slider by using the min and max attributes. You can set the starting value for the slider by using the value attribute. And you can set the amount that the value is increased or decreased when the handle is moved by using the step attribute. It's also common to highlight the portion of the slider bar to the left of the handle as shown in this figure. To do that, you set the data-highlight attribute to "true".

Notice that the current value of the slider in this figure is displayed in a text field to the left of the slider. jQuery Mobile automatically adds this field for you so you can tell the exact value of the slider.

Switches are commonly used on mobile web pages because they provide an easy way for a user to select from one of two options. To create a switch, you code a select element with its data-role attribute set to "slider". Although this may seem counterintuitive since you're creating a switch, not a slider, you can see in this figure that a switch is formatted somewhat like a slider. If you keep that in mind, it will help you to remember how to code the data-role attribute.

Within the select element, you code two options that represent the binary values for the switch. Note that you can code any values you want for these options. Since a switch represents a binary value, though, you'll typically use true/false, on/off, or yes/no values as shown in this figure.

A mobile web page with a slider and a switch

The HTML for the slider and switch

```
<label for="size">Company Size:</label>
<input type="range" name="size" id="size" min="10" max="500" value="300"
    step="10" data-highlight="true"><br>
<label for="currentinstall">Currently installed vSolutions?</label>
<select name="currentinstall" id="currentinstall" data-role="slider">
    <option value="No">No</option>
    <option value="Yes">Yes</option>
</select>
```

How to code the HTML for a slider

- Code a label element with a for attribute that identifies the slider.

- Code an input element with its type attribute set to "range". Set the min, max, and value attributes to identify the minimum, maximum, and initial values. You can also include the step attribute to set the increment or decrement value.

- To highlight the slider bar to the left of the handle, set the data-highlight attribute to a value of "true".

How to code the HTML for a switch

- Code a label element with a for attribute that identifies the switch.

- Code a select element and set its data-role attribute to a value of "slider".

- Code two option elements within the select element that represent the "on" and "off" states for the switch.

Description

- jQuery Mobile automatically converts an input element with a type of "range" to a slider and displays the current value in a text field to the left of the slider.

- A switch is used for binary input and can have only one of two values.

Figure 18-10   How to use sliders and switches

How to use radio buttons and check boxes

Figure 18-11 shows you how to use radio buttons and check boxes. The difference between these two types of controls is that check boxes work independently of each other, but radio buttons are set up so the user can select only one radio button from a group of buttons. In this figure, for example, the user can select only one of the three radio buttons, but any number of the check boxes.

To create a group of radio buttons, you start by coding a fieldset element with its data-role attribute set to "controlgroup". Then, within this element, you code a legend element that identifies the group. After this element, you code an input element for each radio button, and you set its type attribute to "radio". You must also set the name attribute for each radio button in a group to the same value.

Finally, you code a label element that identifies the radio button. You can do that in one of two ways. First, you can code a label element after the input element for the radio button and then set the for attribute of the label to the same value as the id attribute of the radio button. Second, you can wrap the input element in a label element. In that case, you can omit the for attribute.

You use a similar technique to code a group of check boxes. The only difference is that you set the type attribute for each input element to "checkbox". Remember, though, that you don't have to code check boxes in a group since they're independent of one another. If check boxes aren't related to one another, then, you can omit the fieldset and legend elements and just code the individual check boxes and labels.

By default, radio buttons and check boxes are displayed vertically as shown in the first web page in this figure. If you want to, though, you can display them horizontally. In the second web page in this figure, for example, the radio buttons are displayed horizontally. This takes up less space on the page and it can make the buttons easier to tap. To display a group of radio buttons or check boxes horizontally, you simply set the data-type attribute of the fieldset element to "horizontal".

Mobile web pages with check boxes and radio buttons

With vertical controls

With horizontal radio buttons

The HTML for the check boxes and radio buttons on the second page

```html
<fieldset data-role="controlgroup">
    <legend>Which solutions are you interested in?</legend>
    <input type="checkbox" name="vprospect" id="vprospect">
    <label for="vprospect">vProspect</label>
    <!-- add more inputs/labels here -->
</fieldset>
<fieldset data-role="controlgroup" data-type="horizontal">
    <legend>Current infrastructure?</legend>
    <input type="radio" name="infrastructure" id="linux">
    <label for="linux">Linux</label>
    <input type="radio" name="infrastructure" id="mac">
    <label for="mac">Mac</label>
    <!-- add more inputs/labels here -->
</fieldset>
```

How to code the HTML for a group of radio buttons or check boxes

- Code a fieldset element with its data-role attribute set to "controlgroup". To display the controls within the group horizontally, set the data-type attribute to "horizontal".

- Within the fieldset element, code a legend element that contains the text that describes the group.

- Code an input element with its type attribute set to "radio" for each radio button or "checkbox" for each check box. Be sure to code the same name for each radio button.

- Code a label element for each control with a for attribute that identifies the control. Or, code the input element within the label element.

Description

- Because check boxes are independent of one another, you don't need to code them within a fieldset element. It's common to group related controls, though.

Figure 18-11   How to use radio buttons and check boxes

How to use select menus

Figure 18-12 shows how to use select menus, which are similar to drop-down lists. In fact, the HTML for a basic select menu like the one shown here is almost identical to the HTML for a drop-down list. The only difference is that you must include a label element that identifies the select menu.

Although the HTML for a select menu is similar to the HTML for a drop-down list, it's displayed quite differently. This is illustrated in the web page in this figure. Here, when the user taps a select menu, the list of items is displayed by the phone's roulette. Then, the user can spin the roulette or tap the Previous or Next button to display additional items, tap an item in the list to select it, and then tap the Done button to close the roulette and display the selected item in the menu.

You can also group two or more related select menus. For example, suppose you want the user to select a month, day, and year. Then, you can create three select menus and group them so they're described by a single text value.

In the second web page in this figure, for example, you can see a group of two select menus. The first one lets the user select a month, and the second one lets the user select a year. To create a group of menus like this, you wrap the menus in a div element with its data-role attribute set to "fieldcontain", followed by a fieldset element with its data-role attribute set to "controlgroup". Then, before the first select menu, you code a legend element with the text for the group.

By default, the menus in a group of select menus are displayed vertically with the identifying text to the left of the first menu. When you display menus this way, you usually add an option element at the beginning of each list that identifies the contents of that list. For example, you might add options of "Month" and "Year" to the select menus shown in this figure. In most cases, though, you'll display groups of menus horizontally as shown here. To do that, you set the data-type attribute of the fieldset element to "horizontal".

Mobile web pages with select menus

A single menu

A group of menus

The HTML for the first select menu

```
<label for="hearaboutus">How did you hear about us?</label>
<select name="hearaboutus" id="hearaboutus">
    <option value="magazine">Magazine Ad</option>
    <option value="radio">Radio Ad</option>
    <option value="tv">TV Ad</option>
    <option value="word">Word of Mouth</option>
</select>
```

How to code the HTML for a select menu

- Code a label element with a for attribute that identifies the select element.
- Code a select element with name and id attributes.
- Within the select element, code an option element for each menu item. Include a value attribute with an appropriate value.

How to group select menus

- Code a div element with its data-role attribute set to "fieldcontain".
- Within the div element, code a fieldset element with its data-role attribute set to "controlgroup". To create a horizontal group, set the data-type attribute to "horizontal".
- Within the fieldset element, code a legend element with the text you want to display for the group.
- Code the individual select menus as shown above. If necessary, code an additional option element at the beginning of each list with the text to be displayed on the menu.

Description

- When a select menu is tapped, the mobile browser will display the phone's roulette with the list of menu items.

Figure 18-12   How to use select menus

How to submit a form

Figure 18-13 shows you how to submit a jQuery Mobile form. As you can see, this works much the same way that it does for any form. That is, you wrap the controls in a form element and you include an input element with its type attribute set to "submit". Then, when the user taps the submit button, the form is submitted to the server and the script that's identified by the action attribute of the form element is performed.

By default, a jQuery Mobile form is submitted using Ajax. Although using Ajax results in a smoother transition to the resulting page, the added complexity of using Ajax isn't usually worth it. In most cases, then, you'll use a standard HTTP request. To do that, you set the data-ajax attribute of the form element to "false".

Although you haven't seen it in this chapter, you should know that you can include HTML code in your forms that performs client-side validation. For example, you can use the HTML5 required attribute or the CSS3 :required pseudo-class selector to indicate that the user must enter a value into a field. You can also use regular expressions to indicate the pattern that an entry must match. This provides an easy way to validate the data on a form without using client-side or server-side scripting languages.

A mobile web page that submits a form to a server-side script

The HTML for the form and submit button

```
<form action="../scripts/mobile.asp" method="post" data-ajax="false">
    <!-- mobile form elements go here -->

    <input type="submit" value="Submit Form">
</form>
```

Description

- You can use a standard HTML form element for your mobile web pages.
- To submit a form, you can use an input element with its type set to "submit".
- By default, jQuery Mobile submits a form using an Ajax request. Unless you need to use Ajax, you should use a standard HTTP request instead. To do that, set the data-ajax attribute of the form element to "false".

Figure 18-13   How to submit a mobile form

An enhanced mobile web site for Vecta Corp

Now that you've learned how to use the other features of jQuery Mobile, you're ready to see a web site that uses these features. This web site is an enhanced version of the Vecta Corp web site that you saw at the end of the last chapter.

The layout of the web site

Figure 18-14 presents four pages from the enhanced Vecta Corp mobile web site. The pages that aren't shown here are similar to the pages that were shown in the last chapter.

The first change to this web site is that the Solutions page has been updated to use a list view. Then, instead of displaying a dialog when a solution is selected, another page is displayed. In this figure, you can see the page for vProspect. Notice that the header of this page includes a Back button that the user can tap to return to the Solutions page.

The second change is that the Contact Us page has been updated to use a form. You saw many of the elements of this page earlier in this chapter.

Finally, a button has been added to the footer of the Home, Solutions, and Contact Us pages that displays the most recent tweets in a dialog. You can see this button in the footer of the Solutions page in this figure, along with a dialog that shows the tweets. Although this dialog doesn't illustrate any new features of jQuery Mobile, it does illustrate that you can use standard jQuery code in a jQuery Mobile application.

The page layouts for an enhanced mobile web site that uses jQuery Mobile

The Solutions page

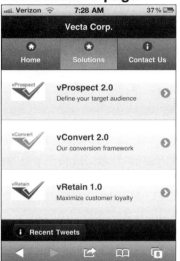

The vProspect page

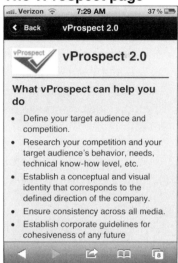

The Recent Tweets dialog

The Contact Us page

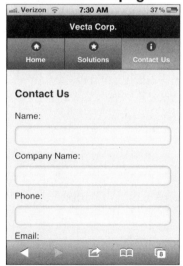

Description

- This Vecta Corp web site provides one page for each solution and a dialog for tweets.
- The Solutions page has been updated to use a basic list view. When the user taps on one of the solutions in this list, the page for that solution is displayed.
- The Contact Us page has been updated to include form elements that can be submitted to the server and processed by a server-side script.
- A button has been added to the footer of the Home, Solutions, and Contact Us pages that displays the Recent Tweets dialog.

Figure 18-14 An enhanced mobile web site for Vecta Corp

The HTML

Figure 18-15 presents the primary HTML for this web site in three parts. Since you've already seen code like this throughout this chapter, you should be able to understand it on your own. In case you're interested, though, here are a few highlights.

Part 1 of this figure shows the HTML for the Solutions page. Within the content section, you can see the list view that's used to format the three solutions. Here, you can see that each list item includes a link to another page. The <a> element for each link includes the image and text that are displayed for that item.

The footer section of this page also includes an <a> element that links to the page named twitter. Because the data-role attribute of this element is set to "button", the link is displayed as a button. And because the data-rel attribute is set to "dialog", the page will be displayed as a dialog. Finally, the data-icon attribute is set to "info", so the letter "i" is displayed on the button as shown in the previous figure.

In part 2 of this figure, you can see the code for the vProspect page. Here, the header element for the page contains the <a> element that defines the Back button. Notice that the data-icon attribute for this element is set to "arrow-1" so a left arrow is displayed on the button, and the data-rel attribute is set to "back" so the previous page is displayed when the user taps this button. Because this page can only be displayed from the Solutions page, this button always returns to that page. Finally, the data-transition attribute for the <a> element is set to "slide" so the Solutions page will slide back into view.

Part 2 also shows the code for the Recent Tweets dialog. As you can see, the content for this page is simply a div element with an id attribute. Then, the jQuery for the page retrieves the recent tweets and assigns them to this element. This code is similar to the code you saw in chapter 15 that displays a timestamp for each tweet.

In part 3 of this figure, you can see the content for the Contact Us page. This page includes all of the form elements you learned about in this chapter. In addition, it includes a submit button that you can use to submit the form to the server.

The style sheet

The developer's style sheet for this application uses simple CSS to apply top borders, margins, and padding to some of the elements in the HTML. If you want to review this style sheet, you can review the file in the downloaded application.

The HTML for the Solutions page

```
<div data-role="page" id="solutions">
    <header data-role="header">
        <h1>Vecta Corp.</h1>
        <div data-role="navbar">
        <ul>
            <li><a href="#home" data-icon="home" data-theme="b"
                data-transition="slide">Home</a></li>
            <li><a href="#solutions" data-icon="star"
                class="ui-btn-active" data-theme="b"
                data-transition="slide">Solutions</a></li>
            <li><a href="#contactus" data-icon="info" data-theme="b"
                data-transition="slide">Contact Us</a></li>
        </ul>
        </div>
    </header>

    <section data-role="content">
        <div class="content-primary">
            <ul data-role="listview">
            <li>
                <a href="#vprospect">
                <img src="images/logo_vprospect.gif" alt="vProspect 2.0">
                <h3>vProspect 2.0</h3>
                <p>Define your target audience</p>
                </a>
            </li>
            <li>
                <a href="#vconvert">
                <img src="images/logo_vconvert.gif" alt="vConvert 2.0">
                <h3>vConvert 2.0</h3>
                <p>Our conversion framework</p>
                </a>
            </li>
            <li>
                <a href="#vretain">
                <img src="images/logo_vretain.gif" alt="vRetain 1.0">
                <h3>vRetain 1.0</h3>
                <p>Maximize customer loyalty</p>
                </a>
            </li>
            </ul>
        </div>
    </section>

    <footer data-role="footer" class="ui-bar">
        <div data-role="controlgroup" data-type="horizontal">
            <a href="#twitter" data-rel="dialog" data-role="button"
                data-icon="info">Recent Tweets</a>
        </div>
    </footer>
</div>
```

Figure 18-15   The HTML for the mobile web site (part 1 of 3)

The HTML for the vProspect page

```
<div data-role="page" id="vprospect">
    <header data-role="header">
        <a href="#" data-role="button" data-icon="arrow-l" data-rel="back"
            data-transition="slide">Back</a>
        <h1>vProspect 2.0</h1>
    </header>

    <section data-role="content">
        <img src="images/logo_vprospect.gif" width="84" height="48">
        <h2>vProspect 2.0</h2>
        <h3>What vProspect can help you do</h3>
        <ul>
            <li>Define your target audience and competition.</li>
            <li>Research your competition and your target audience&rsquo;s
            behavior, needs, technical know-how level, etc.</li>
            <li>Establish a conceptual and visual identity that corresponds
            to the defined direction of the company.</li>
            <li>Ensure consistency across all media.</li>
            <li>Establish corporate guidelines for cohesiveness of any future
            developments.</li>
            <li>Define and/or re-define your service and/or product
            offerings.</li>
            <li>Define expansion plans and strategies.</li>
            <li>Implement search engine optimization of all online
            materials.</li>
        </ul>
    </section>
</div>
```

The HTML for the Recent Tweets dialog

```
<div data-role="page" id="twitter">
    <header data-role="header">
        <h1>Recent Tweets</h1>
    </header>

    <section data-role="content">
        <div id="twitterfeed"></div>
    </section>
</div>
```

Figure 18-15   The HTML for the mobile web site (part 2 of 3)

The HTML for the Contact Us page

```
<div data-role="page" id="contactus">
    <!-- header goes here -->
    <section data-role="content"><h3>Contact Us</h3>
        <form action="mobile.asp" method="post" data-ajax="false">
            <label for="name">Name:</label>
            <input type="text" name="name" id="name">
            <label for="companyname">Company Name:</label>
            <input type="text" name="companyname" id="companyname">
            <label for="phone">Phone:</label>
            <input type="tel" name="phone" id="phone">
            <label for="email">Email:</label>
            <input type="email" name="email" id="email">
            <label for="size">Company Size:</label>
            <input type="range" name="size" id="size" min="10" max="500"
                value="10" step="10" data-highlight="true"><br>
            <label for="currentinstall">Currently installed
                vSolutions?</label>
            <select name="currentinstall" id="currentinstall"
                data-role="slider">
                <option value="No">No</option>
                <option value="Yes">Yes</option>
            </select>
            <fieldset data-role="controlgroup">
                <legend>Which solutions are you interested in?</legend>
                <input type="checkbox" name="vprospect" id="vprospect">
                <label for="vprospect">vProspect</label>
                <input type="checkbox" name="vconvert" id="vconvert">
                <label for="vconvert">vConvert</label>
                <input type="checkbox" name="vretain" id="vretain">
                <label for="vretain">vRetain</label>
            </fieldset>
            <fieldset data-role="controlgroup" data-type="horizontal">
                <legend>Current infrastructure?</legend>
                <input type="radio" name="linux" id="linux">
                <label for="linux">Linux</label>
                <input type="radio" name="mac" id="mac">
                <label for="mac">Mac</label>
                <input type="radio" name="windows" id="windows">
                <label for="windows">Windows</label>
            </fieldset>
            <label for="hearaboutus" class="select">
                How did you hear about us?</label>
            <select name="hearaboutus" id="hearaboutus">
                <option value="magazine">Magazine Ad</option>
                <option value="radio">Radio Ad</option>
                <option value="tv">TV Ad</option>
                <option value="word">Word of Mouth</option>
            </select>
            <label for="questions">Questions/Comments:</label>
            <textarea name="questions" id="questions"></textarea><br>
            <input type="submit" value="Submit Form">
        </form>
    </section>
    <!-- footer goes here -->
</div>
```

Figure 18-15   The HTML for the mobile web site (part 3 of 3)

Perspective

Now that you've completed this chapter, you should be able to use JQuery Mobile to develop a mobile version of your web site that is a nice complement to the full version of your site. Remember, though, that you can also include jQuery features in a jQuery Mobile web site. Together, the jQuery and jQuery Mobile libraries let you bring powerful features to mobile web sites.

Terms

collapsible content block
collapsible set
list view
split button list

inset list
list divider
count bubble
search filter bar

Summary

- The jQuery Mobile documentation is an excellent reference for the components and data attributes that jQuery Mobile provides.

- With jQuery Mobile, you can lay out content in grids that consist of rows and columns.

- You can save space on a page by using *collapsible content blocks* and *collapsible sets*. The difference between the two is that you can display the content for more than one collapsible content block, but you can display the content for only one content block in a collapsible set.

- You can use a *list view* to display a list of items that let you link to other pages. *Split button lists* let you link to one page when the list item is tapped and to another page when the indicator is tapped. *Inset lists* can be used when a page contains other content.

- You can add *list dividers* to a list to divide the list items into groups, and you can include *count bubbles* to indicate the number of items in a group when the list items represent groups.

- A *search filter bar* lets you filter the items in a list so you can find the item you want more easily.

- jQuery Mobile provides many standard form controls for user input, including text fields, text areas, radio buttons, and check boxes. These controls work like their HTML counterparts but are optimized for mobile devices.

- jQuery Mobile also provides for sliders, which work like HTML5 range controls, switches, which can have one of two binary values, and select menus, which work like HTML drop-down lists.

- To submit a mobile form, you code the form controls within a standard form element and you include a submit button.

Exercise 18-1   Review the jQuery Mobile documentation

In this exercise, you'll display the jQuery Mobile web site and review some of the documentation it contains.

Review the components for jQuery Mobile

1. Go to the web site for jQuery Mobile at this URL:

   `http://jquerymobile.com/demos/1.1.1/index.html`

   Notice the list of items under the Components heading. Then, click on the Content Formatting item.

2. From the list that's displayed on the next page, click on the Layout Grids item. Then, review the documentation that's displayed.

3. If you want to, review the documentation for collapsible content blocks and collapsible sets by clicking on those items in the list at the left side of the page. Then, click the Home button in the upper left corner of the page to return to the Home page for jQuery Mobile.

Review the information in the Data Attribute Reference

4. Click on the Data Attribute Reference item under the API heading. Then, scroll through the documentation to see that it lists the data attributes for each type of jQuery Mobile component.

5. Click the header for the slider to see that it takes you to the documentation for that component.

6. Continue experimenting until you're familiar with how the documentation is organized.

Exercise 18-2   Experiment with the mobile web site

In this exercise, you'll first test the mobile version of the Vecta Corp web site that's presented in this chapter. Then, you'll make some modifications to it.

Open and test the mobile web site for Vecta Corp

1. Use your text editor to open the HTML page in this folder:

   `c:\jquery\exercises\ch18\vectacorp\`

2. Test this page and the navigation from one page to another within the site. In particular, use the list items in the list on the Solutions page to display information on the individual solutions, click the Back button in the header of a solution to return to the Solutions page, and click the Recent Tweets button in the footer of the Home or Solutions page to see the Recent Tweets dialog that's displayed. When you're done, close the dialog.

3. Click the Contact Us button in the navigation bar of the Home or Solutions page to display the Contact Us page. Then, complete the form and click the Submit button to see what happens.

Change the switch on the Contact Us page to two radio buttons

4. Replace the switch on the Contact Us page with a group of two horizontal radio buttons. Then, test this change to be sure it works.

5. Change the code you just entered so the input element for each radio button is contained within the label element, and delete the for attribute for the label. Then, test this again.

Change the Solutions page so it uses collapsible content blocks

6. Change the li elements in the list view on this page to div elements that have a data-role attribute set to "collapsible", and delete the ul element for the list view.

7. Delete the <a> and <p> elements from the div elements you just added. Then, move the img element inside the h3 element before the text that element contains.

8. Test this web page to see how it works. When you click one of the content blocks, the paragraph for that block should be displayed. Note that you can display all three of the content blocks at once. Also note that although the formatting for the headings could be improved, they're good enough for now.

9. Replace the <p> element in each content block with the h3 and ul elements from the page for the associated solution. Now when you click on one of the content blocks, all the text that was previously included on a separate page should be displayed.

10. Notice that each content block now starts with two h3 elements. Change the first h3 element in each block to an h2 element and test the page again. Because jQuery mobile always styles the headers the same way, their appearance won't change.

Appendix A

How to set up your computer for this book

This appendix shows how to install the software that we recommend for editing and testing the web pages and applications for this book. That includes Aptana Studio 3 as the text editor for both Windows and Mac OS users, plus the Firefox browser for both Windows and Mac OS users. This appendix also shows you how to download and install the source code for this book.

As you read these descriptions, please remember that most web sites are continually upgraded. As a result, some of the procedures in this appendix may have changed since this book was published. Nevertheless, these procedures should still be good guides to installing the software.

How to install Aptana Studio 3...572
On a Windows system 572
On a Mac OS system 572
How to install Firefox and Firebug...................................574
How to install Firefox 574
How to install Firebug 574
How to install and use the source code for this book....576
For Windows users 576
For Mac OS users 578

How to install Aptana Studio 3

If you're already comfortable with a text editor that works for editing HTML, CSS, and JavaScript, you can continue using it. But otherwise, we recommend that you use Aptana Studio 3. It is a free editor that offers many features, it runs on both Windows and Mac OS systems, and chapter 1 presents a quick tutorial on it that will get you started right.

On a Windows system

Figure A-1 shows how to download and install Aptana Studio 3 on a Windows system.

On a Mac OS system

Figure A-1 also shows how to download and install Aptana Studio 3 on a Mac OS system.

The web site address for downloading Aptana Studio 3

`http://www.aptana.com/products/studio3/download`

How to install Aptana Studio 3 on a Windows system

1. Go to the web site address above.

2. Click on the Download Aptana Studio 3 button near the bottom of the page, click on the Save button in the resulting dialog box, and identify the location where you want the file saved in the Save As dialog box that's displayed.

3. When the Download finishes, use Windows Explorer to find the exe file, and double-click on it to start it.

4. As you step through the wizard that follows, you can accept all of the default settings that are offered.

5. After Aptana Studio 3 is installed, start it, select the check box in the Workspace Launcher dialog box that's displayed to use the same location for the workspace each time you start Aptana, and accept the default location.

6. If you don't have a Git application installed on your system, Aptana will ask you if you want it to install a Portable Git application. Accept that option because Aptana won't run without it.

How to install Aptana Studio 3 on a Mac OS X system

1. Go to the web site address above.

2. Click on the Customize Your Download button, and select Mac OS X.

3. Click on the Download Aptana Studio 3 button, and click on the Save File button in the resulting dialog box.

4. When the Download finishes, double-click on the dmg file in the Downloads folder to display the Aptana Studio 3 window.

5. Use Finder to display the Applications folder. Then, drag the Aptana Studio 3 folder from the Aptana Studio 3 window to the Applications folder.

6. Start Aptana Studio 3. Then, if you don't have a Git application installed on your system, Aptana will ask you if you want it to install a Portable Git application. Accept that option because Aptana won't run without it.

Description

- Aptana runs on Windows, Mac, and Linux systems.

- Git is a source code management tool that Aptana requires. If necessary, Aptana will install it for you when you start Aptana for the first time.

- Chapter 1 of this book presents a tutorial that will get you off to a fast start with Aptana.

Figure A-1   How to install Aptana Studio 3 as your text editor

How to install Firefox and Firebug

When you develop JavaScript applications, you need to test them on all of the browsers that the users of the applications are likely to use. For a commercial application, that usually includes Internet Explorer, Firefox, Safari for Macs, Opera, and Google's Chrome. Then, if an application doesn't work on one of those browsers, you need to debug it.

As you do the exercises and work with the applications in this book, though, you can use just one browser, and the one we recommend is Mozilla Firefox. Then, if you need to debug an application, you can use the Firebug extension to Firefox, which is an excellent debugging tool. Both of these components are free, they don't take long to install, and chapter 4 shows you how to use them.

How to install Firefox

Figure A-2 shows how to download and install Firefox. As you respond to the dialog boxes for the installer, we recommend that you make Firefox your default browser.

How to install Firebug

Figure A-2 also shows how to install the Firebug extension to Firefox, and chapter 4 shows you how to use it.

The web site address for downloading Firefox

`http://www.mozilla.com`

How to install Firefox

1. Go to the web site address above.
2. Click on the Firefox – Free Download button.
3. Save the exe file to your C drive.
4. Run the exe file and respond to the resulting dialog boxes.

How to install the Firebug extension for Firefox

1. Click Tools→Add-ons to open the Add-ons window.
2. Click on the "Get Add-ons" tab at the left side of the window, then click "Browse All Add-ons" at the bottom right of the page.
3. In the search text box, type "Firebug" and then click the Firebug link in the drop-down list that's displayed.
4. Click the "Add to Firefox" button in the page that's displayed.
5. In the Software Installation window, click the Install Now button.
6. When the installation is complete, click the Restart Now button to restart Firefox.
7. When Firefox has restarted, close the Add-ons window.

Description

- We recommend that you use Firefox as your default browser and the Firebug extension as your primary debugging tool.

Figure A-2   How to install Firefox and Firebug

How to install and use the source code for this book

The next two figures show how to install and use the source code for this book. One figure is for Windows users, the other for Mac OS users.

For Windows users

Figure A-3 shows how to install the source code for this book on a Windows system. This includes the source code for the applications in this book, the starting files for the exercises, and the solutions for the exercises.

When you finish this procedure, the book applications, exercises, and solutions will be in the three folders that are listed in this figure. When you do the exercises, you use the subfolders and files in this folder:

`c:\jquery\exercises`

However, the files are also stored in this location:

`c:\murach\jquery\exercises`

That way, you can restore the files for an exercise to their original state by copying the files from the second folder to the first.

As you do the exercises, you may want to copy code from a book application into a file that you're working with. That's easy to do because the applications are in this folder:

`c:\murach\jquery\book_apps`

When you finish an exercise, you may want to compare your solution to ours, which you'll find in this folder:

`c:\murach\jquery\solutions`

You may also want to look at a solution when you're having trouble with an exercise. That will help you get past the problem you're having so you can continue to make progress. Either way, the solutions are an important part of the learning process.

The Murach web site

`www.murach.com`

The Windows folders for the applications, exercises, and solutions

```
c:\murach\jquery\book_apps
c:\murach\jquery\exercises
c:\murach\jquery\solutions
```

The Windows folder for doing the exercises

```
c:\jquery\exercises
```

How to download and install the source code on a Windows system

1. Go to www.murach.com, and go to the page for *Murach's JavaScript and jQuery.*

2. Click the link for "FREE download of the book applications." Then, click the "All book files" link for the self-extracting zip file. This will download a setup file named qury_allfiles.exe onto your hard drive.

3. Use Windows Explorer to find the exe file on your hard drive. Then, double-click this file. This installs the source code for the book applications, exercises, and solutions into the folders shown above. After it does this install, the exe file copies the exercises folder to c:\jquery so you have two copies of the exercises.

How to restore an exercise file

- Copy it from its subfolder in

    `c:\murach\jquery\exercises`

    to the corresponding subfolder in

    `c:\jquery\exercises`

Description

- The exe file that you download stores the exercises in two different folders. That way, you can do the exercises using the files that are stored in one folder, but you have a backup copy in case you want to restore the starting files for an exercise.

- As you do the exercises that are at the ends of the chapters, you may want to copy code from a book application into the file you're working on. That's easy to do because all of the applications are available in the book_apps folder.

- In the solutions folder, you can view the solutions for the exercises.

Figure A-3   How to install the source code for this book on a Windows system

For Mac OS users

Figure A-4 shows how to install the source code for this book on a Mac OS system. This includes the source code for the applications in this book, the starting files for the exercises, and the solutions for the exercises.

When you finish this procedure, the book applications, exercises, and solutions will be in the three folders that are listed in this figure. Then, before you start the exercises, you should copy the exercises folder from:

`documents\murach\jquery`

to

`documents\jquery`

That way, you can restore the files for an exercise to their original state by copying the files from the first folder to the second.

As you do the exercises, you may want to copy code from a book application into a file that you're working with. That's easy to do because the applications are in this folder:

`documents\murach\jquery\book_apps`

When you finish an exercise, you may want to compare your solution to ours, which you'll find in this folder:

`documents\murach\jquery\solutions`

You may also want to look at a solution when you're having trouble with an exercise. That will help you get past the problem you're having so you can continue to make progress. Either way, the solutions are an important part of the learning process.

The Murach web site

www.murach.com

The Mac OS folders for the book applications and exercises

```
documents\murach\jquery\book_apps
documents\murach\jquery\exercises
documents\murach\jquery\solutions
```

The Mac OS folder for doing the exercises

```
documents\jquery\exercises
```

How to download and install the source code on a Mac OS system

1. Go to www.murach.com, and go to the page for *Murach's JavaScript and jQuery*.

2. Click the link for "FREE download of the book applications." Then, click the "All book files" link for the regular zip file. This will download a setup file named qury_allfiles.zip onto your hard drive.

3. Move this file into the Documents folder of your home folder.

4. Use Finder to go to your Documents folder.

5. Double-click the qury_allfiles.zip file to extract the folders for the book applications, exercises, and solutions. This will create a folder named jquery in your documents folder that will contain the book_apps, exercises, and solutions folders.

6. Create two copies of the exercises folder by copying the exercises folder from

   ```
   documents\murach\jquery
   ```

   to

   ```
   documents\jquery
   ```

How to restore an exercise file

- Copy it from its subfolder in

  ```
  documents\murach\jquery\exercises
  ```

  to the corresponding subfolder in

  ```
  documents\jquery\exercises
  ```

Description

- This procedure stores the exercises in two different folders. That way, you do the exercises using the files that are in one folder, but you also have a backup copy.

- If you want to copy code from a book application into an exercise file that you're working on, you can find all of the applications in the book_apps folder.

- In the solutions folder, you can view the solutions for the exercises at the end of each chapter.

Figure A-4   How to install the source code for this book on a Mac OS system

Appendix B

A summary
of the applications
in this book

This appendix summarizes the applications that are presented in this book. That will make it easier to find an application when you want to review or copy its code.

Section 1: JavaScript essentials

Application name	Starting figure	Description
Miles Per Gallon	2-16	A "getting started" app that uses prompt methods to get user entries and alert methods to display the results.
Test Scores	2-17	A "getting started" app that uses prompt methods to get user entries and alert methods to display the results.
Miles Per Gallon	3-10	Gets user entries from text boxes and displays results in text boxes.
Email List	3-11	Gets user entries from text boxes, validates the entries, and displays error messages in span elements.
Enhanced Email List	5-6	Like the previous Email List app but with an array used to validate the state entry.
FAQs (version 1)	6-4	Uses collapsible div elements to hide and show answers beneath questions that are in h2 elements.
FAQs (version 2)	6-6	Like the previous FAQs app, but with improved coding.
FAQs (version 3)	6-8	Like the previous FAQs app, but with improved accessibility.
Image Swap	6-12	Swaps large images when thumbnail images are clicked. To do that, it cancels the default action of the <a> elements, and it preloads the images.
Slide Show	6-15	Uses a timer to display images in a slide show. It also preloads the images.

Section 2: jQuery essentials

Application name	Starting figure	Description
Email List	7-7	Uses jQuery to simplify the Email List app of section 1.
FAQs	7-12	Uses jQuery to simplify the FAQs app of section 1.
Image Swap	7-14	Uses jQuery to simplify the Image Swap app of section 1.
Image Rollover	7-15	Changes the image in an image element when the mouse hovers over it.
FAQs with Effects	8-2	Two versions of the FAQs app of chapter 7 but with effects.
Slide Show	8-3	A Slide Show app with effects.
FAQs and Animations	8-9	Like the earlier FAQs app but with an animated heading and easings.
Carousel	8-11	Uses animation to implement a carousel of books.
TOC	9-5	Generates a TOC in a sidebar from the headings in an article.
Enhanced TOC	9-9	Like the earlier TOC app, but with the TOC moving next to the heading in the article that has been accessed.
Slide Show	9-12	Two versions of a slide show that uses the DOM traversal methods to implement it.
Membership Form	10-5	Data validation of the entries in a membership form using JavaScript and jQuery.
Membership Form	10-8	Data validation of the entries in a membership form using the Validation plugin.
Lightbox	11-4	Demonstrates the use of the Lightbox plugin.
Carousel	11-5	Demonstrates the use of the bxSlider plugin.
Slide Show	11-6	Demonstrates the use of the Cycle plugin.
jLayout	11-7	Demonstrates the use of the jLayout plugin.
Menu Highlighter	11-10	Illustrates a custom plugin that highlights menus.
Vecta Corp	11-11	Shows how you can use multiple plugins (two) for one web page.

Section 3: jQuery UI essentials

Application name	Starting figure	Description
Accordion	12-7	Demonstrates the Accordion widget.
Tabs	12-8	Demonstrates the Tabs widget.
Button and Dialog	12-9	Demonstrates the Button and Dialog widgets.
Autocomplete	12-10	Demonstrates the Autocomplete widget.
Datepicker	12-11	Demonstrates the Datepicker widget.
Slider	12-12	Demonstrates the Slider widget.
Progressbar	12-13	Demonstrates the Progressbar widget.
Vecta Corp	12-14	Shows how you can use multiple widgets (five) for one web page.
Draggable and Droppable	13-2	Demonstrates the Draggable and Droppable interactions.
Resizable	13-3	Demonstrates the Resizable interaction.
Selectable	13-4	Demonstrates the Selectable interaction.
Sortable	13-5	Demonstrates the Sortable interaction.
Individual effects	13-7	Demonstrates individual effects.
Color transitions	13-8	Demonstrates color transitions.
Class transitions	13-9	Demonstrates class transitions.
Visibility transitions	13-10	Demonstrates visibility transitions

Section 4: Ajax, JSON, and API essentials

Application name	Starting figure	Description
XMLHttpRequest	14-4	Shows the use of the XMLHttpRequest object for Ajax.
Load HTML	14-6	Shows the use of the Ajax load method.
Load XML	14-7	Shows the use of the Ajax $.get method with XML data.
Load JSON	14-8	Shows the use of the Ajax $.getJSON method.
Load data	14-11	Shows the use of the $.ajax method to get XML data.
Blogger	14-15	Shows the use of Ajax, JSON, and the Blogger API.
YouTube API	15-3	Lists videos by channel.
	15-4	Lists videos by search term.
	15-5	Plays listed videos in an onsite video player.
Twitter API	15-7	Displays a Twitter feed.
	15-8	Displays a Twitter feed with embedded URLs as links.
	15-9	Displays a Twitter feed with a custom timestamp.
Flickr API	15-12	Shows the use of Flickr as a Content Management System.
	15-13	Shows the use of Flickr for a photo gallery.
Google Maps API	16-3	Displays a Google map on a page.
	16-5	Adds markers to the map.
	16-7	Adds messages to the markers on the map.
	16-8	Adds custom messages to the markers on the map.
	16-9	Adds custom messages that contain Flickr images.
	16-11	Adds driving directions between two points on the map.

Section 5: jQuery Mobile essentials

Application name	Starting figure	Description
Vecta Corp	17-15	A mobile application that uses the basic features of jQuery Mobile.
Vecta Corp	18-14	An enhanced version of the chapter 17 application that uses some of the other features of jQuery Mobile.

Appendix C

How to resolve
$ conflicts

A *$ conflict* occurs when two or more libraries or plugins require the use of the $ sign, and they aren't written in ways that prevent the conflict. Then, the browser doesn't know which library or plugin the use of the $ sign refers to, and that will cause a debugging problem.

Before you go any further, you should know that a $ conflict shouldn't ever occur because libraries and plugins are supposed to be written in ways that prevent these conflicts. For instance, chapter 11 shows how to create a plugin that won't cause a $ conflict. As a result, $ conflicts are extremely rare, and you probably won't ever encounter one. That's why you can think of the solutions that are presented in this appendix as "measures of last resort".

How to avoid $ conflicts

If you are using one or more libraries or plugins in addition to the jQuery, jQuery UI, and jQuery Mobile libraries and you suspect that you may be experiencing a $ conflict, figure C-1 presents two solutions for resolving the conflict. To understand these solutions, you need to know that you can use either the $ sign or "jQuery" to refer to the jQuery library.

As a result, one easy way to resolve a $ conflict is to change all of the $ signs that refer to the jQuery library to "jQuery". This is illustrated by the first example in this figure. That's also a quick way to find out if your debugging problem is a $ conflict. The only trouble with this method is that it can be cumbersome if your code includes many references to jQuery.

The second solution in this figure not only solves the problem but also lets you use the $ sign to refer to jQuery. With this solution, you use the $.noConflict method to relinquish jQuery's control of the $ sign. After that, you use "jQuery" instead of the $ sign to start an event handler for the ready method with $ as the only parameter for the handler. Once you've done that, you can use the $ sign within the ready event handler to refer to jQuery. You can also use the $ sign outside of the ready event handler to refer to other libraries or plugins.

Two ways to refer to jQuery

* $
* jQuery

jQuery code that uses jQuery instead of the $ sign to refer to jQuery

```
jQuery(document).ready(function() {
    jQuery("#selected_item").jqueryMethod();
});
```

jQuery code that uses the $.noConflict method to avoid $ conflicts

```
$.noConflict();                    // relinquishes control of the $ sign
jQuery(document).ready(function($) {
    // code that uses the $ sign to refer to jQuery
    $("#selected_item").jqueryMethod();
});
    // code that uses the $ sign for other libraries or plugins
```

How to write JavaScript code that avoids $ conflicts

* Code the $.noConflict method.

* Use jQuery instead of the $ sign to select the document and create an event handler for its ready event.

* In the parameter for the ready event handler, code $. Then, you can use the $ sign within the ready event handler.

* Write the code for any libraries or plugins that require the $ sign outside of the ready event handler.

Description

* A *$ conflict* can occur when a jQuery application uses other libraries or plugins that require the use of the $ sign. Then, the $ sign can inadvertently refer to a library or plugin other than the one you intended.

* To refer to jQuery, you can use either the $ sign or "jQuery". As a result, you can avoid $ conflicts altogether by using "jQuery" instead of the $ sign to refer to jQuery.

* Another way to avoid $ conflicts is to use the $.noConflict method as shown above.

Figure C-1   How to avoid $ conflicts

Index

$ conflict, 585-587
$.ajax method (Ajax), 424-427, 435, 435
$.each method (Ajax), 414, 415
$.get method (Ajax), 414, 415, 418, 419
$.getJSON method (Ajax), 414, 415, 420, 421
$.noConflict method (jQuery), 586, 587
$.post method (Ajax), 414, 415, 418, 419
$.support.cors property (jQuery), 434, 435, 444, 445

A

Accessibility, 170-173
Accordion (jQuery Mobile), 542, 543
Accordion widget, 356, 357
action attribute (form), 288, 289
addClass method (jQuery), 214, 215, 260, 261, 396, 397
Adding an array element, 144, 145
Address bar, 30, 31
after method (jQuery), 264, 265
Ajax, 405-436
    with Google Maps, 474
alert method (JavaScript), 60, 61
animate method (jQuery), 242, 243, 250, 251
Animation (jQuery), 242-251
Animation queue, 244, 245
Anonymous function, 100, 101
API, 328, 406, 407, 439-466
    Blogger, 428-435
    Flickr, 458-465
    Google Maps, 470, 471
    Twitter, 450-457
    YouTube, 440-449
API key
    Google Blogger, 428, 429
    Google Maps, 470, 471
append method (jQuery), 264, 265
appendTo method (jQuery), 264, 265
Application (JavaScript)
    Email List, 112-115, 152-155
    FAQs, 164-169, 172-173
    Image Swap, 178-181
    Miles Per Gallon, 80-81, 110-111
    Slide Show, 186-189
    Test Scores, 82-83
    Validation, 296-299
Application (jQuery)
    Carousel (animation), 252-255
    Email List, 208-211
    FAQs, 220-221
    FAQs with effects, 234-235

Google Maps directions, 490-491
Google Maps map, 474-475
Google Maps marker, 478-479
Google Maps message, 482-487
Highlighter plugin, 330-333
Image Rollover, 226-227
Image Swap, 222-224
Plugins, 334-337
Slide Show with DOM traversal, 282-283
Slide Show with effects, 236-240
TOC, 268-271, 276-277
Validation (plugin), 304-309
Application (jQuery Mobile), Vecta Corp, 526-531, 562-567
Application (jQuery UI), Vecta Corp with widgets, 370-373
Application Programming Interface (see API)
Application summary, 581-584
Application server, 8, 9
Aptana Studio 3, 34-43
    auto-completion, 40, 41
    change colors, 38, 39
    create project, 34, 35
    error marker, 40, 41, 84, 85
    HTML validation, 136, 137
    installing, 572, 573
    open file, 36, 37
    project, 34, 35
    run application, 42, 43
    save work, 42, 43
    setup exercise, 47
    syntax highlighting, 40, 41
Argument, 100, 101
Arithmetic operator, 64, 65
Array, 141-156
    methods, 150, 151
    object, 142, 143
    element, 142, 143
    index, 142, 143
    length, 142, 143
Assignment operator, 66, 67
Assignment statement, 66, 67
Asynchronous JavaScript and XML, 406, 407
Atom Syndication Format, 442
Attach (event handler), 107
attr method (jQuery), 214, 215, 260, 261
Attribute (see HTML attribute)
Attribute (form), 288, 289
Attribute (HTML5), 290, 291
Attribute (jQuery Mobile)
    class, 516, 517, 518, 519, 522, 523
    data-ajax, 560, 561
    data-filter, 550, 551
    data-highlight, 554, 555
    data-icon, 516, 517, 518, 519

Attribute (continued)
    data-inline, 516, 517
    data-inset, 546, 547
    data-rel, 514, 515
    data-role, 510, 511, 516, 517
    data-split-icon, 546, 547
    data-theme, 516, 517, 518, 519, 522, 523
    data-transition, 514, 515
    data-type, 556, 557
Attribute node, 98, 99, 158, 159
Autocomplete widget, 362, 363
autofocus attribute (HTML5), 290, 291

B

before method (jQuery), 264, 265
bind event method (jQuery), 218, 219
Blogger, 428-435
blur event (JavaScript), 106, 107
blur event method (jQuery), 294, 295
blur method (jQuery), 294, 295
Boolean data type, 62, 63, 68, 69
Boolean variable, 68, 69, 74, 75
Breakpoint, 128, 129
Browser, 4-11
Browser ratings, 32, 33
Bug, 120, 121
Button
    jQuery Mobile, 516, 517
    reset, 288, 289
    submit, 288, 289
Button widget, 360, 361
bxSlider plugin, 322-323

C

Call a method, 60, 61
Call a function, 100, 101
Camel casing, 56, 57
Carousel application (jQuery animation), 252-255
Cascading Style Sheets (see CSS)
Case-sensitive, 54, 55
CDN, 196, 197
    Google Maps, 474, 475
    jQuery, 196, 197
    jQuery Mobile, 508, 509
    jQuery UI, 352, 353
Chaining, 70, 71, 94, 95
    animation methods, 244, 245
change event (JavaScript), 106, 107, 108, 109
change event method (jQuery), 294, 295
change method (jQuery), 294, 295
Check box (jQuery Mobile), 556, 557
Child, 158, 159

childNodes property, 160, 161
children method (jQuery), 278, 279
Class, 472, 473
class attribute, 22, 23
    jQuery Mobile, 516, 517, 518, 519, 522, 523
class selector, 26, 27
Class transitions, 396, 397
clearInterval method (JavaScript), 184, 185
clearTimeout method (JavaScript), 182, 183
click event (JavaScript), 106, 107, 108, 109, 174, 175
click event method (jQuery), 206, 207, 216, 217
Client, 4, 5
Client-side processing, 10
clone method (jQuery), 264, 265
closest method (jQuery), 278, 279
Closing tag, 14
CMS (Content Management System), 458, 459, 460, 463
Collapsible content blocks (jQuery Mobile), 540, 541
Collapsible set (jQuery Mobile), 542, 543
Color transitions, 394, 395
Columns (jQuery Mobile), 538, 539
Comment (JavaScript), 58, 59
Comment node, 98, 99, 158, 159
Comment out, 58, 59
Common JavaScript errors, 122, 123
Compatibility (cross-browser), 32, 33
Compound assignment operator, 66, 67
Compound conditional expression, 72, 73
Concatenate, 68, 69
Concatenation operator, 68, 69
Conditional expression, 72, 73
confirm method (JavaScript), 92, 93
constant (in a Google Maps class), 472, 473
constructor, 472, 473
Content blocks (jQuery Mobile), 540, 541
Content Delivery Network (see CDN)
Content Management System, 458, 459, 460, 463
Contents list (jQuery Mobile), 544, 545
Control statement, 72
Controls (form), 288-293
Core components (jQuery UI), 346, 347
Core effects (jQuery UI), 390, 391
Count bubble (jQuery Mobile), 548, 549
Counter for a loop, 78, 79
Creating a plugin, 328-333
Cross-browser compatibility, 32, 33
Cross-browser security policy, 424, 425, 450, 451
CSS (Cascading Style Sheets), 14, 15
    property, 28, 29
    rule, 28, 29
    rule set, 28, 29
    selector, 26, 27
css method (jQuery), 214, 215, 272, 273
CSS3 media queries, 498, 499
Cycle plugin, 324-325

D

Data attribute (jQuery Mobile), 536, 537
  data-ajax, 560, 561
  data-collapsed, 540, 541
  data-filter, 550, 551
  data-highlight, 554, 555
  data-icon, 516, 517, 518, 519
  data-inline, 516, 517
  data-inset, 546, 547
  data-rel, 514, 515
  data-role, 510, 511, 516, 517, 518, 519
  data-split-icon, 546, 547
  data-theme, 516, 517, 518, 519, 522, 523
  data-transition, 514, 515
  data-type, 556, 557
Data type
  Boolean, 62, 63, 68, 69
  number, 62, 63
  string, 62, 63
Data validation, 10, 11, 296-309
Database server, 8, 9
Date control, 290, 291
Date object, 53, 96, 97
Datepicker widget, 364, 365
dblclick event (JavaScript), 106, 107
dblclick event method (jQuery), 216, 217
Debugging, 120-125
  with Firebug, 126-128
  with Firefox, 126-128
  jQuery apps, 198, 199
Decimal value, 62, 63
Declaration
  DOCTYPE, 12, 13
  variable, 66, 67
Decrement operator, 64, 65
Default action (event), 174, 175
delay method (jQuery), 246, 247
delete operator (JavaScript array), 144, 145
Descendant, 158, 159
Designing mobile web pages, 504, 505
Detect Mobile Browsers, 500, 501
Dialog (jQuery Mobile), 514, 515
Dialog widget, 360, 361
Directions (on map), 488-491
disabled property (JavaScript), 94, 95
div element, 20, 21
DOCTYPE declaration, 12, 13
Document interface, 162, 163
Document object, 92, 93
Document Object Model (see DOM)
Documentation
  Blogger, 430-431
  Google Maps, 470-471
  jQuery Mobile, 536-537

  jQuery UI, 354, 355
  Twitter, 450-451
  YouTube, 440-441
DOM (Document Object Model), 16, 98, 99, 158, 159
  core specification, 158, 159
  manipulation methods, 260-277
  replacement methods, 262, 263
  scripting, 16, 17, 157-190
  traversal methods, 278-283
Domain name, 30, 31
Dot operator, 60, 61
Do-while loop, 76, 77
do-while statement, 76, 77
Download
  book applications, 576, 577
  jQuery UI, 348-353
Draggable interaction, 382, 383
Driving directions (on map), 488-491
Droppable interaction, 382, 383
Dynamic web page, 8, 9

E

each method (jQuery), 214, 215
Easings (jQuery UI), 248, 249, 250, 251, 390, 391
Effect method (jQuery UI), 392, 393
Effect methods (jQuery), 232-235
Effects (jQuery UI), 346, 347, 390-399
Element (see HTML element)
Element interface, 162, 163
Element node, 98, 99, 158, 159
Element of an array, 142, 143
Else clause, 74, 75
Else if clause, 74, 75
email control, 290, 291
Email List application (JavaScript), 112-115, 152-155
Email List application (jQuery), 208-211
Embedded JavaScript, 50, 51
Embedded styles, 24, 25
empty method (jQuery), 266, 267
Empty string, 62, 63
Emulator for mobile device, 504, 505
end method (jQuery), 280, 281
eq method (jQuery), 280, 281
error event method,(jQuery), 216, 217
Error messages (browser), 130, 131
Errors (JavaScript), 120, 121
Escape sequence, 68, 69
Event (JavaScript), 106, 107
Event (jQuery Mobile), 536, 537
Event handler, 106-109
Event method (jQuery), 206, 207
  bind, 218, 219
  blur, 294, 295

Event method (continued)
  change, 294, 295
  click, 206, 207, 216, 217
  dblclick, 216, 217
  error, 216, 217
  focus, 294, 295
  hover, 216, 217
  mouseenter, 216, 217
  mouseout, 216, 217
  mouseover, 216, 217
  one, 218, 219
  ready, 206, 207, 216, 217
  select, 294, 295
  submit, 294, 295
  toggle, 216, 217
  trigger, 218, 219
  unbind, 218, 219
  unload, 216, 217
Exponent, 62, 63
Expression
  conditional, 72, 73
  numeric, 64, 65
Extensible Markup Language (XML), 408, 409, 412,
    413, 418, 419
External JavaScript file, 50, 51
External style sheet, 24, 25

F

fadeIn method (jQuery), 232, 233
fadeOut method (jQuery), 232, 233
fadeTo method (jQuery), 232, 233
fadeToggle method (jQuery), 232, 233
FAQs application
  JavaScript, 164-169, 172-173
  jQuery, 220-221
  jQuery effects, 234-235
Field, 288-293
Filename, 30, 31
Filter bar (jQuery Mobile), 550, 551
filter method (jQuery), 280, 281
find method (jQuery), 278, 279
Firebug, 126, 127
  debugging, 126-128
  breakpoint, 128, 129
  installing, 574, 575
  with jQuery, 198, 199
Firefox
  debugging, 126-128
  Error Console, 84, 85
  error messages, 84, 85
  installing, 574, 575
first method (jQuery), 280, 281
firstChild property (JavaScript), 98, 99, 160, 161

First-in, first-out array, 150, 151
Flash, 504, 505
Flickr, 458-465
  image on map, 486-487
Floating-point arithmetic problems, 122, 123
Floating-point value, 62, 63, 66, 67
focus event (JavaScript), 106, 107
focus event method (jQuery), 294, 295
focus method
  JavaScript, 94, 95
  jQuery, 204, 205, 294, 295
for attribute, 22, 23
For loop, 78, 79
  with array, 146, 147
for statement, 78, 79
  with array, 146, 147
For-in loop, 148, 149
for-in statement, 148, 149
Form (jQuery), 287-310
Form (jQuery Mobile), 560, 561
Function (JavaScript), 100-103

G

Geocoding, 476, 477
get method (form), 288, 289, 410, 411
getAttribute method (JavaScript), 162, 163
getDate method (JavaScript), 96, 97
getElementById method (JavaScript), 92, 93
getElementsByClassName method (JavaScript), 162,
    163
getElementsByName method (JavaScript), 162, 163
getElementsByTagName method (JavaScript), 162, 163
getFullYear method (JavaScript), 96, 97
getMonth method (JavaScript), 96, 97
Global object, 60, 61, 70, 71, 92, 93
Global variable, 104, 105
  problem with, 122, 123
Google Auto Suggest, 406, 407
Google Blogger, 428-435
Google Maps, 469-492
  API, 470, 471
  applications, 474-475, 478-479, 482-487, 490-491
  classes, 472, 473, 476, 477, 480, 481
Grid (jQuery Mobile), 538, 539

H

Handler (event), 106-109
has method (jQuery), 280, 281
hasAttribute method (JavaScript), 162, 163
hasClass method (jQuery), 260, 261
height method (jQuery), 272, 273

hide method (jQuery), 214, 215, 232, 233
Highlighter plugin, 330-333
hover event method (jQuery), 216, 217
HTML (Hypertext Markup Language), 7, 12, 13
HTML attribute, 22, 23
    class, 22, 23
    for, 22, 23
    form, 290, 291
    HTML5, 290, 291
    id, 22, 23
    name, 22, 23
    title, 22, 23
HTML element, 12
    div, 20, 21
    form, 290, 291
    link, 24, 25, 352, 353, 508, 509
    script, 50-53, 196, 197, 352, 353, 474, 475, 508, 509
    span, 20, 21
html method (jQuery), 262, 263
HTML validation, 136, 137
HTML5
    attribute, 290, 291
    browser ratings, 32, 33
    compatibility, 32, 33
    controls, 290, 291
    semantic elements, 18, 19
HTTP (Hypertext transport protocol), 6, 7
    request, 6-11
    response, 6-11
Hypertext Markup Language (see HTML)
Hypertext transport protocol (see HTTP)

I

id attribute, 22, 23
id selector, 26, 27
Identifier (JavaScript), 56, 57
IE (Internet Explorer)
    compatibility issues, 32, 33, 434, 435, 444, 445
    cross-browser security policy, 434, 435, 444, 445
    error messages, 130, 131
If clause, 74, 75
if statement, 74, 75
IIFE, 328
Image preloading, 176, 177
Image rollover, 10, 11
Image Rollover application (jQuery), 226-227
Image swap, 10, 11, 178
Image Swap application (JavaScript), 178-181
Image Swap application (jQuery), 222-224
Immediately Invoked Function Expression, 328
Increment operator, 64, 65, 66, 67
Index
    for a loop, 78, 79

for an array, 142, 143
indexOf method (JavaScript), 96, 97
Individual effects (jQuery UI), 392, 393
Info window (Google map), 480-483
innerHeight method (jQuery), 272, 273
innerWidth method (jQuery), 272, 273
insertAfter method (jQuery), 264, 265
insertBefore method (jQuery), 264, 265
Inset list (jQuery Mobile), 546, 547
Installing
    Aptana, 572, 573
    book downloads, 576, 577
    Firebug, 574, 575
    Firefox, 574, 575
Integer, 62, 63
Interactions, 346, 347, 380-389
Interface, 158, 159
    document, 162, 163
    element, 162, 163
Interface node, 160, 161
Internet, 4, 5
Internet Explorer (see IE)
Internet service provider (ISP), 4, 5
Interval timer, 184, 185
isNaN method (JavaScript), 72, 73
ISP (Internet service provider), 4, 5

J

JavaScript, 10, 11
    application, 12-17
    Boolean data type, 62, 63
    comment, 58, 59
    common errors, 122, 123
    control statements, 72-79
    conventions, 56, 57
    data, 62-71
    Date object, 53
    embedded, 50, 51, 52, 53
    engine, 10, 11
    errors, 84, 85
    external, 50, 51
    function, 100-103
    identifier, 56, 57
    method, see Method (jQuery)
    naming conventions, 56, 57
    number data type, 62, 63
    object, 92-99
    primitive data type, 62, 63
    reserved word, 56, 57
    shim (see shiv)
    shiv, 18, 19, 32, 33
    statement, 54, 55
    string data type, 62, 63

syntax, 54-61
variable, 66, 67, 68, 69
JavaScript Object Notation, 408, 409
JavaScript statement
assignment, 66, 67
do-while, 76, 77
for, 78, 79, 146, 147
for-in, 148, 149
if, 74, 75
while, 76, 77
jLayout plugin, 326-327
join method (JavaScript), 150, 151
jQuery, 196-202
coding plan, 270, 271
event method, see Event method (jQuery)
method, see Method (jQuery)
plugin, 200, 201, 313-338
selectors, 202, 203, 212-213
jQuery Mobile, 506-532
accordion, 542, 543
buttons, 516, 517
check box, 556, 557
collapsible content blocks, 540, 541
collapsible set, 542, 543
columns, 538, 539
contents list, 544, 545
count bubble, 548, 549
dialog, 514, 515
documentation, 536-537
filter bar, 550, 551
form, 560, 561
grid, 538, 539
link element, 508, 509
list divider, 548, 549
radio button, 556, 557
script element, 508, 509
select menu, 558, 559
slider, 554, 555
style sheet, 508, 509
styles, 520, 521
swatch, 522, 523
switch, 554, 555
text area, 552, 553
text field, 552, 553
theme, 522, 523
ThemeRoller, 524, 525
transition, 514, 515
jQuery UI, 200, 201, 341-376, 379-400
components, 346, 347
core components, 346, 347
documentation, 354, 355
download, 348-353
easings, 248, 249, 250, 251, 390, 391
effects, 346, 347, 390-399
interactions, 346, 347, 380-389

link element, 352, 353
method, see Method (jQuery UI)
script element, 352, 353
ThemeRoller, 350, 351
themes, 344, 345, 350, 351
widgets, 354-375
jqXHR object, 424, 425
JSON, 408, 409, 420, 421
JSON editor, 432, 433
JSONP, 424, 425, 450, 451, 452, 453

K

Keyword, 56, 57
this (JavaScript), 166, 167
this (jQuery), 220, 221

L

LAN (Local area network), 4, 5
last method (jQuery), 280, 281
lastChild property (JavaScript), 160, 161
Last-in, first-out array, 150, 151
Length of an array, 142, 143
length property (JavaScript), 96, 97, 144, 145
Lightbox plugin, 320-321, 464, 465
link element, 24, 25
jQuery Mobile, 508, 509
jQuery UI, 352, 353
List divider (jQuery Mobile), 548, 549
List view (jQuery Mobile), 544, 545
Listener (Google Maps), 488-491
Literal
numeric, 66, 67
string, 68, 69
load event (JavaScript), 106, 107, 108, 109
load method (Ajax), 414, 415, 416, 417
Local area network (LAN), 4, 5
Local variable, 104, 105
location property (JavaScript), 60, 61
Logic error, 120, 121
Logical operator, 72, 73

M

Map (Google), 469-492
Marker (on map), 476-479
media attribute (link element), 24, 25
Media queries, 498, 499
Member, 410, 411
meta element
charset, 12, 13
for mobile devices, 502, 503

Method, 60, 61, 472, 473
Method (JavaScript)
    alert, 60, 61
    clearInterval, 184, 185
    clearTimeout, 182, 183
    confirm, 92, 93
    focus, 94, 95
    getAttribute, 162, 163
    getDate, 96, 97
    getElementById, 92, 93
    getElementsByClassName, 162, 163
    getElementsByName, 162, 163
    getElementsByTagName, 162, 163
    getFullYear, 96, 97
    getMonth, 96, 97
    hasAttribute, 162, 163
    indexOf, 96, 97
    join, 150, 151
    parseFloat, 70, 71, 92, 93
    parseInt, 70, 71, 92, 93
    pop, 150, 151
    preventDefault, 174, 175
    print, 60, 61
    prompt, 60, 61
    push, 150, 151
    removeAttribute, 162, 163
    setAttribute, 162, 163
    setInterval, 184, 185
    setTimeout, 182, 183
    shift, 150, 151
    substr, 96, 97
    toDateString, 96, 97
    toFixed, 94, 95
    toLowerCase, 96, 97
    toString, 150, 151
    toUpperCase, 96, 97
    unshift, 150, 151
    write, 92, 93
    writeln, 92, 93
Method (jQuery), 204, 205
    $.ajax (Ajax), 424-427, 434, 435
    $.each (Ajax), 414, 415, 420, 421
    $.get (Ajax), 414, 415, 418, 419
    $.getJSON (Ajax), 414, 415
    $.noConflict, 586, 587
    $.post (Ajax), 414, 415, 418, 419
    addClass, 214, 215, 260, 261, 396, 397
    after, 264, 265
    animate, 242, 243
    append, 264, 265
    appendTo, 264, 265
    attr, 214, 215, 260, 261
    before, 264, 265
    blur, 294, 295
    change, 294, 295

children, 278, 279
clone, 264, 265
closest, 278, 279
css, 214, 215, 272, 273
delay, 246, 247
each, 214, 215
empty, 266, 267
end, 280, 281
eq, 280, 281
fadeIn, 232, 233
fadeOut, 232, 233
fadeTo, 232, 233
fadeToggle, 232, 233
filter, 280, 281
find, 278, 279
first, 280, 281
focus, 204, 205, 294, 295
has, 280, 281
hasClass, 260, 261
height, 272, 273
hide, 214, 215, 232, 233
html, 262, 263
innerHeight, 272, 273
innerWidth, 272, 273
insertAfter, 264, 265
insertBefore, 264, 265
last, 280, 281
load (Ajax), 414, 415, 416, 417
next, 204, 205, 214, 215, 278, 279
nextAll, 278, 279
nextUntil, 278, 279
not, 280, 281
offset, 274, 275
offsetParent, 278, 279
outerHeight, 272, 273
outerWidth, 272, 273
parent, 278, 279
parents, 278, 279
parentsUntil, 278, 279
position, 274, 275
prepend, 264, 265
prependTo, 264, 265
prev, 214, 215, 278, 279
prevAll, 278, 279
preventDefault, 224, 225
prevUntil, 278, 279
remove, 266, 267
removeAttr, 260, 261
removeClass, 214, 215, 260, 261, 396, 397
replaceAll, 262, 263
replaceWith, 262, 263
scrollLeft, 274, 275
scrollTop, 274, 275
select, 294, 295
serialize (Ajax), 422, 423

Method (continued)
    serializeArray (Ajax), 422, 423
    show, 214, 215, 232, 233
    siblings, 278, 279
    slice, 280, 281
    slideDown, 232, 233
    slideToggle, 232, 233
    slideUp, 232, 233
    stop, 246, 247
    submit, 204, 205, 294, 295
    text, 204, 205, 262, 263
    toggle, 232, 233
    toggleClass, 214, 215, 260, 261, 397
    trim, 292, 293
    unwrap, 266, 267
    val, 204, 205, 262, 263, 292, 293
    width, 272, 273
    wrap, 266, 267
    wrapAll, 266, 267
    wrapInner, 266, 267
Method (jQuery UI)
    effect, 392, 393
    switchClass, 396, 397
Method (jQuery Mobile), 536, 537
method attribute (form), 288, 289
Miles Per Gallon application (JavaScript), 80-81, 110-111
Mobile web site, 498-505
    design and testing, 504, 505
Mobile web site application, 526-531, 562-567
Modal, 360, 361
Modulus operator, 64, 65
mouseenter event method (jQuery), 216, 217
mousein event (JavaScript), 106, 107
mouseout event (JavaScript), 106, 107
mouseout event method (jQuery), 216, 217
mouseover event (JavaScript), 106, 107
mouseover event method (jQuery), 216, 217

N

name attribute, 22, 23
    for form, 288, 289
Named function, 102, 103
Naming conventions, 56, 57
    plugins, 329
NaN, 70, 71, 92, 93
Nested if statements, 74, 75
Network, 4, 5
new keyword, 97, 142, 143, 176, 177
next method (jQuery), 204, 205, 214, 215, 278, 279
nextAll method (jQuery), 278, 279
nextElementSibling property (JavaScript), 160, 161
nextUntil method (jQuery), 278, 279

Node interface, 160, 161
nodeValue property (JavaScript), 98, 99, 160, 161
noscript element, 52, 53
not method (jQuery), 280, 281
Number control, 290, 291
Number data type, 62, 63
Number object (JavaScript), 94, 95
Numeric expression, 64, 65
Numeric literal, 66, 67
Numeric variable, 66, 67

O

Object, 60, 61
Object (browser)
    jqXHR, 424, 425
    XHR, 406, 407, 410, 411, 412, 413
    XMLHttpRequest, 406, 407, 410, 411, 412, 413
Object (JavaScript), 92-99
    Date, 96, 97
    document, 92, 93
    global, 92, 93
    Number, 94, 95
    String, 96, 97
    Textbox, 94, 95
    window, 60, 61, 92, 93
Object chaining, 70, 71, 94, 95
offset method (jQuery), 274, 275
offsetParent method (jQuery), 278, 279
one event method (jQuery), 218, 219
One-time timer, 182, 183
Opening tag, 14
Operator
    arithmetic, 64, 65
    assignment, 66, 67
    compound assignment, 66, 67
    concatenation, 68, 69
    logical, 72, 73
    relational, 72, 73
Order of precedence
    arithmetic expression, 64, 65
    conditional expression, 72, 73
outerHeight method (jQuery), 272, 273
outerWidth method (jQuery), 272, 273

P

Parameter, 60, 61, 100, 101
Parent, 158, 159
parent method (jQuery), 278, 279
parentNode property (JavaScript), 160, 161
parents method (jQuery), 278, 279
parentsUntil method (jQuery), 278, 279

parseFloat method (JavaScript), 70, 71, 92, 93
parseInt method (JavaScript), 70, 71, 92, 93
Path, 30, 31
Pattern (regular expression), 290, 291
pattern attribute (HTML5), 290, 291
placeholder attribute (HTML5), 290, 291
Plugin (jQuery), 313-338
    API standards, 329
    application (jQuery), 334-337
    bxSlider, 322-323
    creating, 328-333
    Cycle, 324-325
    Highlighter, 330-332
    jLayout, 326-327
    Lightbox, 320-321, 464, 465
    naming conventions, 329
    Redirection, 500, 501
    Validation, 300-309
pop method (JavaScript), 150, 151
position method (jQuery), 274, 275
post method (form), 288, 289, 410, 411
Preloading images, 176, 177
prepend method (jQuery), 264, 265
prependTo method (jQuery), 264, 265
prev method (jQuery), 214, 215, 278, 279
prevAll method (jQuery), 278, 279
preventDefault method
    JavaScript browsers, 174, 175
    jQuery, 224, 225
prevUntil method (jQuery), 278, 279
Primitive data type, 62, 63
print method (JavaScript), 60, 61
Progressbar widget, 368, 369
prompt method (JavaScript), 60, 61
Property, 28, 29, 60, 61
    returnValue (IE), 174, 175
    viewport metadata, 502, 503
Property (JavaScript)
    location, 60, 61
    disabled, 94, 95
    firstChild, 98, 99
    length, 96, 97, 144, 145
    nodeValue, 98, 99
    value, 94, 95
Property (jQuery), 434, 435, 444, 445
Property (Node interface), 160, 161
    firstChild, 160, 161
    lastChild, 160, 161
    nextElementSibling, 160, 161
    nodeValue, 160, 161
    parentNode, 160, 161

Properties map, 242, 243
Protocol, 30, 31
push method (JavaScript), 150, 151

Q

Queue (animation), 244, 245

R

Radio button (jQuery Mobile), 556, 557
Range control, 290, 291
ready event method (jQuery), 206, 207, 216, 217
Redirection plugin, 500, 501
Redirection to mobile web site, 498, 499, 500, 501
Refresh button, 42, 43
Regular expression, 290, 291, 454, 455
Relational operator, 72, 73
Reload button, 42, 43
remove method (jQuery), 266, 267
removeAttr method (jQuery), 260, 261
removeAttribute method (JavaScript), 162, 163
removeClass method (jQuery), 214, 215, 260, 261, 396,
    397
Rendering
    driving directions, 488-491
    web page, 6, 7
replaceAll method (jQuery), 262, 263
replaceWith method (jQuery), 262, 263
required attribute (HTML5), 290, 291
Reserved word, 56, 57
Reset button, 288, 289
Resizable interaction, 384, 385
return statement (JavaScript), 100, 101
returnValue property (IE), 174, 175
Retweet, 450, 451, 452
Round trip, 8, 9
Router, 4
Rule, 28, 29
Rule set, 28, 29
Runtime error (JavaScript), 120, 121

S

Scale of viewport, 502, 503
Scope, 104, 105
script element, 50-53
    Google Maps, 474, 475
    jQuery, 196, 197
    jQuery UI, 352, 353
    jQuery Mobile, 508, 509
Scripting language, 10, 11
scrollLeft method (jQuery), 274, 275

scrollTop method (jQuery), 274, 275
select event (JavaScript), 106, 107
select event method (jQuery), 294, 295
Select menu (jQuery Mobile), 558, 559
select method (jQuery), 294, 295
Selectable interaction, 386, 387
Selector
    CSS, 26, 27
    jQuery, 202, 203, 212-213, 292, 293
serialize method (Ajax), 422, 423
serializeArray method (Ajax), 422, 423
Server, 4-11
Server-side processing, 8
setAttribute method (JavaScript), 162, 163
setInterval method (JavaScript), 184, 185
setTimeout method (JavaScript), 182, 183
shift method (JavaScript), 150, 151
shim (see shiv)
shiv, 18, 19, 32, 33
show method (jQuery), 214, 215, 232, 233
Sibling, 158, 159
siblings method (jQuery), 278, 279
Simulator for mobile device, 504, 505
slice method (jQuery), 280, 281
Slide show, 10, 11
Slide Show application
    JavaScript, 186-189
    jQuery DOM traversal, 282-283
    jQuery effects, 236-240
slideDown method (jQuery), 232, 233
Slider widget, 366, 367
Slider (jQuery Mobile), 554, 555
slideToggle method (jQuery), 232, 233
slideUp method (jQuery), 232, 233
Sortable interaction, 388, 389
Source-code viewing, 134, 135
span element, 20, 21
Split button list (jQuery Mobile), 546, 547
src attribute (script element), 50, 51
Stack (array), 150, 151
Start slide show, 240, 241
Statement (JavaScript), 54, 55
    assignment, 66, 67
    do-while, 76, 77
    for, 78, 79, 146, 147
    for-in, 148, 149
    if, 74, 75
    while, 76, 77
Static web page, 6, 7
Step through application, 128, 129
stop method (jQuery), 246, 247
Stop slide show, 240, 241
String, 62, 63
    concatenation, 68, 69
    data type, 62, 63

    literal, 68, 69
    object, 96, 97
    variable, 68, 69
Style sheet, 24, 25
    jQuery Mobile, 508, 509
    jQuery UI, 352, 353
styles (jQuery Mobile), 520, 521
Submit button, 288, 289, 560, 561
submit event method (jQuery), 294, 295
submit method (jQuery), 204, 205, 288, 289, 294, 295
substr method (JavaScript), 96, 97
swatch (jQuery Mobile), 522, 523
Switch (jQuery Mobile), 554, 555
switchClass method (jQuery UI), 396, 397
Syntax
    common errors, 84, 85
    JavaScript, 54-61, 120, 121

T

Tabs widget, 358, 359
Tag, 14
tel control, 290, 291
Test Scores application, 82-83
Testing, 42, 43, 120-125
    JavaScript application, 30, 31
    jQuery application, 198, 199
    phases, 120, 121
    mobile web pages, 504, 505
Text area (jQuery Mobile), 552, 553
Text field (jQuery Mobile), 552, 553
text method (jQuery), 204, 205, 262, 263
Text node, 98, 99, 158, 159
Textbox object (JavaScript), 94, 95
Theme
    jQuery Mobile, 522, 523
    jQuery UI, 344, 345, 350, 351
ThemeRoller
    jQuery Mobile, 524, 525
    jQuery UI, 350, 351
this keyword
    JavaScript, 166, 167
    jQuery, 220, 221
time control, 290, 291
Timer, 182-185
title attribute, 22, 23
    HTML5, 290, 291
TOC application (jQuery), 268-271, 276-277
toDateString method (JavaScript), 96, 97
toFixed method (JavaScript), 94, 95
toggle event method (jQuery), 216, 217
toggle method (jQuery), 232, 233
toggleClass method (jQuery), 214, 215, 260, 261, 396, 397

toLowerCase method (JavaScript), 96, 97
Top-down coding, 124, 125
Top-down testing, 124, 125
toString method (JavaScript), 150, 151
toUpperCase method (JavaScript), 96, 97
Tracing, 132, 133
Transition, 394-399
   jQuery Mobile, 514, 515
trigger event method (jQuery), 218, 219
trim method (jQuery), 292, 293
Tweet, 450-457
Twitter, 450-457
type attribute (script element), 50, 51
type selector, 26, 27

U

unbind event method (jQuery), 218, 219
Undeclared variable, 122, 123
Uniform Resource Locator (URL), 30, 31
unload event method (jQuery), 216, 217
unshift method (JavaScript), 150, 151
unwrap method (jQuery), 266, 267
URL (Uniform Resource Locator), 30, 31
url control, 290, 291
Usability, 170, 171

V

val method (jQuery), 204, 205, 262, 263, 292, 293
Validation (HTML), 136, 137
Validation application
   JavaScript, 296-299
   plugin, 304-309
Validation plugin, 300-309
value property (JavaScript), 94, 95
Variable, 66, 67, 68, 69
   global, 104, 105, 122, 123
   local, 104, 105
   undeclared, 122, 123
Vecta Corp application with widgets, 370-373
Video applications, 440-449
Viewing source code, 134, 135
Viewport, 502, 503
Visibility transition, 398, 399

W

W3C Markup Validation Service, 137
WAN (Wide area network) 4, 5
Watch expression, 128, 129
Web browser, 4-11
Web server, 4-11

While loop, 76, 77
while statement, 76, 77
Whitespace, 54, 55
Wide area network (WAN), 4, 5
Widget, 354-375
width method (jQuery), 272, 273
window object, 60, 61, 70, 71, 92, 93
wrap method (jQuery), 266, 267
wrapAll method (jQuery), 266, 267
wrapInner method (jQuery), 266, 267
write method (JavaScript), 53, 92, 93
writeln method (JavaScript), 92, 93

XYZ

XHR object, 406, 407, 410, 411, 412, 413
XML, 408, 409, 412, 413, 418, 419
XMLHttpRequest object, 406, 407, 410, 411, 412, 413
YouTube, 440-449

What software you need for this book

- To enter and edit JavaScript, HTML, and CSS, you can use any text editor, but we recommend Aptana Studio 3 for both Windows and Mac OS users. It is a free editor with many excellent features.

- To help you get started with Aptana Studio 3, chapter 1 provides a short tutorial.

- To test the JavaScript and jQuery applications that you develop, we recommend that you use Firefox. Then, to debug your applications, you can use the Firebug extension to Firefox. Both the browser and the extension are free.

- To help you install these products, appendix A provides the web site addresses and procedures that you'll need.

The downloadable applications and files for this book

- All of the applications that are presented in this book.
- The starting files for the exercises in this book.
- The solutions to the exercises.

How to download the applications and files

- Go to www.murach.com, and go to the page for *Murach's JavaScript and jQuery*.

- Click the link for "FREE download of the book applications."

- If you're using a Windows system, click the "All book files" link for the self-extracting zip file. That will download an exe file named qury_allfiles.exe. Then, find this file in Windows Explorer and double-click on it. That will install the files for this book in this directory: c:\murach\jquery.

- If you're using a Mac, click the "All book files" link for the regular zip file. That will download a zip file named qury_allfiles.zip onto your hard drive. Then, move this file into the Documents folder of your home directory, use Finder to go to your Documents folder, and double-click on the zip file. That will create a folder named jquery that contains all the files for this book.

- For more information, please see appendix A.

www.murach.com